MW01631006

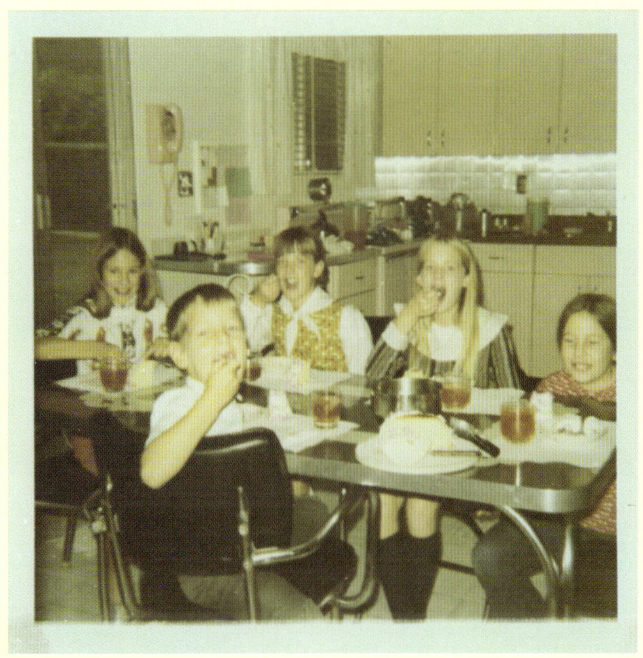

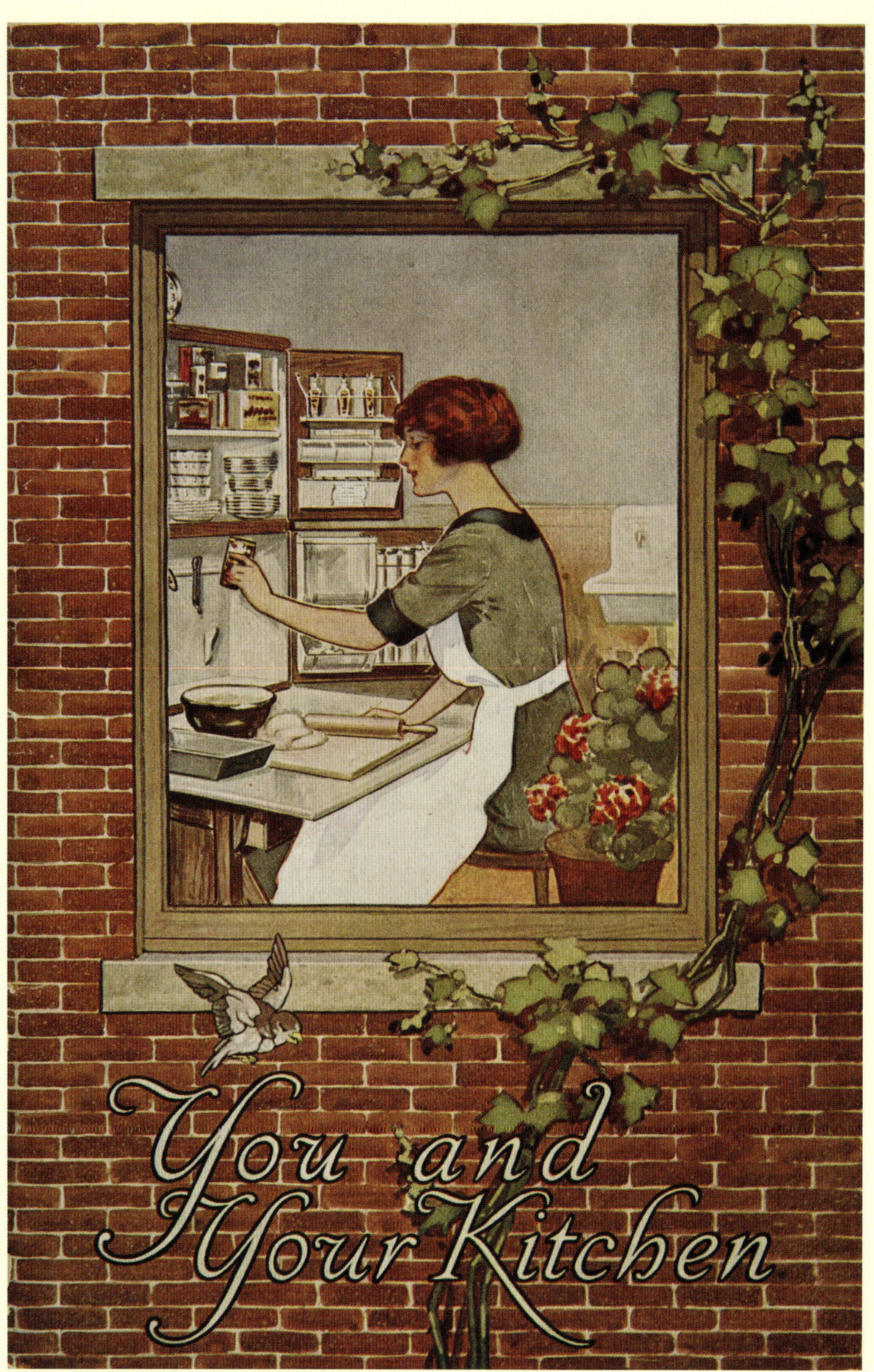
You and
Your Kitchen

# AMERICA'S KITCHENS

NANCY CARLISLE *and*
MELINDA TALBOT NASARDINOV
*with* JENNIFER PUSTZ

HISTORIC NEW ENGLAND

Boston 2008

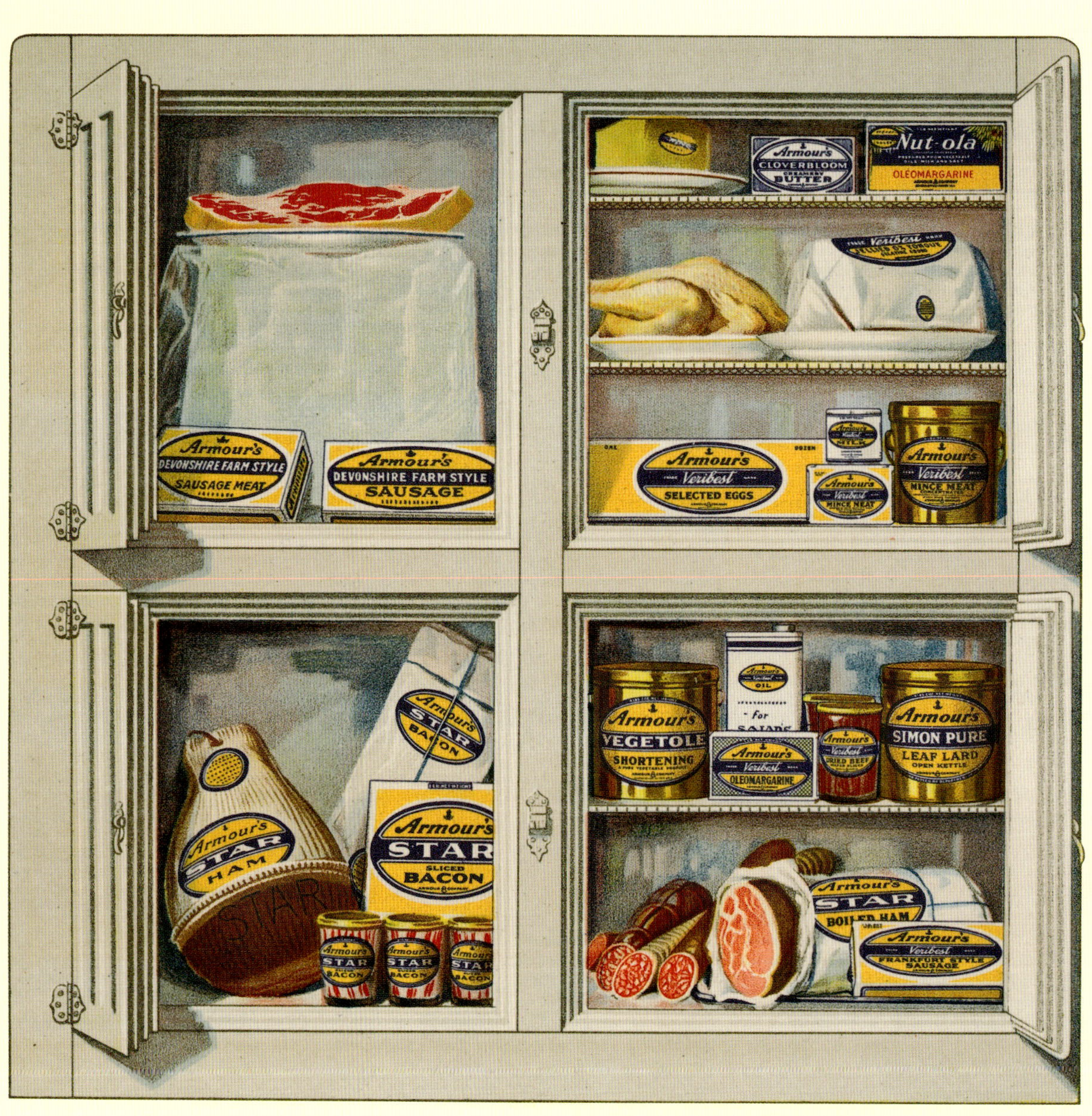
Armour's
DEVONSHIRE FARM STYLE
SAUSAGE MEAT
Armour's
DEVONSHIRE FARM STYLE
SAUSAGE
Armour's
CLOVERBLOOM
CREAMERY
BUTTER
Nut-ola
OLEOMARGARINE
Veribest
Armour's
Veribest
SELECTED EGGS
Armour's
Veribest
MINCE MEAT
Armour's
Veribest
MINCE MEAT
Armour's
STAR
BACON
Armour's
STAR
HAM
STAR
Armour's
STAR
SLICED
BACON
Armour's
STAR
BACON
Armour's
STAR
BACON
Armour's
VEGETOLE
SHORTENING
Armour's
Veribest
OIL
for
Armour's
Veribest
OLEOMARGARINE
Armour's
Veribest
DRIED BEEF
Armour's
SIMON PURE
LEAF LARD
OPEN KETTLE
Armour's
STAR
BOILED HAM
Armour's
Veribest
FRANKFURT STYLE
SAUSAGE

# CONTENTS

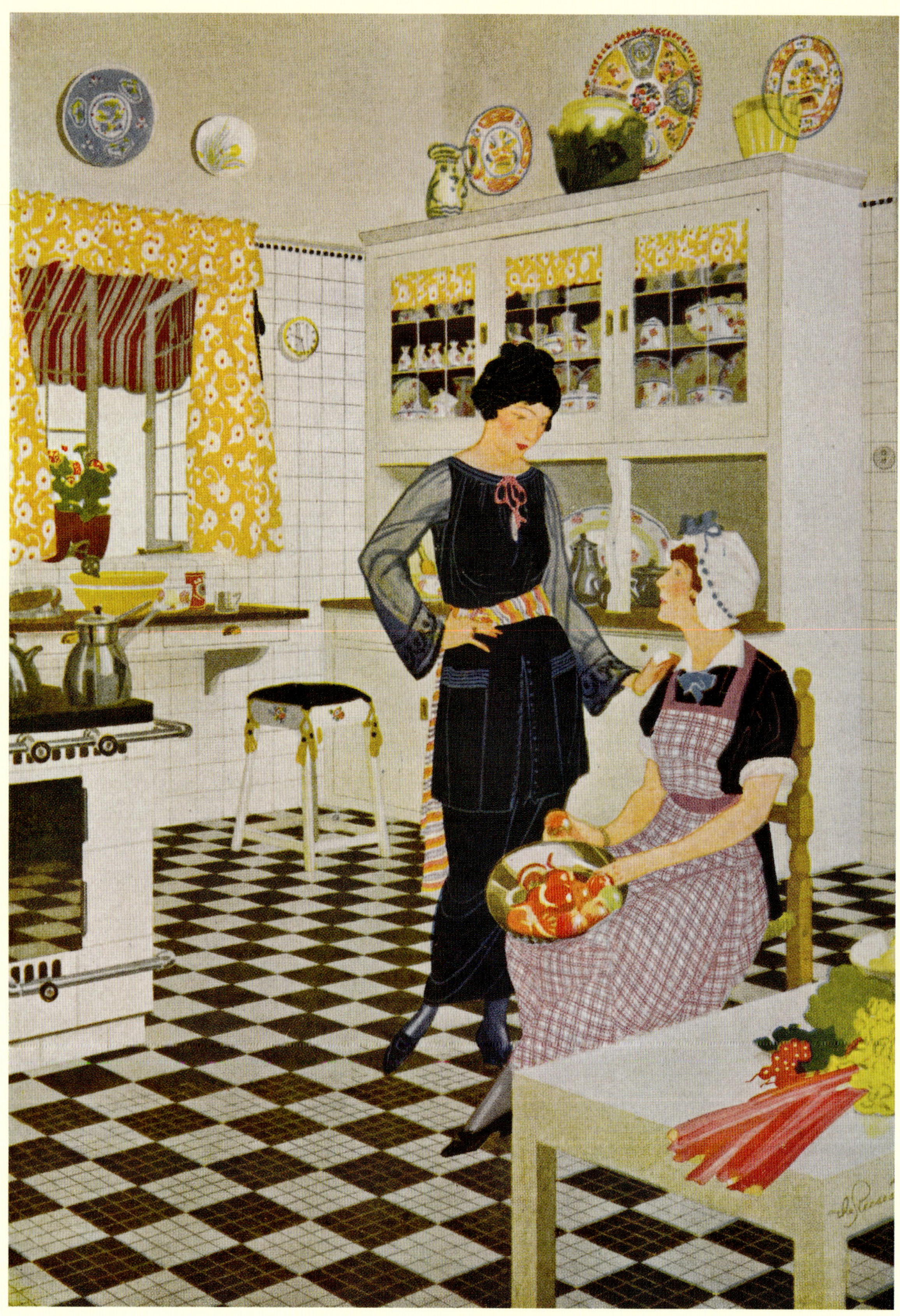

# FOREWORD

Memories of home usually include memories of time spent in the kitchen. Whether we remember the smells of favorite dishes cooking on the stove, family time while a meal was being prepared, homework being done at the kitchen table, or parents who either loved or hated the role of family chef, most of us can recall experiences that put the kitchen at the center of home life.

Historic New England's vast collections contain thousands of domestic artifacts related to the kitchen. Our historic houses contain well-documented kitchens from many periods, and many of these properties at one time had kitchen gardens. Our study collections feature an endless array of items used for food preparation or food service. Our Library and Archives has a wealth of historic photographs, ephemera, and documents describing the development and use of the kitchen.

In the effort to preserve and share stories of New England life during four centuries, Historic New England seeks themes that are of interest to diverse audiences. Because the topics of kitchens and food resonate with people in all geographic, economic, and ethnic groups, we decided to expand the content of this book to include other regions besides New England. Kitchens in the Plantation South, the Midwest, and the Southwest, offer revealing comparisons to those of this region. In the years since the Second World War, rapid societal changes and technological developments have made the nation's kitchens more homogeneous, making it all the more crucial to document and recall the particular character of each locale.

With this book, we invite you to learn more about the history of the kitchen, to compare your own experiences to those of other times, and to plan to visit some of the historic sites that are represented here. The story of America's kitchens continues to develop, and you are part of it.

*America's Kitchens* is the second in a series begun, under the inspiration and guidance of Series Editor Richard Cheek, with *The Camera's Coast: Historic Images of Ship and Shore in New England*. The purpose of the series is to present sound historical information, illustrated in large part by Historic New England collections, in a lively fashion that appeals to all. The trustees and staff of Historic New England are committed to making our collections fully accessible, and are pleased to share them in this format. Historic New England is grateful to all who contributed to this project.

CARL R. NOLD

President and CEO

HISTORIC NEW ENGLAND

Boston, Massachusetts

# EDITOR'S NOTE

To move from the shores of New England into the kitchens of America is quite a transition for the second volume of Historic New England's new book series, but this shift reflects the wide range of popular subjects we plan to cover as we continue to explore the rich resources of our Library and Archives.

Carefully researched and written by scholars in the field, each title is lavishly illustrated with the most evocative images that can be found. The three authors of this volume, Nancy Carlisle, Melinda Talbot Nasardinov, and Jennifer Pustz, first distilled vast quantities of research to produce essays that are both highly readable and rich in historical insight. They then worked with the Library and Archives staff to fill *America's Kitchens* with photographs, paintings, and drawings as well as personal letters and diary pages, printed and handwritten recipes, and myriad advertisements for food and kitchen equipment, all of which were selected to convey the vitality and variety of American family life as it has been expressed at the heart of the nation's homes: the kitchen.

As she did for our first title, *The Camera's Coast*, designer Julia Sedykh incorporated all of these diverse images in a layout that is highly imaginative and distinctive in conception, reflecting the differences in illustrative material between the two books and adding a new level of visual appeal.

Our ability to publish the series successfully continues to be enhanced by our publishing consultant, Stephen Pekich, whose experience and patient optimism are invaluable.

RICHARD CHEEK

Series Editor

# ACKNOWLEDGMENTS

A*merica's Kitchens* has been part of a multiyear project that includes, in addition to this publication, a regional traveling exhibition, and a reassessment of many of the kitchens at Historic New England's thirty-six historic properties. No project of this sort can be accomplished by one or even three people, and the authors owe a debt of gratitude to the hundreds of men and women encountered during our research. To the staff of the dozens of museums and libraries where we looked for objects, images, and stories of kitchens across America, and to those who supplied many of the images published here, thank you. The willingness and energy with which people shared their historical resources were inspirational. We owe thanks as well to the many people who answered our initial questionnaire seeking out intact historical kitchens. Thanks also to those who responded to the invitation on our website to send in images and stories of their own kitchens. We had many wonderful images to choose from and wish we could have included more.

We are deeply indebted to numerous supporters and donors: An Anonymous Foundation, The Acorn Foundation, Mars Foundation, the National Endowment for the Humanities, Betsy and Richard Cheek, and Susan Paine. We are also grateful to those who attended the Food and Friends dinners, and even more indebted to those who hosted them or plan to host them: Barbara and Theodore Alfond, Deborah Allinson and Thomas Lamb, Maureen and Edward Bousa, Deborah and Philip Edmondson, Toni and Joseph Junkin, Arleyn and Newton Levee, Kimberly and John McDowell, Andrew Spindler-Roesle and Hiram Butler, Tracy and William Veillette, and to Historic New England staff members who helped organize these events, Melinda Cheston and Denise Trapani.

We are especially grateful to all the consultants who helped shape the direction of our research and writing. In four separate meetings, held over a two-year period, we were greatly informed by the expertise and insight of the participants: James Ayres, Donna Braden, Priscilla Brewer, Ruth Schwartz Cowan, Elizabeth Cromley, Marcie Cohen Ferris, Neil Foley, Donna Gabaccia, Stephen Long, Nancy McCoy, Jane Nylander, Cynthia Robinson, Edwin (Ted) Selker, Ellen Snyder-Grenier, Hilary Anderson Stelling, and Camille Wells. We are indebted to the experts and editors who read the manuscript in whole or in part: Barbara Carson, Neil Foley, Cheryl Foote, Barbara Haber, Sandy Oliver, Laura Shapiro, Leni Sorensen, Luise Erdmann, Thomas Kozachek, and Caroline Sloat.

We had four wonderful research assistants who helped with various parts of the project. Abigail Carroll did two studies for us, one searching through the Tucker family papers to learn about the kitchen at Castle Tucker, and the other investigating the history of food preservation in the United States. Cheryl Foote provided insightful new research into the history of kitchens in New Mexico. Andrea Hawkes conducted an inventory analysis of eighteenth-century probate records in Essex County, Massachusetts. Lynne Paschetag looked into the history of cookbooks in America and tracked down many documentary photographs.

We have featured a number of kitchens across the country in the chapters that follow, and are grateful to the people who shared their stories of living in these kitchens as well as to the families and staffs of the historical organizations that preserve them. Thanks are due to Ati Gropius Johansen, Sally and Jack Sondesky, Crystal Marra, Olivia and Spiros Sintros, and Stewart Smith, as well as to Curt Miner at the Pennsylvania State Museum, Marcia Young and her staff at the David Davis Mansion, and Jana Gottshalk, Carol Hilgers, and Julie Anna Lopez at El Rancho de las Golondrinas. We are also grateful to Leo J. Shapiro & Associates, and especially to George Rosenbaum, who worked tirelessly to answer our questions about kitchen use today.

We owe thanks to a number of talented photographers and one wonderful illustrator. To David Carmack, Kurt Gittings, Peter Harholdt, and Ken Kashian, thank you for your sensitive photographs of rooms and objects often overlooked. And many thanks are due to Gerald Foster, whose wonderful and imaginative drawings enable us to show how these kitchens might have looked in their heyday.

From the start we have been helped by colleagues at Historic New England. We are especially grateful to President and CEO Carl Nold for his unwavering support of the project. Thanks are also due to the members of the staff advisory team: Cheryl Aldridge, Nancy Curtis, Peter Gittleman, Ken Turino, and Diane Viera. We have been continually supported by members of the collections services team at Historic New England, who not only helped with the details of the exhibition and book but also picked up the slack while we were immersed in this project: Megan MacNeil, Richard Nylander, Adrienne Sage, Michael Schuetz, and Julie Solz. We are equally grateful to the conservators who evaluated and treated some of Historic New England's kitchen-related collections: Judith Bohan, John Childs, Michaela Neiro, and Teresa Williams.

Finally, to the project team who worked on all aspects of the book's production, we are eternally grateful. We had wonderful assistance seeking out, organizing, tracking, and ordering the many images that illustrate these pages. Thank you to Joanne Flaherty, Jeanne Gamble, and Alyce Perry. Emily Novak Gustainis has been invaluable in organizing illustrations and managing permission requests. We are especially indebted to Series Editor Richard Cheek, whose astute eye and encyclopedic knowledge of ephemera helped us locate precisely those images that were most appropriate to our narrative. Above all, we are deeply indebted to Lorna Condon, curator of Library and Archives at Historic New England, whose reliable wisdom and efficiency guided this publication to a successful conclusion.

NANCY CARLISLE

MELINDA TALBOT NASARDINOV

JENNIFER PUSTZ

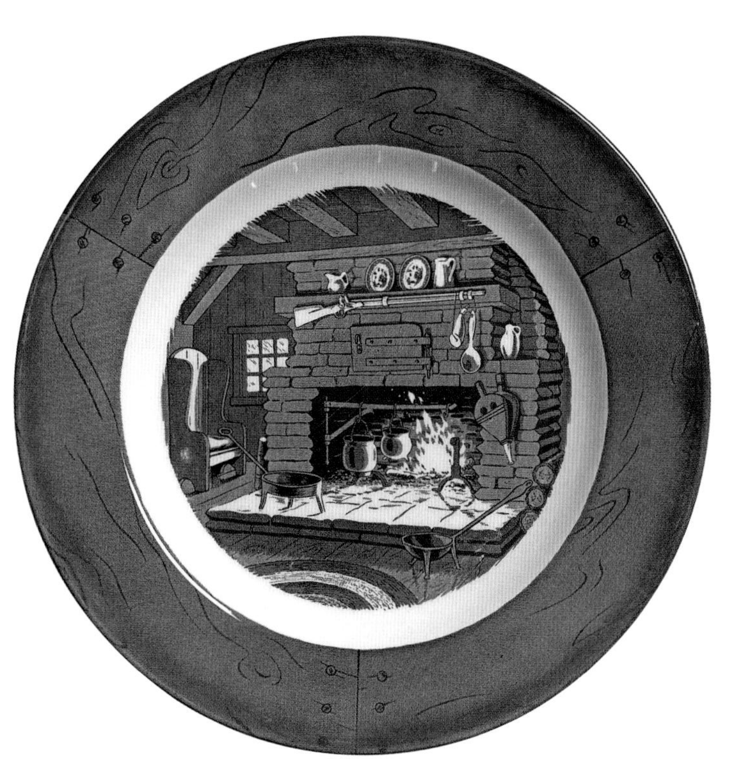

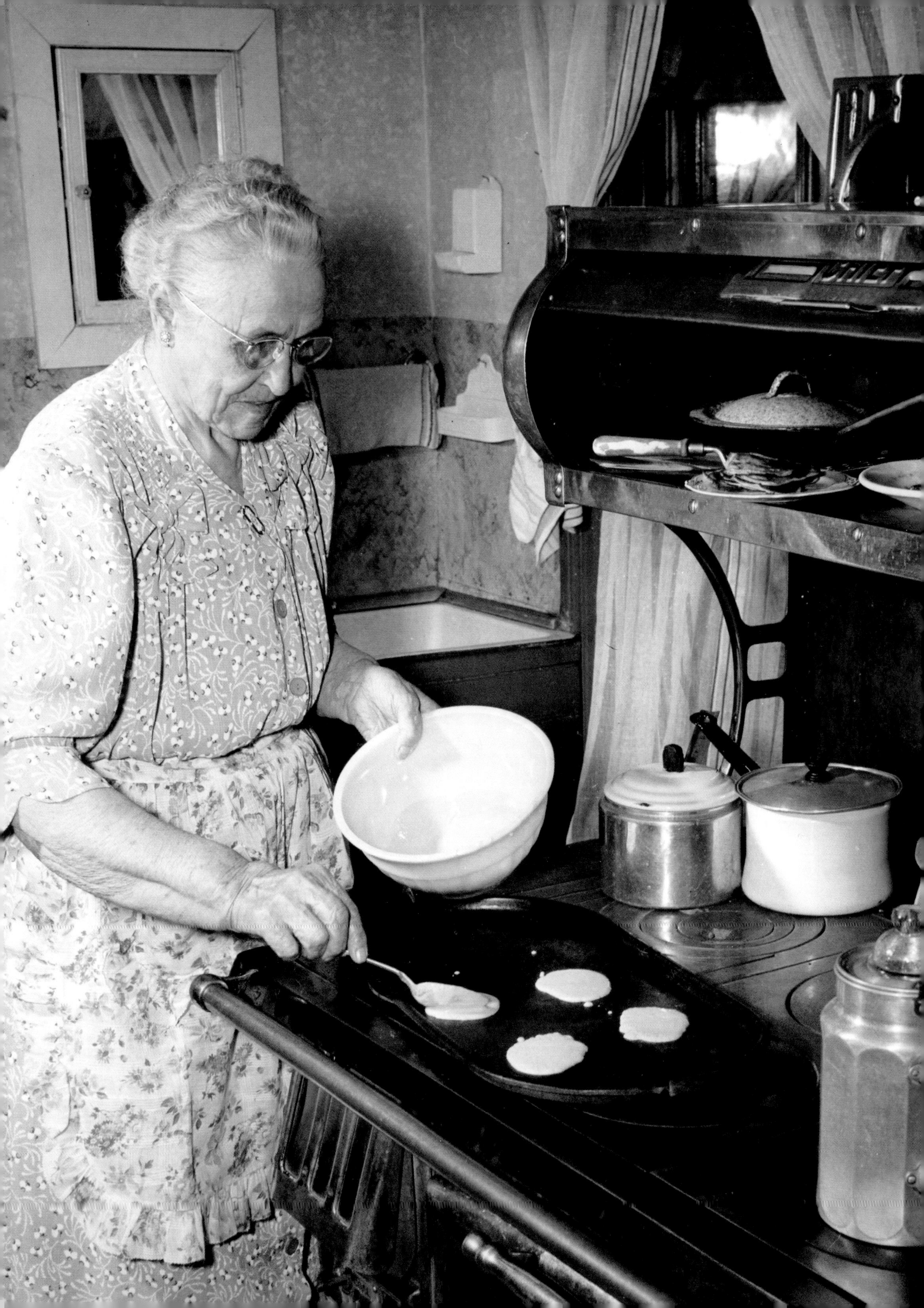

# THE KITCHEN IN AMERICAN LIFE

## *Why Kitchens Matter*

In an essay published in 1956, noted author E. B. White focused on one room when he described his home on the coast of Maine: "From morning till night, sounds drift from the kitchen, most of them familiar and comforting, some of them surprising and worth investigating. On days when warmth is the most important need of the human heart, the kitchen is the place you can find it; it dries the wet socks, it cools the hot little brain."[1]

Indeed for many, the kitchen is the first room that comes to mind when they think of home. It is the room where family, friends, and pets gather. It is the locus of long-held family traditions, the site of celebrations and solace, and the place of day-to-day life. As White explains: "[Our kitchen] teems with life of all sorts—cookery, husbandry, horticulture, canning, planning. It is an arsenal, a greenhouse, a surgical-dressing station, a doghouse, a bathhouse, a lounge, a library, a bakery, a cold-storage plant, a factory, and a bar, all rolled up into one gorgeous ball, or ballup."[2] While the room is the center of activities of all sorts, it also plays an important role in the imagination. Many people think about the kitchen in ways that are highly charged with nostalgia and with idealized visions of comfort and mother's love.

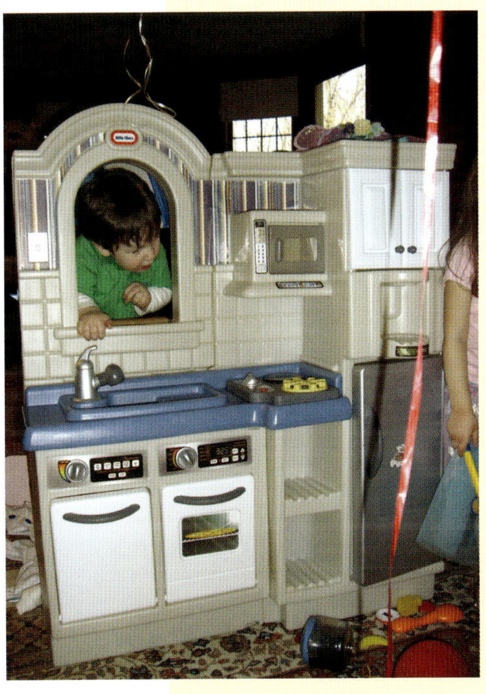

Kitchen memories begin early. Here, a two-year-old boy plays with the toy kitchen he and his sister received for Christmas.

For much of American history, it was a virtual certainty that the women in the family, or, for the privileged class, female servants, were responsible for feeding members of the household. The history of the kitchen is thus also the history of women—a history that survives not so much in words but in spaces, artifacts, routines, and recipes. Knowing what went on in the kitchen is the closest many of us will come to knowing our grandmothers' grandmothers.

More than any other room in the house, the kitchen symbolizes the best of family life, engendering memories of warmth, comforting smells, and family celebrations—dancing to the radio while drying dishes; stuffing ravioli with grandparents, parents, children, and

Throughout the book, quotations retain their original spelling and punctuation.

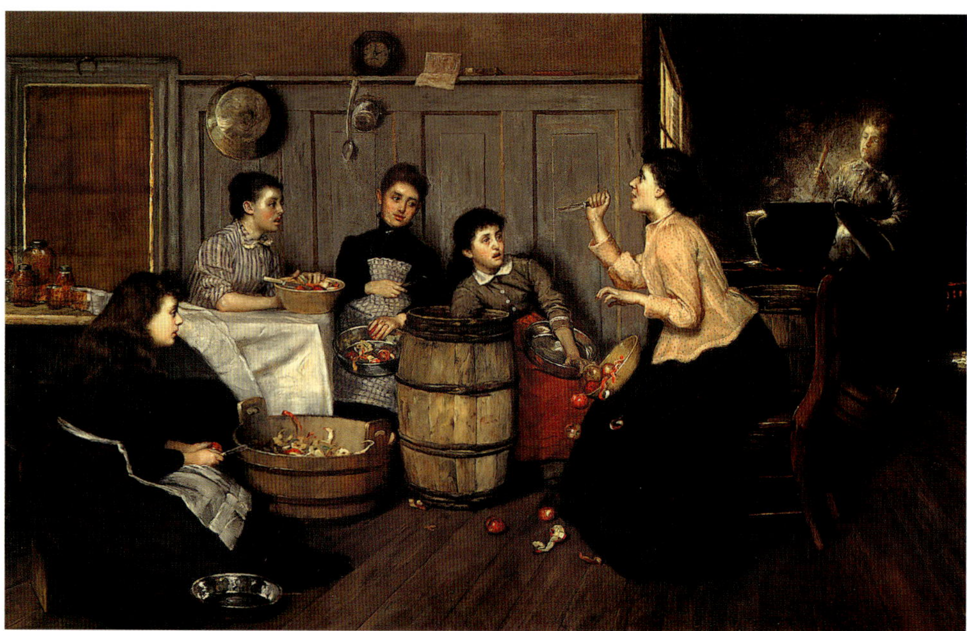

*The Ghost Story*, painted about 1895 by William Verplanck Birney, records the kitchen as a female-dominated space, where women and girls entertain each other while they work.

cousins; playing board games at the kitchen table. Yet it has always been a work site—not only for the women who lived in the house but also, in some households, for paid servants or enslaved cooks. For these women, the kitchen was the center of their working lives and, for the ones who lived in, it could be the center of their nonworking lives as well. For generations of women the kitchen was both a sanctuary and a prison.

Kitchens have also witnessed many moments of conflict and sorrow. As a source of sustenance and heat, the room draws people together. What happens once they come together is as varied as the people themselves.

## The Heart of the Home?

Many things besides cooking take place in the kitchen. This painting by F. W. Edmonds, about 1858, shows a father in the kitchen carving a toy windmill for his son.

As the symbolic center of the home, the kitchen gives meaning to family life. It is a place where parents nurture their children, families gather at breakfast and dinner, share chores, and discuss the world outside. Women especially see it as the space that connects them to past generations.

Daily domestic rituals can forge powerful bonds among generations. In *Miriam's Kitchen*, author Elizabeth Ehrlich writes about her mother-in-law, a survivor of the Holocaust, who moved to the United States and raised a family in the Midwest. For Miriam, the kitchen was a place to honor the family members she had lost: "A keeper of rituals and recipes, and of stories, she cooks to recreate a lost world, and to prove that unimaginable loss is not the end of everything. She is motivated by duty to ancestors and descendants, by memory and obligation and an impossible wish to make the world whole."[3] Ehrlich herself, raised in a

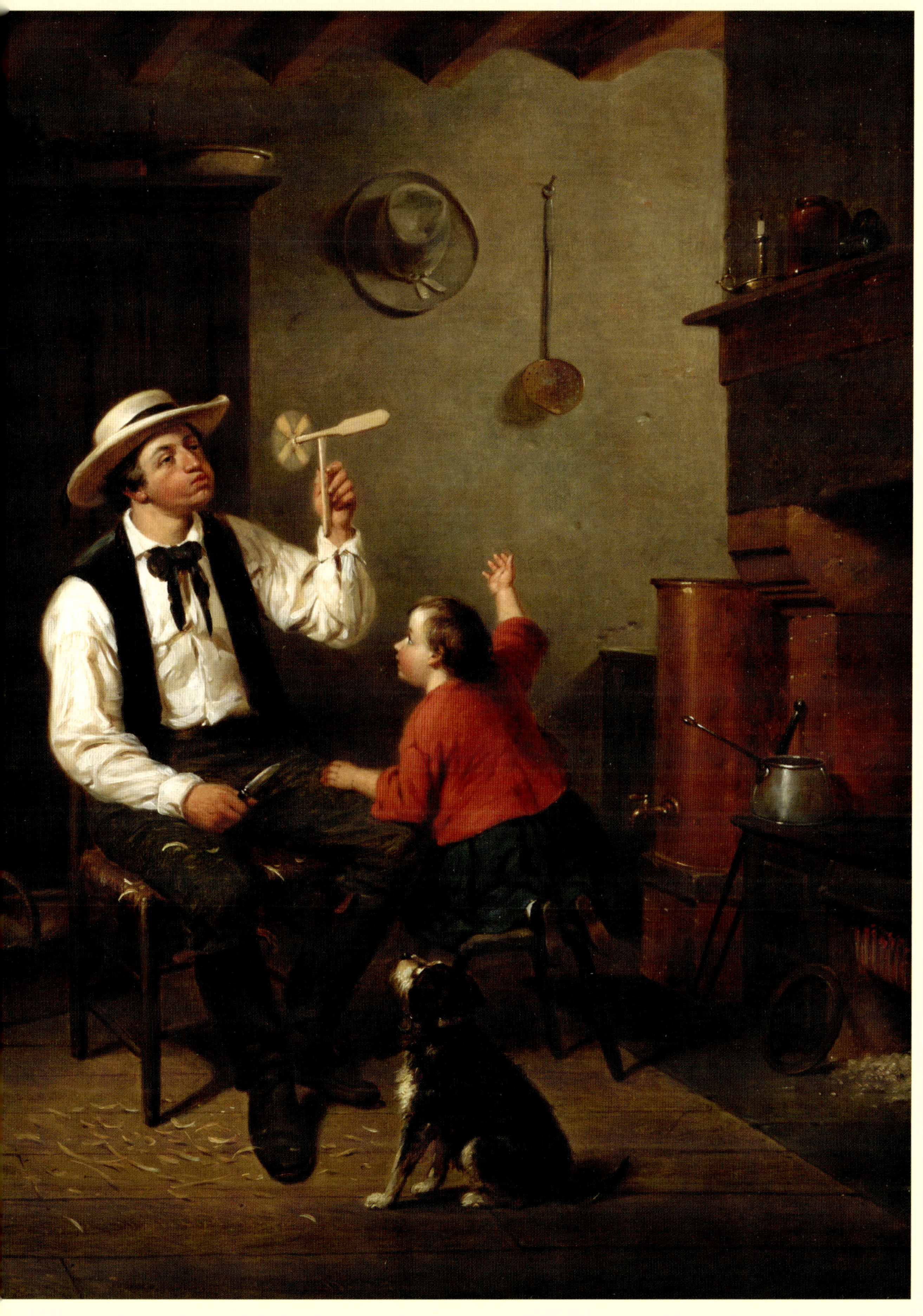

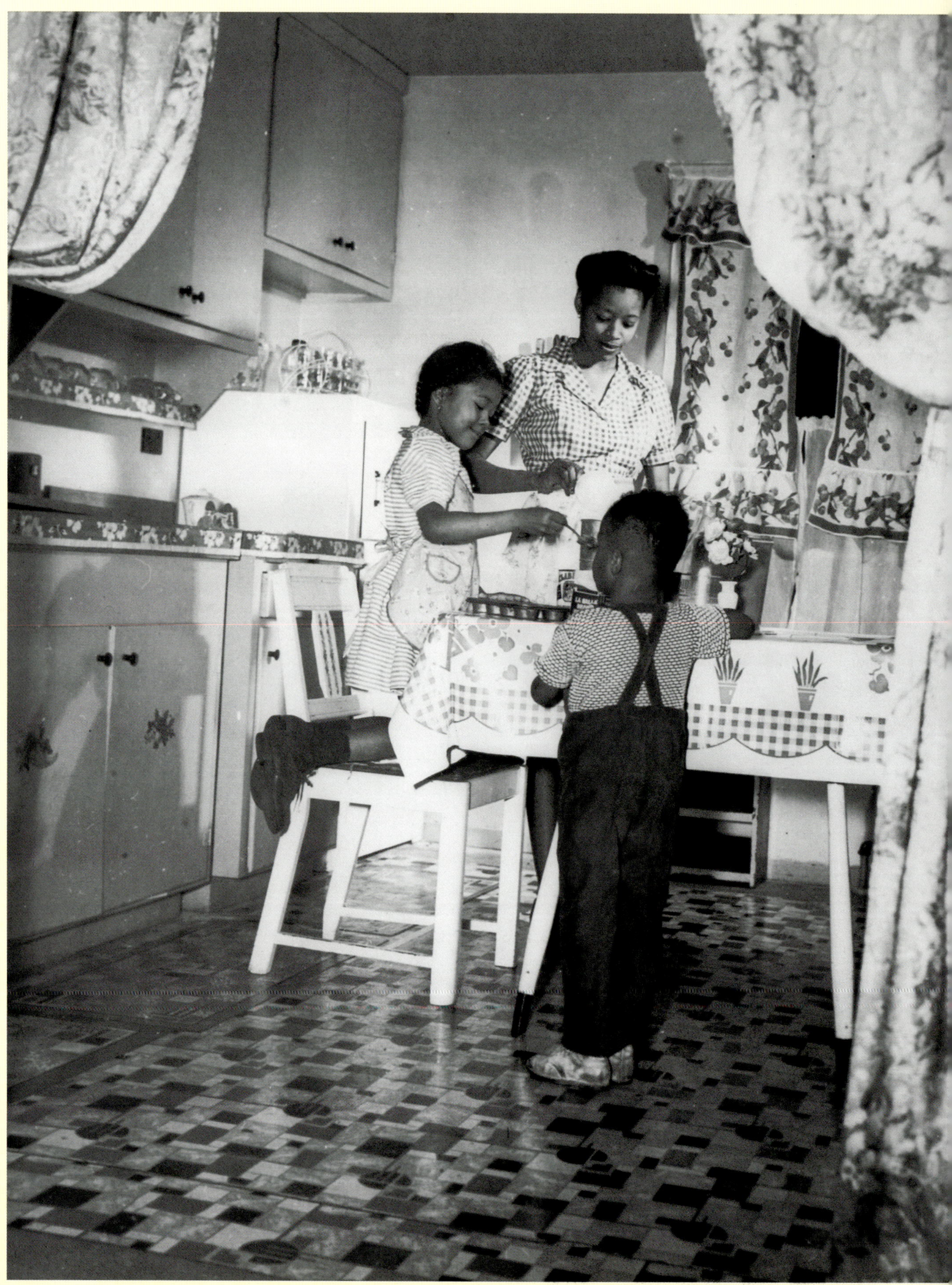

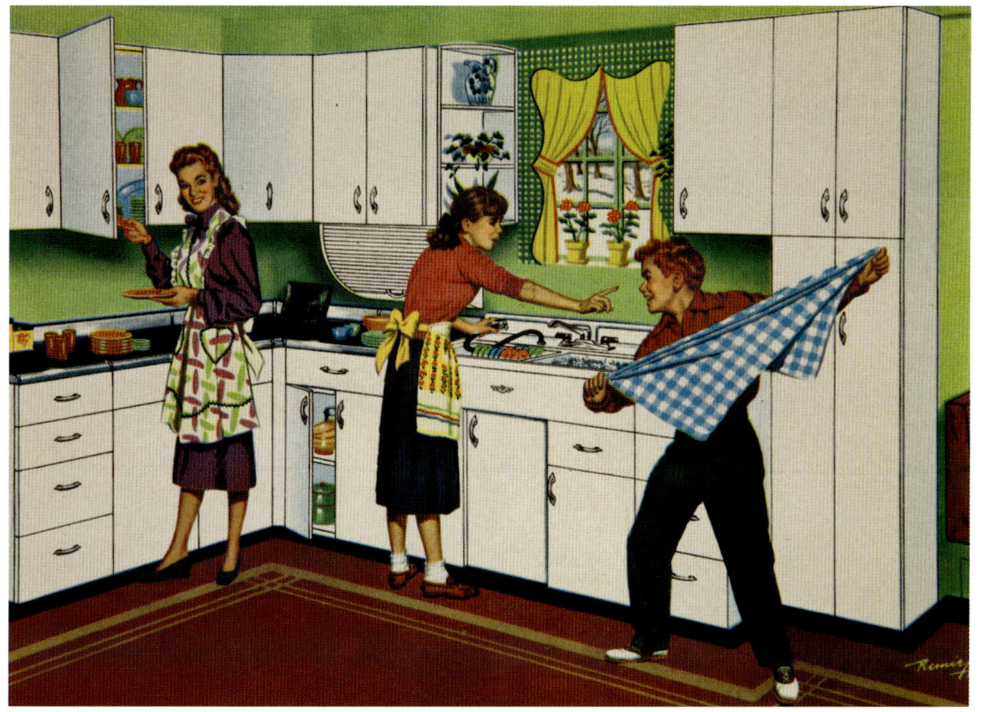

In a 1948 pamphlet for Youngstown Kitchens, manufacturers of metal kitchen cabinets, the advertisers describe one of their kitchens as "an inviting, family kitchen where work is really a pleasure."

non-kosher household, decided to honor her husband's family by learning to follow the laws of kashruth: "With ambivalence and some sense of irony, I light a candle, recite a prayer, grate a potato, and move toward making my kitchen kosher. Thus, I forge links from my grandparents, and my husband's grandparents, to my children."[4]

> If women ever stopped to figure out how many dishes they would have to wash for the rest of their lives, all the world would live in boarding houses.
>
> Earle E. Whitehorne, *House Beautiful*, July 1920

Of all the rooms in the home, the kitchen is uniquely suited to linking the past, present, and future. The actress and singer Pearl Bailey wrote of her kitchen in Philadelphia, "My kitchen is a mystical place, a kind of temple for me. It is a place where the surfaces seem to have significance, where the sounds and odors carry meaning that transfers from the past and bridges to the future."[5] Whether through recipes, rituals, stories, or meals, traditions from the past are preserved and passed on as new traditions are forming.

Most women know all too well how many dishes they wash and meals they prepare. The relentless nature of the work is a common complaint.

The kitchen can also be the place where family problems are played out. Ruth Reichl, the editor in chief of *Gourmet Magazine*, recalled that as a child she could determine the state of her mother's fragile mental health by looking in the refrigerator. When she found a suckling pig surrounded by tiny apples, she knew it was going to be a good day.[6] Louise DeSalvo wrote about growing up in a home where the kitchen was a battleground. Her childhood experience stood in sharp relief to the idealized image of a young girl learning to cook at

Kitchens offer women a place to work and play with their children. This mother is baking with her children in their kitchen in Altgeld Gardens, an early public housing project, built in Chicago in 1945 for the families of African American veterans.

her mother's side: "The kitchen, when my mother is cooking, is not a place I want to be. And so. No cookie-baking in the kitchen. No rolling out pie dough together. No lessons in how to make sauce."[7]

For many women, both now and in the past, the relentless nature of meal preparation—day after day, week after week, and month after month—kept them tied to a room they grew to hate. In the late nineteenth century, Ellen Swallow Richards, one the founders of the home economics movement in America, recognized the problem: "You cannot make women contented with cooking and cleaning and you need not try."[8] She believed that if women understood the principles behind domestic work better, they would feel less like drudges. Certainly, many women have looked to technological and design advances in the kitchen to reduce the amount of time needed to cook, clean up, and preserve foods.

## The Kitchen Defined

Put simply, a kitchen is the domestic space where food is prepared. It may be a room that serves a host of other functions, but its most basic role is for the preparation of food. Of course, food can also be prepared outside, whether in simple fire pits or in luxuriously fitted outdoor spaces with gas grills and refrigerators. But fundamentally, the kitchen is an indoor space, the place people go to chop, mix, roast, boil, and bake.

For most Americans, the basic building blocks of a kitchen are the same. A stove, refrigerator, sink, cabinets, and countertops are required even in the smallest urban galley kitchens. But few if any of these amenities existed historically. In kitchens in the country's colonial period, a fireplace stood in place of a stove; large tubs instead of a sink; and a table, lap, or floor instead of countertops. Built-in storage usually consisted of the simplest shelves and provisions were stored around the house in the areas best suited for their preservation—a cool cellar for fruits and vegetables, an attic for dried goods, a dairy room for milk and cheese, a smokehouse for meats.

This 1624 engraving from Theodor de Bry's *Les Grands Voyages* shows an imagined scene of two Eastern Woodland Indians cooking succotash, a corn stew usually made with beans and occasionally fish or meat.

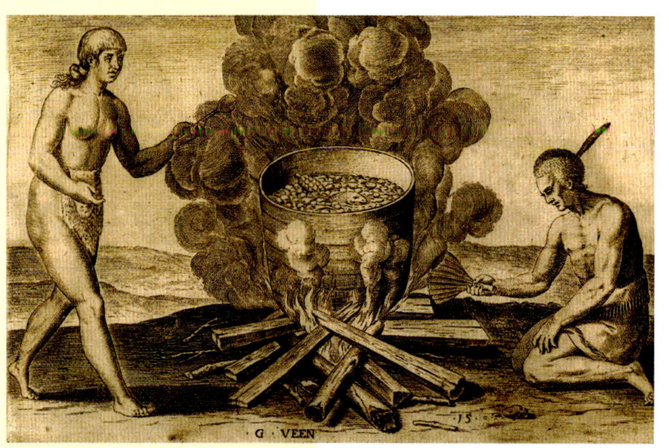


For centuries before the arrival of European settlers, American Indians had been cooking outdoors in pots made of wood or clay or in tightly woven baskets, in which they prepared porridges, stews, soups, and puddings. Depending on the local custom, they ate wild and cultivated foods raw, baked, roasted, dried, or, for those with plentiful water, boiled. The women in many tribes dried foods and stored them for times of scarcity.[9]

Sixteenth- and seventeenth-century colonists most often prepared meals in a particular room, though that room might equally be used for a host of other purposes—processing tex-

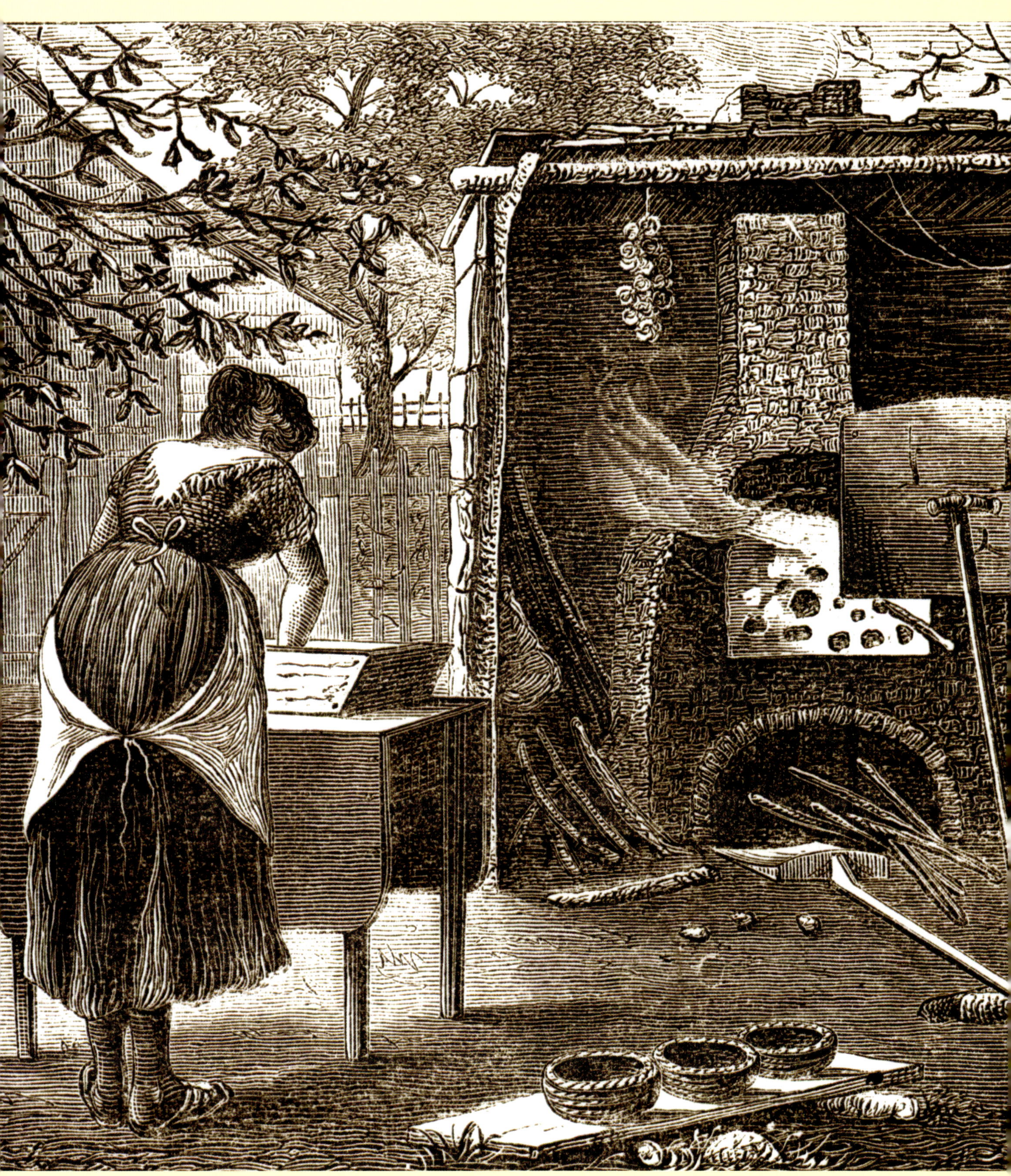

In many parts of the country, bake ovens were built outside and protected under a shed roof, like this one depicted in the June 1873 edition of the *American Agriculturist*.

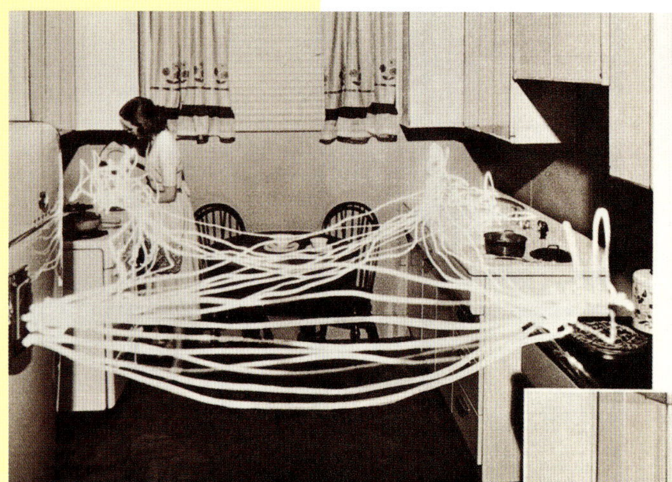

*when a kitchen works for and against you--*

**The camera charts unmistakably the value of planning to conserve effort and time.**

THE properly-planned kitchen works *for* you. The badly-arranged kitchen, replete though it may be with good appliances, is your foe in daily combat. It saps your energy, it makes the day seem twice as long. This is, in brief, the philosophy of kitchen planning.

These striking photographs are illustrative of this philosophy and reveal—as no words could—the contrast between two kitchens, properly and improperly arranged. The camera has charted the patterns made (by strapping lights to the homemaker's wrists) in the preparation of a soup. Here is graphic proof that, even with top-flight appliances, a kitchen may be woefully inefficient!

In both kitchens, the cabinets, range and sink are made by Murray while the refrigerator is an International Harvester. In the photograph above, the homemaker has no work surface at any of the appliances (there is a gap between the base cabinet and the range). Notwithstanding the heavy traffic between range and sink, she must hurdle the table and chairs positioned so awkwardly. (Originally it did seem like such a good idea to have a table for snacks just there.)

In the properly planned kitchen at right, all appliances have been shifted, work surfaces have been added—and this area is now in the popular and efficient U-shape.

Now—there is no backtracking, no confused web almost every strand of which chains the homemaker to a wasteful routine, struggle as she may. Preparing a dish or a meal is done in the shortest possible time—and in the most convenient manner—by following a neat, orderly pattern which saves time—*and saves the homemaker!* •

80

81

The authors of the 1952 booklet, *Today's Woman Prize Kitchens*, use camera chart photography to support their assertion that a badly designed kitchen "is your foe in daily combat. It saps your energy, it makes the day seem twice as long."

tiles, making candles and soap, repairing tools, praying, schooling, sleeping. A few homes had rooms reserved specifically for cooking, whether a large open space that accommodated multiple laborers or a small lean-to abutting the main living space. In some parts of the country, those who could afford to had their kitchens in separate buildings entirely. Food was also often prepared out of doors, particularly during the hot summer months, when cooking indoors would cause suffocating heat throughout the house. Food preparation took place in smokehouses, butchering sheds, dairies, and outdoor bake ovens as well as in the kitchen.

While kitchens continued to serve many purposes into the nineteenth century, increasingly they were devoted primarily to cooking. In some houses, they were placed at the back to isolate noise, heat, and smells from the more public spaces at the front. Many nineteenth-century kitchens were dominated by massive cast-iron cookstoves, apt symbols of the Industrial Age that produced them, instead of by open fireplaces. Instead of gathering in the kitchen for a range of activities, upper- and middle-class families now moved out of the kitchen and into the parlor, while women, some of them servants, were left laboring in a back room.

The kitchen has been affected by changing technology more than any room in the house. The introduction of electricity in the early twentieth century meant not only the development of new gadgetry, but a transformation in the way food was preserved as electric refrigerators eventually proved far more reliable than ones cooled by ice.

As kitchens came to be used exclusively for cooking, efficiency became the highest priority for layout and design. Domestic reformers advocated small, well-lit spaces. Kitchens decreased in size to allow cooks easy access to food and equipment. Especially for farm women who lived at the edge of exhaustion each step saved was critical. For a time early in the twentieth century, the ideal kitchen was a well-ordered, hygienic laboratory. Running water and refrigeration were essential. Tile, valued because it was easily cleaned, was increasingly used on floors and walls. The availability of mass-produced canned goods and other convenience foods began to ease women's work load.

> It looks as if the iceless refrigerator—along with the horseless carriage, wireless telephone and fireless cooker—has come to stay. Now that the seeming miracle of washing, cooking, sweeping, sewing and dishwashing by electricity has been accomplished, the restless American mind is inquiring whether domestic refrigeration by electricity is practicable.
>
> Clara Zillessen, *House Beautiful*, April 1920.

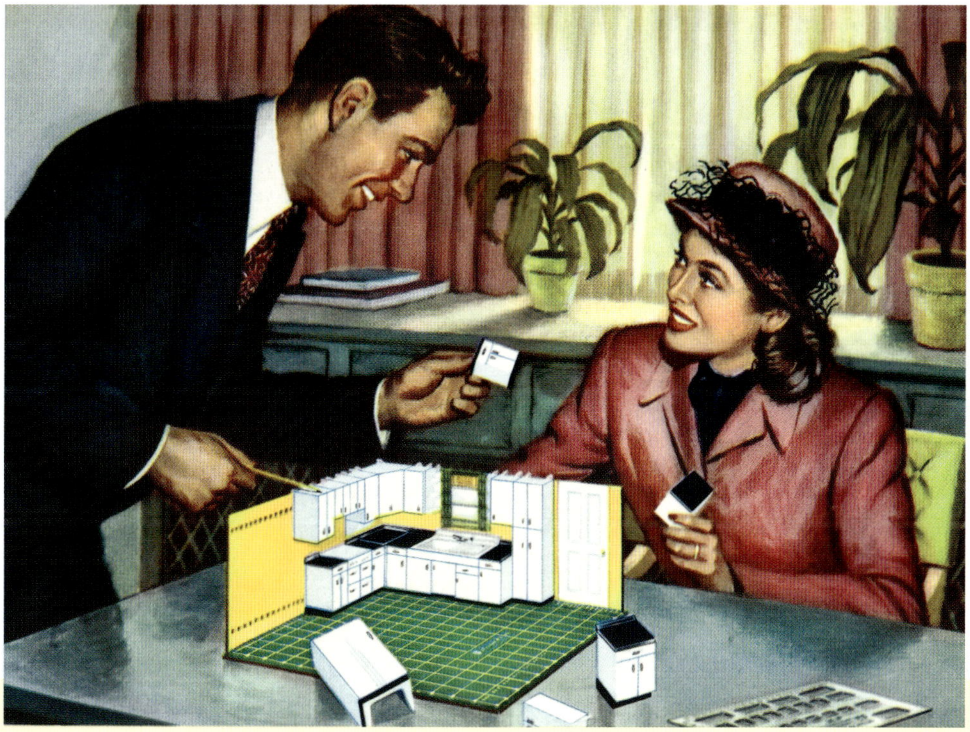

By the middle of the twentieth century, the greatest need in kitchen design was to reintegrate the kitchen into the rest of the house. In an age without servants, women objected to being isolated from their families at the back of the house, and designers responded by creating the now almost universal open plan. However, at a time when the ideal kitchen in the popular imagination was the suburban kitchen of the television program *Leave It to Beaver*, many women, especially those living on farms, were still cooking on woodstoves and pumping water into their sinks. In a few of the country's largest cities, apartments still had bathtubs in the kitchen, covered by a board that served as a table or countertop when the tub was not in use.

Advertisers of the Youngstown Kitchen boasted in a 1948 pamphlet that their dealers could provide plastic models that customers could arrange and rearrange "until you have the snuggest, best looking, most compact kitchen possible."

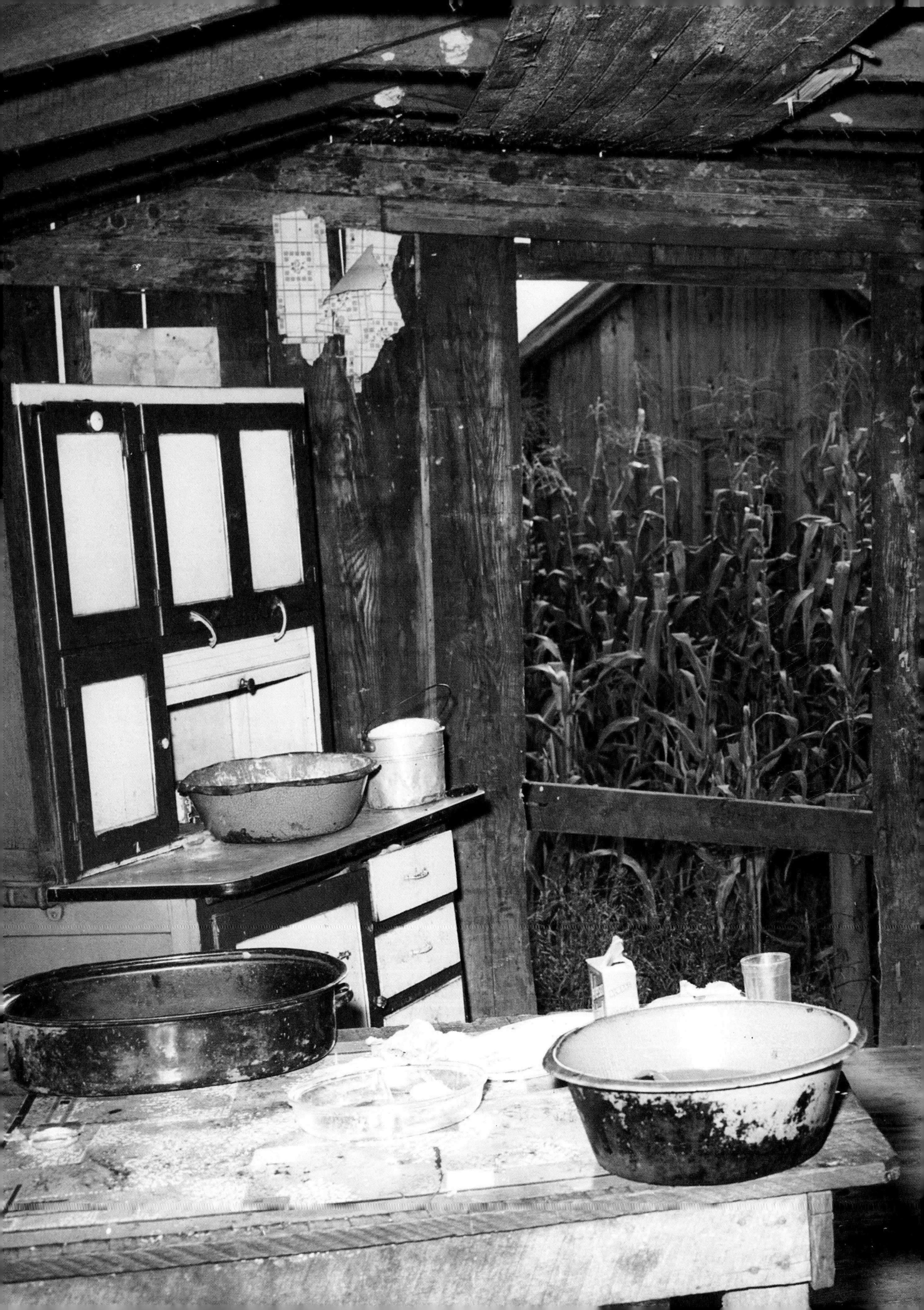

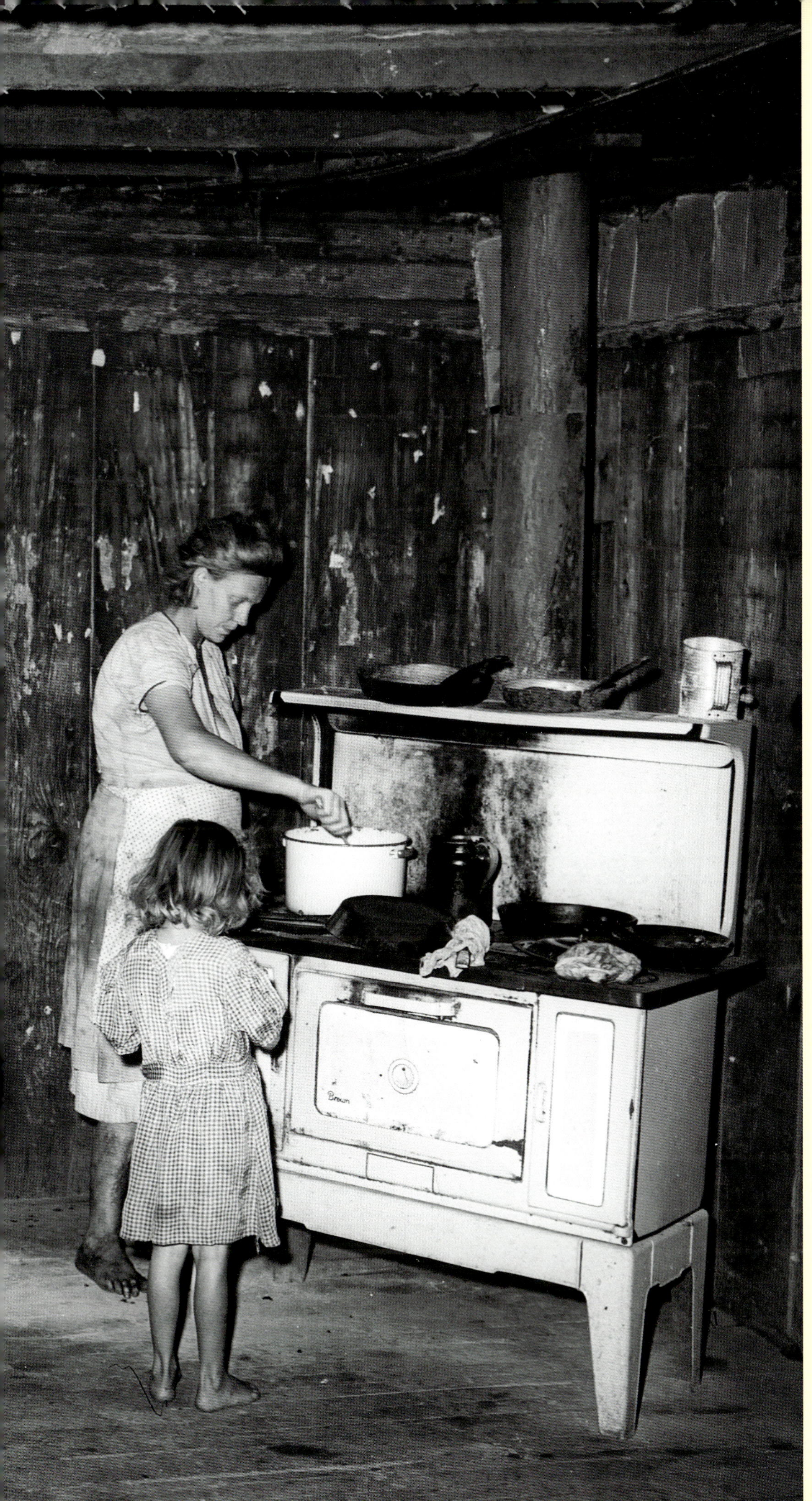

Not everyone took part in the prosperity following World War II. In a Kentucky mining town in 1946, Mrs. Monroe Jones prepared a meal while her daughter watched.

During the 1960s, many women boycotted their potholders at the same time that they burned their bras. Increasingly finding work outside of the home, they looked for ways to liberate themselves from kitchen drudgery. The success of Julia Child's cooking programs and cookbook, *Mastering the Art of French Cooking*, however, suggests that some women were perfecting rather than abandoning their culinary skills. In the years since, as more and more women leave their homes to work full time, the kitchen has become a place of shortcuts, where new appliances like the microwave, crockpot, and food processor, and prepared and frozen foods contribute to lessening the amount of time needed to prepare meals.

## Kitchens Today

Nancy Barker, of Anniston, Alabama, one of an estimated six million American homeowners who renovated their kitchens in 2006,[10] asked her contractor to replace her stove with a desk. He was reluctant, so according to Barker, "he left it so a drop-in range could be added later. But I assure you that won't be necessary." Between heating frozen meals in her microwave and eating out regularly she had no use for a stove.[11]

The most important difference between the way people use their kitchens today and the way previous generations used them is the range of options that make it possible *not* to cook. Many cooks rely on prepackaged frozen foods for some, if not all, of their meals. Other options include take-out from local restaurants or pizza delivery. There are nationally franchised companies such as Dream Dinners and Let's Dish! that provide meal assembly kitchens where women can go to prepare a week's worth of dinners from precut, premeasured ingredients, while the staff takes care of the cleanup. They could buy prepared foods for roughly the same price, but many women feel that assembling the meals themselves makes them better wives and mothers.

Certainly the widespread availability of frozen and packaged prepared foods has transformed the way daily meals are prepared. From health- and calorie-conscious frozen entrées and rotisserie chickens to bagged salad greens, there are now endless shortcuts for family meals. Recent studies suggest, however, that most people routinely also use fresh unprocessed ingredients.[12] One study found that in a typical week in 2007, the average family cooked and ate nearly five dinners out of a possible seven at home. One meal a week was eaten at a restaurant, and fewer than one was a take-out meal.[13] (Using take-out food to alleviate the daily chore of cooking is not new: in many cities, it has been available for a century or more.)

More often than not, someone is in the modern American kitchen cooking. The question is, who? In a 2007 study of a group of households in the Los Angeles region, one meal in five of those prepared was cooked in whole or in part by men.[14] Another nationwide survey suggests that only half of all women are responsible for cooking all of their family's meals and nearly half of all men do half or more of the cooking.[15] Indeed, not all men cook, and

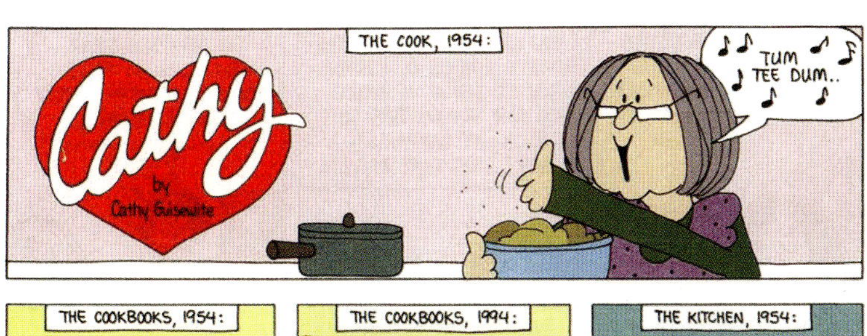


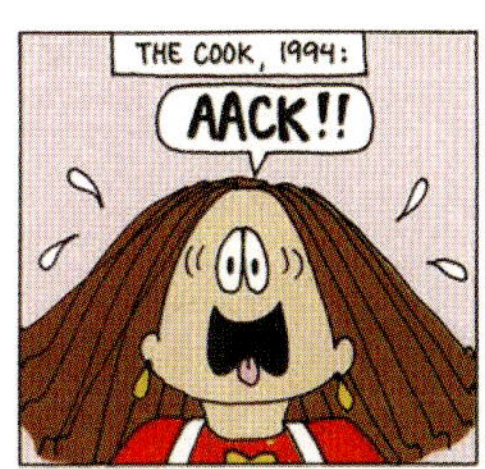


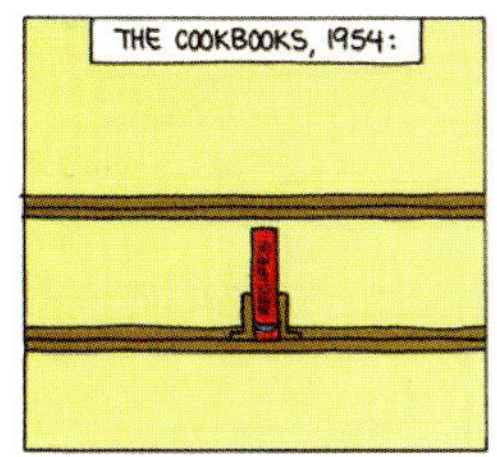

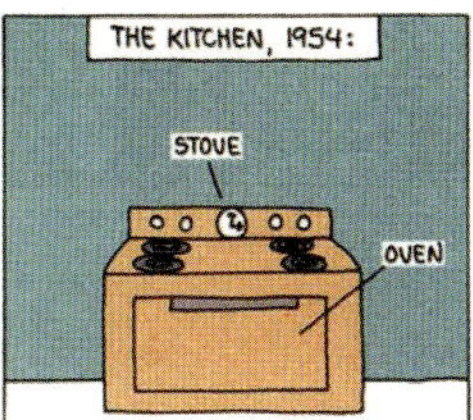


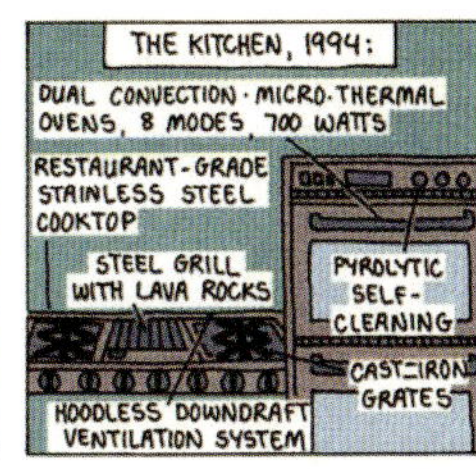


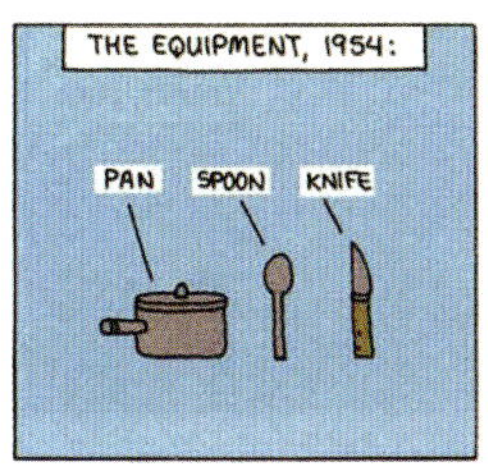


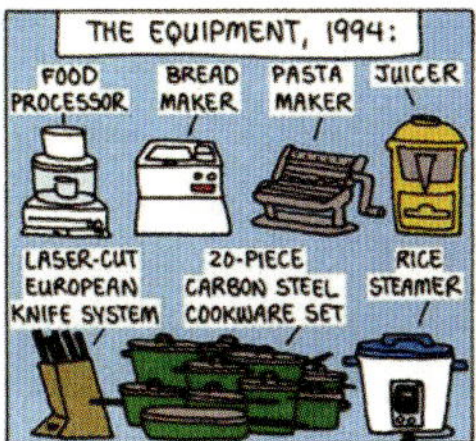


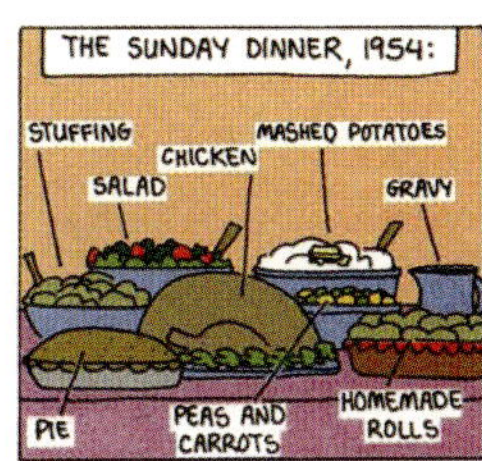


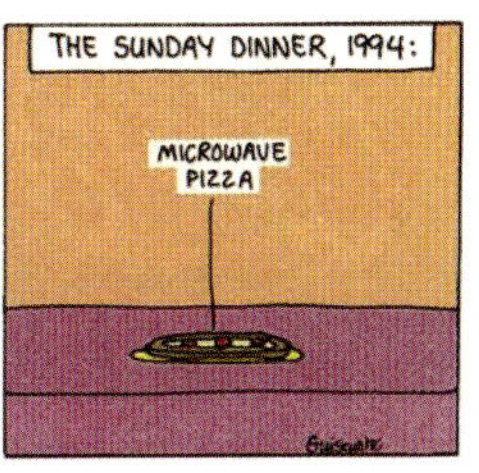


Cartoonist Cathy Guisewite perfectly captures the irony of late-twentieth-century kitchens. 

not all men who do cook do anything more than contribute the occasional special meal or barbecued entrée. But the numbers are growing. A 2006 Pew Research Center study found that 32 percent of men say that they very much enjoy cooking, up from 25 percent in 1989.[16] In addition, thanks in part to microwave ovens, older children occasionally make their own meals. This means that many American women are cooking less often then their mothers and grandmothers did.

Paradoxically, at a time when women are cooking fewer meals and the preparation of these meals is less complex, kitchens are reaching new technological and design heights, with so-called professional-grade appliances that can cost as much as a car. Shelter magazines and food programs on cable television bombard homeowners with information about the latest kitchen gadgetry and design.[17] While the costliest appliances are still out of range of most homeowners' budgets, appliance companies are producing less expensive versions with many of the same features. The result is that increasing numbers of people can have kitchens with the most up-to-date high-tech equipment.

Many see investing in their homes as sound financial strategy, with the added benefit of providing a showcase in which to entertain. Russell Morash, the creator of one of the first home remodeling programs, *This Old House*, notes, "We've moved away from the well-mannered, out-of-the-way appliances to in-your-face kitchen as theater."[18] Not surprisingly, as men take more notice of the kitchen, the amount that families spend on equipping the space is more generous than when the room was the exclusive domain of women. Accord-

Koppel, quoted in Pilar Guzman, "Hey Man, What's for Dinner?" *New York Times*, August 28, 2002, is convinced that the reason many domestic kitchens have become sites of such over-the-top conspicuous consumption is that increasing numbers of men are cooking.

> It's only since men have been cooking that you can justify the $275 knife.
>
> Ross Koppel, Department of Sociology, University of Pennsylvania

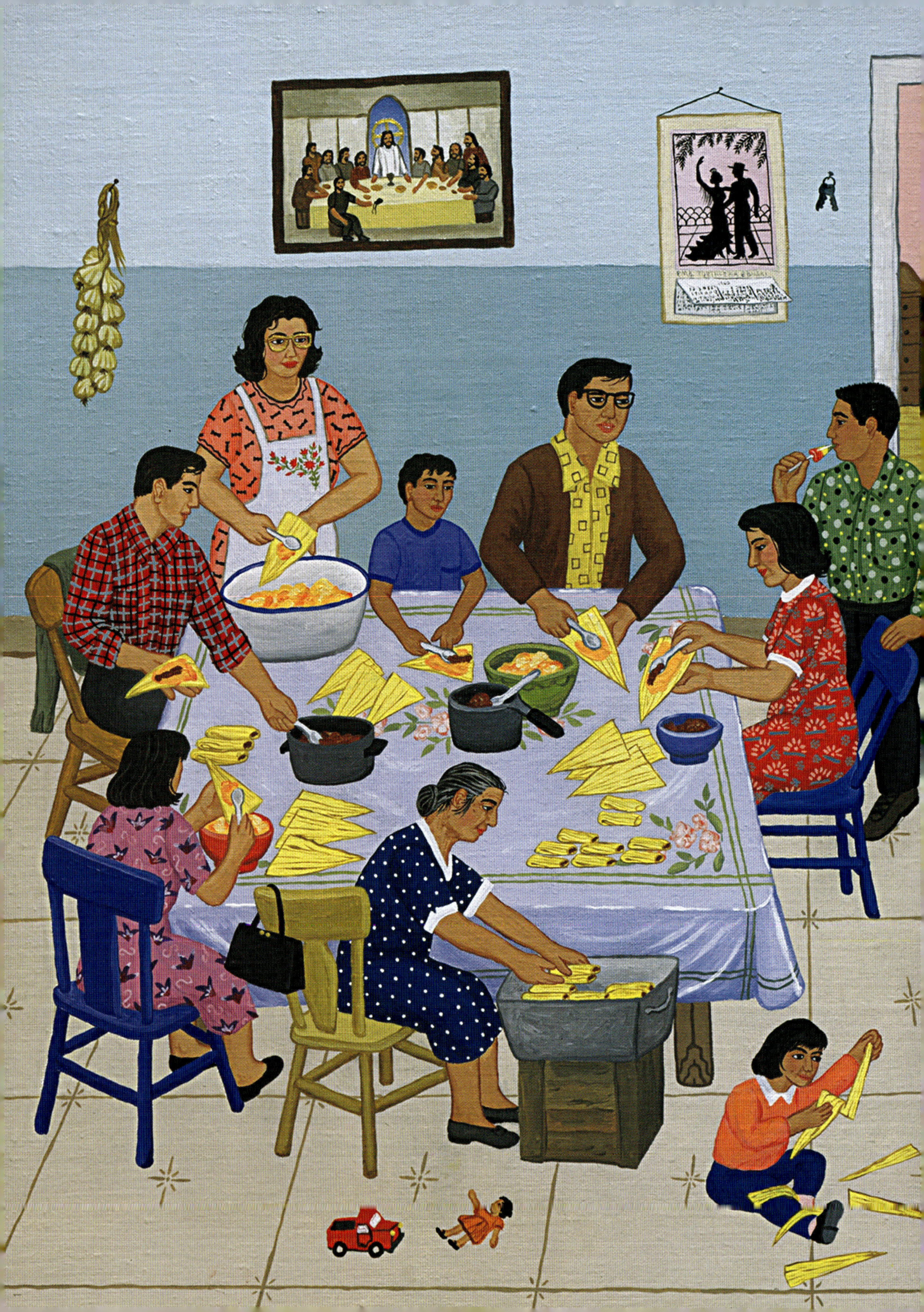

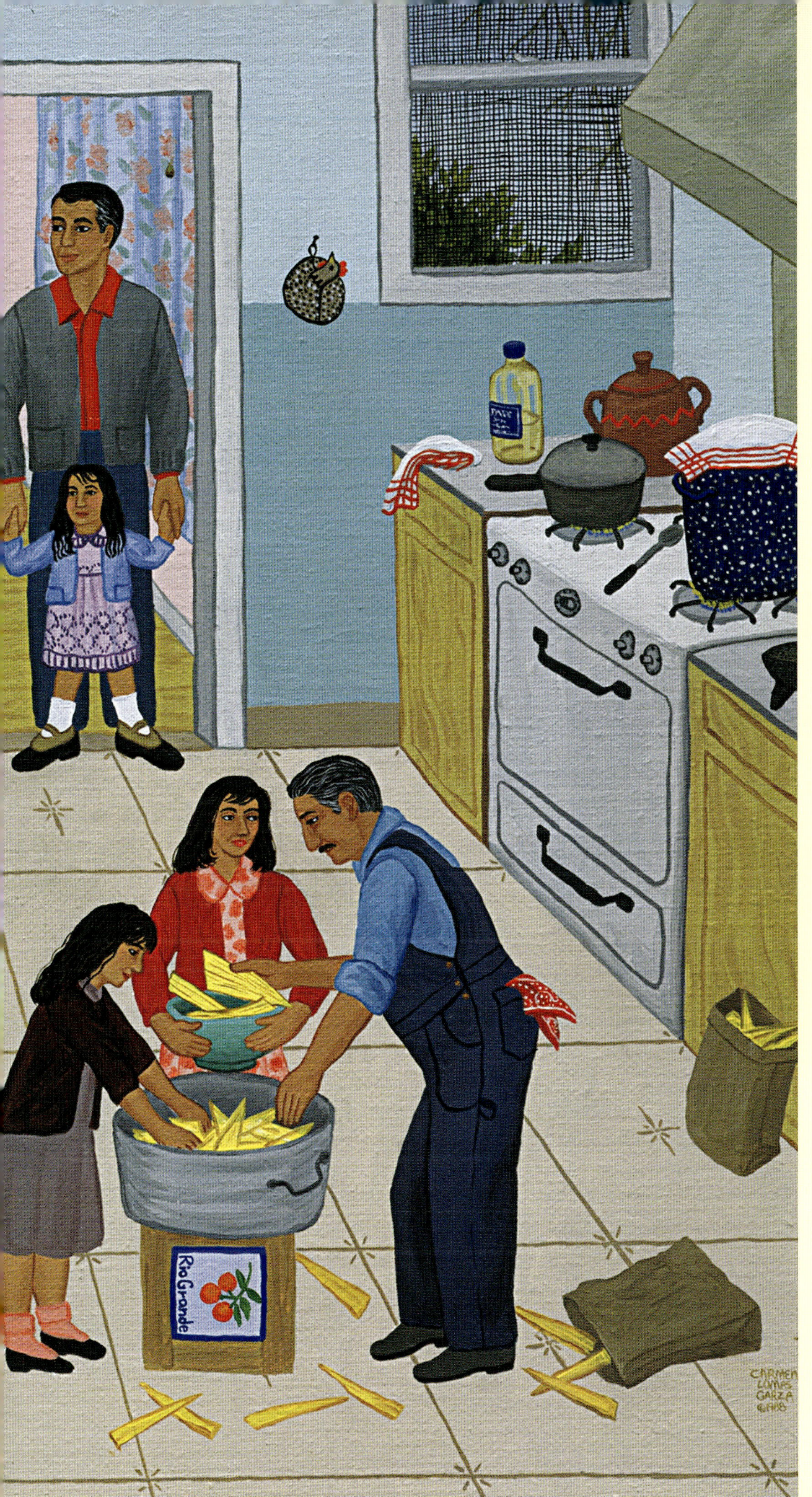


Chicana artist Carmen Lomas Garza's painting recalls her parents' rural South Texas kitchen. The extended family has gathered to make tamales for the Christmas season. In many Latino communities, *tamaladas*—tamale-making parties—are a traditional precursor of Christmas.

ing to design critic Thomas Hine, "Men have taken to cooking and made it into a hobby and a locus of consumption and gadgetry."[19] Martyn Straw, a New York advertising executive, commented on the cultural shift: "Cooking was once domestic, kind of homely. Now it's sexy and it's all about entertainment."[20]

The ideal kitchen is typically pictured as a large open space that is the center of family life and entertaining. Formal living and dining rooms have given way to large so-called great rooms with a kitchen at the center. The space revolves around an island, where people can sit and interact with the cook. Workstations for cleaning produce, chopping, mixing, cooking, preparing drinks, and cleanup replace the traditional triangular arrangement of stove, sink, and refrigerator. The result is intentional redundancy, sometimes involving multiple stoves, sinks, dishwashers, and refrigerators.

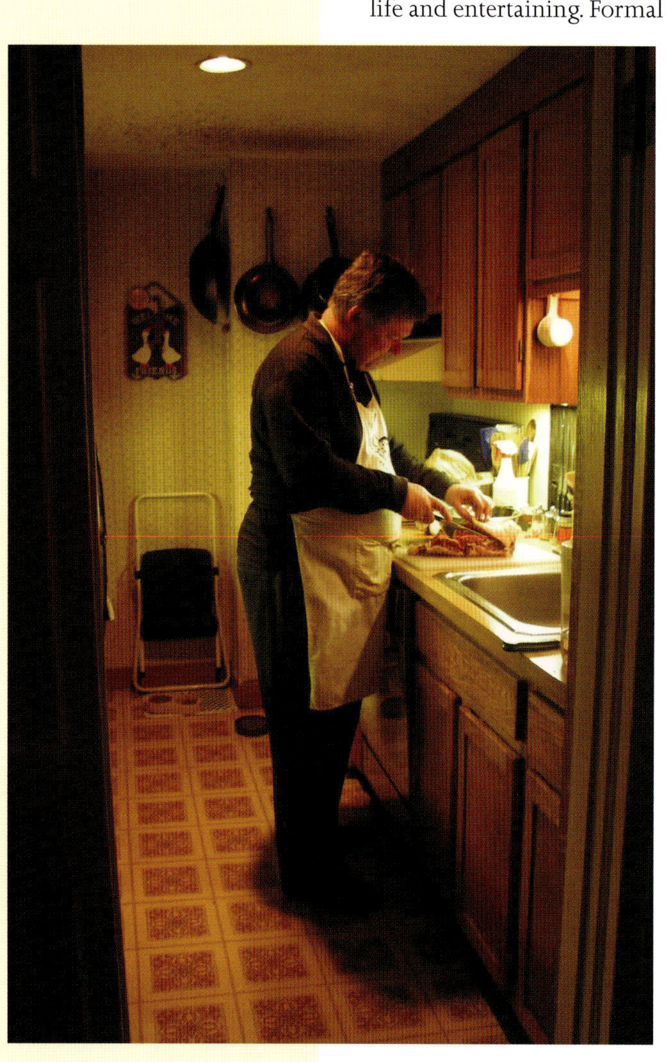

Glossy magazines give the impression that most Americans live with huge kitchens dominated by beautiful granite-topped central islands, however, many cooks manage to produce excellent meals in cramped quarters. Here, chef J.T. Aldridge prepares to cure bacon in the thirty-year-old galley kitchen in his Boston home.

Often these kitchens include space for a computer and portable electronic devices. Cooks can look up recipes online or order a complete list of groceries. Even the mobile phone has affected families' food habits; women, still the traditional grocery shoppers, can delegate errands to husbands and teenage children, who can call from the store to make sure they are getting the right cut of meat or brand of mustard.[21]

In kitchen design, a growing concern for building "green" has meant using renewable resources like fast-growing bamboo for flooring; reusing old materials or refacing cabinetry to keep things out of landfills; and selecting energy-efficient appliances and lighting. Organic foods, perceived as more healthful and much better for the environment, are becoming increasingly mainstream, and there is a trend to buy produce locally, both to support small farms and reduce one's carbon footprint.

Of course not everyone can afford a new kitchen, and not everyone wants one. Apartment dwellers, accustomed to efficient galley kitchens, still manage to produce good meals and entertain their guests in another room. Some recent immigrants must manage with limited facilities and get by with microwaves, hot plates, crockpots, or electric grills to create comforting home-cooked meals.[22]

While new immigrants have faced challenges, later generations do as well. In Texas, Crystal Marra faces a daily balancing act between her American upbringing, her mother and grandmother's Mexican traditions, and her husband's Italian and Argentinean roots. As a child growing up in the 1970s, Marra never developed a taste for the "heavy, fat-laden foods that my grandparents enjoy," or for the "lengua (tongue), cow brains, and other strange concoctions." She admits that she is "not all that great about seeing my meats close to their natural state—I prefer plastic wrapped, on a little Styrofoam tray with a price sticker and nutrition information. Very American." She and her husband have adapted her family's way of making *migas* (a breakfast dish of fried tortillas with egg, salsa, and cheese) substituting more healthful ingredients, using corn tortillas instead of wheat, olive oil instead of lard, vegetables, and low-fat cheese. "In the end, it was migas in spirit, but it looked and tasted nothing like the migas my grandma prepares." While adapting the recipe to suit her tastes, clearly, preserving a link with her family's traditions is important.[23]

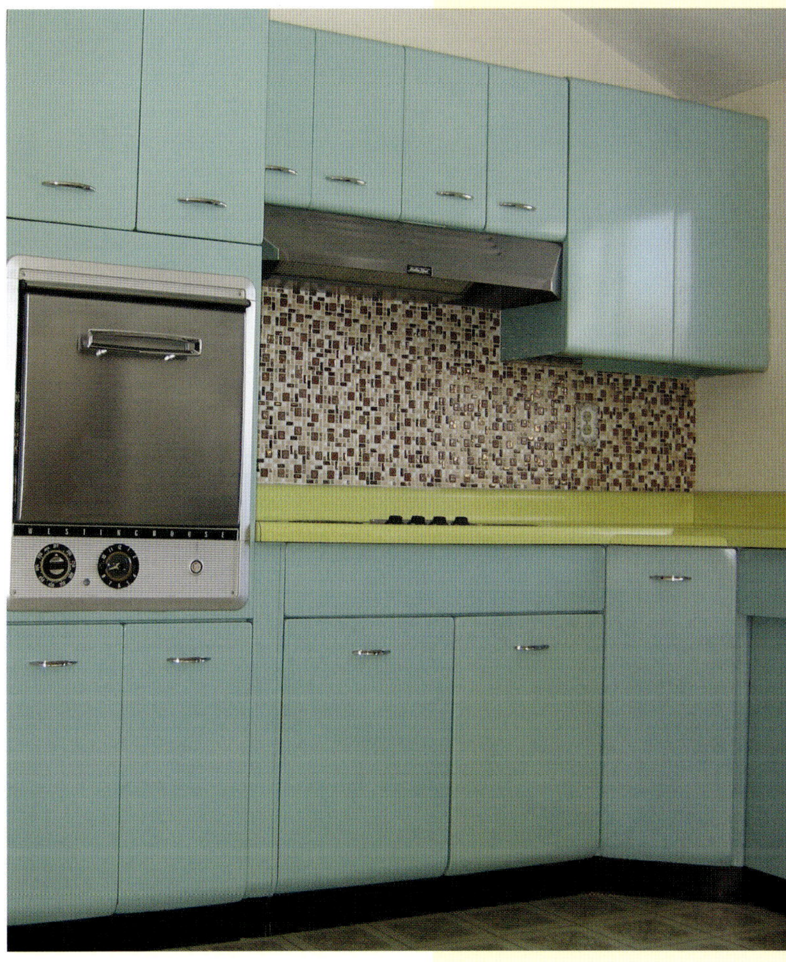

Olivia Sintros's parents installed this kitchen in their newly built home in Andover, Massachusetts, in 1957, but rarely used it. Instead, they did most of their cooking in a second kitchen in the basement.

In 2007, when the Sintros family of Massachusetts decided to remodel their kitchen, they replaced one that was nearly as pristine as it had been the day it was installed fifty years earlier. Like many Greek and Italian immigrant families, the Sintroses had two kitchens, one in the basement for everyday use, and a second show kitchen used only on special occasions.[24] Having already remodeled the basement kitchen, and in spite of the fact that she rarely cooked, Olivia Sintros insisted it was now time to renovate their show kitchen; having grown up with two kitchens, she felt the house would not be complete without both.

The Marra and Sintros stories are emblematic of the importance of food and family traditions in the lives of Americans. More than just a place to cook, the kitchen is where these traditions are honored, celebrated, and passed from one generation to the next. The following chapters explore kitchens from the East Coast to the Midwest and Southwest, from the eighteenth century to the twentieth, and show how the room has varied from place to place and over time. While new technologies and their effects will be part of the story, more important is the way women have lived in and used the space. While certain universals pertain, the variety of ways that individuals use their kitchens is boundless. By exploring these spaces, readers may gain a greater appreciation for their own kitchens as well as for the women who have taught us all how to live in them.

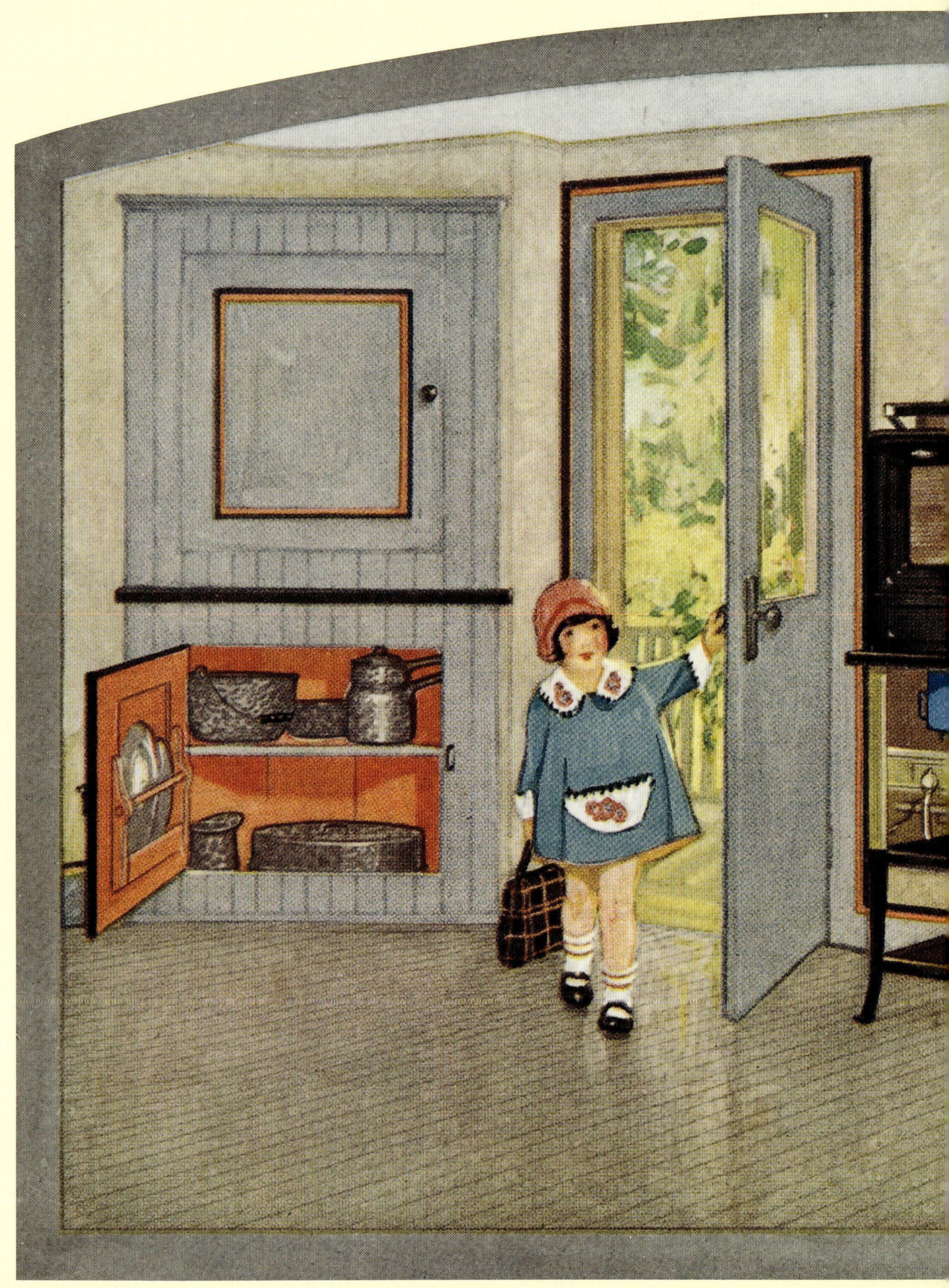

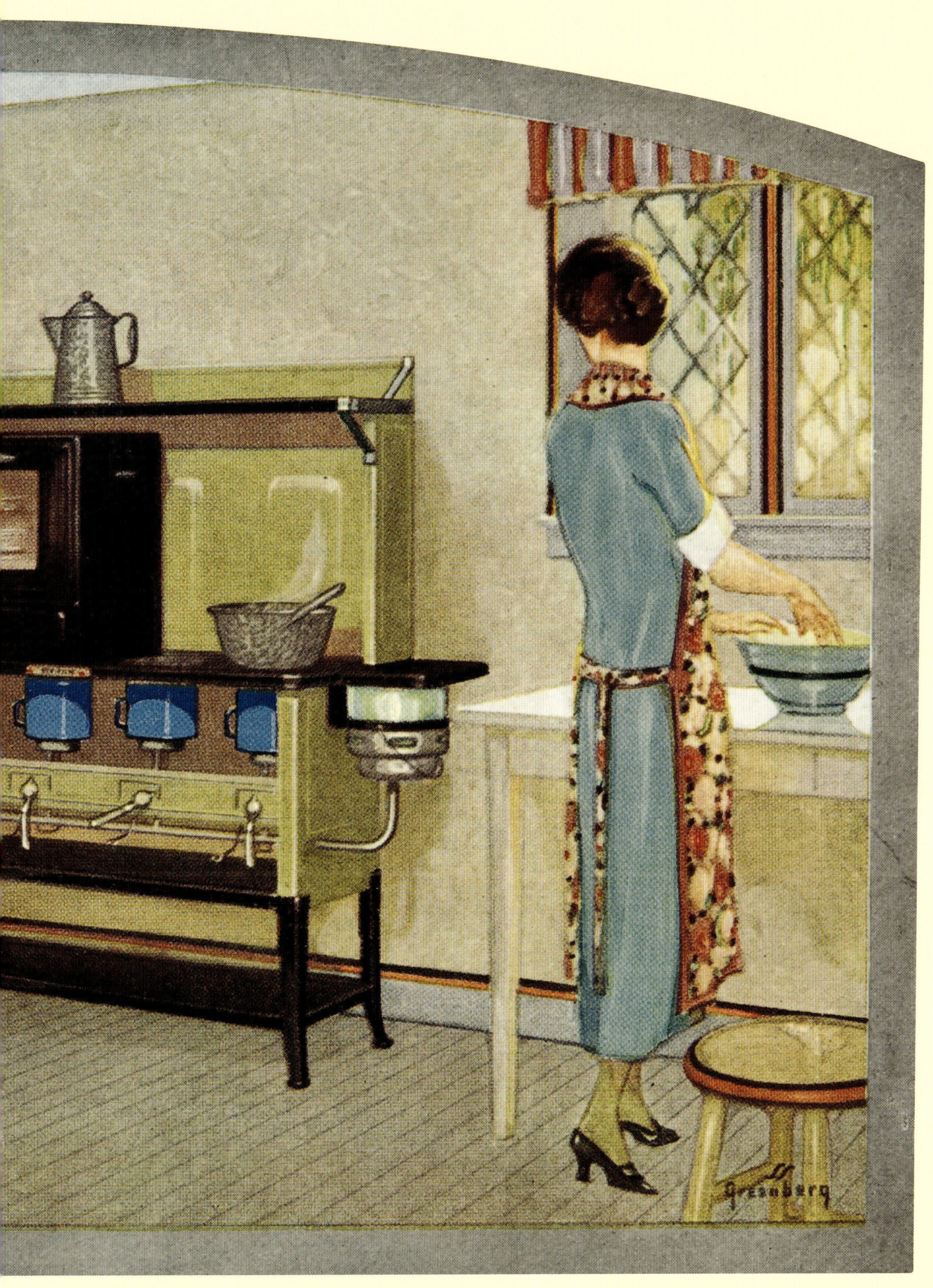

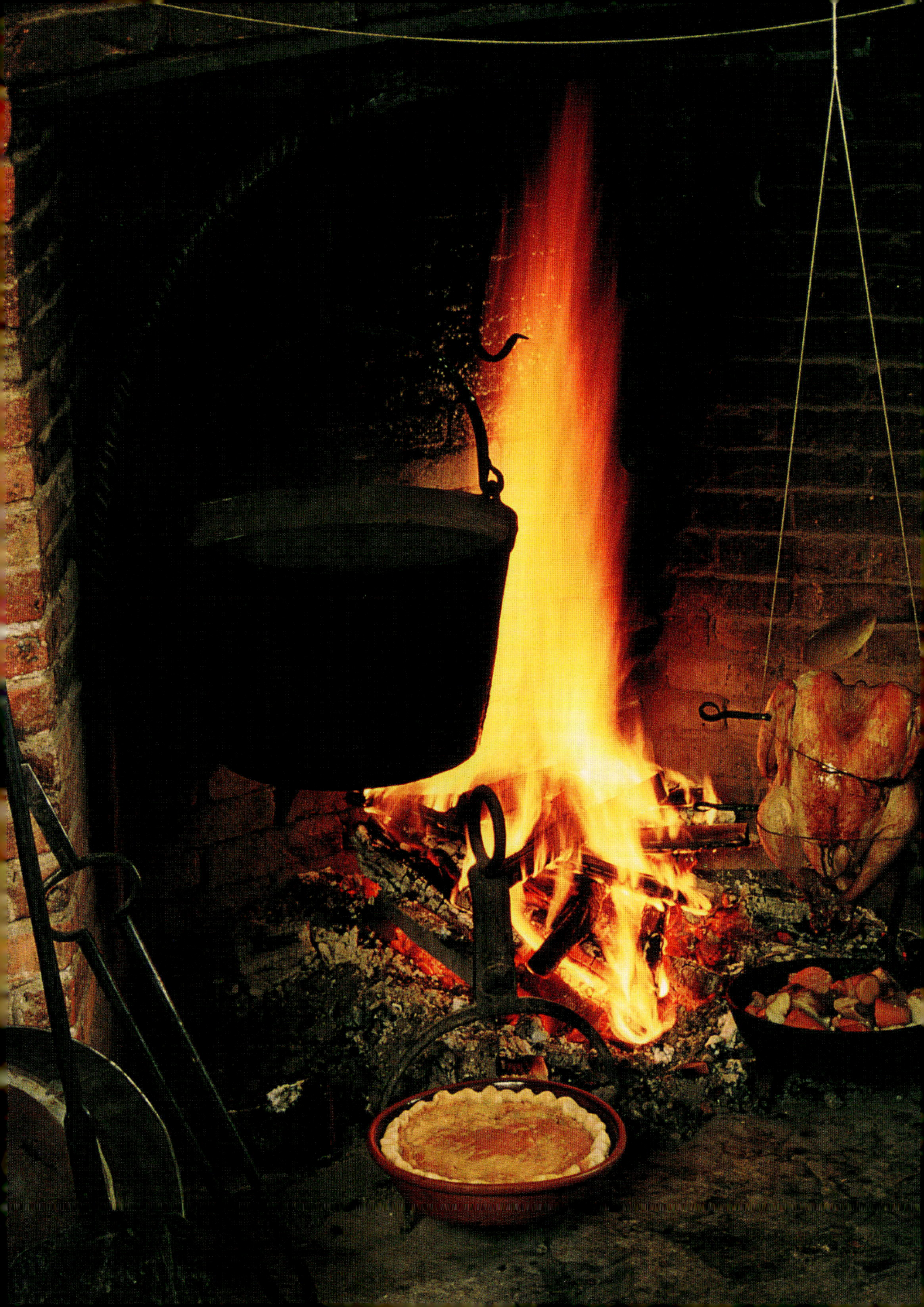

# THE NEW ENGLAND HEARTH

## {1720–1840}

### The Coffin Family Homestead

In the Coffin family's large, rambling house in Newbury, Massachusetts, two cooking hearths stood back to back.[1] In the years leading up to the Revolution, one kitchen was used by Margaret Coffin and her husband, Joseph, and the other by their son Joshua, his wife, Sarah, and their children. Although it might have conserved both effort and fuel if mother-in-law and daughter-in-law had shared one kitchen, it is more likely that each cooked at her own hearth.[2] Sarah Anna Emery, the well-known nineteenth-century chronicler of life in early Newbury, described a similar arrangement in even closer quarters. When Daniel Colman married Nancy Pike,

> *the young couple commenced housekeeping in half of Col. Jeremiah Colman's house. . . . A large L was soon added to the house, giving accommodations to the two families; but for some months the two sisters-in-law shared the kitchen, one having a fire in one corner of the capacious fireplace and the other in the opposite, the brick oven being used alternately. Mrs. Jeremiah Colman was fond of adverting to this period, always ending her recital with "and we never had one word of difference."*[3]

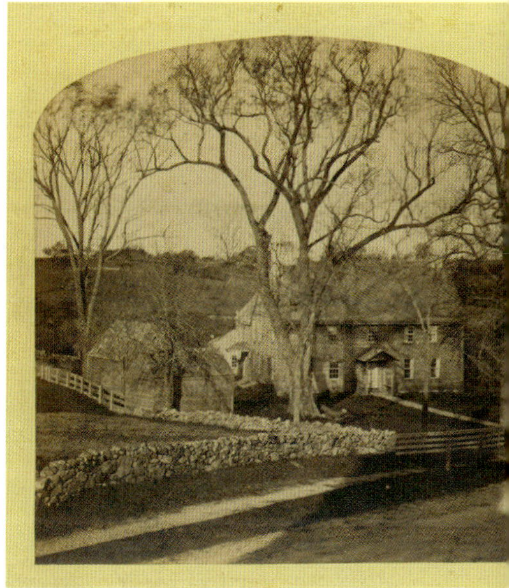

Throughout most of its history, the Coffin house in Newbury, Massachusetts, housed more than one family—several generations of Coffins or, later, the families of siblings. The original two-and-a-half-story structure of 1678 more than tripled in size in 1713, with an addition to the front that reoriented the house toward the road.

Women in the Coffin and Colman families enjoyed sovereignty over their own kitchen fires and their own resources. After Margaret and Sarah Coffin were both widowed, Sarah carefully noted when Margaret owed her for something as slight as a half pound of coffee.[4] Serving separate meals and keeping accurate accounts helped protect both women in the event of a conflict.

The relationship between Joseph and Joshua Coffin, and therefore between their wives, appears to have been tense. Even though father and son lived in the same house and worked together in the family's tanyard, Joshua wrote to his father in 1764 to ask for permission

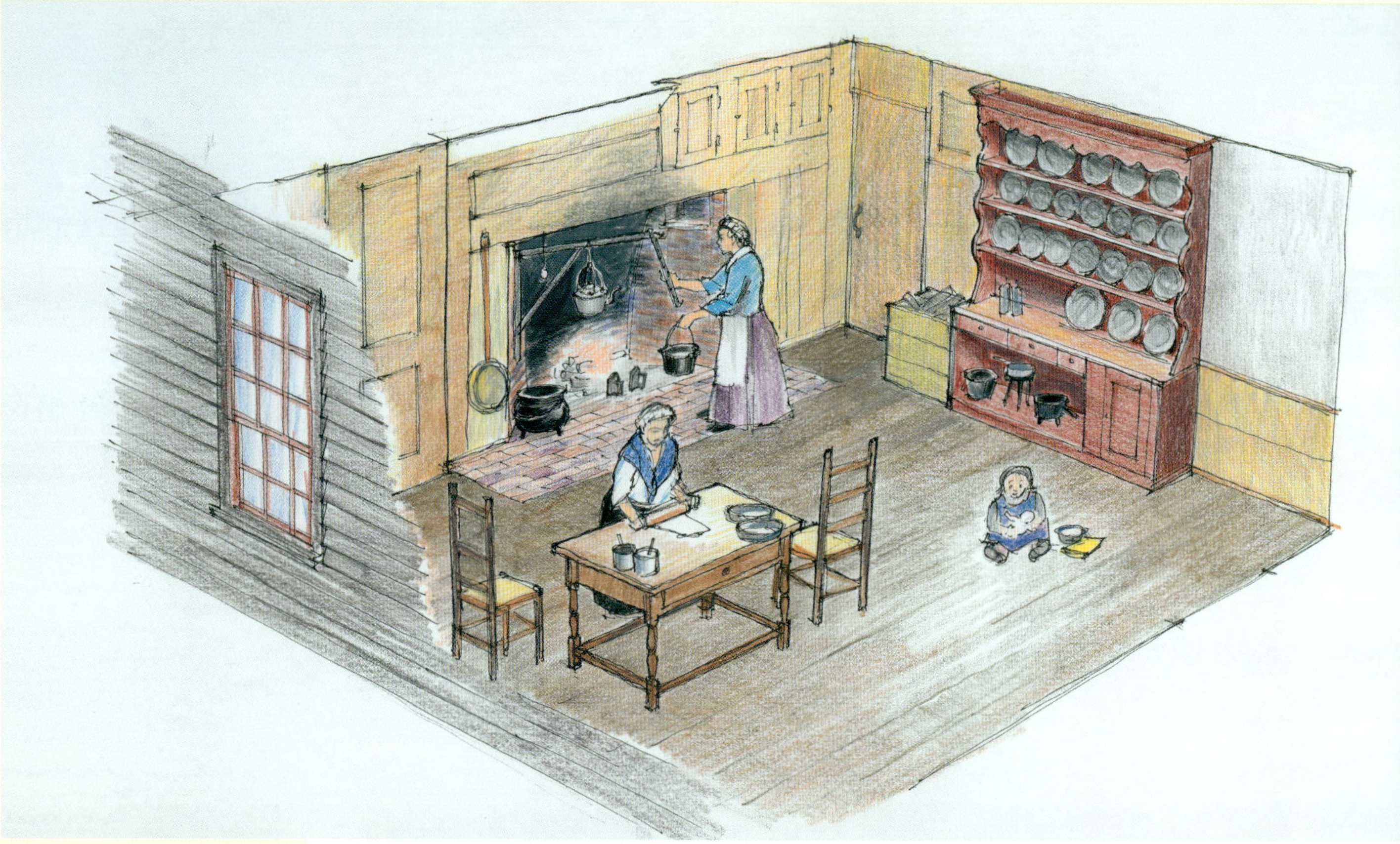

This kitchen is one of two in the Coffin house. It was updated in the 1760s with wall paneling and a dresser. It is not clear whether the older or younger Mrs. Coffin occupied this space.

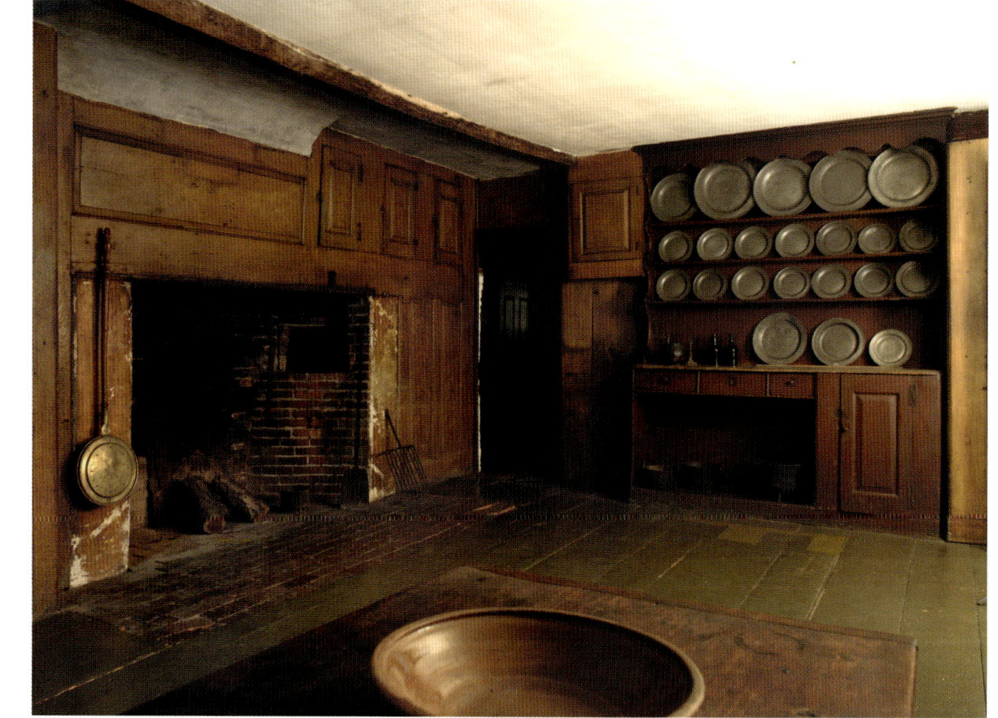

Caleb Huse, a Coffin descendant, fondly recalled the kitchen of his youth in the 1840s: "I remember distinctly the great fireplace in the kitchen . . . and at the right as you entered was the Dresser, with its shelves well filled with very bright pewter platters[,] plates and 'porringers.'" Today the kitchen survives as part of a historic house museum operated by Historic New England.

to make improvements to the house at his own expense.[5] This carefully worded request seems to have had the desired effect, as it was about this time that one of the kitchens was divided to create a separate sitting room and updated with paneled walls and the installation of a built-in dresser.[6]

Eighteenth-century New England kitchens were hubs of activity. The hearth, a source of light and heat, drew members of the household to eat, work, and even to sleep. With its large size and two cooking hearths, the home the Coffins lived in was not typical, but the activities that took place in the kitchens were similar to those that took place throughout the region.

## "Some things which my daughter . . . had of me"

Some women began housekeeping with little more than a knife, a spoon, and an iron pot. The Coffins' daughters Sarah and Susanna were better equipped. At the time of their marriages, Joseph Coffin gave both daughters the items they needed to set up households of their own.[7] Although no inventory of their "portions" seems to exist, each was valued at £863, a sizable sum. While their brothers were given land, houses, and schooling, the sisters probably received a variety of new and used but serviceable bed and table linens, furnishings for every room in the house, and possibly livestock, as well.[8] Their cooking equipment probably varied little from what their grandfather Nathaniel Coffin had listed nearly thirty years earlier as part of their aunt Jane's portion: an assortment of pots and kettles for boiling, pans for stewing and frying, a spit for roasting, a gridiron for broiling, tools for tending the fire, and platters for serving the meal.[9] In addition to household goods, Joseph Coffin noted that he gave each daughter "part of a Negro girl Lucy," each part valued at £45.[10]

Slavery was a legal, familiar, and vital part of the colonial New England economy.[11] Not only did merchants prosper from the slave trade and related goods, but individual households, farms, and businesses depended on the labor of enslaved Native Americans and

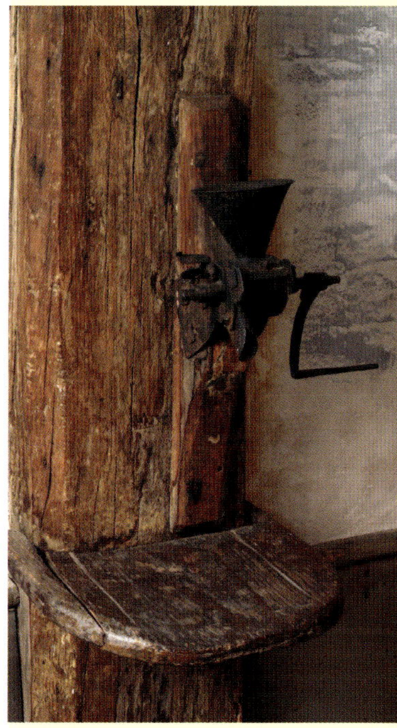

Although the probate inventory taken after the death of Joshua Coffin in 1774 does not indicate the location of the goods within the house, it includes food-related items that were presumably used in and around the kitchen, including a coffee mill that may be the same one that survives in the house to this day. The values are in English pounds, shillings, and pence.

### Estate of Joshua Coffin Esq. late of Newbury, 1774

| | |
|---|---|
| Iron hollow ware 15/ frying pan & Ladle 7/ brass & copper ware 26/ | 2. . . 8. . . 0 |
| Trammels andirons & other Ironware 35/1 Coffee Mill 2/ | 1. . . 17. . . 0 |
| 1 Warming pan 3/2 pr bellows 4/1 dozn knives & forks 9/ | 0. . . 16. . . 0 |
| 1 box Iron & heaters 3/6 4 dozn bottles 12/8 quintle fish 40/ | 3. . . 3. . . 6 |
| Old Cask 10/2 Candle sticks & 9 baskets 10/scieves milk pans woodware 10/ | 1. . . 10. . . 0 |

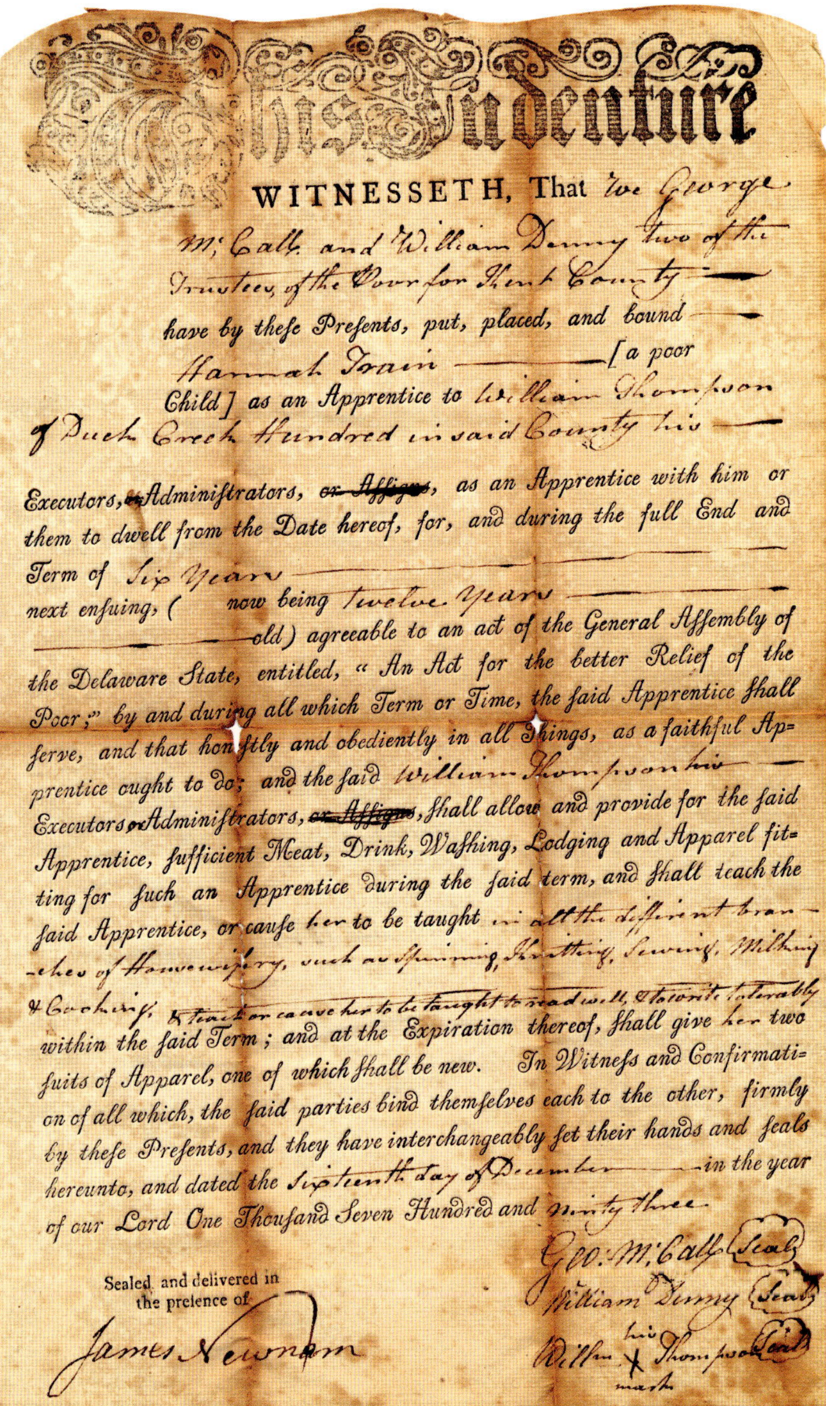

This Indenture

WITNESSETH, That we George M'Call and William Denny two of the Trustees of the Poor for Kent County — have by these Presents, put, placed, and bound Hannah Train —— [a poor Child] as an Apprentice to William Thompson of Duck Creek Hundred in said County his — Executors, ~~or~~ Administrators, ~~or Assigns~~, as an Apprentice with him or them to dwell from the Date hereof, for, and during the full End and Term of Six Years —— next ensuing, ( now being twelve Years —— old) agreeable to an act of the General Assembly of the Delaware State, entitled, « An Act for the better Relief of the Poor;" by and during all which Term or Time, the said Apprentice shall serve, and that honestly and obediently in all Things, as a faithful Apprentice ought to do; and the said William Thompson his — Executors ~~or~~ Administrators, ~~or Assigns~~, shall allow and provide for the said Apprentice, sufficient Meat, Drink, Washing, Lodging and Apparel fitting for such an Apprentice during the said term, and shall teach the said Apprentice, or cause her to be taught in all the different branches of Housewifery, such as Spinning, Knitting, Sewing, Milking & Cooking, & teach or cause her to be taught to read well, & to write tolerably within the said Term; and at the Expiration thereof, shall give her two suits of Apparel, one of which shall be new. In Witness and Confirmation of all which, the said parties bind themselves each to the other, firmly by these Presents, and they have interchangeably set their hands and seals hereunto, and dated the Sixteenth day of December —— in the year of our Lord One Thousand Seven Hundred and ninety three.

Sealed and delivered in the presence of
James Newnam

Geo: M'Call (Seal)
William Denny (Seal)
William his + mark Thompson (Seal)

This 1793 legal indenture, typical of the period, recorded that twelve-year-old Hannah Train, "a poor Child," was bound as an apprentice to William Thompson of Kent County, Delaware, for a period of six years. Thompson agreed to provide her with an education "in all the different branches of Housewifery, such as Spinning, Knitting, Sewing, Milking & Cooking."

African Americans. The enslaved girl, Lucy, either lived with one of Joseph Coffin's married daughters or moved back and forth between the two. Depending on her age, she may have helped look after the children or carried out more demanding chores, such as laundry, freeing the sisters to do other work.

In 1742 the appraisers of the estate of Benjamin Moreshead of nearby Salem clearly thought that "One Negro Girl Call'd Rose ab't 15 years old" belonged in the kitchen, listing her in the inventory just above the pots and kettles.[12] While Joseph Coffin's married daughters clearly shared an enslaved girl, it is not certain whether his wife, Margaret, or daughter-in-law, Sarah, ever had a slave working in her kitchen, but it is quite possible. Nearly a century later, Joseph Coffin's great-grandson, the historian and abolitionist Joshua Coffin, wrote: "With few exceptions, all classes of people [in Essex County], merchants, farmers, mechanics, professors of religion, and ministers of the gospel, bought and sold slaves, apparently without the slightest idea of the enormity of the sin, and on the same principle that they would purchase a horse, a sheep, or a piece of land. They thus necessarily sanctioned the slave trade, and all its unspeakable abominations."[13] The Coffins were also accustomed to hiring help when they needed it. At times they paid a widow or a young neighbor to work for a day, a week, or longer. In 1774, for example, Sarah hired her twenty-year-old niece for £40 a year even though she still had four daughters at home.[14]

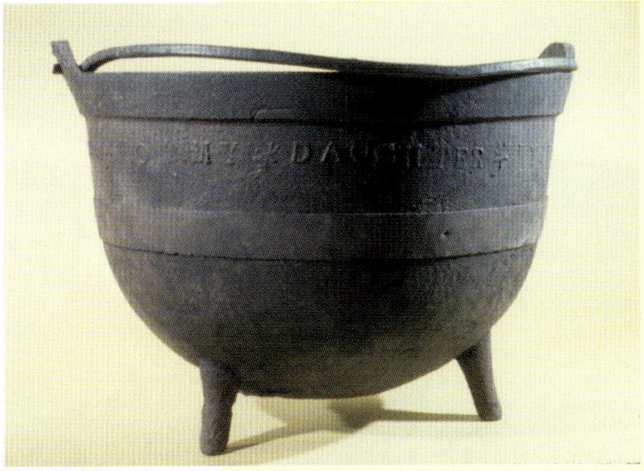

This iron kettle bears the inscription "This I give to my daughter Lydia J. Clap, 1801, R. Cady." Fathers transferred wealth to their daughters at their marriage by giving them the items they needed when they "went to housekeeping."

## An account of some things which my daughter Jane had of me, 1728

| | | | |
|---|---|---|---|
| to a Brass kittle two Iron pots two skillits two basons and two porringers | 03 | 00 | 00 |
| to a chafen dish a Box Iron & two kandle sticks | 00 | 18 | 00 |
| to eight platters | 03 | 01 | 06 |
| to bails for y$^{e}$ pots | 00 | 02 | 06 |
| to two skillit frams | 00 | 05 | 00 |
| to a gridiron & flesh fork | 00 | 08 | 00 |
| to a fire shovle | 00 | 06 | 00 |
| two porringers | 00 | 05 | 06 |
| a pair of belows | 00 | 04 | 00 |
| a puding pan 7$^{d}$ | 00 | 00 | 07 |
| a brass kittle | 05 | 16 | 00 |
| a belmetle skilit | 01 | 02 | 00 |

Nathaniel Coffin kept a list of the goods he gave to his daughter Jane at the time of her marriage. Like most fathers of the period who could afford to do so, Coffin set his daughter up for her role as a housewife. This excerpt from Coffin's list suggests that Jane's kitchen was well equipped.

## "All the different branches of Housewifery"

Eighteenth-century women rarely questioned their role, which both complemented and deferred to that of men.[15] Men would cut and split wood, bank fires, carry water, and help with seasonal projects such as paring apples for apple butter, but most kitchen work fell to women. There was never a shortage of work: daily chores like cooking and dishwashing, weekly rounds of laundry and baking, seasonal activities such as gardening and preserving, and the seemingly never-ending tasks of sewing, spinning, and caring for the young, ill, and infirm. These activities took housewives to the well, cellar, garret, dairy yard, kitchen garden, smokehouse, and beyond, but the demands of housekeeping generally kept women, and therefore children, close to the kitchen hearth. The skills of housewifery were usually learned by a young girl at her mother's side.

### A Nice Indian Pudding

3 pints scalded milk, 7 spoons fine Indian meal, stir well together while hot, let stand till cooled; add 7 eggs, half pound raisins, 4 ounces butter, spice and sugar, bake one and half hour.

Amelia Simmons, *American Cookery*, 1798

One of three recipes Simmons includes in her cookbook for Indian Pudding, the main ingredient is "Indian," or cornmeal. Corn was introduced to colonists by the native population nearly two centuries earlier and had become a staple ingredient in every American household.

Good housewives kept their kitchens clean and orderly. Equipment was stored when not in use to keep work areas clear. Wood chips, soot, creosote, ashes, food spills, and dirt from frequent foot traffic called for sweeping, scrubbing, and, in many households, an occasional application of whitewash. The floor was scoured, sometimes with a layer of sand left to absorb spills and drips. Sarah Anna Emery recalled that her aunt swept the sand into patterns: "Seizing the broom, she drew the freshly-strewn sand on the kitchen floor into a remarkable combination of zig-zags."[16]

Good housewifery also required the constant monitoring of supplies. Urban households had access to markets for some of their food, but in rural areas, provisions were stored in and around the house: dried corn in garrets, vegetables in root cellars, hams in smokehouses. Throughout the year, housewives inspected stores of meat, grains, produce, butter, and cheese for signs of insect and rodent infestation and spoilage.

Turkey had yet to be codified as a traditional Thanksgiving meal; this is the first printed recipe that pairs the dish with cranberry, or, as written here, "cramberry."

### To Stuff and Roast a Turkey, or Fowl

One pound soft wheat bread, 3 ounces beef suet, 3 eggs, a little sweet thyme, sweet majoram, pepper and salt, and some add a gill of wine; fill the bird therewith and sew up, hang down to a steady solid fire, basting frequently with salt and water, and roast until a steam emits from the breast, put one third of a pound of butter into the gravy, dust flour over the bird and baste with the gravy; serve up with boiled onions and cramberry-sauce, mangoes, pickles or celery.

Amelia Simmons, *American Cookery*, 1798

AMERICAN COOKE

OR THE ART OF DRESSING

VIANDS, FISH, POULTRY and VEGETABLES,

AND THE BEST MODES OF MAKING

PASTES, PUFFS, PIES, TARTS, PUDDINGS, CUSTARDS AND PRESERVES,

AND ALL KINDS OF

CAKES,

FROM THE IMPERIAL PLUMB TO PLAIN CAKE.

ADAPTED TO THIS COUNTRY,

AND ALL GRADES OF LIFE.

By Amelia Simmons,

AN AMERICAN ORPHAN.

PUBLISHED ACCORDING TO ACT OF CONGRESS.

*HARTFORD:*

PRINTED BY HUDSON & GOODWIN,

FOR THE AUTHOR.

1796.

Eliza Smith's *The Compleat Housewife*, first published in London in 1727 and printed in Virginia in 1742, was the first cookbook printed in America. More than fifty years elapsed before Amelia Simmons's *American Cookery* was published, the first cookbook written by an American, using American ingredients. At least three printings of the book appeared in the eighteenth century.

## Early Kitchens and Kitchen Hearths

Early New England farmers and artisans often had large households, but most lived in relatively small houses. Family members, apprentices, servants, and slaves lived together in just a few rooms. The room where the cooking took place was sometimes called the "hall" rather than the "kitchen." In the smallest houses, the kitchen, sitting room, and bedroom were one. When a family gained more resources, the functions of cooking and dining might be separated when the kitchen moved to a lean-to or, less frequently, to a basement or outbuilding. However, for most people in the eighteenth and early nineteenth centuries, the room used for cooking continued to serve many purposes.

The hearth was the focal point of any kitchen, but its design varied over time and according to region and tradition. Some cooking fireplaces built early in the eighteenth century were nearly ten feet wide. Lucy Larcom of Beverly, Massachusetts, recalled: "The fireplace was deep, and there was a 'settle' in the chimney corner, where three of us youngest girls could sit together and toast our toes on the andirons . . . while we looked up the chimney into a square of blue sky, and sometimes caught a snow-flake on our foreheads."[17] In some households, cooking pots and kettles were hung on lug poles made of green wood set in the chimney and replaced as needed. In more well-to-do homes the pots were hung on a swinging iron crane attached to the jamb or side wall of the fireplace that could be swung out from the fire for easier and safer access. In 1704, when she visited New York City, Madam Sarah Kemble Knight of Boston observed that the Dutch hearths were different from those she was used to: "The fire places have no Jambs (as ours have) But the Backs run flush with the walls, and the Hearth is of Tyles."[18] A projecting hood, often hung with textiles, guided the smoke up the chimney. The hearths of German immigrants were raised above floor level. By the end of the eighteenth century, most households in the Northeast had smaller, English-style hearths with angled jambs to conserve energy. Fuel was one of the highest costs of housekeeping; a typical household used twenty to forty cords of wood a year for cooking as well as heating, exhausting supplies very quickly in thickly settled areas.[19]

### An Oat-Pudding to Bake

Of oats decorticated take two pounds, and new-milk enough to drown it, eight ounces of raisins of the sun stoned, an equal quantity of currants neatly picked, a pound of sweet suet finely shred, six new laid eggs well beat: season with nutmeg, beaten ginger, and salt; mix it all well together: it will make a better pudding than rice.

Hannah Glasse, *The Art of Cookery Made Plain and Easy*, 1784

The oats called for in this recipe had been successfully cultivated in Massachusetts, New York, and Virginia since early in the seventeenth century. Hannah Glasse's *The Art of Cookery*, first published in 1747 and republished in twenty subsequent eighteenth-century editions, was one of the most popular cookbooks in England and was equally popular in America. The book's transatlantic success suggests the close link between American and English cooking.

English pamphlets, like this one published in 1622, advised people emigrating to the colonies to bring cookware with them. These were the items considered necessary for a modestly well-equipped kitchen. This same equipment would have been considered adequate for kitchens over the next 150 years.

# THE INCONVENIENCIES THAT HAVE HAPPENED TO SOME PERSONS WHICH HAVE TRANSPORTED THEMSELVES

from *England* to *Virginia*, vvithout prouiſions neceſſary to ſuſtaine themſelues, hath *greatly hindred the Progreſſe of that noble Plantation: For preuention of the like diſorders* heereafter, that no man ſuffer, either through ignorance or miſinformation; it is thought requiſite to publiſh this ſhort declaration: wherein is contained a particular of ſuch neceſ-*ſaries, as either priuate families or ſingle perſons ſhall haue cauſe to furniſh themſelues with, for their better ſupport at their firſt landing in* Virginia; *whereby alſo greater numbers may receiue in part, directions how to prouide themſelues.*

### *Apparrell.*

*Apparrell for one man, and ſo after the rate for more.*

| | li. | s. | d. |
|---|---|---|---|
| One Monmouth Cap | 00 | 01 | 10 |
| Three falling bands | — | 01 | 03 |
| Three ſhirts | — | 07 | 06 |
| One waſte-coate | — | 02 | 02 |
| One ſuite of Canuaſe | — | 07 | 06 |
| One ſuite of Frize | — | 10 | 00 |
| One ſuite of Cloth | — | 15 | 00 |
| Three paire of Iriſh ſtockins | — | 04 | — |
| Foure paire of ſhooes | — | 08 | 08 |
| One paire of garters | — | 00 | 10 |
| One doozen of points | — | 00 | 03 |
| One paire of Canuaſe ſheets | — | 08 | 00 |
| Seuen ells of Canuaſe, to make a bed and boulſter, to be filled in *Virginia* 8.s. One Rug for a bed 8. s. which with the bed ſeruing for two men, halfe is | — | 08 | 00 |
| Fiue ells coorſe Canuaſe, to make a bed at Sea for two men, to be filled with ſtraw, iiij.s. One coorſe Rug at Sea for two men, will coſt vj. s. is for one | — | 05 | 00 |
| | — | — | — |
| | 04 | 00 | 00 |

### *Victuall.*

*For a whole yeere for one man, and ſo for more after the rate.*

| | li. | s. | d. |
|---|---|---|---|
| Eight buſhels of Meale | 02 | 00 | 00 |
| Two buſhels of peaſe at 3.s. | — | 06 | 00 |
| Two buſhels of Oatemeale 4.s. 6.d. | — | 09 | 00 |
| One gallon of *Aquauitæ* | — | 02 | 06 |
| One gallon of Oyle | — | 03 | 06 |
| Two gallons of Vineger 1. s. | — | 02 | 00 |
| | 03 | 03 | 00 |

### *Armes.*

*For one man, but if halfe of your men haue armour it is ſufficient ſo that all haue Peeces and ſwords.*

| | li. | s. | d. |
|---|---|---|---|
| One Armour compleat, light | — | 17 | 00 |
| One long Peece, fiue foot or fiue and a halfe, neere Musket bore | 01 | 02 | — |
| One ſword | — | 05 | — |
| One belt | — | 01 | — |
| One bandaleere | — | 01 | 06 |
| Twenty pound of powder | — | 18 | 00 |
| Sixty pound of ſhot or lead, Piſtoll and Gooſe ſhot | — | 05 | 00 |
| | 03 | 09 | 06 |

### *Tooles.*

*For a family of 6. perſons and ſo after the rate, for more.*

| | li. | s. | d. |
|---|---|---|---|
| Fiue broad howes at 2.s. a piece | — | 10 | — |
| Fiue narrow howes at 16.d. a piece | — | 06 | 08 |
| Two broad Axes at 3.s. 8.d. a piece | — | 07 | 04 |
| Fiue felling Axes at 18.d. a piece | — | 07 | 06 |
| Two ſteele hand ſawes at 16.d. a piece | — | 02 | 08 |
| Two two-hand-ſawes at 5. s. a piece | — | 10 | — |
| One whip-ſaw, ſet and filed with box, file, and wreſt | — | 10 | — |
| Two hammers 12.d. a piece | — | 02 | 00 |
| Three ſhouels 18.d. a piece | — | 04 | 06 |
| Two ſpades at 18.d. a piece | — | 03 | — |
| Two augers 6.d. a piece | — | 01 | 00 |
| Sixe chiſſels 6.d. a piece | — | 03 | 00 |
| Two percers ſtocked 4.d. a piece | — | 00 | 08 |
| Three gimlets 2.d. a piece | — | 00 | 06 |
| Two hatchets 21.d. a piece | — | 03 | 06 |
| Two froues to cleaue pale 18.d. | — | 03 | 00 |
| Two hand bills 20. a piece | — | 03 | 04 |
| One grindleſtone 4.s. | — | 04 | 00 |
| Nailes of all ſorts to the value of | 02 | 00 | — |
| Two Pickaxes | — | 03 | — |
| | 06 | 02 | 08 |

### *Houſhold Implements.*

*For a family of 6. perſons, and ſo for more or leſſe after the rate.*

| | li. | s. | d. |
|---|---|---|---|
| One Iron Pot | 00 | 07 | — |
| One kettle | — | 06 | — |
| One large frying-pan | — | 02 | 06 |
| One gridiron | — | 01 | 06 |
| Two skillets | — | 05 | — |
| One ſpit | — | 02 | — |
| Platters, diſhes, ſpoones of wood | — | 04 | — |
| | 01 | 08 | 00 |

| | li. | s. | d. |
|---|---|---|---|
| *For Suger, Spice, and fruit, and at Sea for 6. men* | 00 | 12 | 06 |
| So the full charge of Apparrell, Victuall, Armes, Tooles, and houſhold ſtuffe, and after this rate for each perſon, will amount vnto about the ſumme of | 12 | 10 | — |
| The paſſage of each man is | 06 | 00 | — |
| The fraight of theſe prouiſions for a man, will bee about halfe a Tun, which is | 01 | 10 | — |
| *So the whole charge will amount to about* | 20 | 00 | 00 |

*Nets, hookes, lines, and a tent muſt be added, if the number of people be greater, as alſo ſome kine.*

*And this is the vſuall proportion that the* Virginia *Company doe beſtow vpon their Tenants which they ſend.*

Whoſoeuer tranſports himſelfe or any other at his owne charge vnto *Virginia*, ſhall for each perſon ſo tranſported before Midſummer 1625. haue to him and his heires for euer fifty Acres of Land vpon a firſt, and fifty Acres vpon a ſecond diuiſion.

Imprinted at London by FELIX KYNGSTON. 1622.

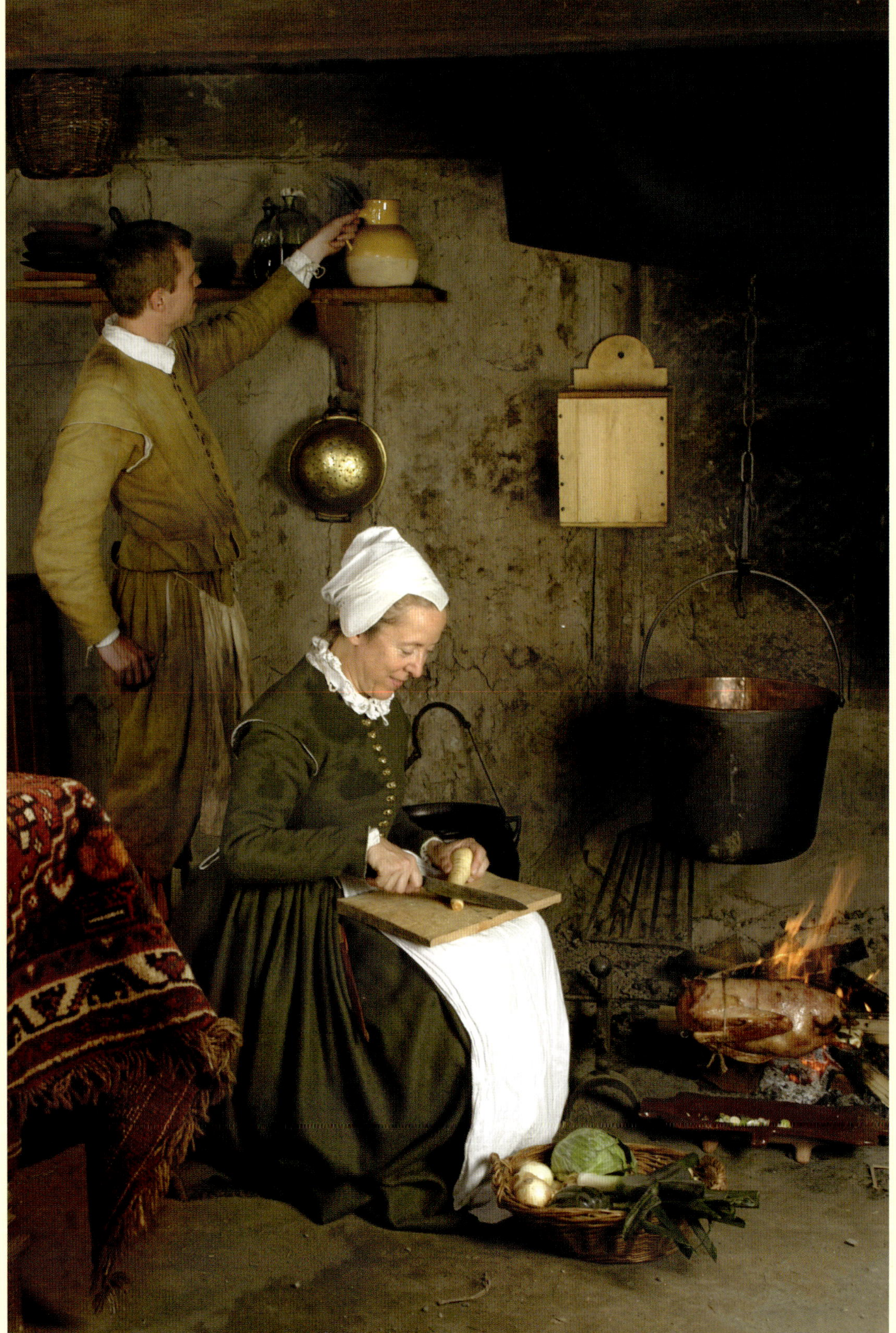

Because no images of seventeenth- or eighteenth-century American cooks exist, modern reenactments of colonial cooking and contemporary European sources can provide useful information. At Plimoth Plantation in Plymouth, Massachusetts, a costumed museum interpreter demonstrates 1620 hearth cooking techniques, using appropriate tools and ingredients. The 1678 painting by Dutch artist Pieter Gierritz van Roestraten of a woman making pancakes shows that although hearth cooking required a different set of skills and lower posture than modern cooking, a woman could be competent and comfortable around the hearth, even while minding an infant and a small child.

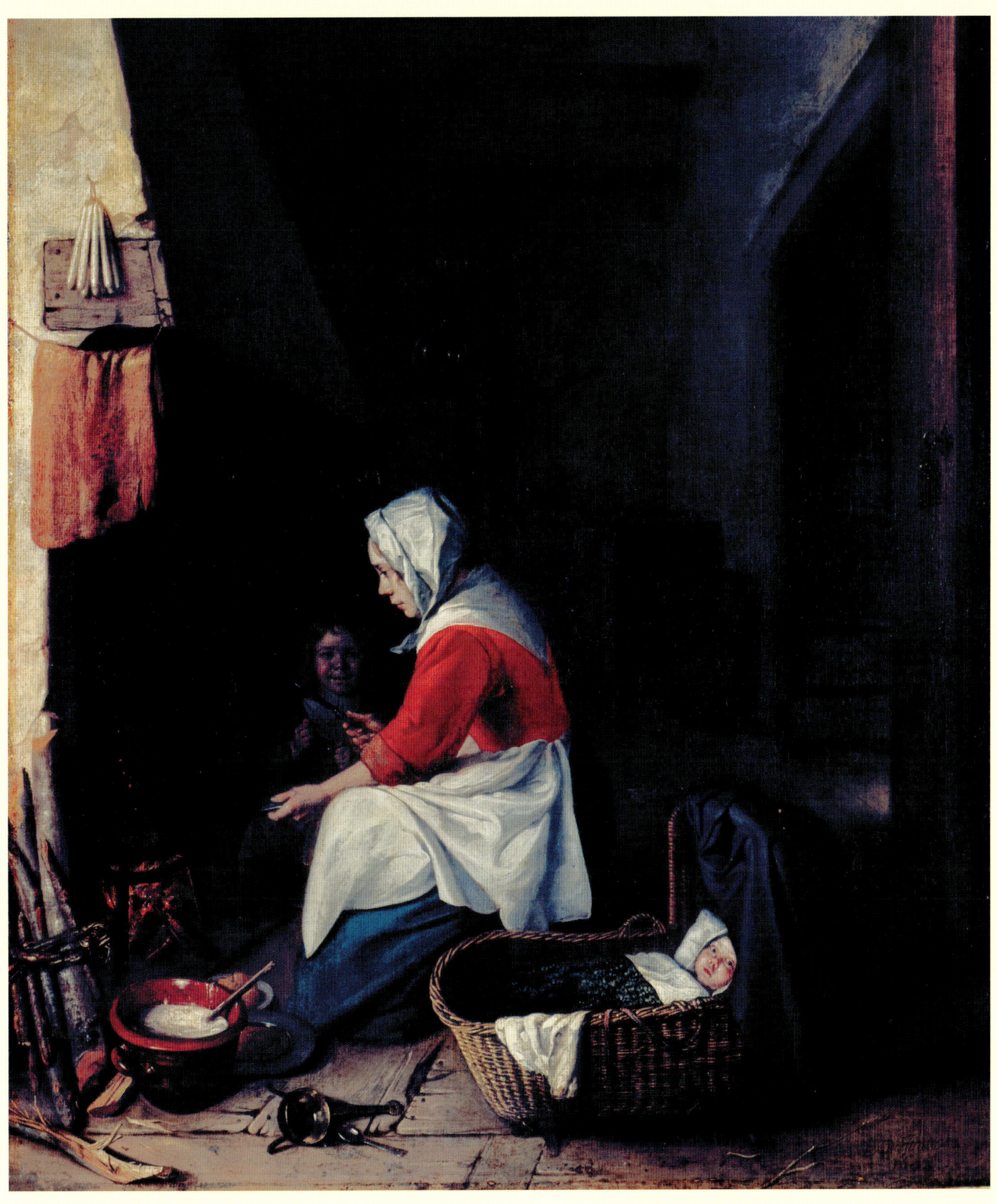

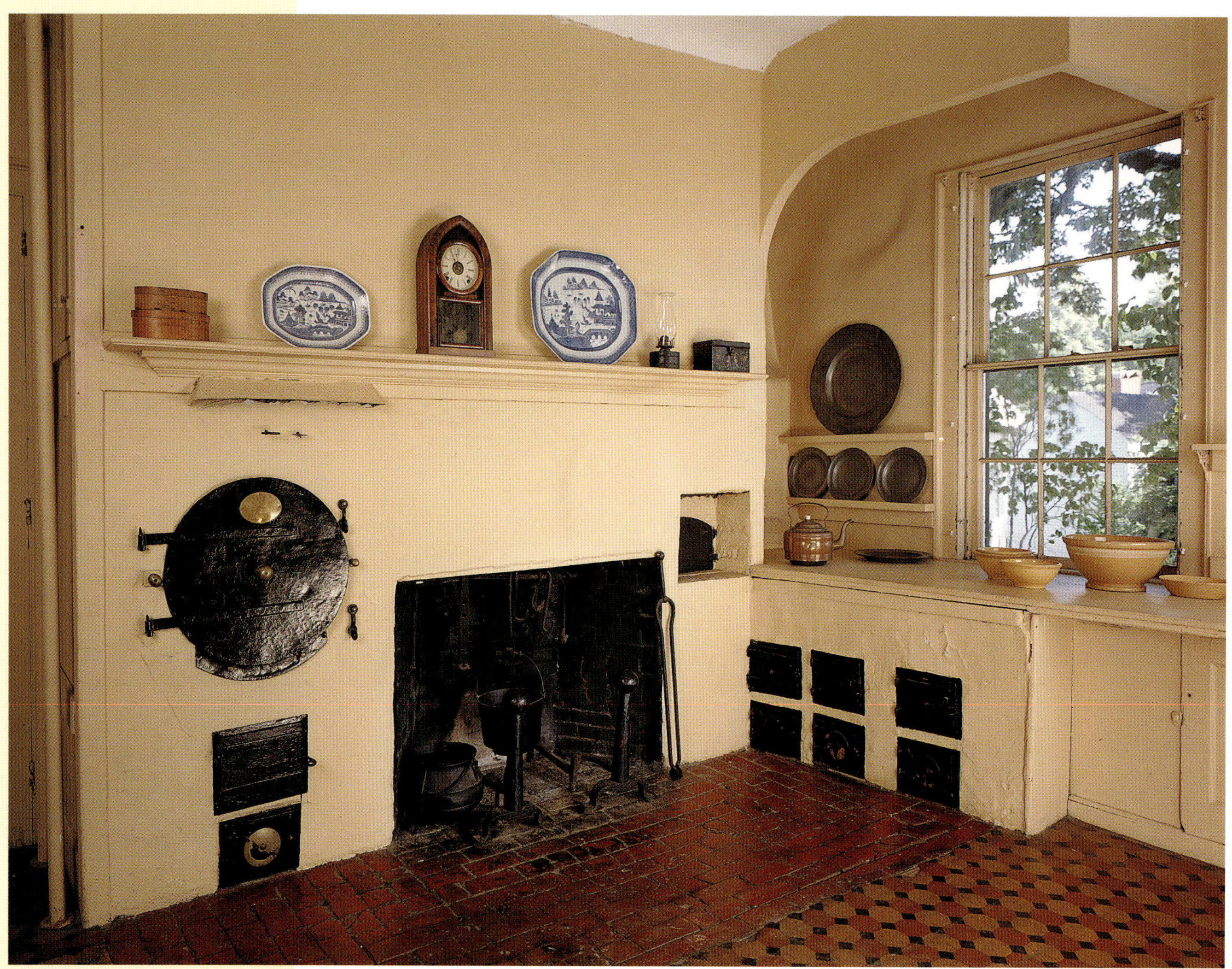

The Rundlet family installed a Rumford kitchen in their home in Portsmouth, New Hampshire, in 1807. The roaster is to the left of the fireplace. To the right is a bake oven, and under the window is the stew stove, now hidden below a wooden countertop.

Bake ovens were sometimes built outdoors, often with roofs to protect them from the weather, but by the eighteenth century, ovens in New England were generally built into a wall of the cooking fireplace. Even more advantageous was an oven built beside the fireplace with its own flue, an arrangement that was common by the end of the eighteenth century and continued into the next.

In addition to hearths and bake ovens, some early American households did part of their cooking on masonry stoves called stew stoves, *estufas* in Spanish colonial regions, or *potagers* after the French variety.[20] Stew stoves had burnerlike grates set over iron baskets that held charcoal. These stoves offered several advantages, such as more precise heat control and a higher work surface, but they were expensive to build and required specialized cooking techniques, fuel, and utensils. It is likely that stew stoves were used mostly in affluent households that could afford highly trained cooks and more complex meals. For example, an

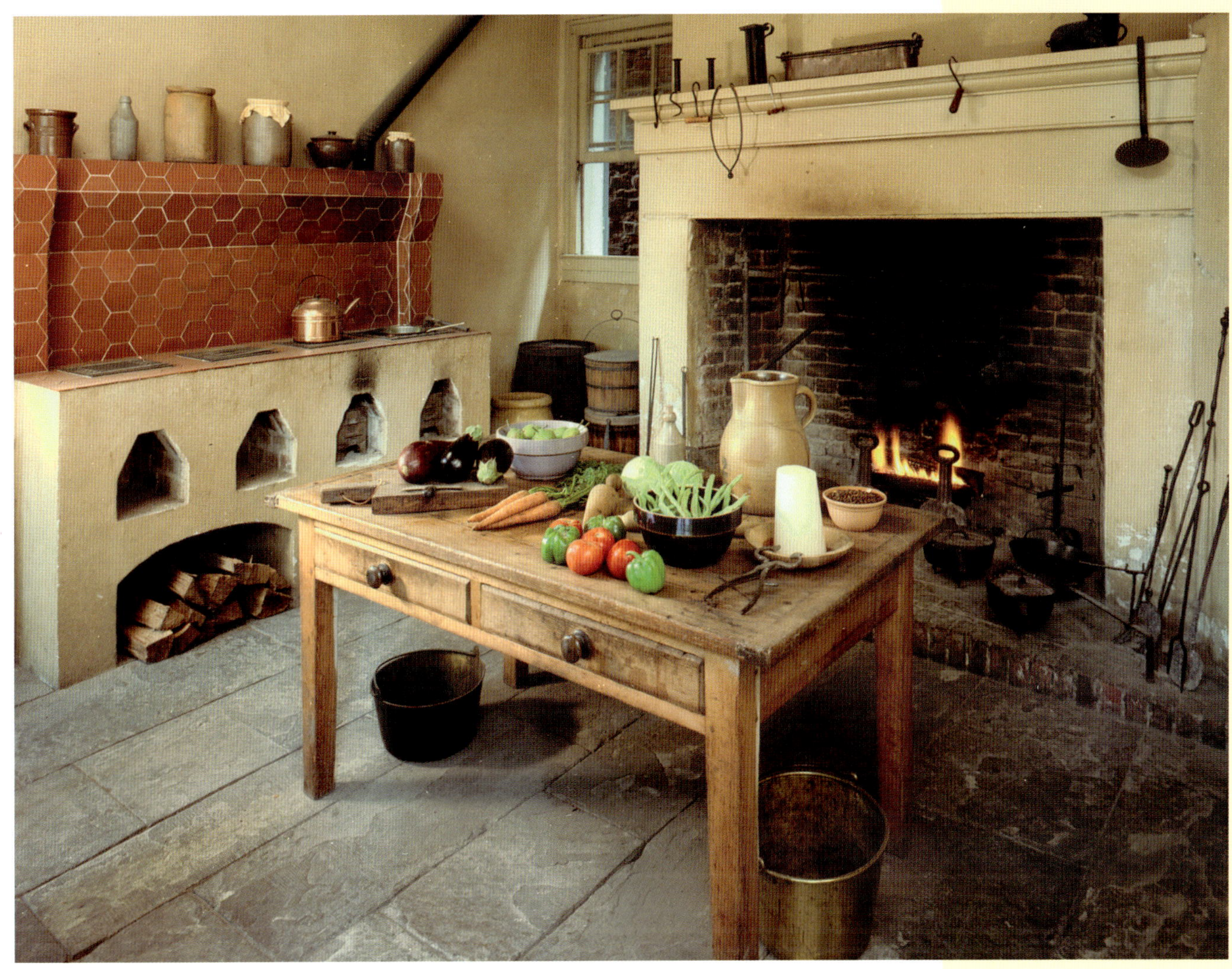

eighteenth-century stew stove survives in the Wentworth-Coolidge Mansion in Portsmouth, New Hampshire. Governor Benning Wentworth employed a French cook, John King, who may have offered advice on building the stove.[21] In the early nineteenth century, Thomas Jefferson's kitchen at Monticello in Charlottesville, Virginia, had a stew stove, where his enslaved cooks Peter Hemings, Edith Hern Fossett, and Fanny Gillette Hern prepared meals in the French manner.[22]

Certain well-to-do progressive families furnished their kitchens early in the nineteenth century with the latest technology. The full Rumford kitchen, named after its inventor, Benjamin Thompson, Count Rumford, included a cooking range, much like a traditional stew stove, and an enclosed roaster.[23] With its cast-iron elements and elaborate flues, this kitchen system was expensive and, although never widely adopted, it characterized a spirit of innovation in kitchen design.[24]

Nineteenth-century cooks in the Hermann household in New Orleans, Louisiana, used four burnerlike stew holes as well as the hearth and a brick bake oven. The stew holes were well suited to French and Creole cookery, which often called for a slow simmer. The Hermann-Grima House stove has been reconstructed based on documentary evidence.

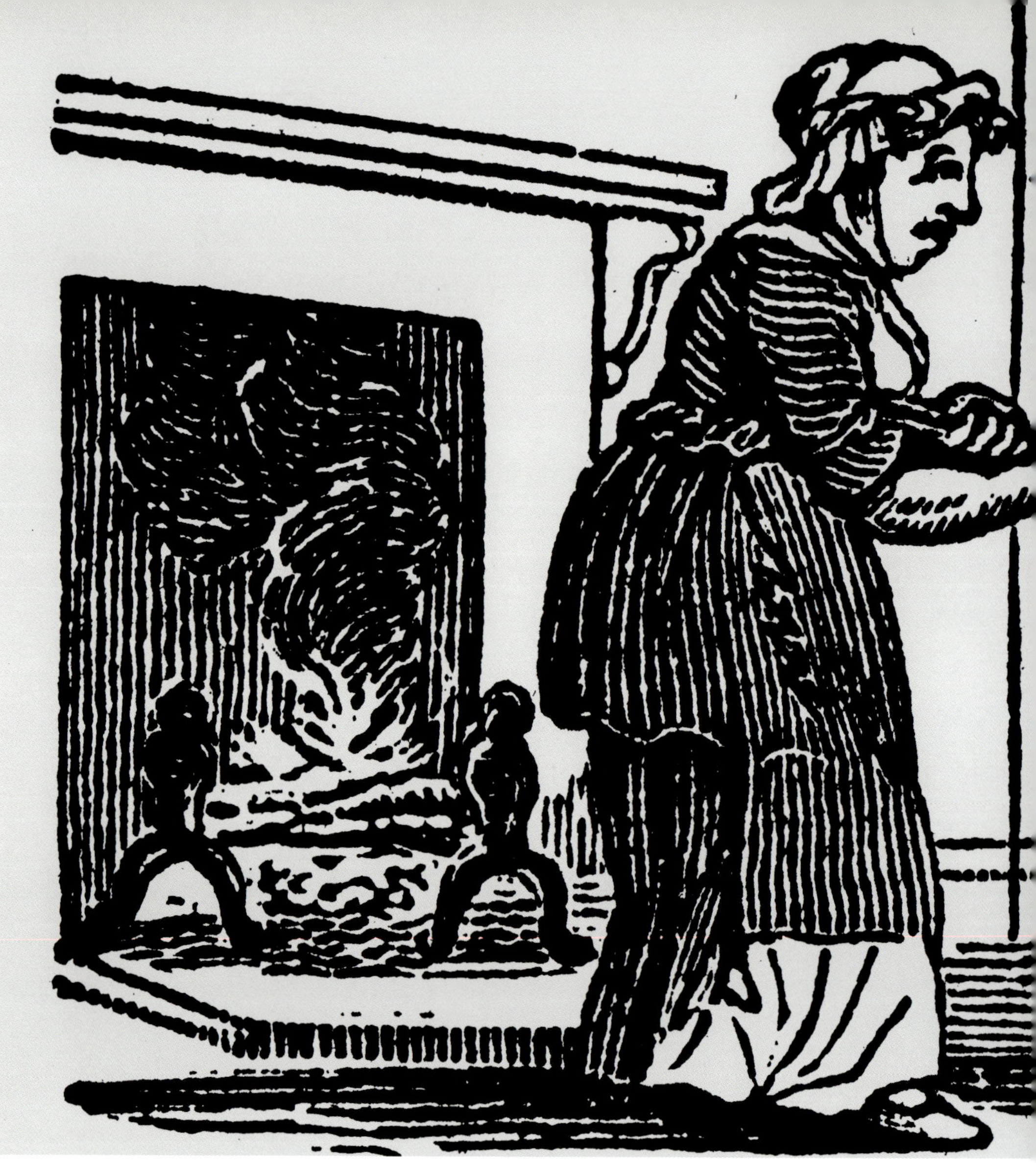

## *Working with Fire*

Housewives generally rose early to rekindle the fire on the kitchen hearth, using bellows to coax a flame from embers hidden under banked ashes the night before. Building and managing fires was second nature. A fire that was not well supplied with air or fuel was in danger of going out, in which case someone would have to ignite some tinder with a spark from a flint and steel or go to a neighbor's house to borrow live coals.

Most women had a comfort and familiarity with fire that allowed them to work safely around the hearth. Clothes in this period were usually made of wool and linen rather than more flammable cotton, so if women's clothing did catch a spark, it smoldered rather than flared. Burns must have been commonplace, but tragic accidents were unusual and newsworthy. On December 16, 1786, the *New-Hampshire Gazette* reported the following accident:

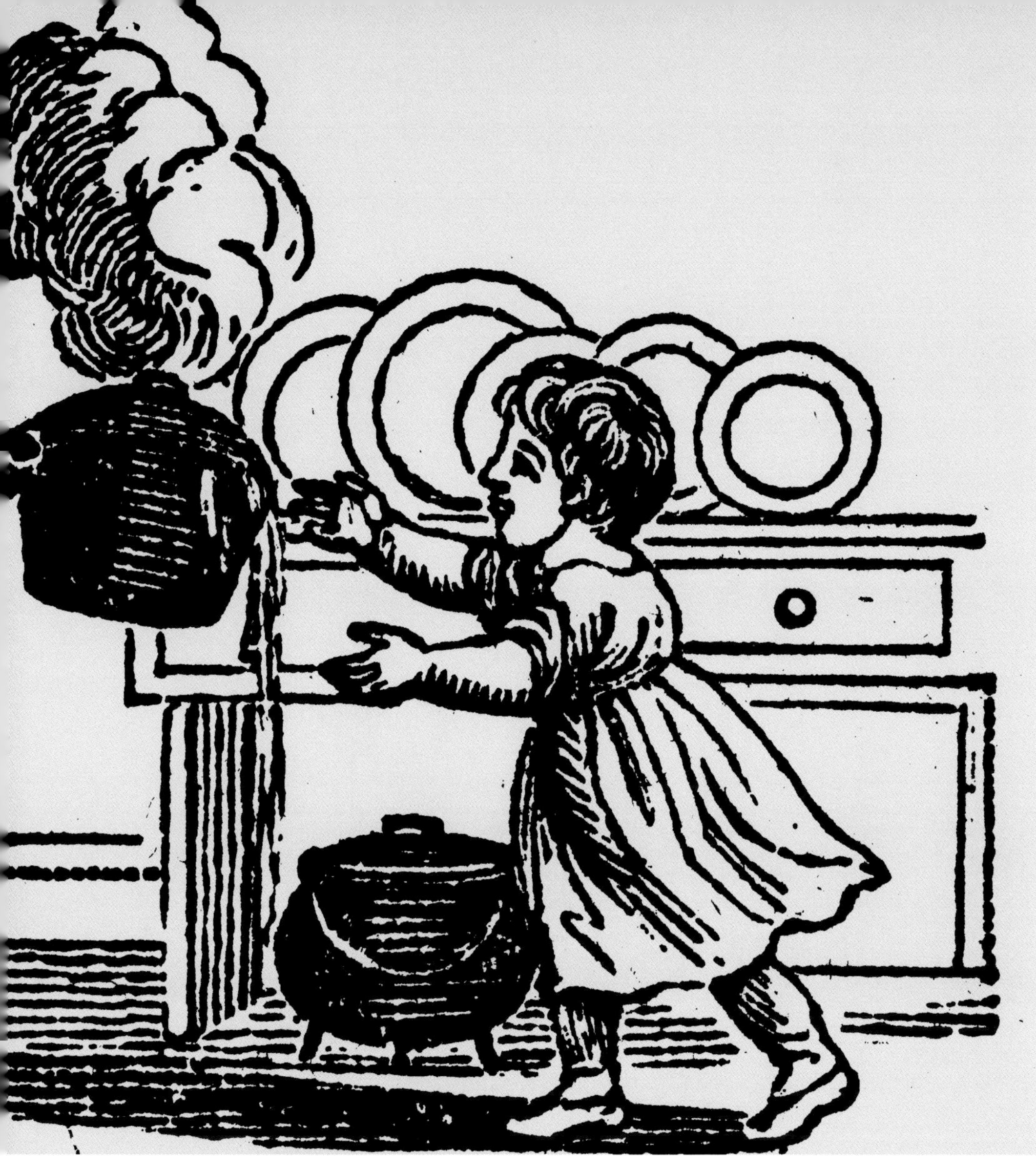

Tragic accidents involving adults around the hearth were not common, but severe scaldings and burns, especially affecting children, occurred more often, as this illustration from a nineteenth-century children's book warns.

> Charleston, (S.C.) Oct. 31
> *Last week Mrs. Moses, of King Street, leaning too forwardly over a fire, where she was cooking some rice, the heat overcame her and she fell into the fire, which burnt the poor woman so excessively that she expired in a few minutes.* [25]

Not only was this shocking news more than a month old, it took place a thousand miles away. In most reports, adults who were burned fell into the fire as a result of intoxication, a seizure, or an apoplectic fit.

Kitchen accidents involving children, however, were more common. In 1742 at least three newspapers reported a tragic event that took place at the home of Captain Daniel Denny of Leicester, Massachusetts, when the pole from which a kettle hung was burned through:

> *A large Kettle of boiling Water . . . being over the Fire, and the Trammel-Stick happening to be burnt the Kettle fell down and spilt the Liquor upon Four Children who sat or lay upon the Hearth, (some of whom were asleep) which scalded them in so terrible a manner, that one died presently after, and another's Life is despaired of; but the other two, tho' much scalded, 'tis hop'd may recover.* [26]

## Cooking and Food

A cook might begin her work by building a good-sized fire on the hearth, but once the logs had burned to coals, she moved these burning embers around, adding carefully selected pieces of wood as needed to produce different kinds of heat, often having several small fires going at once. Piles of live embers on the hearth were like burners on a stove; a gridiron set over a pile of coals could be used for broiling; a pan set over coals on a trivet could be used for frying; and coals could be piled over and under a Dutch oven for baking.

The easiest technique was cooking in iron pots hung above the fire from a lug pole or crane on adjustable hooks, chains, or trammels, some of which raised and lowered vessels with a ratcheting mechanism. Busy housewives often made one-pot meals from simple ingredients that required little attention, such as meat and vegetables boiled together in the same pot with a starchy pudding tied in a piece of cloth. Baking root vegetables or other foods buried in the embers was another simple cooking method.

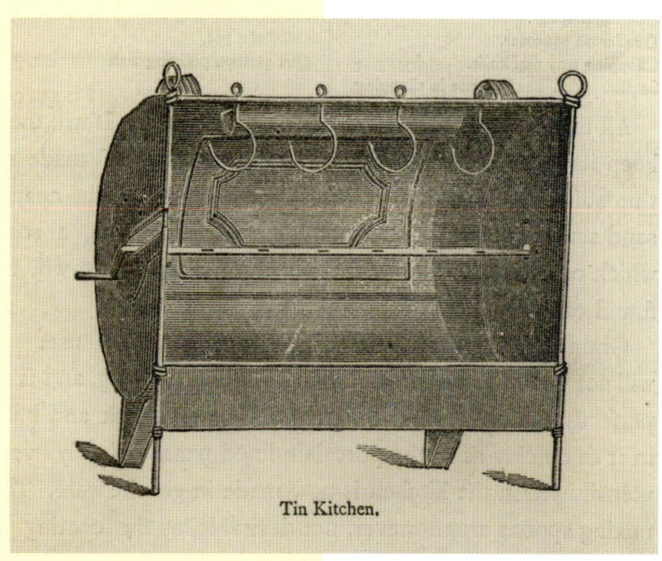


By the end of the eighteenth century, more and more households were equipped with tin kitchens for roasting. The cook put the fowl or meat on the spit and set the reflective half cylinder with the open side toward the fire, periodically rotating the spit a fraction of a turn and lifting a small door in the back to baste.

Cooks roasted fowl and large pieces of fresh meat in front of the fire, either on a spit or suspended on a piece of twine that could be twisted periodically to keep it spinning.[27] Twisting the string or turning the spit might be the job of a child or assistant, but the wealthiest households had mechanical jacks with geared mechanisms, like those in a clock, that turned the spit automatically.[28] A few elite households may have had turnspit dogs, which were trained to turn the spit by running on a wheel.[29]

The typical eighteenth-century New England breakfast consisted of leftovers from the day before, bread or porridge, and milk. Dinner, the main meal of the day, eaten between noon and three o'clock in most households, included meat, often beef, with cabbage, squash, peas, beans, or root vegetables, and condiments such as vinegar and pickles. Fish, butter, cheese, and molasses rounded out the fare. Supper was served in the evening and was usually much like breakfast.[30] Adults and children alike consumed cider and small beer (with a low alcohol content) daily, as well as fruits and vegetables, either preserved or in season. Those who could afford them ate imported goods such as raisins, nuts, spices, sugar, wine, coffee, tea, and chocolate.

This nineteenth-century frontispiece from Esther Howland's *New England Economical Housekeeper* (1845) shows an ideal kitchen with work tables, shelves for storage, and a large tin roaster in front of the hearth.

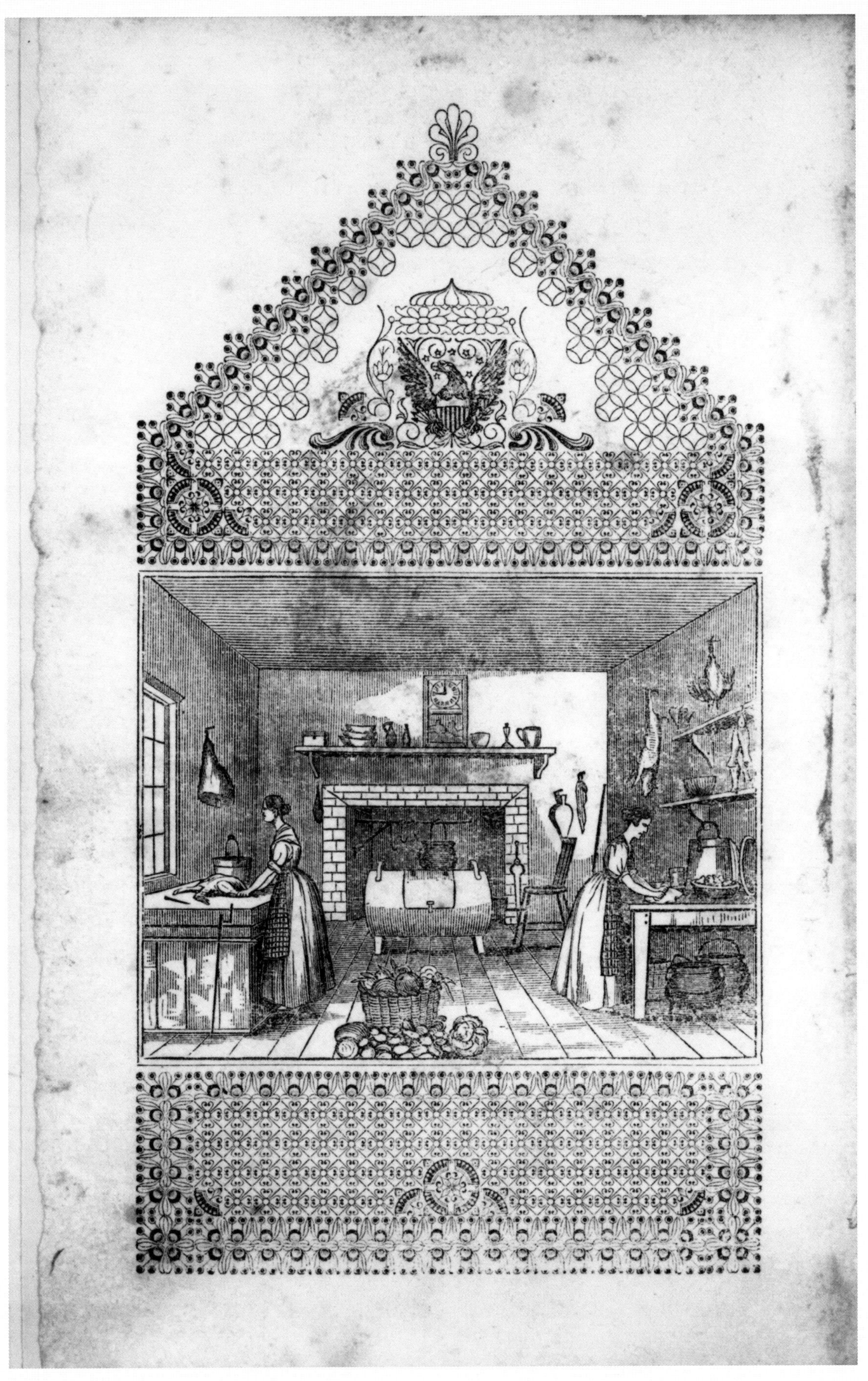

## The Rhythm of Work

Kitchen work followed a daily, weekly, and seasonal pattern. Twice a day for much of the year many women milked cows, carried the milk inside to be strained, and poured it into shallow pans to allow the cream to rise. Later they skimmed off the cream and churned it into butter or made cheese. Sharing milk could balance the workload of the household dairy. Sarah Anna Emery recalled that her family had six cows and her grandmother had four, so her mother and aunt combined the milk: "The milk being from the ten cows, my mother made cheese four days, Aunt Sarah having the milk the remainder of the week."[31]

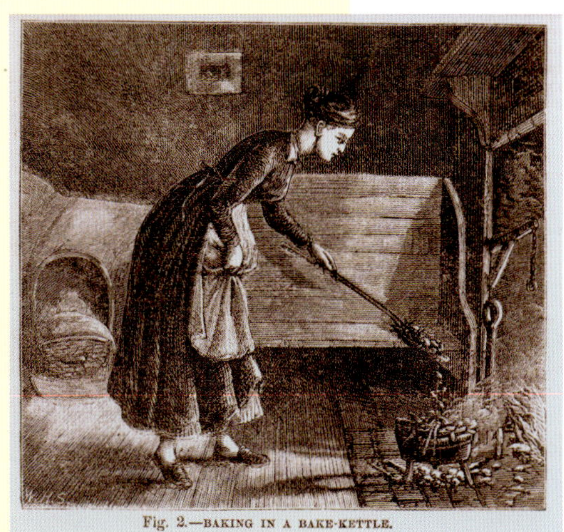


Women baked in small quantities by setting a bake kettle, or Dutch oven, over a pile of coals on the hearth and shoveling more coals on top of its lipped lid.

Depending on the size of the household, women generally baked in brick ovens once or twice a week, as it took about two hours and a large amount of fuel to heat a typical "beehive" oven. Baking was often done on Saturday in order to prepare foods for Sunday, when some cooks took their rest.[32] On other days, women baked on the hearth in bake kettles, or Dutch ovens, which was quick and convenient. Some made bread out of meal and water and baked it on a board propped up in front of the fire. Bread made from a combination of cornmeal, referred to as "Indian meal," rye, and wheat flour was common in New England. Most cooks saved their wheat flour for the best cakes and breads because, although it made the finest pastry, it was costly.[33] On baking day, dinner was often simpler than usual, but it might include a warm pudding or pie. Women often combined baking with brewing, since both required yeast, and brewing produced a new supply.

Food supplies and routines changed with the seasons. Spring and early summer were the leanest times of year, with supplies running short. Garden produce was more plentiful in late summer, but fresh meat was impractical in warm weather, as it spoiled too quickly. Instead, families ate salted meat, which was well suited to boiled dinners and could be cooked largely unattended. Boiled meals did not provide enough relief from the heat of cooking for Ruth Henshaw Bascom, a minister's wife in Leicester, Massachusetts. After eight days of high temperatures in late July, she hired a cook, "the

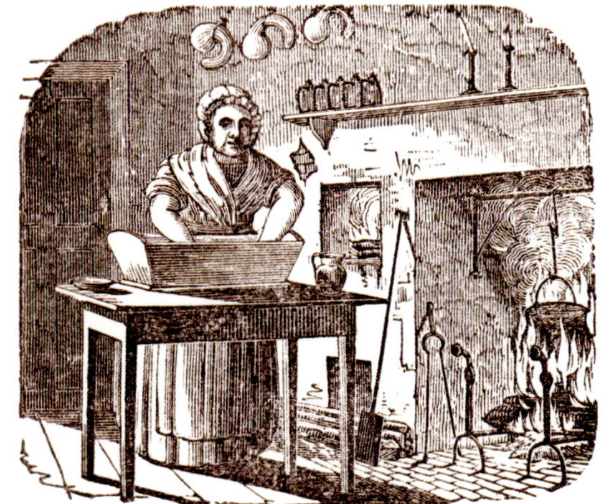

In this mid-nineteenth-century illustration, a woman kneads her bread dough while a fire burns in the bake oven. Once the oven was hot, she would remove the coals, fill it with goods to be baked, and close it up to keep in the heat.

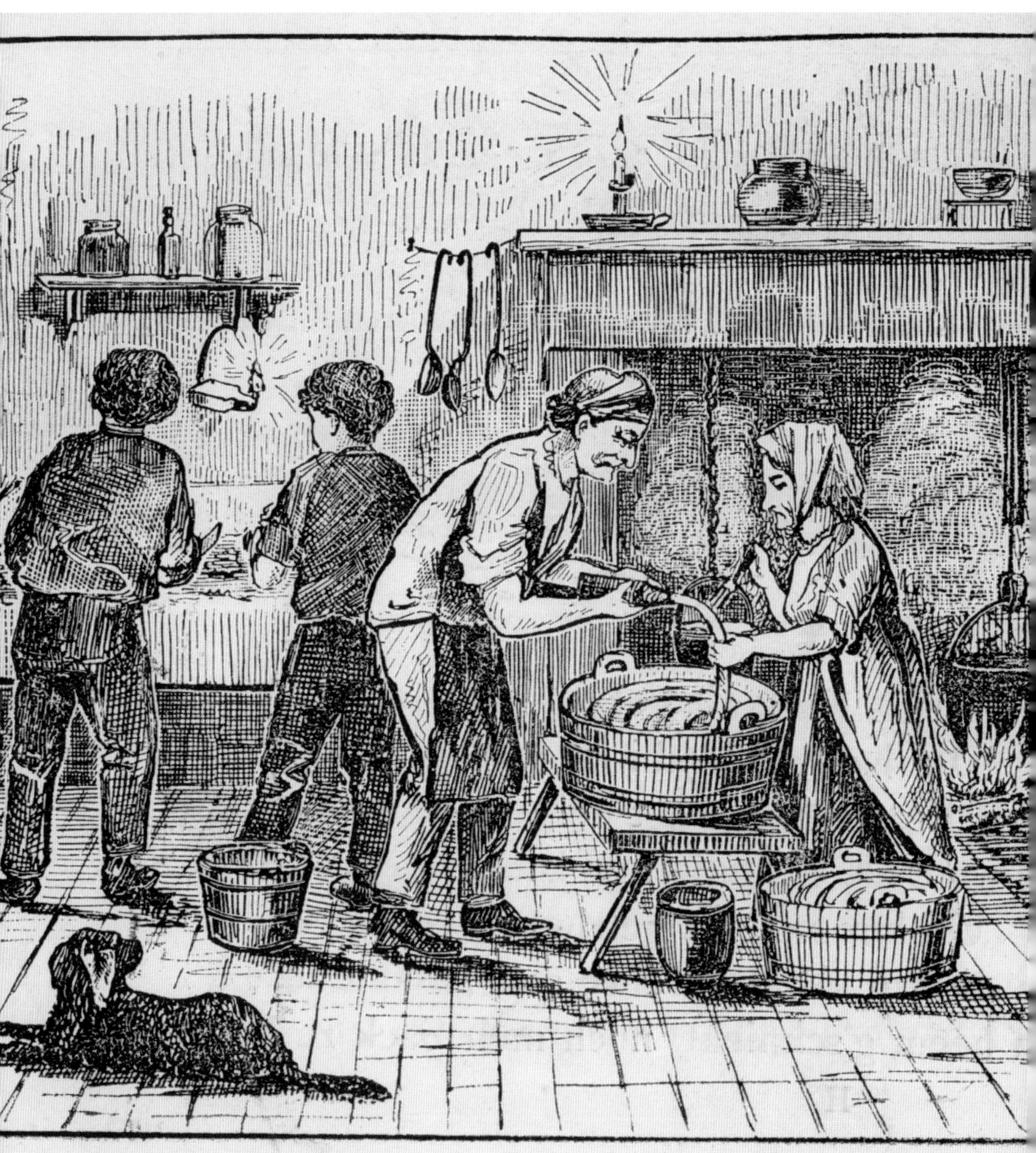

Tasks such as making sausage, shown in Henry Barrat's 1879 woodcut of a Pennsylvania German family, were a group effort. As the burning candle and hanging lamp suggest, every member of the household worked well into the night.

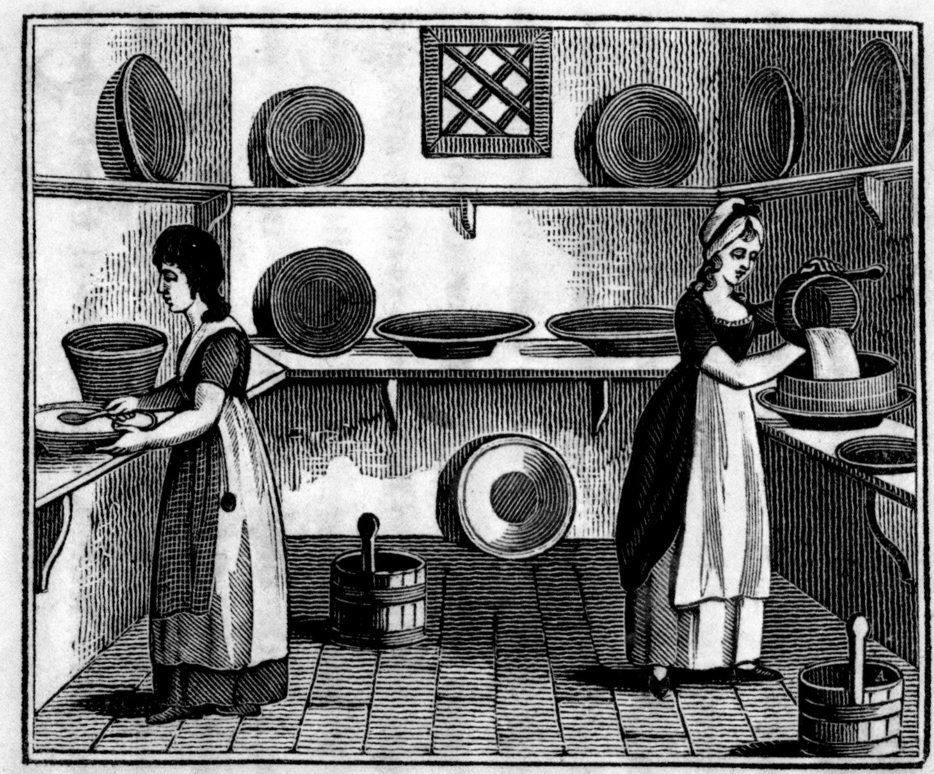


Dairying was a laborious process, requiring many steps. In this scene, the woman on the right strains the milk through a sieve into a shallow pan. The girl on the left skims the cream off the top of the milk.

cooking of meat & vegetables these sultry days being repugnant to my inclination if not to my health."[34] Winter in the kitchen could be equally uncomfortable, for many fireplaces carried the heat up the chimney. Sarah Anna Emery recalled a season when "plates set to drain in the process of dishwashing froze together in front of the huge logs, ablaze in the wide kitchen fireplace."[35] Preserving fruits and vegetables at harvest time was one of the seasonal projects that involved every member of the household, and sometimes friends and neighbors, to lighten the work.

This cycle of domestic life—tied closely to the land and the seasons—was practically unchanged for several generations of New Englanders until a world transformed by technology, new modes of transportation, and new rhythms of work reshaped most kitchens. In many cases, the hearth and its traditions were replaced by the cast-iron stove, which brought with it new roles for many members of the household. In other regions, however, the hearth way of life persisted, particularly in the South, where slave labor and an agricultural economy slowed the pace of advancing domestic technology.

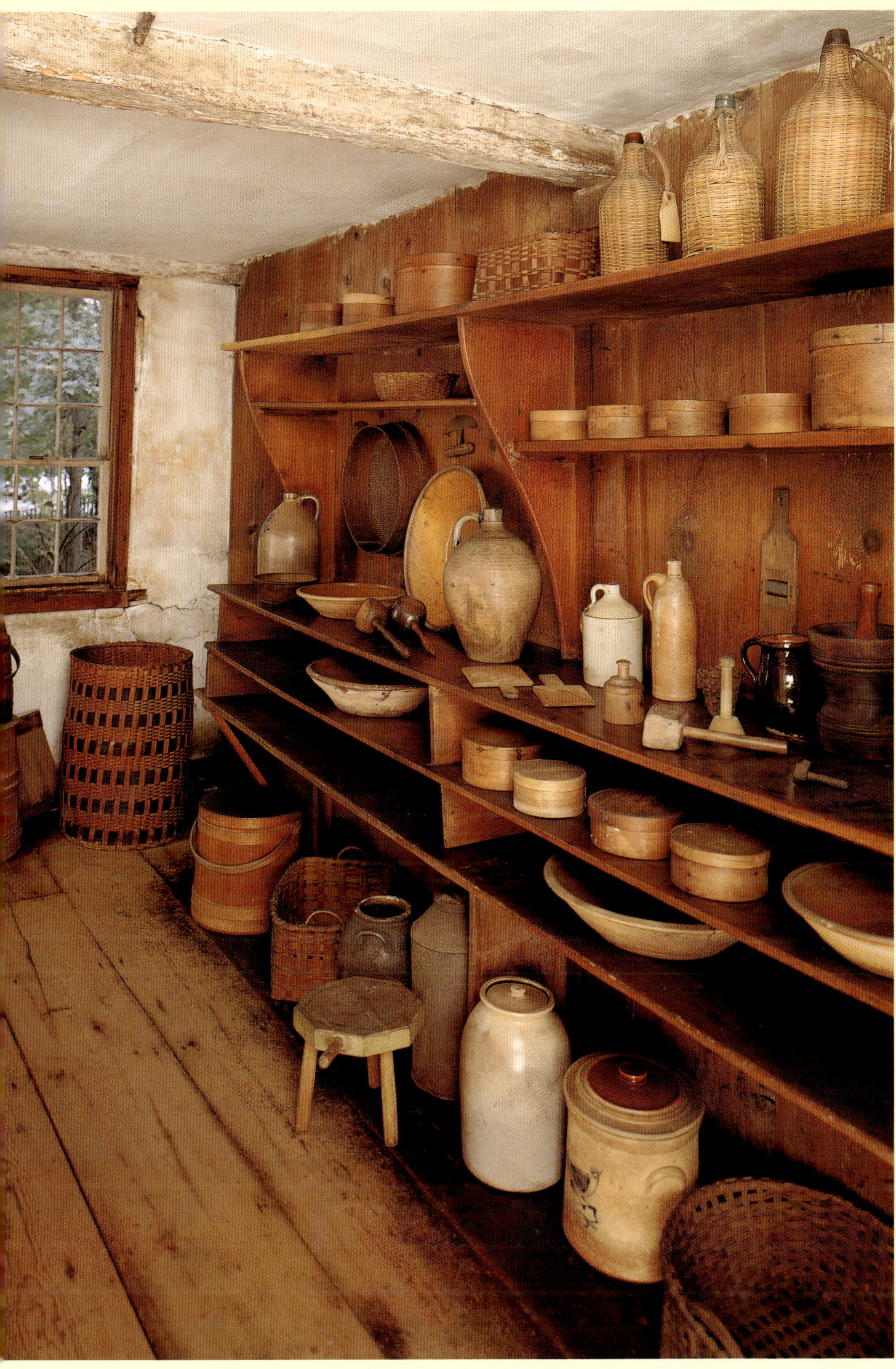

The buttery in the Coffin house, close to the two kitchens, was used for storage and for processing dairy products. It was kept scrupulously clean to avoid contaminating the milk. The cheeses were stored on the shelves and were monitored, turned, and rubbed daily.

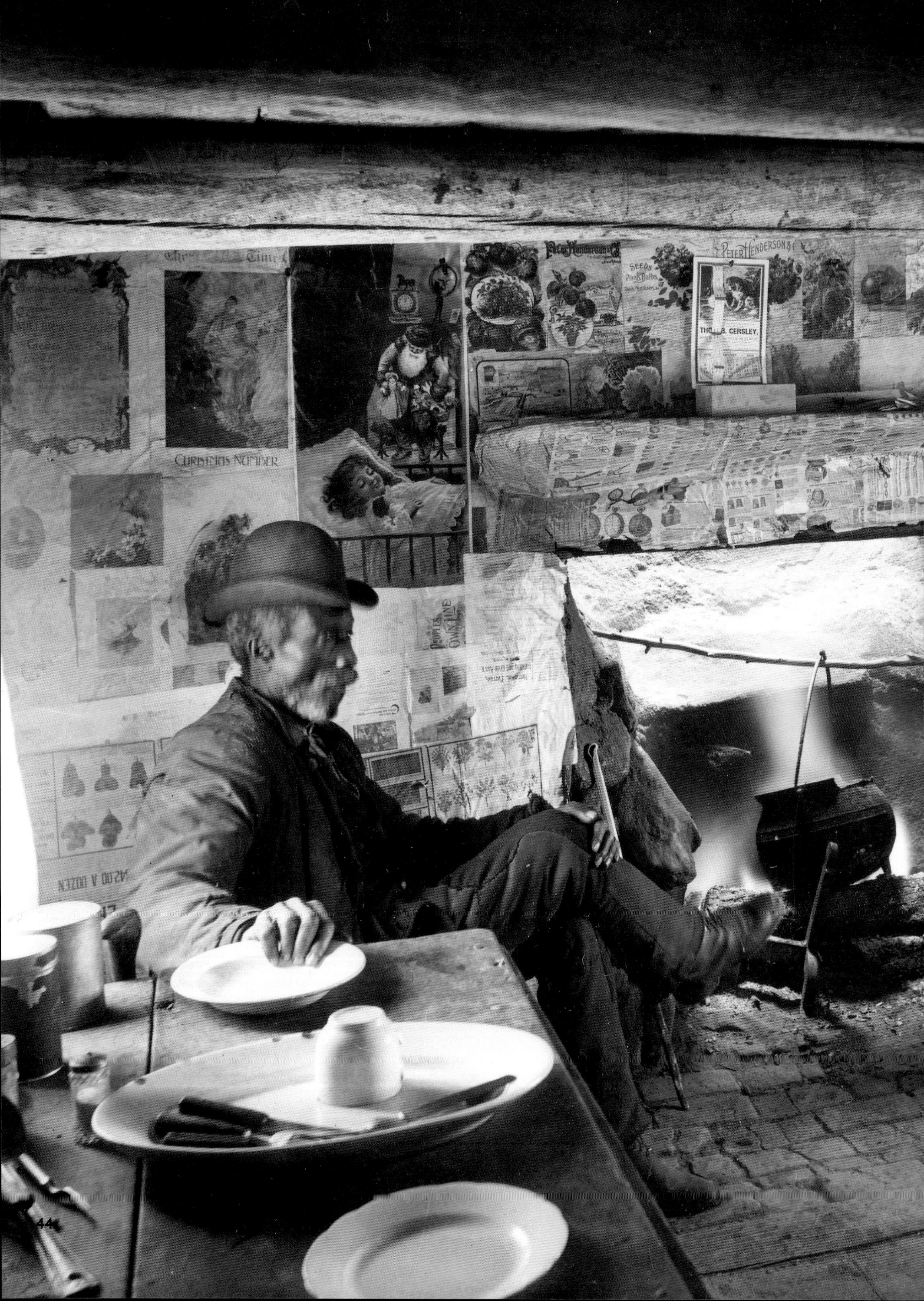
CHRISTMAS NUMBER
PETER HENDERSON &
PEOPLES OWN LINE

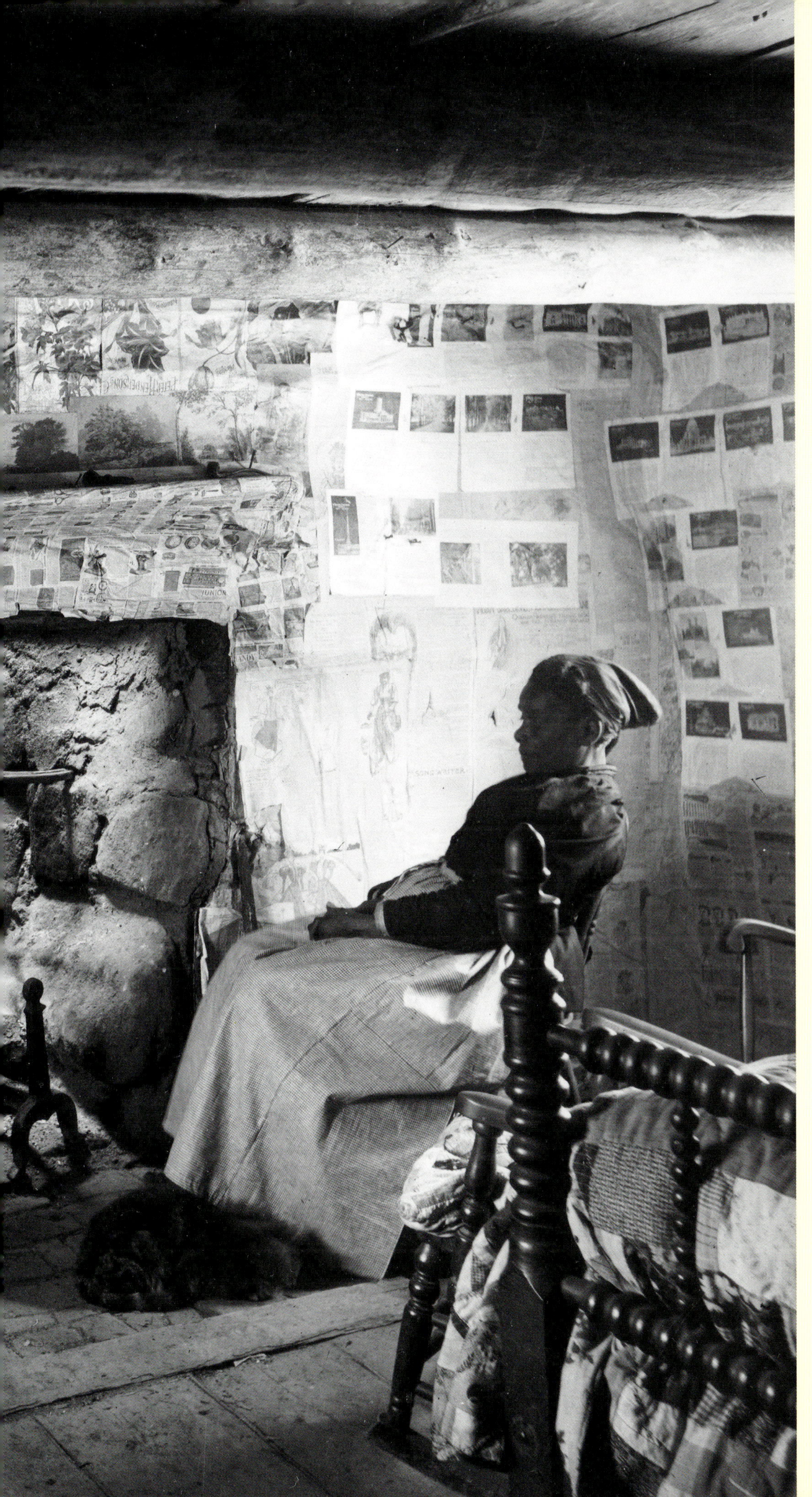

The hearth way of life persisted into the twentieth century, mostly in rural households. This 1898 photograph shows a couple at their hearth in Richmond, Virginia, the walls neatly papered with newspaper and magazine clippings.

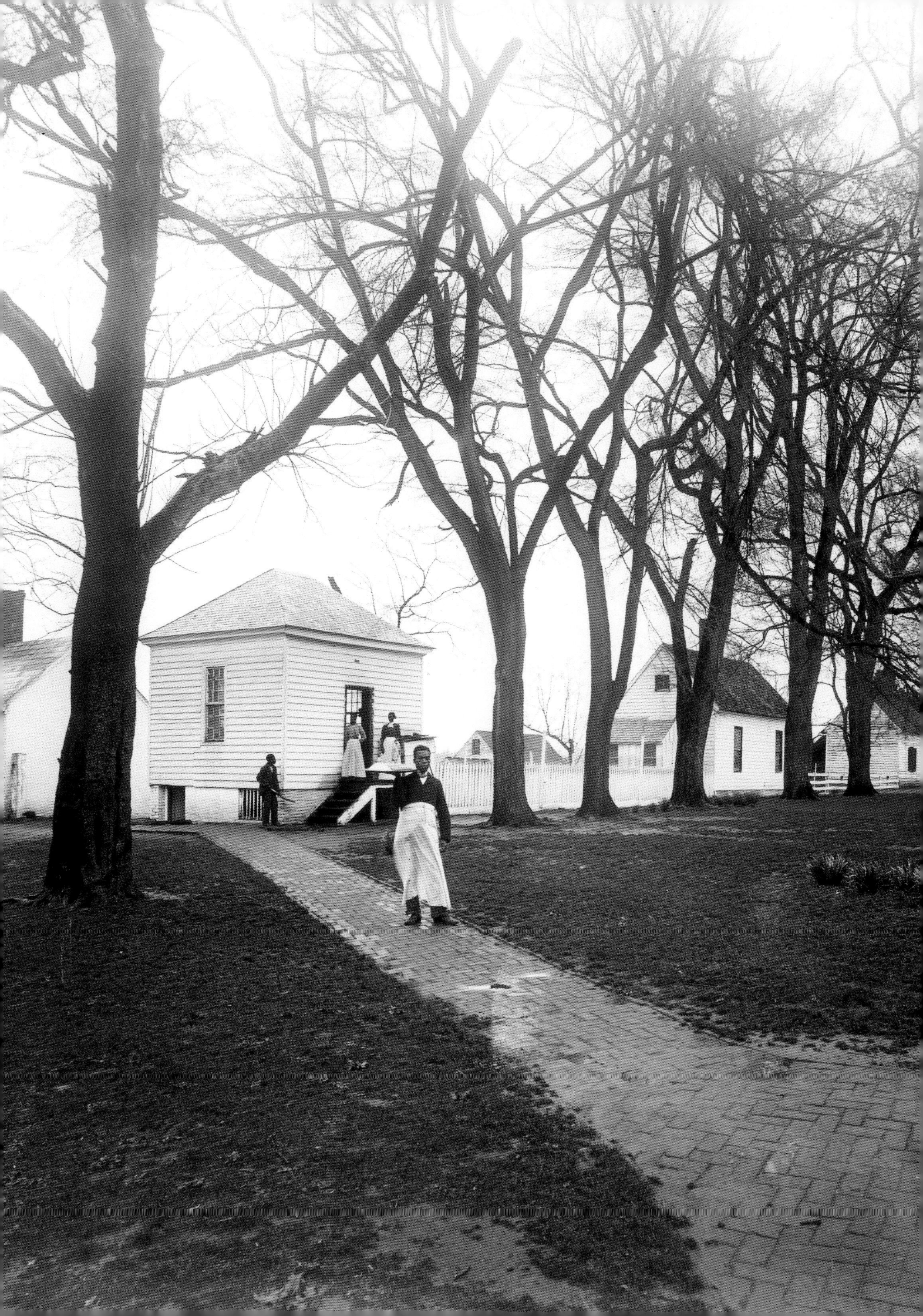

# KITCHENS IN THE PLANTATION SOUTH

## {1830–1860}

### *Green Hill Plantation, Campbell County, Virginia*

A massive stone chimney is all that remains of the kitchen building at Green Hill Plantation, in Campbell County, Virginia. The kitchen was part of a complex of buildings known as "Upper Town," which included structures for food storage, laundry, animals, and quarters for household slaves. It was also the center of activity for a few of the 150 enslaved people who lived and worked on the plantation. In this detached kitchen, enslaved cooks prepared meals for the Pannill family, owners of Green Hill, and perhaps for themselves and the residents of Upper Town. The extant cobblestone walkways that connect the remains of the kitchen to the planter's house and the other outbuildings make it easy to imagine servers carrying food to the Big House's dining room or basement kitchen and the mistress, Judith Pannill, visiting the kitchen and storehouses to monitor supplies and oversee the activities of the slaves.[1] Provisions were locked up in the basement, the icehouse, the dairy, and the smokehouse, and Judith Pannill held the keys. Mrs. Pannill's routine at Green Hill may have been similar to the one described by Marion Harland, an author raised in the antebellum South:

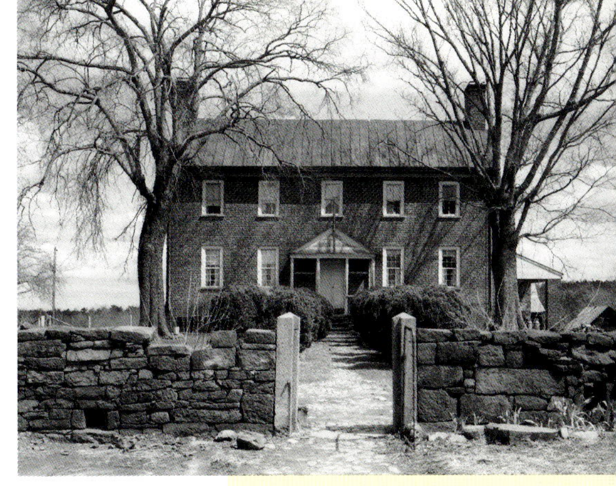

The Pannills' house at Green Hill in Campbell County, Virginia, was more modest than some plantation houses, but it held a commanding position on a hill above the Staunton River.

> *Every morning the cook was summoned as soon as breakfast was fairly over, appearing with a big wooden tray under her elbow, sundry empty "buckets" slung upon her arm, and often a pail on her head, carried there because every other available portion of her person was occupied. The two [mistress and cook] went together to the storeroom, and materials for the daily food of white and black households were measured into the various vessels.*[2]

After her mistress's departure, the Pannills' cook would have started preparing the day's meals using centuries-old cooking techniques.

The kitchen at Green Hill Plantation, shown here about 1960, was eighty feet east of the dwelling house. Today, all that remains is the chimney.

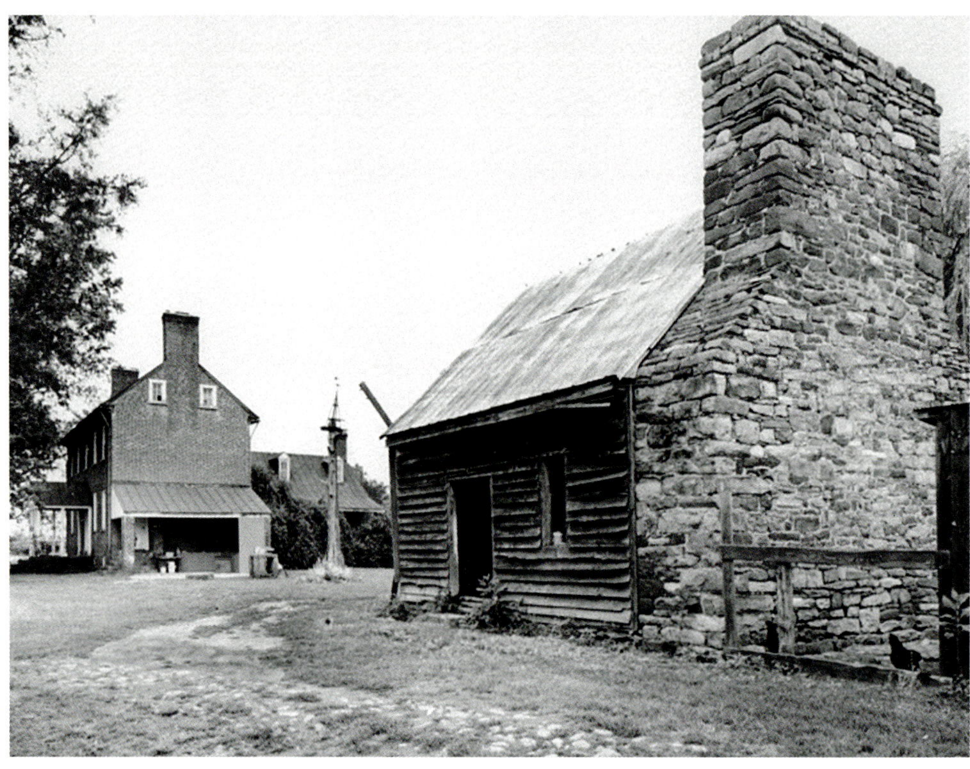

In Green Hill's detached kitchen, members of the slave community worked together to prepare food for the plantation owners and perhaps other residents of Upper Town.

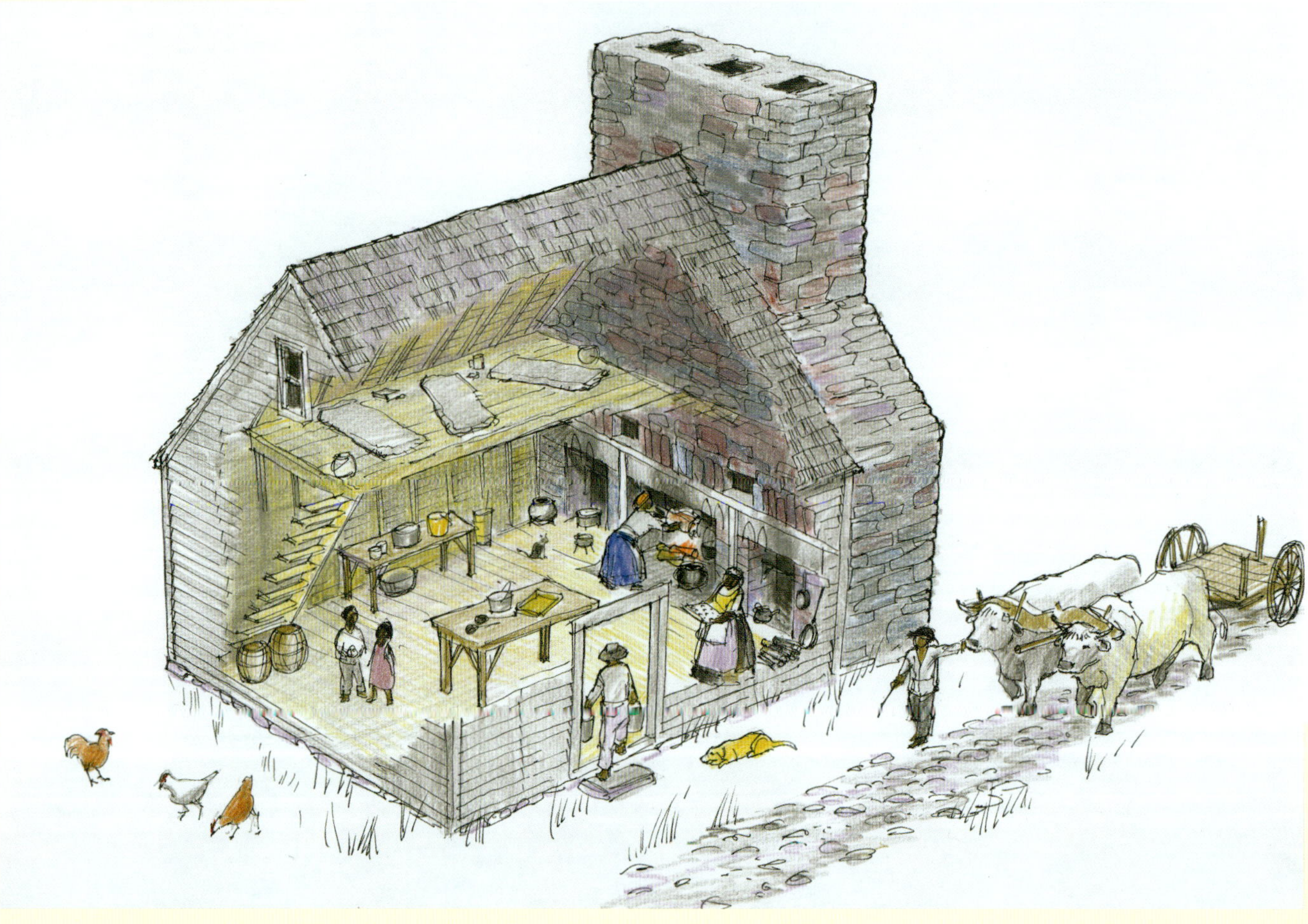

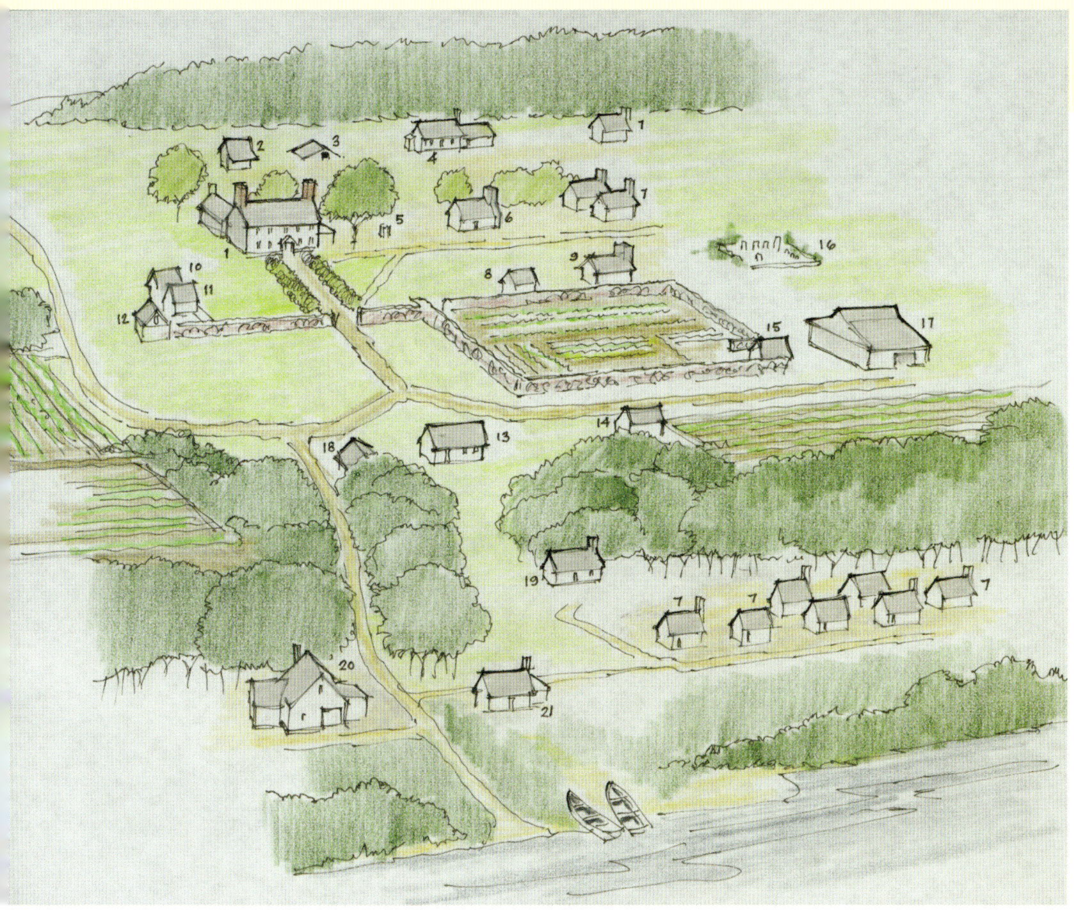

Outbuildings in Upper Town supported the domestic needs of food and clothing; those in Lower Town provided the plantation's economic center and housing for most of Green Hill's enslaved population. This illustration is based on extensive surviving evidence of the layout and location of buildings in Upper Town. However, because little evidence is available to document Lower Town's slave quarters, the depiction and location of these structures is based on speculation.

1. Main House
2. Office
3. Icehouse
4. Brick House
5. Mounting Block
6. Kitchen
7. Slave Quarters
8. Duck House
9. Laundry
10. Frame Barn
11. Log Barn
12. Carriage House
13. Stables
14. Carriage House
15. Granary
16. Cemetery
17. Tobacco Barn
18. Outbuilding
19. Tenant House
20. Grist Mill
21. Miller's House

Large plantations like Green Hill were governed by complex relationships not only among white owners and black slaves but also among slaves working in different parts of the plantation. The wealth that supported the Pannills' privileged way of life was generated by the slaves who lived and worked in Green Hill's Lower Town and the surrounding fields. They produced cotton, tobacco, wheat, corn, and other crops that were shipped down the river on bateaux—part of a transportation system created by the Roanoke Navigation Company, which was headed by Green Hill's owner, Samuel Pannill.[3] Some slaves worked as skilled tradesmen—carpenters, shoemakers, blacksmiths, and coopers.[4] Others worked in the house or in the kitchen and supported the family's high standard of living.

The Pannill plantation was not a typical household in the mid-nineteenth-century South. Only about a quarter of white southern families owned slaves; those that did not frequently hired slaves to do the laundry, cooking, and agricultural work.[5] Very few slaveholders owned more than twenty

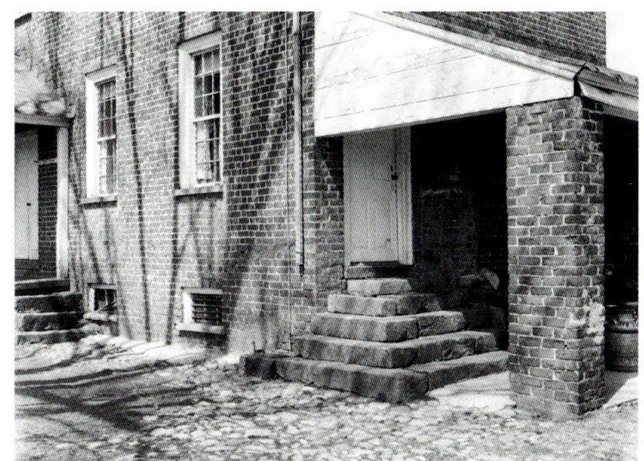

The original dining room in the Pannills' house at Green Hill had an exterior door so that slaves could deliver food directly from the detached kitchen. To the right of the door, concealed in this view by the brick post, was the entrance to the basement kitchen and storerooms, which were also accessible from inside the house.

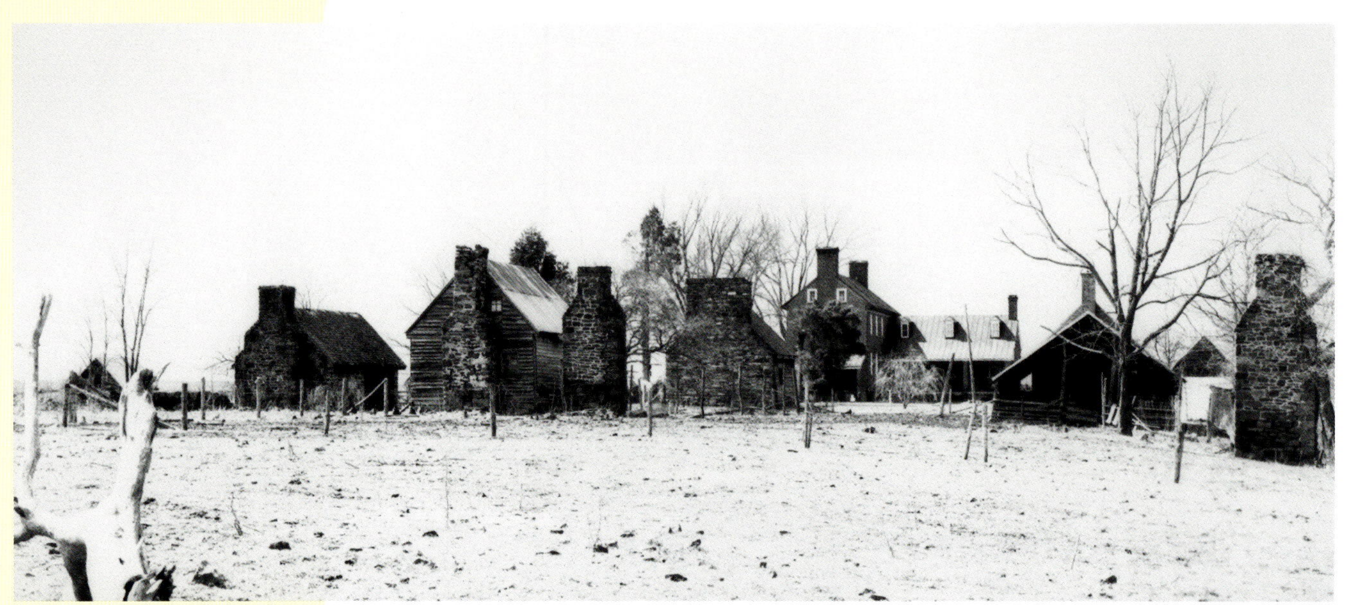

Visitors routinely described plantations as looking like villages, an apt description as this photograph of the remains of Green Hill's Upper Town shows. The buildings were used for laundry, weaving, food storage, and other purposes.

slaves, usually considered the minimum number for a plantation. By the eve of the Civil War, there were nearly four million African American slaves in the South, most of them concentrated in the Deep South on large plantations producing sugar, rice, and cotton. The plantations were owned by wealthy white families, but most of the people who lived and worked there were African Americans, who maintained their own culture despite a wide variety of living and working conditions and personal experiences. Of the many places where white and black plantation residents interacted, the kitchen was among the most critical. In this space, the relationship between the mistress and her enslaved cook could be simultaneously cooperative and contested.

## Detached Kitchens

A distinctive feature of the southern plantation kitchen was its physical separation from the family dwelling. The practice of building a detached kitchen was established by the end of the seventeenth century in the Chesapeake region.[6] These structures were often referred to as "Big House kitchens" to distinguish them from kitchens in tenant dwellings and slave quarters. Big House kitchens were generally one- or two-room log or frame buildings with brick or stone chimneys.[7] A second room or loft above often housed the cook's family. Green Hill's kitchen was a frame building of typical size—about sixteen by eighteen feet and one and a half stories high—but it had an unusually massive stone chimney and three fireplace openings. The enormous hearth allowed the cook to prepare a number of dishes at once for the family, their guests, and possibly the enslaved residents of Upper Town.

Although most were not as elaborate as the one at Green Hill, plantation kitchens generally had large cooking hearths, despite the growing popularity of cookstoves in the nineteenth century. Most masters were not inclined to update their kitchens, for human labor was plentiful and cash was scarce. Simple furnishings, rarely little more than basic shelves and tables, were found in all but the finest kitchens. The best had elaborate sets of cookware, specialized tools and equipment, ovens, and occasionally stew stoves. Like the one at Green Hill, many kitchens had dirt floors and a root cellar concealed by boards, dug near the hearth, where vegetables would be protected from freezing in the winter.

Plantation kitchens (and kitchens in well-to-do urban households in the South) were traditionally detached from the Big House for several reasons. In the southern climate, families were more concerned with keeping the heat of the cooking fire out of the house during the warmer months than they were with the risk of a house fire. In 1705 historian Robert Beverley commented, "All their Drudgeries of Cookery, washing, Daries, etc. are perform'd in Offices detacht from their Dwelling-Houses, which by this means are kept more cool and Sweet."[8] Detached kitchens also kept food and its accompanying mess closer to the fields, coops, barns, and outbuildings, the places where it was grown, processed, and stored. The most important reason, however, for detaching the kitchen from the Big House was the increasing desire to separate the races as the system of chattel slavery became better defined in the late seventeenth century. This move reinforced the division between master and slave and limited the slaves' access to the Big House.[9]

> They build also a separate kitchen, a separate house for the Christian slaves, one for the Negro slaves, and several to dry the tobacco, so that when you come to the home of a person of some means, you think you are entering a fairly large village.
>
> Durand de Dauphine, 1686

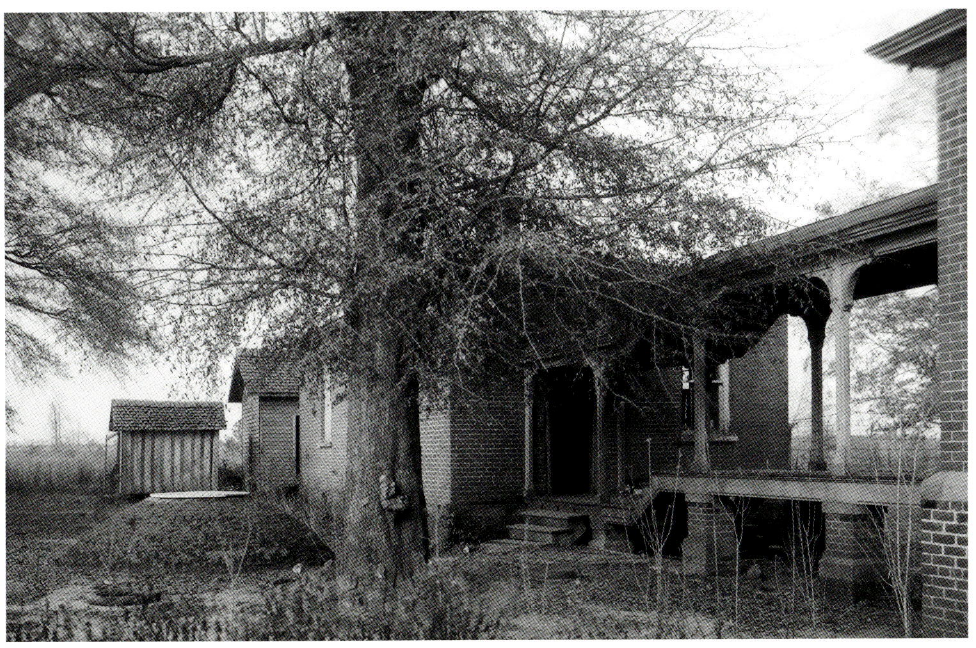

Some plantation kitchens, like this one at Kenworthy Hall in Perry County, Alabama, were attached to the house by covered walkways, which kept food and people dry in inclement weather. Open walkways were more problematic; food was usually covered, but the slaves who carried it were not.

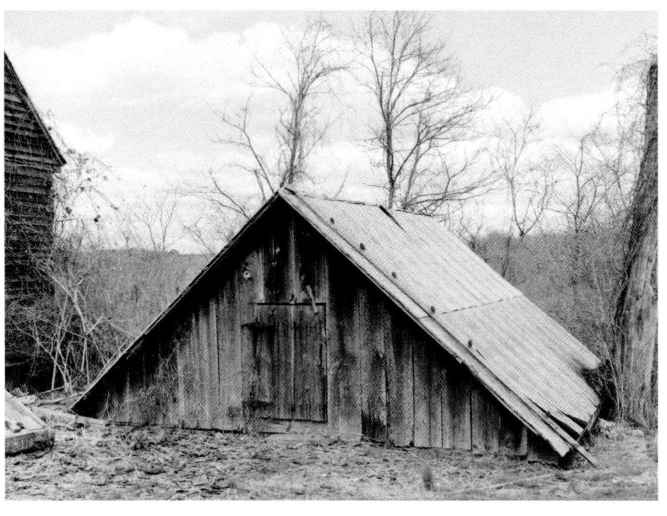
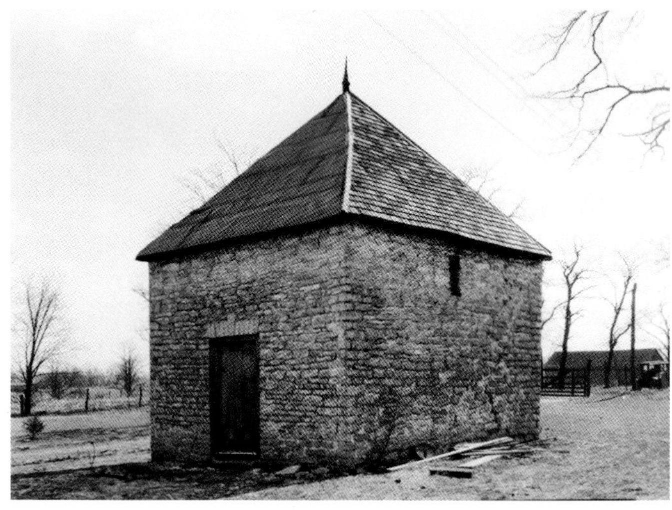
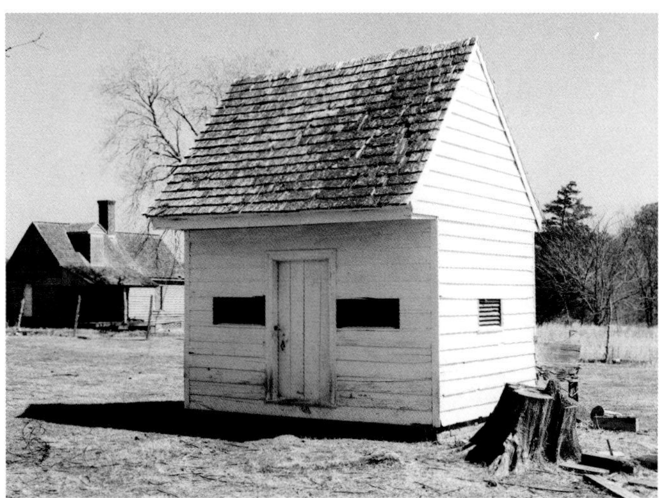
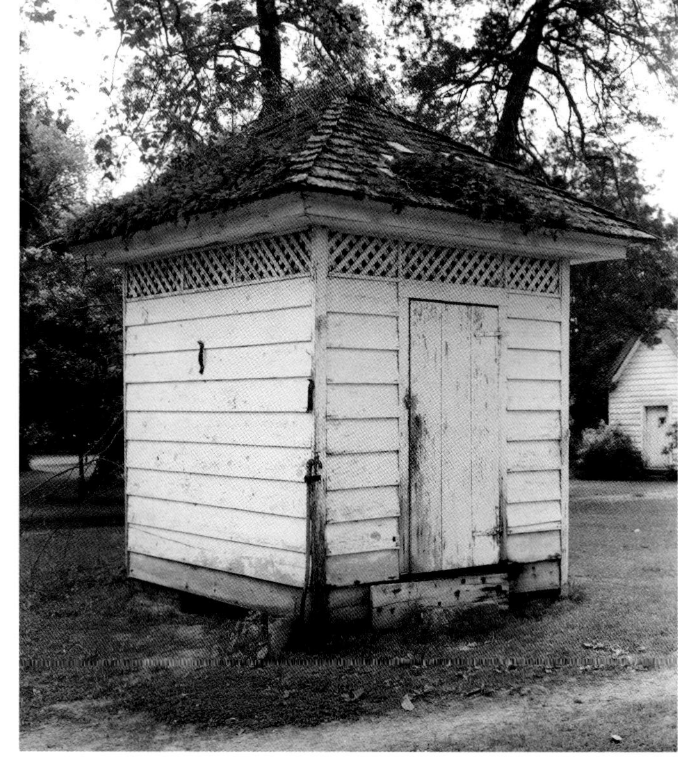
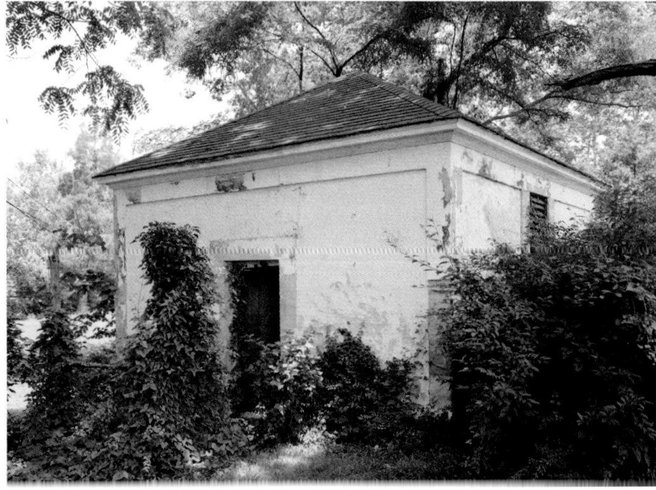

Most large plantations had numerous outbuildings for processing and storing food. Here, clockwise, from the upper left, are the icehouse at Green Hill, Campbell County, Virginia; the Mt. Lebanon smokehouse, Bourbon County, Kentucky; and three dairies, at Hayes Manor, Chowan County, North Carolina; Mount Airy, Richmond County, Virginia; and Woodlands, Northampton County, Virginia.

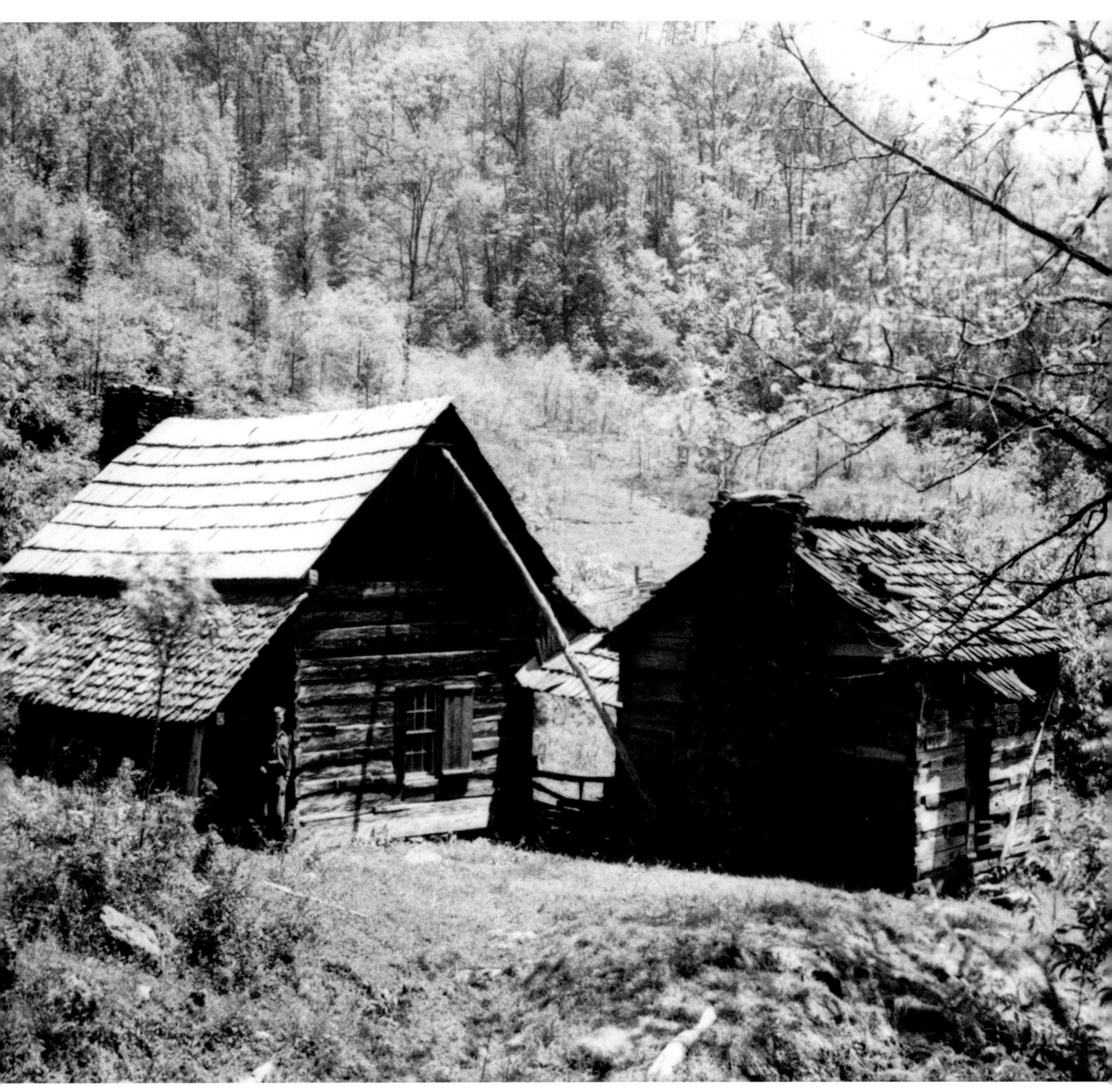

Prompted by practical reasons or by a desire to emulate the slave-owning classes, white families in southwestern North Carolina commonly lived in a one-room house with a separate kitchen, often similar in size. This arrangement, illustrated by this 1937 photograph of the Ephraim Bumgarner cabin and kitchen in Deep Creek, North Carolina, was commonly referred to as "Big House and kitchen."

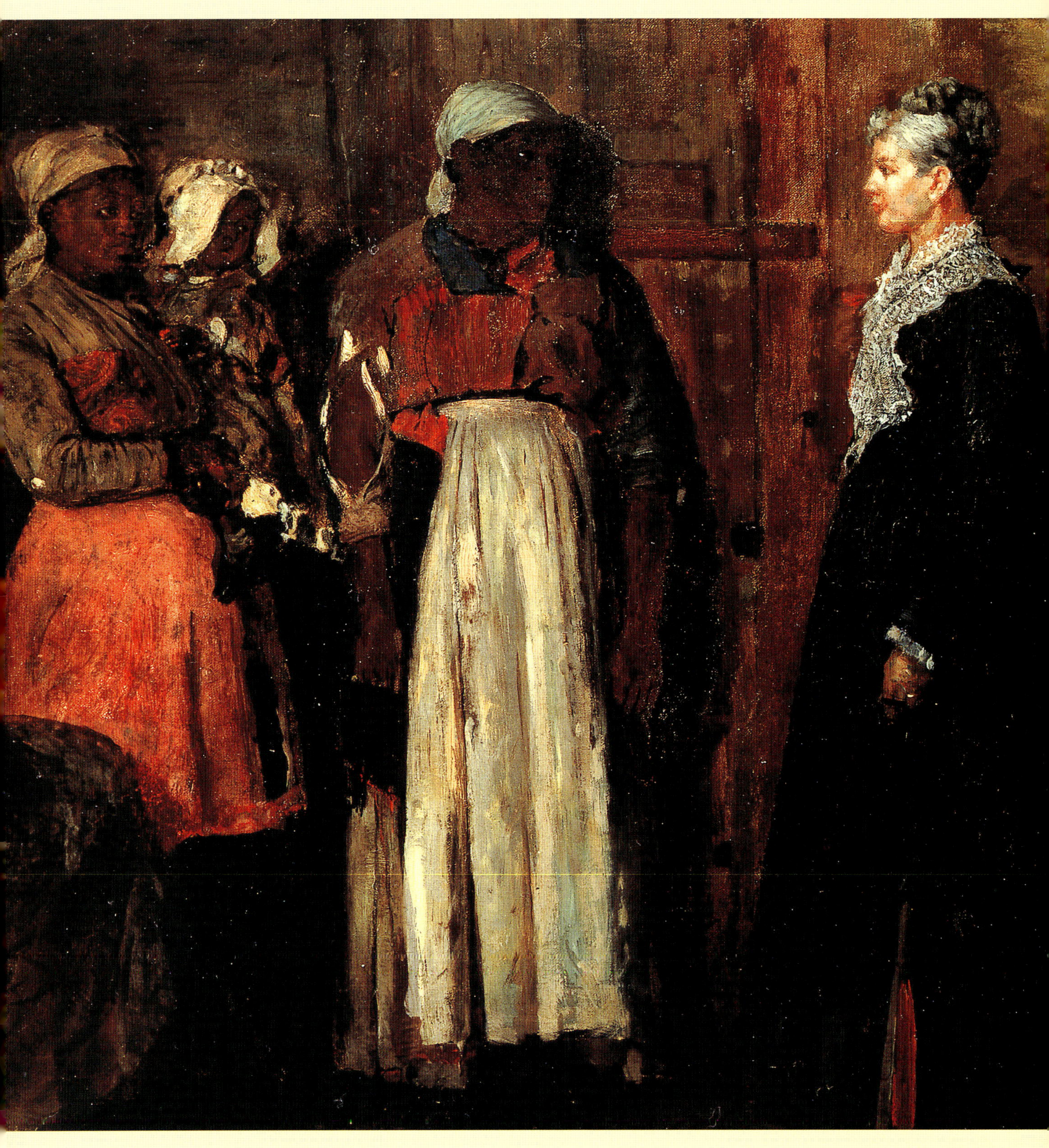

Winslow Homer's *A Visit from the Old Mistress* (1876) shows the tension between the former mistress and her former slaves in their kitchen. The women are probably making work plans, but the freed women's posture reveals their bargaining power.

## *Mistresses and Slaves*

The relationships between plantation mistresses and the slaves who worked in their kitchens were full of contradiction. They could be antagonistic and intimate at the same time. Backed by her husband's authority, a mistress was dominant, but slaves had subtle ways of rebelling. Those who openly challenged their mistresses suffered harsh consequences.

Despite working closely with their owners, the thoughts and feelings of domestic slaves were often invisible to whites. Mistresses convinced themselves that they understood their slaves and then expressed surprise when they left following Emancipation. "My life long," wrote one, "I have been laboring and caring for them, and since the war have labored with all my might to supply their wants, and expended everything I had upon their support, directly or indirectly; and this is their return." Some mistresses believed that they were "slaves of slaves."[10]

The everyday responsibilities of the mistresses involved managing people and supplies to ensure that everyone in the plantation community would be clothed and fed and the economic vitality of the plantation protected. Mistresses had to be skilled in planning and monitoring their storerooms, dairies, icehouses, smokehouses, poultry yards, gardens, and orchards. The preservation and storage of foods was a responsibility that few entrusted to slaves. Mistresses often did the work of putting up pickles and preserves and making sausages, processing lard, salting and smoking meat—critical tasks that had long-term consequences for feeding the household.[11] As a young mistress, Mary Withers lamented, "Now I have turned housekeeper for to my sorrow I know there is no romance in going from the smoke house to the store room and from there to the cellar half a dozen times a day."[12] As a symbol of their authority, mistresses carried keys to the household locks and maintained inventories in notebooks and diaries.

Early each day, the mistress discussed the menu with the cook and distributed the food to be prepared for her family and sometimes for the slaves. It was the housewife's duty to know "to a fraction how much of the raw products went to the composition of each dish she ordered. So much flour was required for a loaf of rolls, and so much for a dozen beaten biscuits; a stated quantity of butter was for cake or pudding."[13] Such familiarity with the

> To my smoke house my Dairy Pantry kitchen & cellar like famished wolves they come breaking locks & whatever is in their way. The thousand pounds of meat in my smoke house is gone in a twinkling my flour my meal my lard butter eggs pickles of various kinds both in vinegar & brine. Wine jars & jugs are all gone. My eighteen fat turkeys my hens chickens & fowls. My young pigs are shot down in my yard & hunted as if they were rebels themselves.
>
> Dolly Burge, 1864

The extent of a mistress's knowledge of her provisions is illustrated in a list kept by Dolly Burge of Newton County, Georgia, describing what was lost when Yankee troops raided her plantation in November 1864.

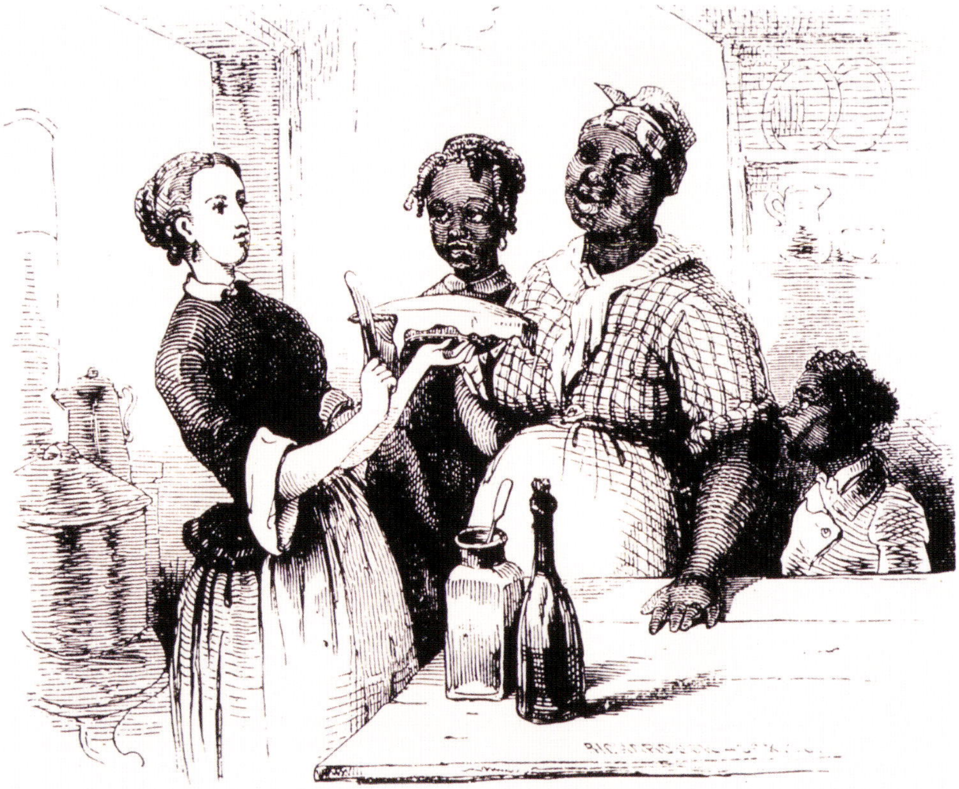

This illustration from an 1854 *Harper's Weekly* short story depicts the unlikely scene of a young mistress demonstrating a simple technique to the chief cook, Aunt Dilly. Aunt Dilly is described as watching "in proud humility—proud of serving such a mistress, humble at seeing herself outdone by one of only half her age," a description that insults the cook's culinary skills and her dignity.

THE VIRGINIA HOUSEKEEPER

recipes left little room for error or nibbling on the part of the cook—and little chance that many leftovers would make their way back to the kitchen.

After receiving the ingredients, the cook began preparing dinner, the main meal of the day. Some cooks had one or more assistants—either cooks in training or people too young or old for other work—to help prepare vegetables, pluck chickens, or turn the spit, but the cook herself was responsible for orchestrating the meal and sending dishes to the dining room. Cooks often prepared a second meal for themselves, their families, and other slaves, which they ate when they could. In the midst of all this activity, cooks nursed their babies and looked after older children. Cooks often cared for the children whose enslaved parents were otherwise occupied and occasionally the white children as well. On some plantations they were also responsible for the laundry, spinning, weaving, gardening, and other tasks.

Some cooks were men, but the kitchen was predominately a female space, one over which slaves could exert a little control. While the mis-

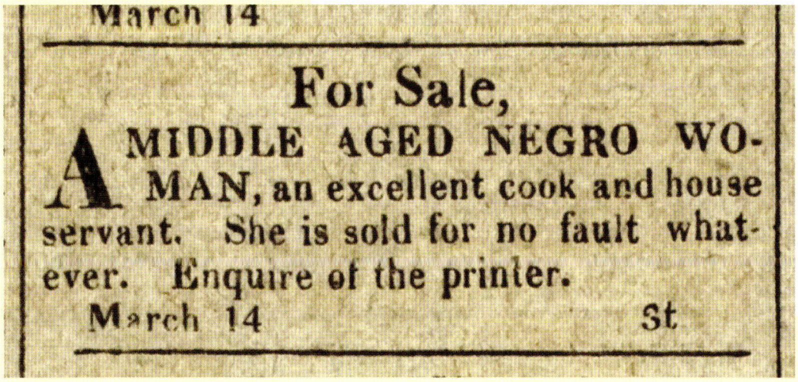

March 14

For Sale,

A MIDDLE AGED NEGRO WOMAN, an excellent cook and house servant. She is sold for no fault whatever. Enquire of the printer.

March 14 3t

This notice was published in the *Alexandria Gazette & Daily Advertiser* in 1818. Good cooks were sought after and fetched a high price on the auction block.

tress had ultimate authority and would drop in unannounced to order meals, distribute and monitor supplies, and supervise the cooking (as Caroline Howard Gilman put it in 1838, "to stimulate her cook to neatness and activity"), she was usually glad to leave as soon as she felt her presence was not needed.[14] Caroline E. Merrick described how as a young mistress her efforts to exert her authority were deflected by her older, more experienced cook, who resisted supervision by feigning interest in her mistress's comfort and concern for her ladylike sensitivity: "*Go* inter de *house*, Miss Carrie! Yer ain't no manner er use heah only ter git yer face red wid de heat. I'll have dinner like yer wants it. Jes' read yer book an' res' easy til I sen's it ter de dining room."[15]

Household slaves had more contact with the white family than those who worked in the fields, which occasionally gained them favored access to food, clothing, and housing. In some accounts, slaves and their mistresses developed true friendships, although both were always aware of their inequality. Personal experiences varied widely, but underlying all of these relationships was the threat of violence.[16] Constantly on call, slaves were often in the path of the worst moods of the master or mistress. Former slave Emmaline Heard recalled, "Just before dinner, the mistress would come in to inspect the cooking. If the food in any of the pots was not cooked to her satisfaction, she would sometimes lose her temper, remove her slipper and strike the cook."[17] In 1937 Cornelia Andrews of North Carolina, a former slave then eighty-seven years old, recalled a severe beating, "I wuz whupped public . . . for breaking dishes an' bein' slow. I wuz at Mis' Carrington's den, an' it wuz jist 'fore de close o' de war. I wuz in de kitchen washin' dishes an I draps one. De missus calls Mr. Blount King, a patteroller [patroller], an' he puts de whuppin' yo' sees de marks of on me."[18]

"Mary Jane, put some warm water in this jug, and clean it for molasses," I say before tea. After tea, I say again, "Mary Jane, put some warm water in this jug, and clean it for molasses." I go to bed. In the morning, I say, "Mary Jane, put some warm water in this jug, and clean it for molasses." Two days afterwards I clean it myself.

Lucy Chase, 1863

Ignoring directions was a common way for slaves to resist authority. Such actions tested a mistress's patience, as even abolitionist Lucy Chase learned when she moved to the South to work with former slaves.

There was a side of slave life that white families rarely saw, though it often took place in their kitchens, right under their noses. Some used rituals to shroud their secrets; Lizzie Johnson of Arkansas explained: "When company would come they would turn the pot down and close the shutters and doors. They had preaching and prayed that way. The pot was to drown out the sound."[19] Archaeological excavations of kitchens have uncovered groups of objects, including beads, pins, buttons, bones, and glass, used by enslaved African Americans in conjuring. Bundles of objects were placed in hearths and doorways to induce the spirits that passed through to control anyone who entered the space, most notably the mistress.[20]

Because cooks had control over their masters' food, some plantation owners lived in fear of being poisoned, particularly in the wake of slave rebellions. Writing to her husband in 1838, Eliza Bruce, a plantation mistress in south-central Virginia, mentioned a near-tragic event on a neighboring plantation, "A servant girl . . . made an attempt the other day to poison Mr. Sowers's family by putting a large lump of *white lead* in the coffee pot."[21] None of the family was harmed, for the poison was discovered before they drank much of it. If her enslavement were not a sufficient motive, what prompted the girl to take such a risk is unknown, as is what became of her. She was probably whipped, sent to work in the fields, or sold. In her diary, Keziah Goodwyn Hopkins Brevard of South Carolina constantly complained that her slaves did not like or respect her. Concerned about the taste of a cup of coffee, she wrote, "Can it be possible it was an attempt to poison—somehow I can't think so," but, with little humor, she warned those who read her diary, "If I should be suddenly taken off after a meal—remember the coffee."[22] Despite a lingering uncertainty about the safety of the food on their tables, these women were not about to do the cooking themselves.

Most instances of slave resistance were less dramatic. Pretending to be forgetful or not to hear, breaking or "losing" objects, being disorganized, running away, feigning illness, burning the dinner, and otherwise slowing the workings of the house were common expressions of resistance, unspoken negotiations that helped a slave feel greater autonomy. Mistresses might use persuasion or force to make their slaves obey, but resistance was possible because slaves knew how much they were needed. A cook, who had burned a batch of bread, hid in the woods for two weeks to avoid punishment. When she returned, her master did whip her but not severely, as "he was glad to git her back."[23]

> As a great many ladies have wished to know how I have such good success in making my cakes so light, I will say, I first heat the oven hot enough for cooking, set in my cake, and open the door; and for a common sized cake leave the door open for about fifteen minutes, and for a large one, about twenty minutes. When the cake begins to raise, close the door.
>
> Malinda Russell, *A Domestic Cook Book: Containing a Careful Selection of Useful Receipts for the Kitchen*, 1866

Malinda Russell authored the first cookbook known to be written by an African American. The daughter of a free black family from Tennessee, Russell worked for many years as a cook and also kept a boarding house and pastry shop. Her numerous recipes for elegant cakes and baked goods highlight her talent for preparing pastries and the diversity of southern foods.

Cooks were often taught by family members or older slaves and only rarely received professional training. Their culinary ability, authority, and access to the master's family and food elevated their status in the plantation community. Of one cook, Aunt Rachel, it was recalled: "All de niggers have to stoop to Aunt Rachel jes' like dey curtsy to Missy."[24] But cooks were forced to show respect to their mistresses. One woman remembered how the mistress had come to the kitchen to "scold my mammy 'bout de sorry way mammy done clean de chitlins." The mother had to deflect the child's effort to stand up for her: "Little ez Ah wuz ... I sez tuh Miss Millie, 'Doan you no' Mammy is boss of dis hyar kitchen. You cyan' cum a fussin' in hyar.'" Miss Millie laughed, but Lucy's mother grabbed a switch "en gin ticklin' my laigs" to show the mistress that she knew her place and would be responsible for disciplining her own child.[25]

Some accounts of the Old South honored African American cooks for their culinary talents while simultaneously insulting them as human beings. "The negroes are born cooks," Charles Gayarre declared in 1887. The cook "was simply inspired; the god of the spit and

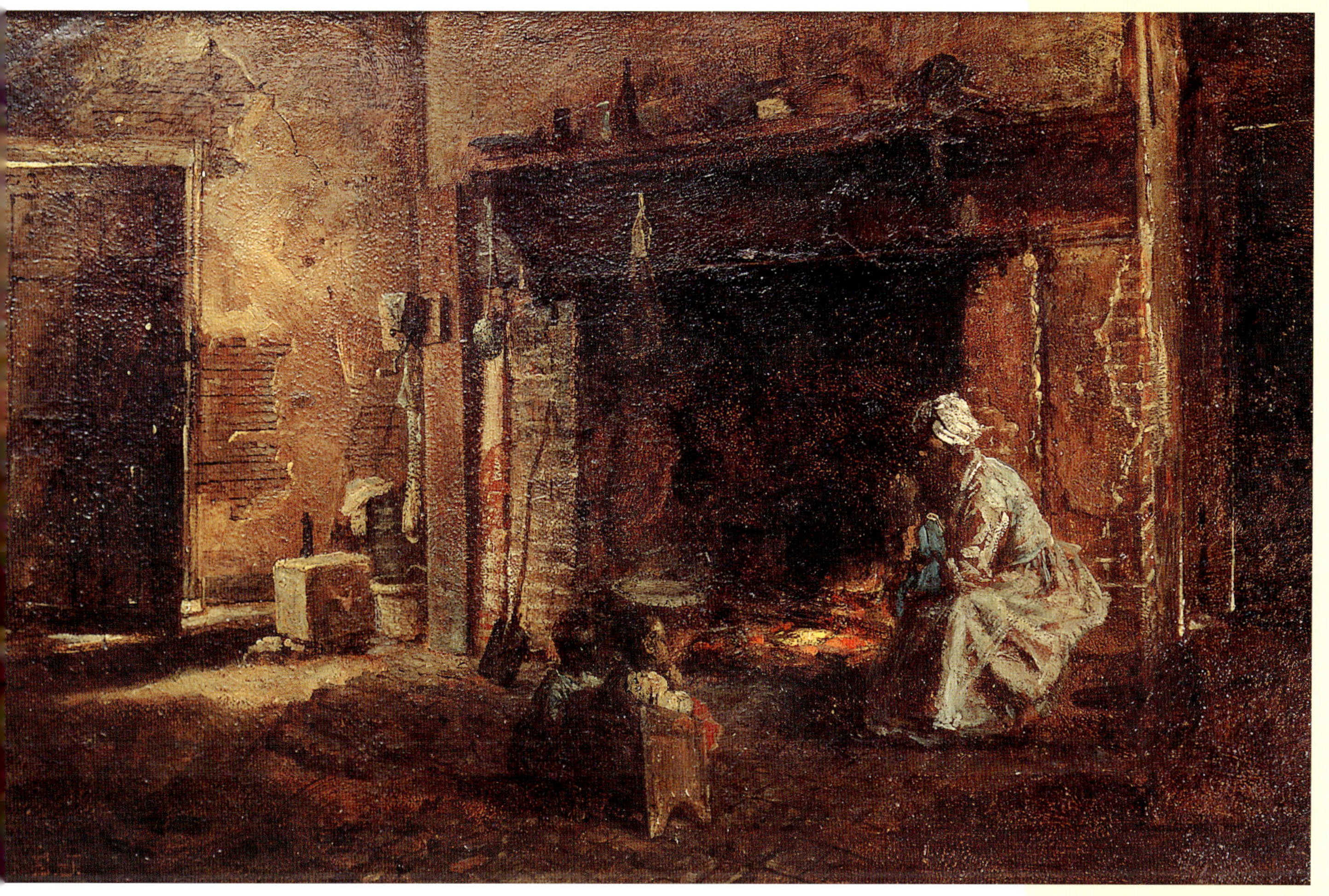

the saucepan had breathed into him."[26] Such comments were two racist insults masked: that African Americans passively gained their skill through instinct (rather than through study, hard work, and intellect) and—the more subtle and derogatory assertion—that they were best suited for kitchen work rather than jobs with more power or prestige. In 1841 Frederick Douglass told a story about a white woman who had been in a trance and thought she had gone to heaven. When asked if she saw any black people there, she replied, "Oh! I didn't go into the kitchen!"[27] The image of beaming Aunt Jemima on boxes of pancake mix is a lingering example of this stereotype.[28]

Eastman Johnson painted this scene of an enslaved African American family around a cooking hearth at Mount Vernon about 1857. By that time, the former home of George Washington had fallen into picturesque disrepair.

While some black cooks undoubtedly had a genuine gift, daily practice enabled them to become more proficient cooks than their mistresses, who generally had little practical experience. After her cook's departure, Malvina Gist Waring wished that she "had been taught to cook instead of how to play on the piano."[29] The extent of slaves' contribution to the smooth operation of the plantation became apparent after Emancipation.

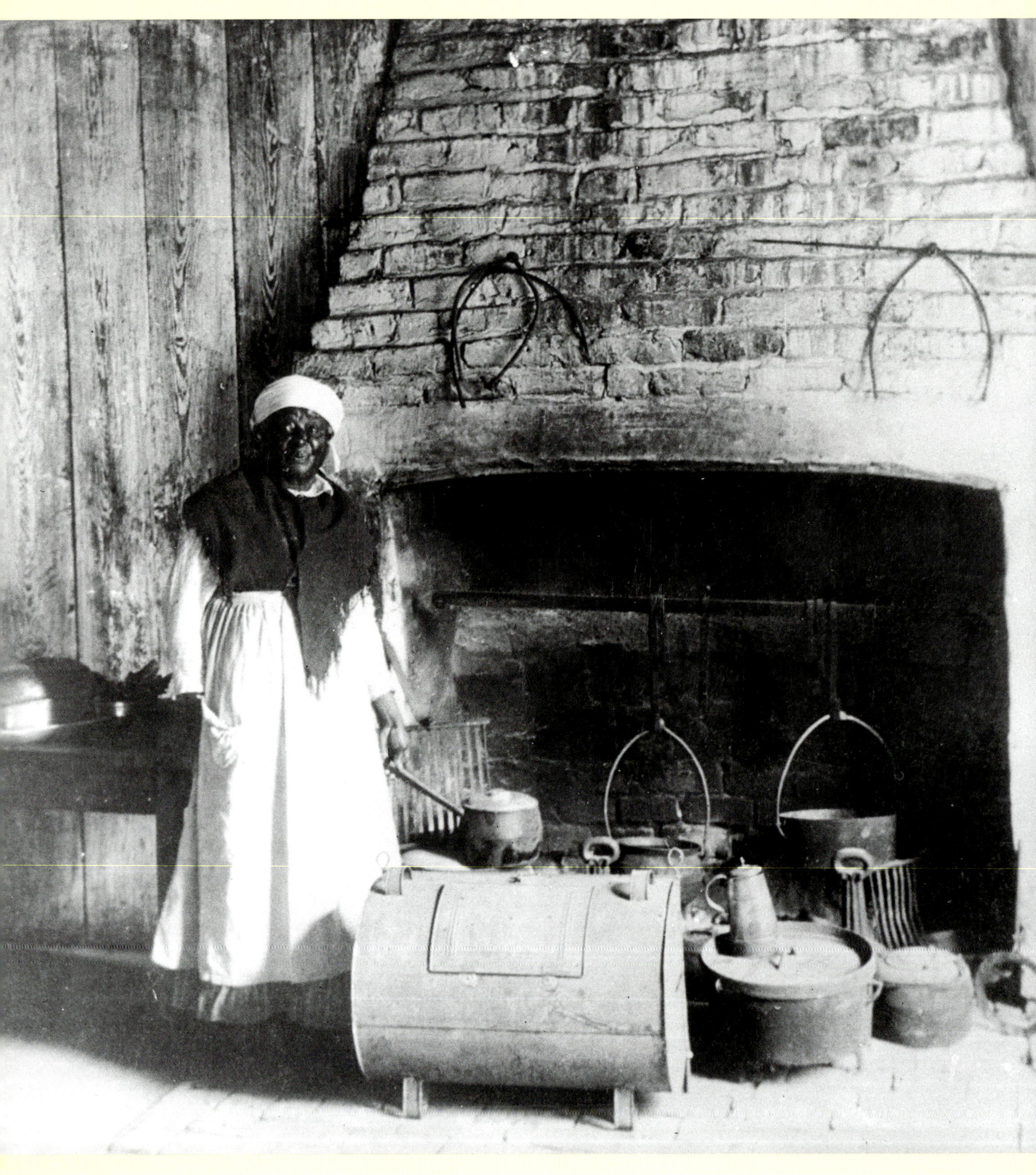

This undated photograph of a woman in the kitchen at Refuge Plantation in Camden County, Georgia, shows the type of cooking equipment still in use in plantation kitchens during much of the nineteenth century.

## Plantation Fare

Corn and pork were the cornerstones of the southern diet. In their simplest forms, mush or baked pone—made from cornmeal, salt, and water—and bacon served as everyday fare, and corn bread or cakes made rich with milk, butter, and eggs and ham cut into the most delicate slivers were presented to fine company. Corn and pork were accompanied by other kinds of domestic poultry and meat, wild game, and fish. In most areas, wheat flour was secondary to cornmeal; costly, it was reserved for biscuits, pastries, and cakes rather than bread. Lucy Chase wrote approvingly of Virginia corn bread: "If you could eat the negroes corn-cake, you would no longer ask for scalding water, milk, eggs, soda, or yeast for your 'Indian-cake.'"[30] Rice, grown along the coast of South Carolina and Georgia, was common in those regions. Southerners ate vegetables such as sweet potatoes, turnips, peas, beans, cabbage, and greens, and fruits such as apples, peaches, berries, and melons, fresh in season and preserved for later use.[31] Some of the most famous southern foods required considerable labor. For example, the dough for beaten biscuits was pounded for half an hour or more until it was tender.

> Not until you come here can you imagine how entirely different is their mode of living. They live more heartily. There must always be two or three different kinds of meats on Mrs. Williams' table for breakfast & dinner. Red pepper is much used to flavor meat with the famous "barbecue" of the South & which I believe they esteem above all dishes is roasted pig dressed with red pepper & vinegar. Their bread is corn bread, just meal wet with water & without yeast or saleratus [leavening], & biscuit with shortening and without anything to make them light and beaten like crackers. The bread and biscuit are always brought to the table hot.
>
> Sarah Frances Hicks Williams, 1853

Sarah Frances Hicks Williams, a new bride in North Carolina, described southern food to her family in New York.

The meals served in the Big House dining room might be elaborate displays of abundance, such as a memorable breakfast table on a Louisiana plantation that included "a profusion of dishes—grilled fowl, prawns, eggs and ham, fish from New Orleans, potted salmon from England, preserved meats from France, claret, iced water, coffee and tea, varieties of hominy, mush, and African vegetable preparations."[32] On the other hand, Keziah Goodwyn Hopkins Brevard, who was constantly at odds with her cook, described serving a more modest meal to guests: "Had a Ham—boiled & roast mutton—two fowls & vegetables for dinner." She added, "all done up in the worst order—the soup passable—I am mortified every time I have a dining."[33] While traveling in Mississippi, landscape architect Frederick Law Olmsted noted a typical meal presented to him that was more modest still: "Bacon, corn-bread and coffee invariably appeared at every meal; but, besides this . . . a fried fowl, 'biscuit' of wheat flour, with butter were added. . . . Molasses usually, honey frequently, and as a rare exception, potatoes and green peas were added to the board. Whiskey was seldom offered me, and only once any other beverage except the abominable preparation which passes for coffee."[34]

## *Slave Cooking and Diet*

Most planters provided adequate food for their slaves, both to maintain their health and to discourage them from stealing. Although mistresses were responsible for tracking supplies, masters or overseers usually distributed rations, particularly to field slaves, who had little contact with the mistress.[35] The content of the weekly rations varied by region and the wealth and generosity of the master but generally consisted of a peck of cornmeal, three or four pounds of meat, and often molasses. Slaves were given the less desirable cuts and quality of meat, usually pork or beef, but sometimes mutton and goat, often from animals that had otherwise outlived their usefulness.

Despite this, accounts indicate that the diets of many slaves were surprisingly varied. Some were permitted to grow vegetables for themselves, such as collard greens, cabbage, turnips, and sweet potatoes, and raise chickens and eggs for themselves or to sell, sometimes to their own masters. They tended their gardens on moonlit nights, and in any available free time. Slaves gathered wild nuts, berries, and greens, fished, and hunted wild animals—possums, raccoons, and rabbits. They stored produce in root cellars. Except for the produce and animals they raised for themselves, however, slaves had little food in their houses.

Many slaves had a few iron and ceramic vessels for cooking, storing, and serving food, as well as wooden or iron utensils. Charred pieces of pottery recovered from archaeological sites suggest that slaves in parts of the South used ceramic vessels for cooking. Excavated animal bones indicate that the slaves generally chopped meat into pieces for stewing in pots. This was partly due to tradition and partly because the cuts of meat were generally not of a quality for roasting.

For the management of plantation Servants, I have adopted a system, which works so entirely to my satisfaction, that I have determined to send it to you, to be disposed of as you may deem best. If others will adopt it, and carry it out in a proper spirit, I have no doubt they will be equally gratified. . . .

Diet—Three and a half pounds of sides and a peck of meal is given out every Saturday night, to every grown hand and others in proportion to their ages. In addition, they are supplied with yams, Southern pea, and garden vegetables. It is held to be the duty of every one to take care of his provisions; and they know full well that should they, from negligence or other cause, fall short, they will get no more until next Saturday. This rule is rigidly enforced. To pursue a different course would encourage the negligent and produce great trouble. Each family takes charge of its own provisions. They cook their own breakfasts and suppers, but their dinners are prepared by a common cook who sends it to the field at 12 o'clock. This plan they prefer, and it works well.

"Management of Servants," *Southern Cultivator*, 1853

Some planters, like the author of this article, approached the provisioning of their slaves as a way of reinforcing their own authority as much as a means of nourishment.

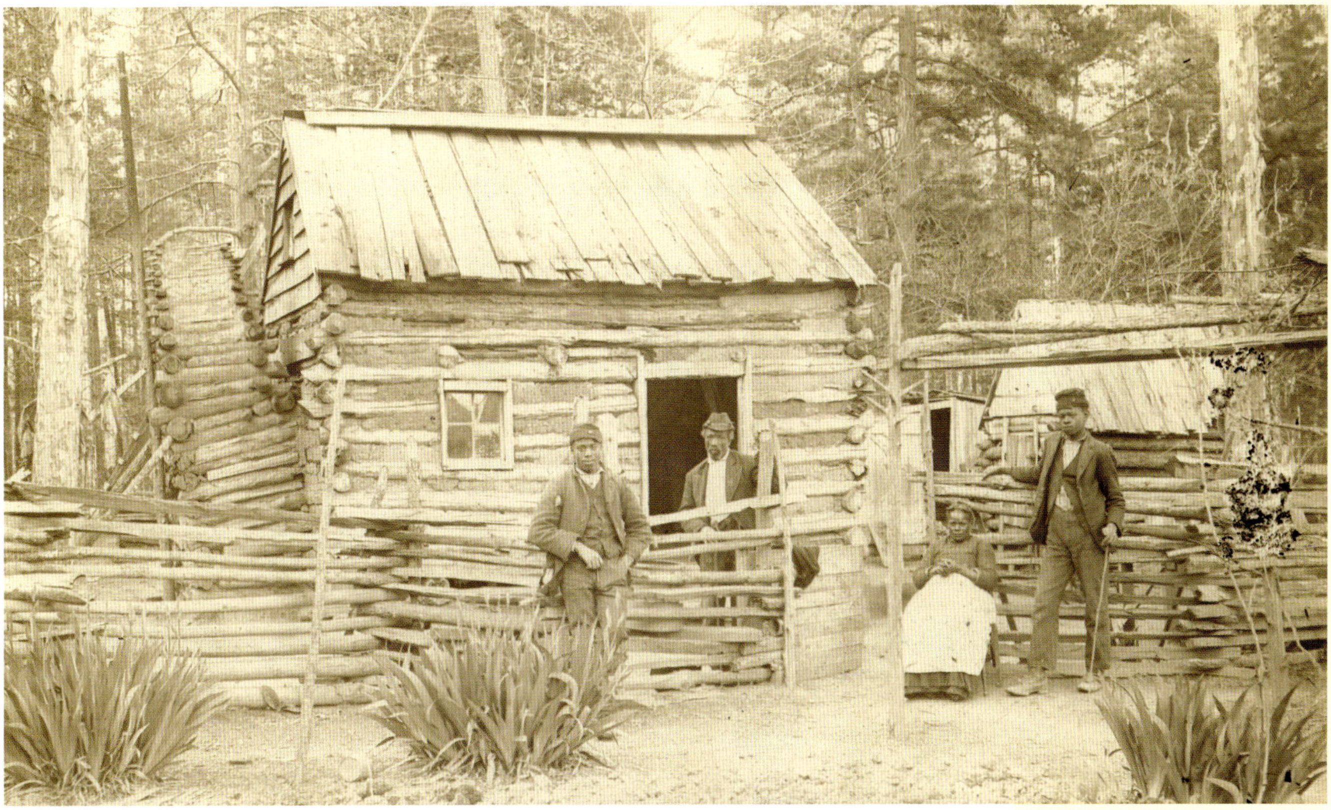

This nineteenth-century photograph shows a type of house typically used as slave quarters. These cabins often had wooden chimneys that narrowed toward the top and were daubed with mud. Residents might cook at the hearth or outside in the yard.

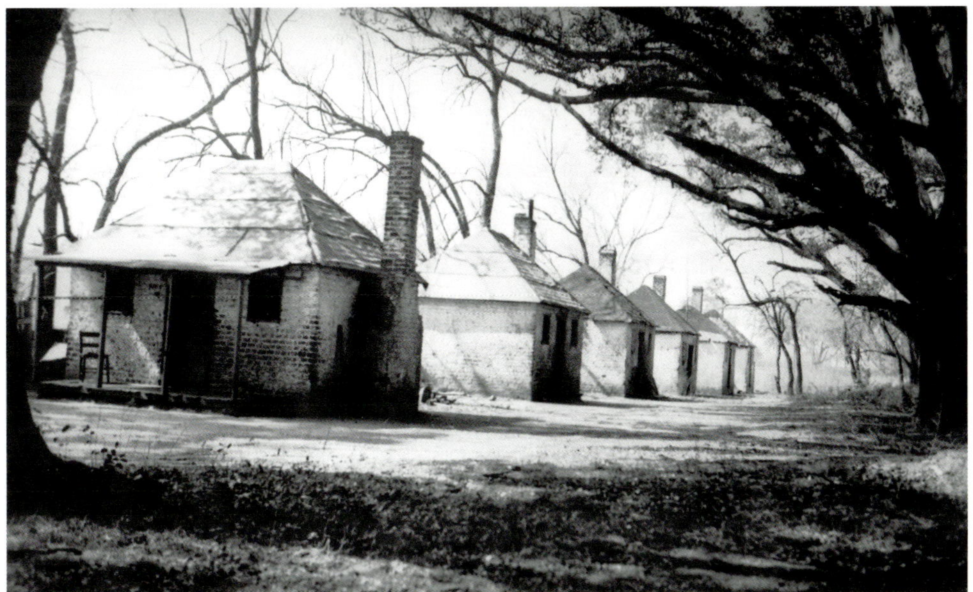

Dwellings for field workers were generally set apart from the planter's house. Some, such as these at the Hermitage Plantation in Chatham County, near Savannah, Georgia, were single-family dwellings with fireplaces for cooking and heating, while others housed several families. In the nineteenth century, wealthy planters built more orderly, commodious quarters, in part to deflect criticism about slaveholding.

Although by the nineteenth century most slaves had been born in the Americas, many continued to cook foods similar to those their ancestors had known in their homeland. West African peoples generally ate flat and bland breads or porridges made from starchy grains, roots, or legumes, served with roasted or boiled meat and stews made from vegetables such as leafy greens, okra, and squashes. With some substitutions, these meals translated easily into the foods slaves could make from their rations: preparations of corn, including flat hoe cakes (said to have been baked on the flat iron head of a hoe propped up in front of the fire, although they were also baked on griddles), hominy, and ash-cakes (corn dough baked in the ashes), served with vegetables seasoned with meat and pepper.[36] In some parts of the South, slaves ate their stew with rice.

Consciously or purely by habit, slaves perpetuated food traditions from one generation to the next and introduced them to white families. These recipes eventually made their way into mainstream American culture. For example, African American cooks, although uncredited, clearly influenced Mary Randolph's cookbook, *The Virginia Housewife* (1824). The book includes recipes for okra and field peas, both native to West Africa. The recipe for field peas calls for mashing them and frying them into cakes, a typical West African preparation.[37] Unfamiliar with the concept of mashing beans, Lucy Chase complained: "Home from school and into the kitchen, to find Mary Jane mashing the beans into pulp . . . . Sarah said she was tired of mush, and had hoped to find variety in beans, but there was mush again."[38]

This hearth in a former slave cabin at Thornhill Plantation in Greene County, Alabama, photographed in 1934, is similar to the modest hearths that most slaves, as well as poorer white families, had in their small cabins.

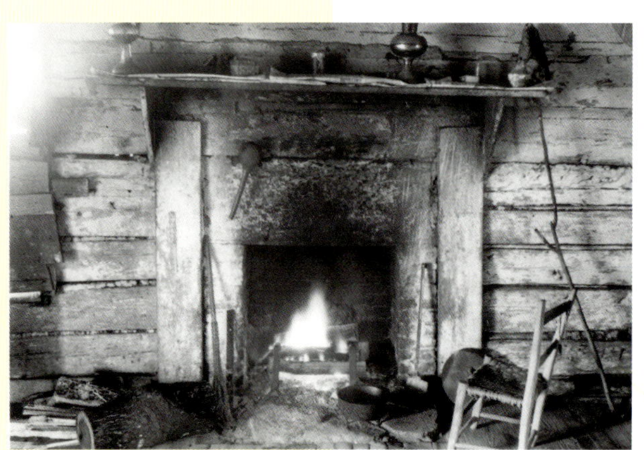

Cooks had better access to the master's supplies of food than most slaves and sometimes surreptitiously distributed it to others. Sarah Fitzpatrick, from Tuskegee, Alabama, recalled that the slaves felt entitled to the food they stole: "Dey didn't call it stealin,' dey called it takin.'" The evidence was carefully concealed: "If you got it [a chicken] you stole it when de white folks wus sleep at night an' den you had to be careful an' bury all de feathers in de groun' 'cause if you burned 'em de white folks would smell 'em."[39]

This recipe for "Ochra Soup" demonstrates how new cultural influences enter through the kitchen door. Many of the recipes in *The Virginia Housewife*, first published in 1824 and still in print, were clearly influenced by those of enslaved African American cooks, although none is credited.

## Ochra Soup

Get two double handsful of young ochra, wash and slice it thin, add two onions chopped fine, put it into a gallon of water at a very early hour in an earthen pipkin, or very nice iron pot; it must be kept steadily simmering, but not boiling: put in pepper and salt. At 12 o'clock, put in a handful of Lima beans; at half-past one o'clock, add three young cimlins [squashes] cleaned and cut in small pieces, a fowl, or knuckle of veal, a bit of bacon or pork that has been boiled, and six tomatos, with the skin taken off; when nearly done, thicken with a spoonful of butter, mixed with one of flour. Have rice boiled to eat with it.

Mary Randolph, *The Virginia Housewife*, 1838

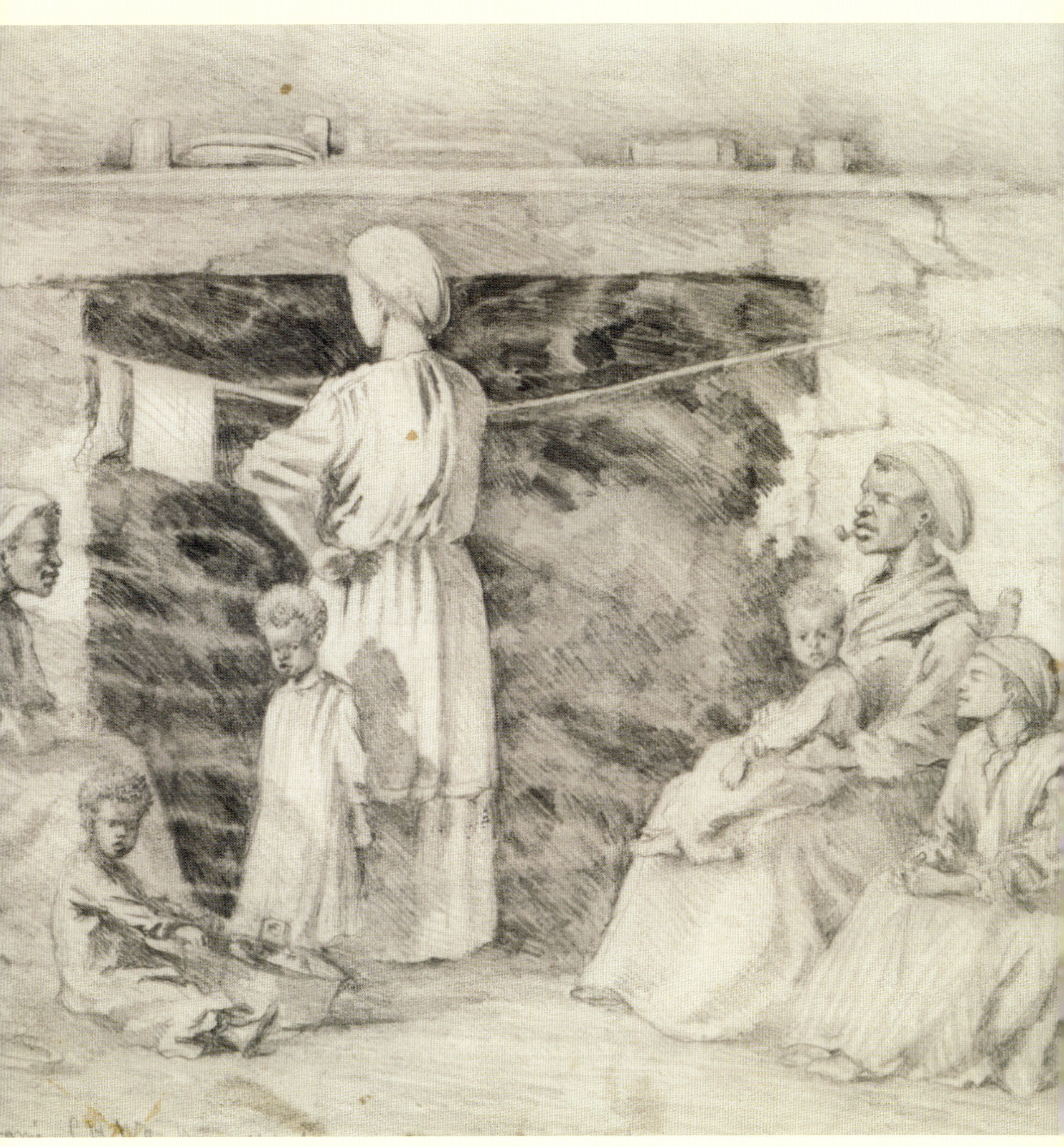

In 1864 Edwin Forbes depicted an enslaved African American family gathered around their hearth in Spotsylvania, Virginia. Like many white families, they would have used this hearth for heating their home, as well as for cooking and, as shown, drying laundry.

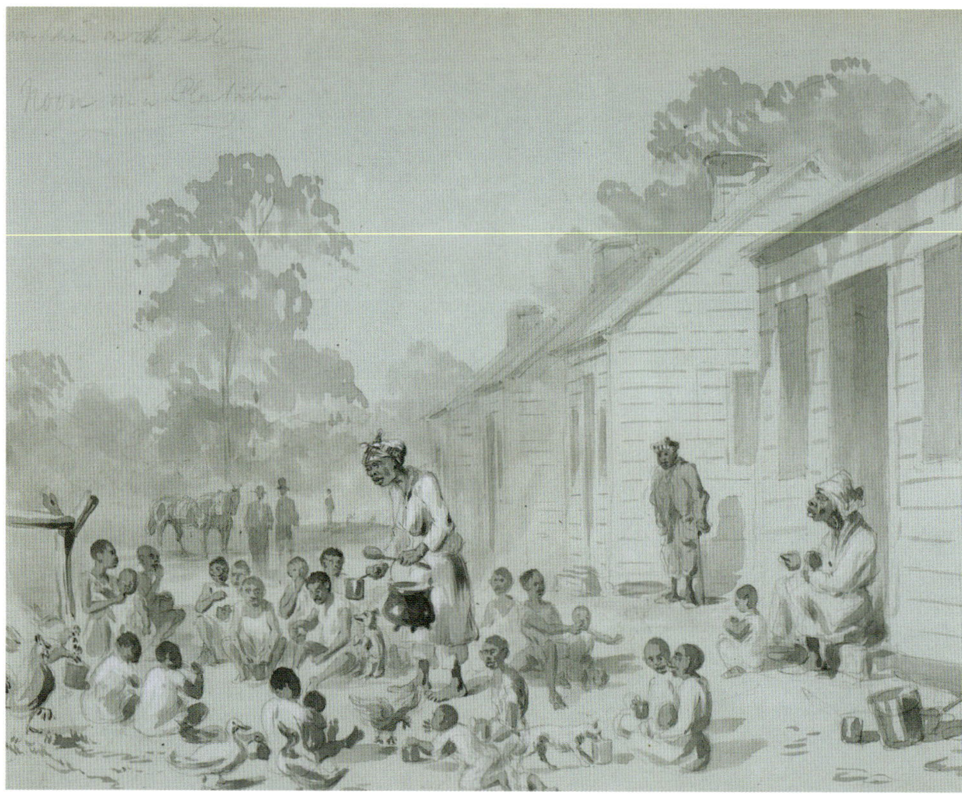

The children of slaves were often fed in a central location by a slave who was too old to work in the fields. In William Waud's watercolor from the 1860s, they are depicted in the yard outside the quarters preparing to eat a meal that was probably cooked outdoors.

Some slaves, particularly those who worked in or near the Big House, ate food that the cook prepared for them in the master's kitchen, occasionally supplemented by leftovers from the master's table. Others received meals from a cookhouse or prepared at least some of their meals for themselves in their quarters.[40] In slave households, men hunted and fished, stole food, and prepared meat, but women generally did the cooking, returning home during the course of the day to tend the pot.

Slaves often prepared one-pot meals in their cabins, which would cook all day and were ready when families returned from the fields in the evenings.

Slaves were accustomed to eating what they could whenever they could find the time. Booker T. Washington recalled, "I cannot remember a single instance during my childhood . . . when our entire family sat down to the table together, and God's blessing was asked, and the family ate a meal in a civilized manner. . . . Sometimes a portion of our family would eat out of the skillet or pot, while some one else would eat from a tin plate held on the knees, and often using nothing but the hands with which to hold the food."[41] Slaves often ate outdoors in good weather, either close to where they worked or in the yards.

> Dey was in de fiel' fore de sun rose an' dere' till after it went down—fum sun to sun. Dem dat had families done dere own cookin' an' dere was a special cook fer de single ones. De women whut had families would git up soon in de mornin's 'fore time to go to de fiel' an' put de meat on to boil an' den dey would come in at dinner to . . . put de vegetables in de pot to cook an' when dey come home in de evenin' dey would cook some corn bread in de ashes at de fireplace.
>
> Amanda Jackson, *WPA Slave Narratives Project, Georgia Narratives*, 1938

Some masters insisted that enslaved children be fed in a central location, sometimes the Big House, often the kitchen, where the cook or an elderly slave could oversee their care and free their parents for other work. Former slave Lina Hunter remembered that "Granny Rose had 'em [the children] all day, and she had to see dat dey had de right sort of victuals to make chillun grow fast and strong."[42] Other accounts indicate that children were sometimes fed much like animals:

> *Dere was a great long trough what went plum 'cross de yard, and dat was whar us et. For dinner us had peas or some other sort of veg'tables, and cornbread. Aunt Viney crumbled up dat bread in de trough and poured de veg'tables and pot-likker over it. Den she blowed de horn and chillum come a-runnin' from evvy which away. . . . At nights, she crumbled de cornbread in de trough and poured buttermilk over it. Us never had nothin' but cornbread and buttermilk at night. Sometimes dat trough would be a sight, 'cause us never stopped to wash our hands, and 'fore us had been eatin' more dan a minute or two what was in de trough would look lak de red mud what had come off of our hands.*[43]

Frederick Douglass wrote of his extreme hunger during childhood: "I have often been so pinched with hunger, that I have fought with the dog . . . for the smallest crumbs that fell from the kitchen table, and have been glad when I won a single crumb in the combat."[44] Succumbing to temptation, one woman stole a bite of the master's food: "We couldn't eat all the different kinds of victuals the white folks et and one mornin' when I was carryin' the breakfast to the big house we had waffles that wuz a pretty golden brown and pipin' hot. They wuz a picture to look at and Ah jest couldn't keep frum takin' one, and that wuz the hardest waffle fur me to eat befo' I got to the big house I ever saw. Ah jest couldn't git rid of that waffle 'cause my conscience whipped me so."[45] Food was a great divider.

## *After the Civil War*

With the emancipation of slaves and the economic uncertainty that followed the Civil War, all Southerners, free and newly free, had to adapt to changed circumstances. On plantations, some mistresses were forced to cook for their own families. "The first & only meal my mother ever cooked," one woman remembered, was the "day after the negroes all left. Mother went into the kitchen to cook breakfast. She sifted some flour into the tray and stood, thinking what to do next—when an old negro man appeared at the window & said 'law mistis is you cooking breakfast.' 'No I am not come in here and get it for me' which he did." Another described her determination to learn: "I have gone to regular *hard* work. I am learning to do every thing, from making wine, preserves, pickles, &c, down to baking a hoe-cake. I think I *excell* in cooking: but poor little Floy often wishes 'we could get a good cooker.' The dear child *feels* the change, sensibly, though she is unconscious of the great loss she has sustained." And, after making her own meals for ten days, a South Carolina woman exulted that she had found a cook: "Newport has taken the cooking, and we are all ladies again."[46]

Even women who resigned themselves to doing the work on their own found it nearly impossible. Samuel Pannill's grand-niece described how the arrangement of her plantation—designed for slave labor—no longer functioned satisfactorily after the war:

> *It will take some time for us to get fixed to do our own house work or to do with a few servants. For instance, my kitchen is about forty five yards from the dwelling house; my spring about two hundred yards, and other things to correspond. We have no wood house, washing machine, cooking stove,—in short, none of the conveniences that you Northern people have been so long accustomed to, and worse than all, we have no money to fix these things.*[47]

Even in elite southern households, the kitchens were eventually absorbed back into the main body of the house—with the possible exception of summer kitchens, which continued to be used mainly on farms for heavy or hot chores.

For Americans of African descent, life after Emancipation continued to be difficult. Their freedom was eroded by Jim Crow laws that segregated, disenfranchised, and failed to protect them from violence. They may have gained greater privacy and better control of their own kitchens, but their housing conditions were poor. Many African Americans migrated to other parts of the country or to towns and cities, where the women, with limited access to jobs, continued to work in other women's kitchens.

## Chow Chow

Take one cabbage, a large one, and cut up fine. Put in a large jar or keg, and sprinkle over it thickly one pint of coarse salt. Let it remain in salt twelve hours, then scald the cut-up cabbage with one gallon of boiling vinegar. Cut up two gallons of cucumbers, green or pickled, and add to it; cut in pieces the size of the end of little finger. Then chop very fine two gallons more of cucumbers or pickles and add to the above. Seasonings: One pound of brown sugar, one tablespoonful of cayenne pepper, one tablespoonful of black pepper, two gallons of pure wine vinegar, two tablespoonfuls of tumerick, six onions, chopped fine or grated. Then put it on to cook in a large porcelain kettle, with a slow fire, for twelve hours. Stir in occasionally to keep it from burning. You can add more pepper than is here given if you like it hot.

Abby Fisher, *What Mrs. Fisher Knows about Old Southern Cooking*, 1881

After Emancipation, Abby Fisher moved out of the South and settled in California. Like many former slaves, she earned her living as a cook. Mrs. Fisher became well-known for her pickles, preserves, and southern fare, recipes which she dictated to an uncredited writer for this publication.

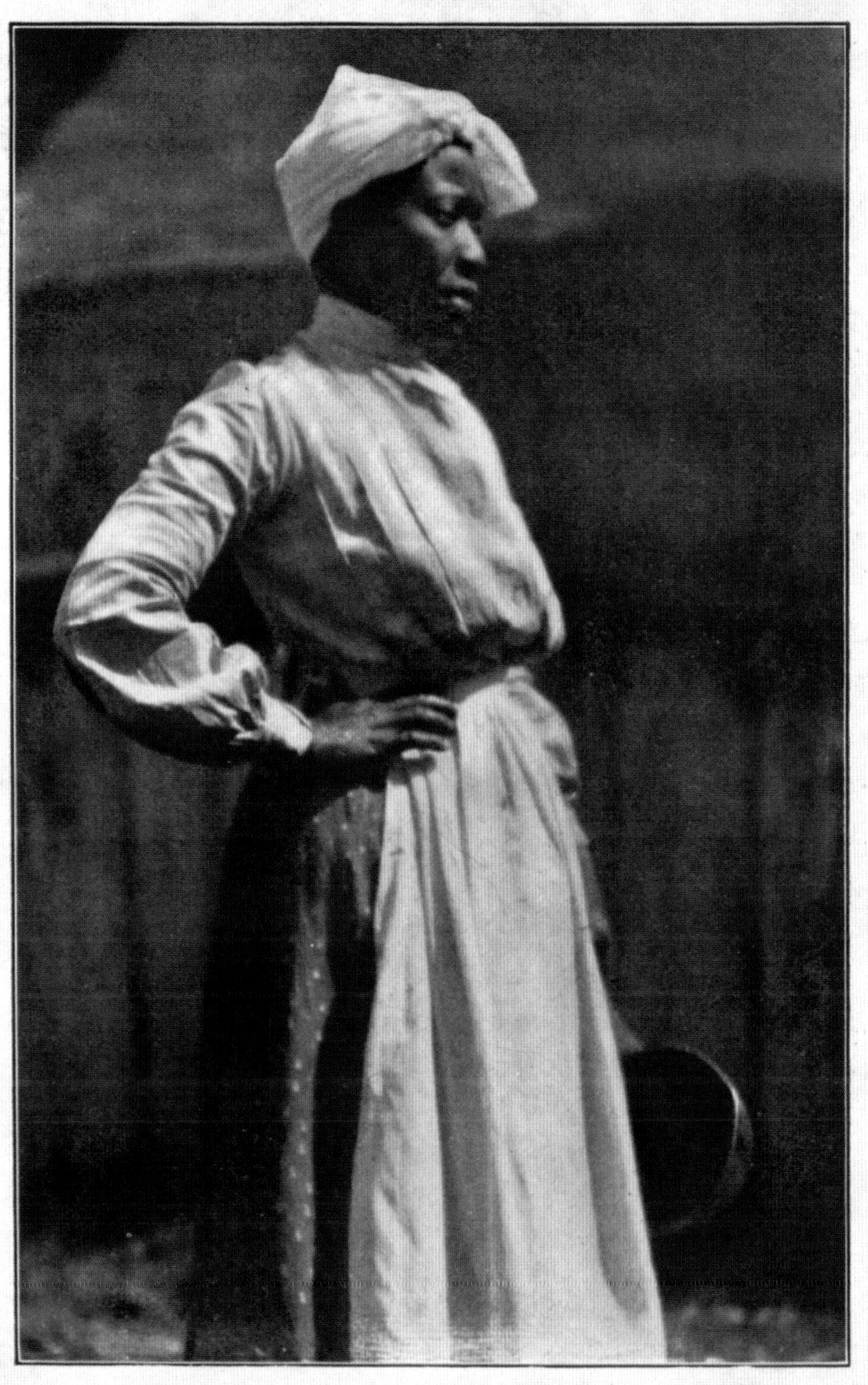

"THE TURBANED MISTRESS OF A KENTUCKY KITCHEN"

Minnie C. Fox's *Blue Grass Cook Book* (1904) includes portraits of mostly anonymous black cooks such as this one.

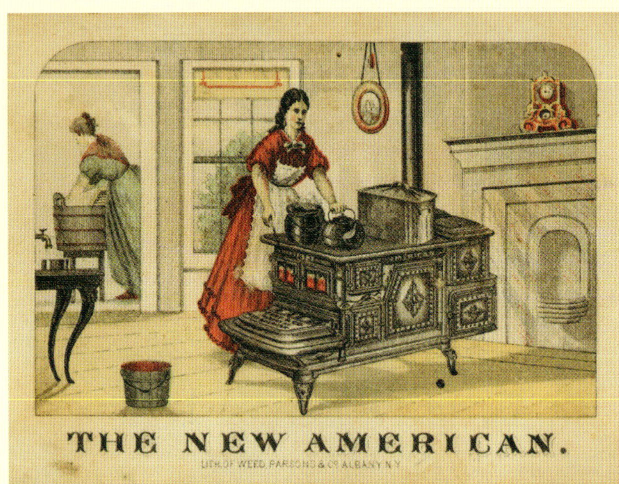
THE NEW AMERICAN.
LITH. OF WEED PARSONS & CO. ALBANY N.Y.

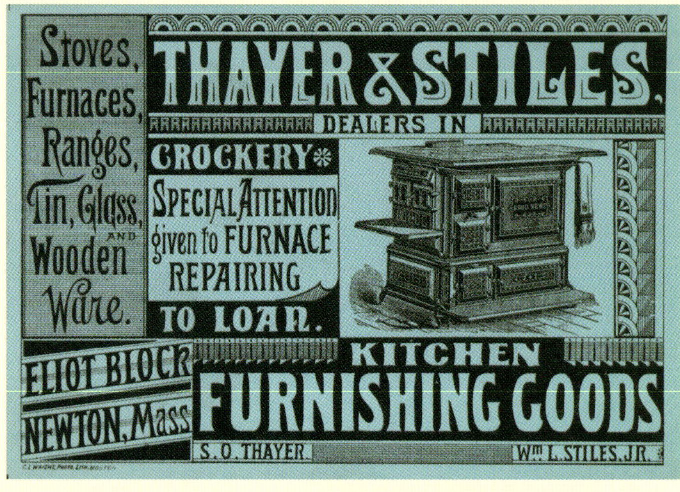
Stoves, Furnaces, Ranges, Tin, Glass, AND Wooden Ware.
THAYER & STILES,
DEALERS IN
CROCKERY
Special Attention given to FURNACE REPAIRING
TO LOAN.
ELIOT BLOCK NEWTON, Mass.
KITCHEN FURNISHING GOODS
S. O. THAYER.
Wm. L. STILES, JR.

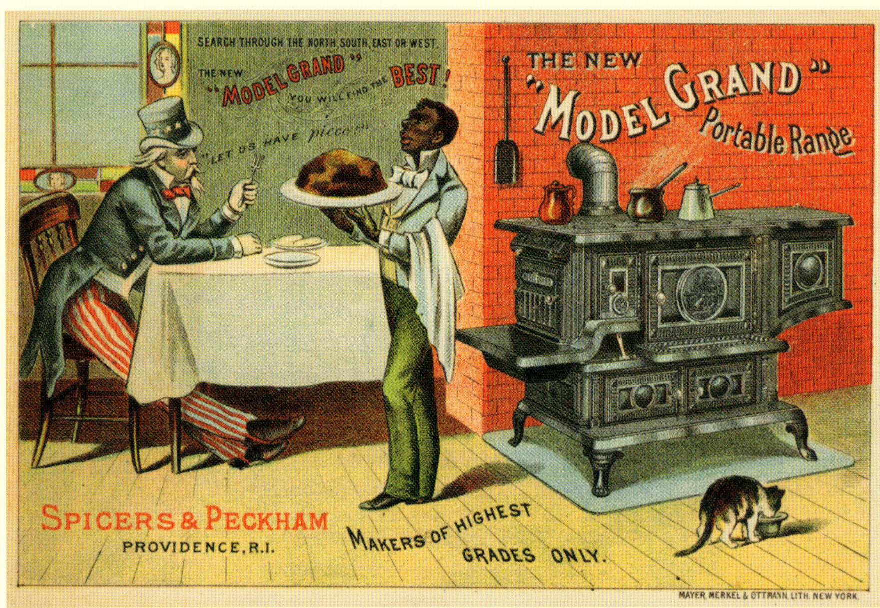
SEARCH THROUGH THE NORTH, SOUTH, EAST OR WEST.
THE NEW "MODEL GRAND" YOU WILL FIND THE BEST!
"LET US HAVE piece"
THE NEW "MODEL GRAND" Portable Range
SPICERS & PECKHAM
PROVIDENCE, R.I.
MAKERS OF HIGHEST GRADES ONLY.
MAYER, MERKEL & OTTMANN, LITH. NEW YORK

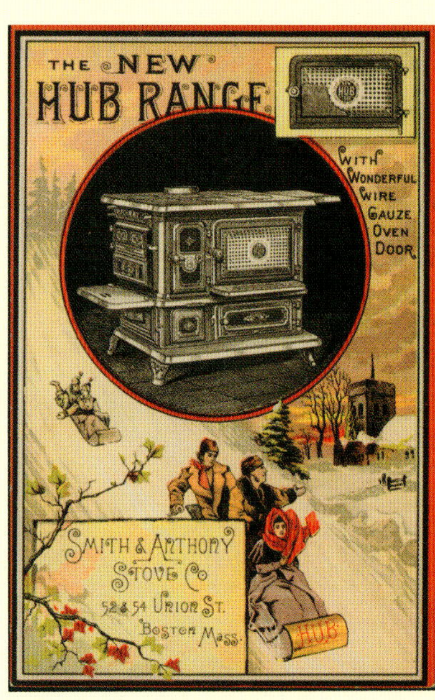
THE NEW HUB RANGE
WITH WONDERFUL WIRE GAUZE OVEN DOOR.
SMITH & ANTHONY STOVE Co
52 & 54 UNION ST.
BOSTON MASS.
HUB

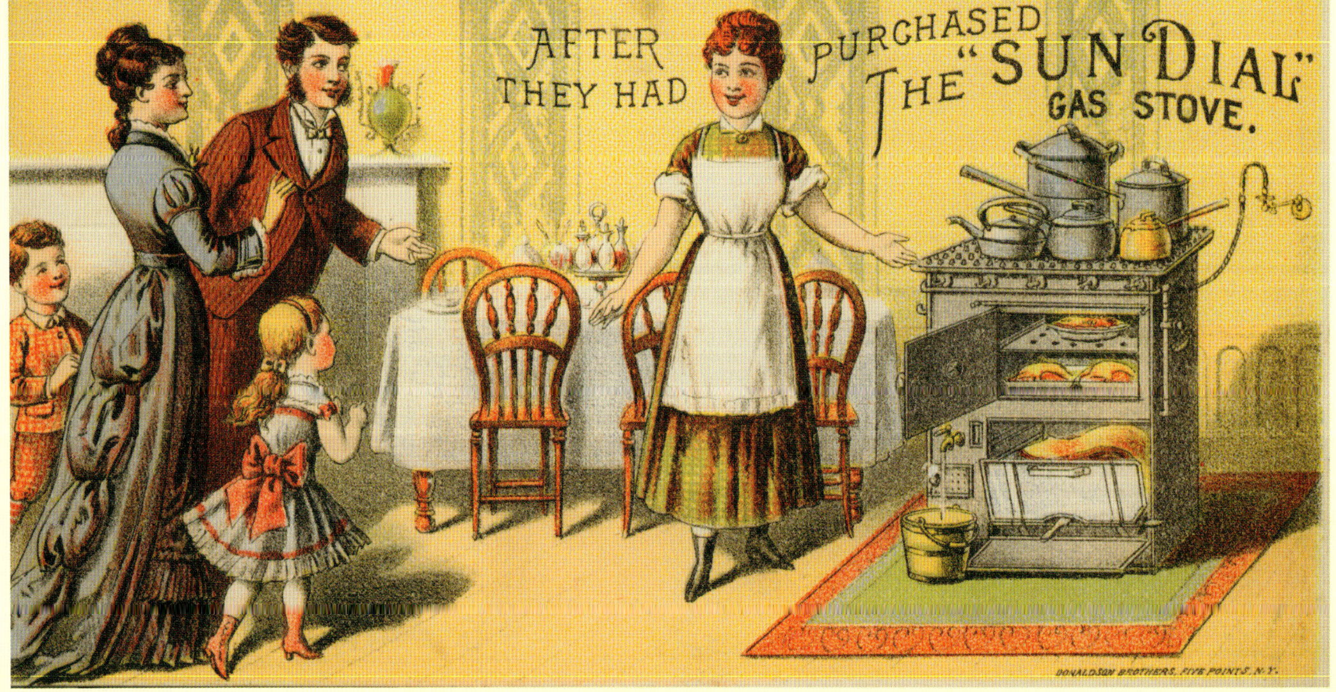
Indade Mum, the Breakfast will always be ready on time since you got the "SUN DIAL", sure the work's so aisy now, I was thinking Mum I wouldn't object to a small reduction of my wages.
AFTER THEY HAD PURCHASED THE "SUN DIAL" GAS STOVE.
DONALDSON BROTHERS, FIVE POINTS, N.Y.

# COOKSTOVES AND SERVANTS

## {1850–1890}

### The Cookstove

Not long after the Civil War, Sarah and David Davis began building a new home in Bloomington, Illinois. Sarah oversaw the work and made most of the decisions. She kept her husband, a justice of the U.S. Supreme Court, informed about the construction by mail. The budget for the house was quickly surpassed, as Sarah chose materials and finishes to suit one of the state's wealthiest families. When it was time to outfit the kitchen, Sarah's plumber suggested she look at the built-in cast-iron range recently installed by her neighbors, the Gridleys. A month later the Davises installed their own magnificent range, made by the Magee Stove Company of Boston.[1]

The Davis family's mansion, designed by Springfield, Illinois, architect Alfred Piquenard, was an imposing residence, befitting the status of its owners. Work began on the building in 1869. The family moved in three years later.

Cast-iron stoves were in use in Pennsylvania in the eighteenth century, but it was not until the 1840s that they became more commonplace in other regions. The initial impetus behind the development of the cookstove was not to improve the cooking process but to achieve greater fuel efficiency. Although fireplaces had become increasingly small, they still consumed more wood than most people could supply from their own lots. Merchants advertised that their stoves would require half as much wood, an incentive even for families who were not well off, as the savings in fuel would soon pay for the stove.[2]

By transforming kitchen work, the cookstove served notice that the technological advances of the Industrial Revolution were now entering the home. This was a laborsaving device; it allowed better regulation of the heat, and raised the work surface to a more comfortable height. Because stoves consumed less fuel than hearths, installing one meant less time would be spent cutting and hauling wood, an important advantage when men increasingly were employed away from home.

> Of the numerous varieties of cooking stoves, and of the mode of managing each, it is impossible to attempt a description. They all find favor in some kitchens, and lose it in others, according to the taste and habits of the family and the cooks.
>
> Eliza Leslie, *Miss Leslie's Lady's House-Book*, 1850

By the middle of the nineteenth century, the variety of cookstoves available was extraordinary. Merchants used colorful advertisements to compete for sales.

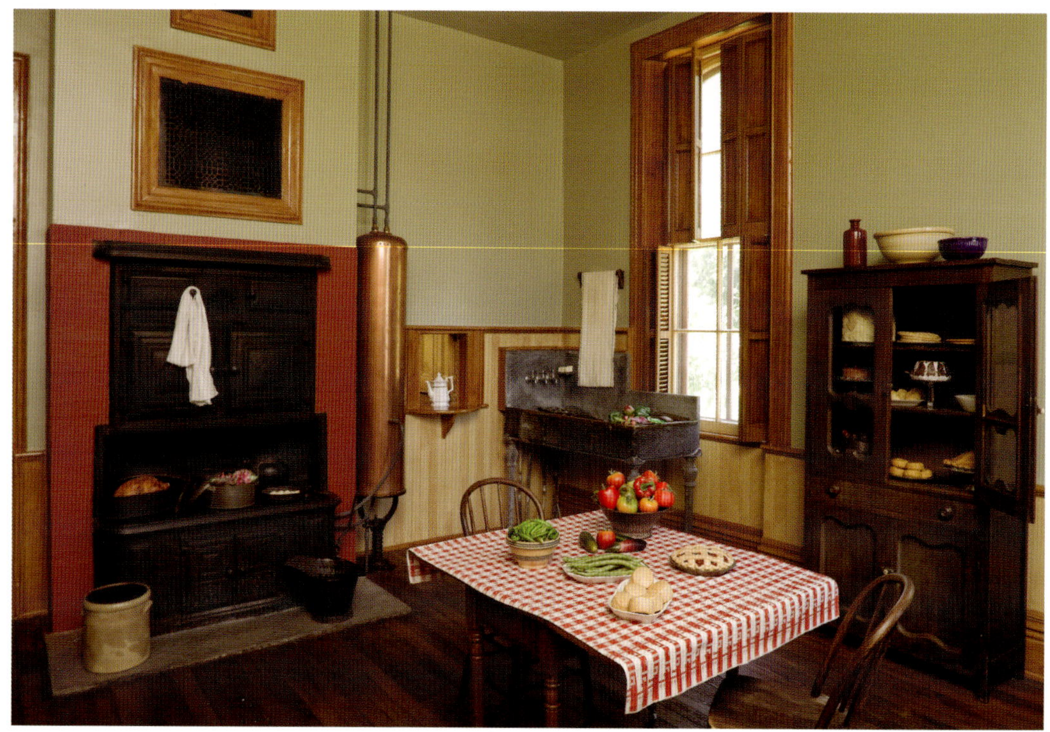

The Davises' kitchen survives relatively unchanged, a premiere example of an ideal Victorian kitchen. The property is operated as a State Historic Site by the Illinois Historic Preservation Agency.

Although the cookstove gradually became widely accepted, some women continued to work over an open hearth. Throughout the country there were countless families who could not afford the initial investment. In the South, few white families and virtually no black ones cooked on a stove. Pioneer families journeying west learned that the lighter their wagons, the easier they traveled; the stove was often the first thing jettisoned. Once a family was settled, it might be years before they could purchase a stove, so many women on the frontier continued to cook on a hearth. In 1865, when Mary Borst moved into her well-equipped home in Centralia, in the Washington Territory, she boasted, "My cookstove was the envy of all my women visitors."[3]

> It was the inauguration of a new era in the culinary kingdom—the pleasant old fire-place with the swinging crane of well filled pots and kettles, hearth spiders with legs and bake-kettles and tin-bakers to stand before the blazing logs and bake custard pies in—all went down at once and disappeared before that first stove without so much as a passing struggle.
>
> Abby Maria Hemenway, *Vermont Historical Gazetteer*, 1877

Abby Hemenway of Vermont recalled the transformation of her family's kitchen when their first stove arrived.

Not everyone adjusted easily to the cookstove. Many feared that poorly made stoves might blow up or that the stoves would poison the air around them. Others complained of a "burnt, disagreeable odor."[4] By the time stoves were accepted, many people began to miss the camaraderie of an open hearth. Nathaniel Hawthorne saw no beauty in the cookstove and lamented its introduction, worrying that with the demise of the kitchen hearth, "there will be nothing to attract children to one center. Domestic life . . . will seek its separate corners."[5] Like Hawthorne, many complained that the end of the hearth meant the end of traditional family life. In reacting to the onslaught of change brought about by industrialization and massive immigration, much of the nostalgia for an earlier age centered on memories of the hearth. More often than not, however, it was men rather than their wives who were nostalgic. In one of her short stories, Sarah Orne Jewett described a man who waited until his wife was away and, after a drink or two with a friend, took the stove apart piece by piece and disposed of it. Jewett observed that women "knew better than their husbands did the difference this useful invention had made in their every-day work."[6]

While a cookstove made some aspects of cooking easier, its care resulted in new chores. Good housekeepers cleaned and blacked their stoves at least once a week; if they did not, the dust from the ashes quickly competed with emerging rust on the surface. With some regularity stoves would suddenly begin to smoke badly, which meant the stovepipe needed cleaning. This miserable, filthy task frequently fell to the man of the house. One Connecticut husband, when asked to clean the stovepipe, "immediately became plunged in an anxious bustle, and was obliged to meet a man on important business," leaving his wife to do the chore alone.[7]

The Davis household with its Magee range was spared this bothersome task because theirs, like all ranges, was built directly into the chimney. Ranges had both advantages and disadvantages over freestanding cookstoves. A range took up less space and had a larger cooking surface, so more food could be prepared and, most important, larger quantities of water could be heated. However, a range used

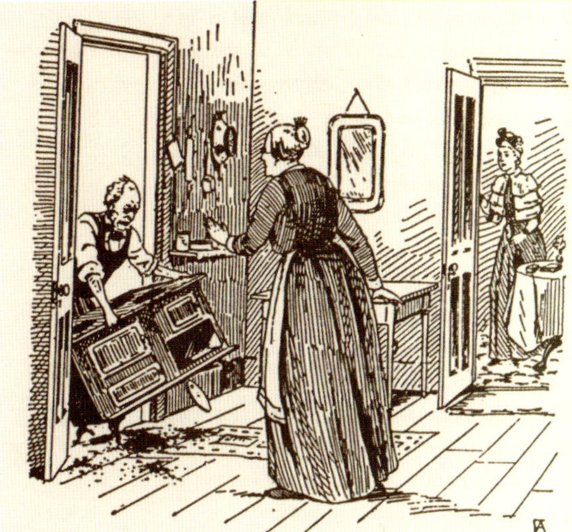

Some families moved their cookstoves to an outbuilding in the spring to avoid adding heat to their homes in the summer. In his essay, "Putting Up Stoves," Mark Twain wrote, "The job is as severe and vexatious as humanity can possibly endure."

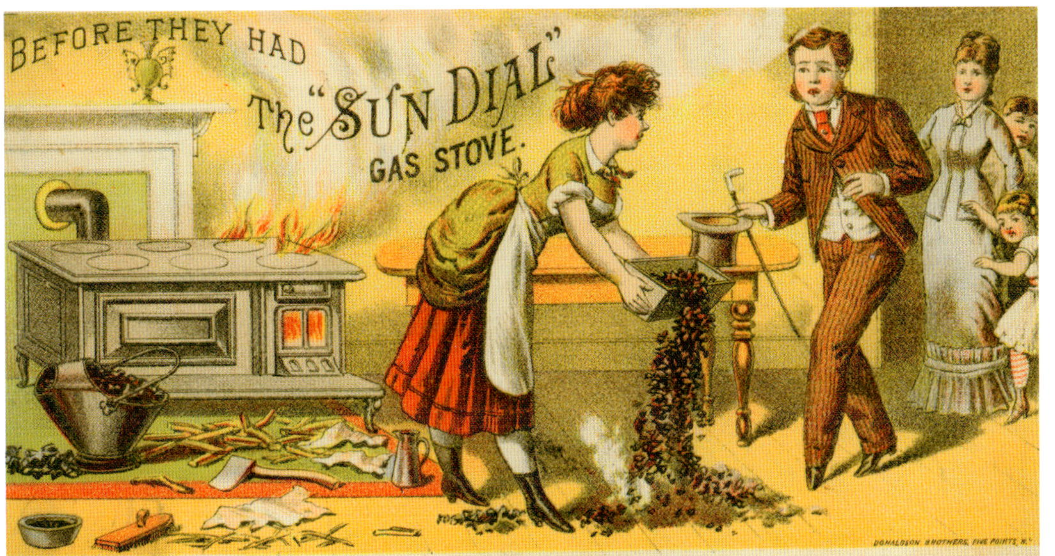


With little instruction newly arrived immigrants employed as domestic servants suddenly found themselves responsible for preparing meals on cookstoves with which they had no experience. Even experienced cooks sometimes had trouble with recalcitrant stoves. This image shows a young Irish servant dealing with an early morning smoky disaster.

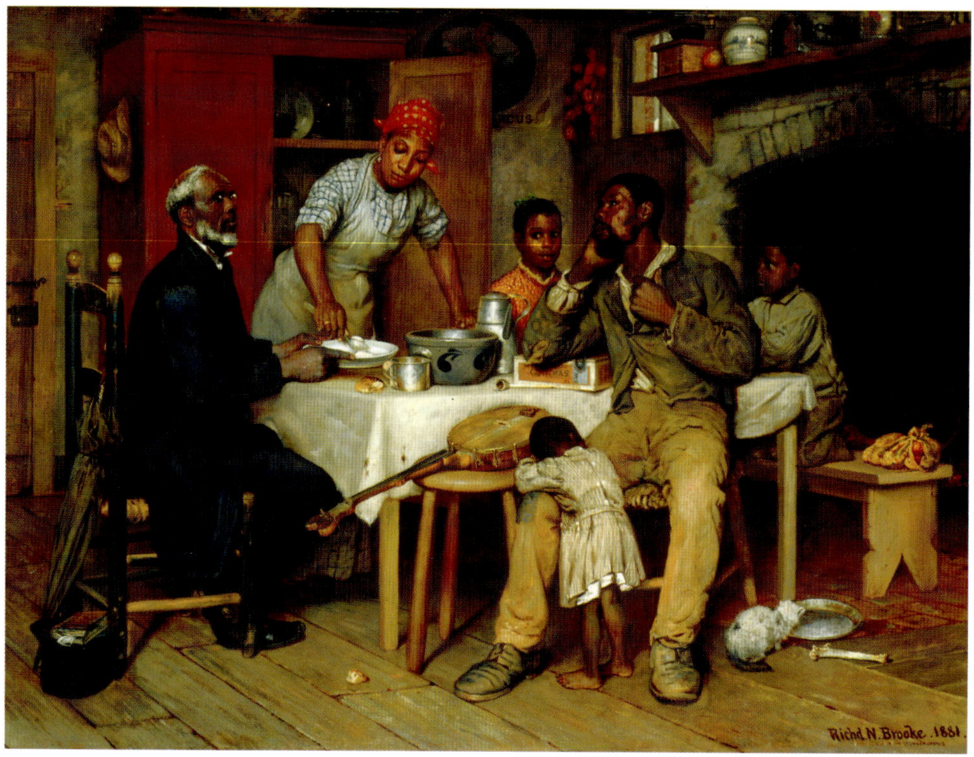

Even as the cookstove was becoming commonplace in much of the country, many, like the northern Virginia family depicted in this painting by Richard Norris Brooke in 1881, continued to work over an open hearth.

more fuel and took longer to heat than a stove, and, since it could be used only from the front, not the sides, cooking on it was more difficult.[8] Ranges were also more expensive than cookstoves and were permanently installed; families could neither move them to a new home nor move them to an outbuilding to keep the house cool in the summer. Cookbook writers recommended that whether a family wanted a range or a stove, they should choose the simplest model with well-fitting parts to ensure it would draw well and with the plainest surface so that it would be easy to clean.[9]

Most women eventually embraced the cookstove, but learning to use it was often an ordeal. Women cooking on a hearth could see when new logs should be added, but it was easy to forget about the cookstove fire, which was hidden from plain sight. Controlling the airflow was more complicated. Women who had learned to cook at a hearth understood that sometimes more air rather than more wood was needed to increase the heat; they would move the fuel around for better airflow. In a stove's small firebox, it was harder to move the wood and harder still to manipulate pieces of coal. Instead, the cook had to acquire the skill of controlling the flow of air by setting and adjusting the stove's drafts and dampers.

By the middle of the nineteenth century, more and more stoves were built to accommodate coal, which created a longer-lasting fire and was cheaper to use than wood. Here the Beecher sisters, authors of one of the century's most successful domestic advice books, describe the benefits of a coal-burning stove.

> With proper management of dampers, one ordinary-sized coal-hod of anthracite coal will, for twenty-four hours, keep the stove running, keep seventeen gallons of water hot at all hours, bake pies and puddings, etc. . . .
>
> Catharine Beecher and Harriet Beecher Stowe, *The American Woman's Home*, 1869

Some people bemoaned the loss of a roaring fire on a large open hearth. This 1869 painting of a mother and child by Eastman Johnson, however, suggests that the warmth of the kitchen stove still drew family members together.

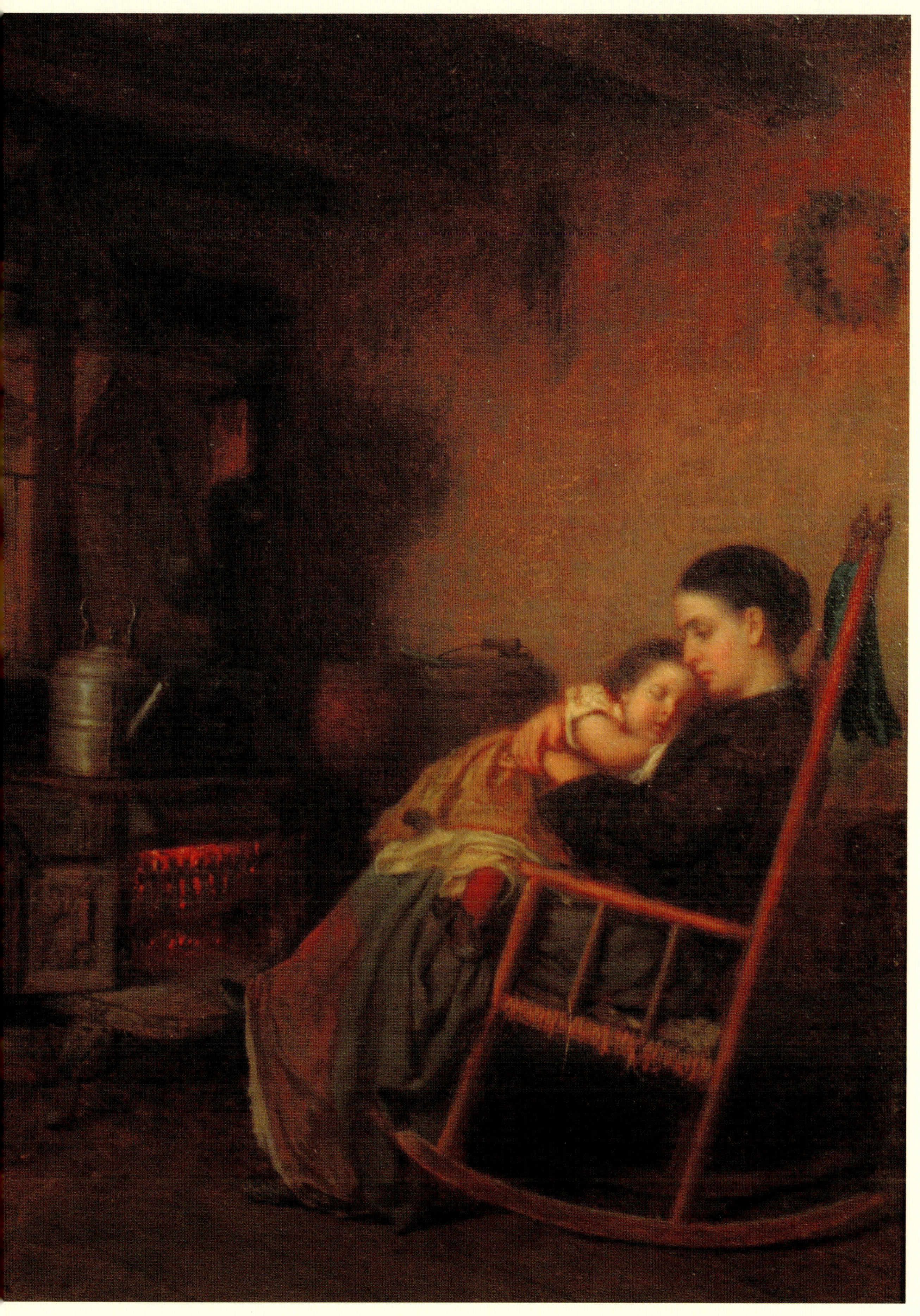

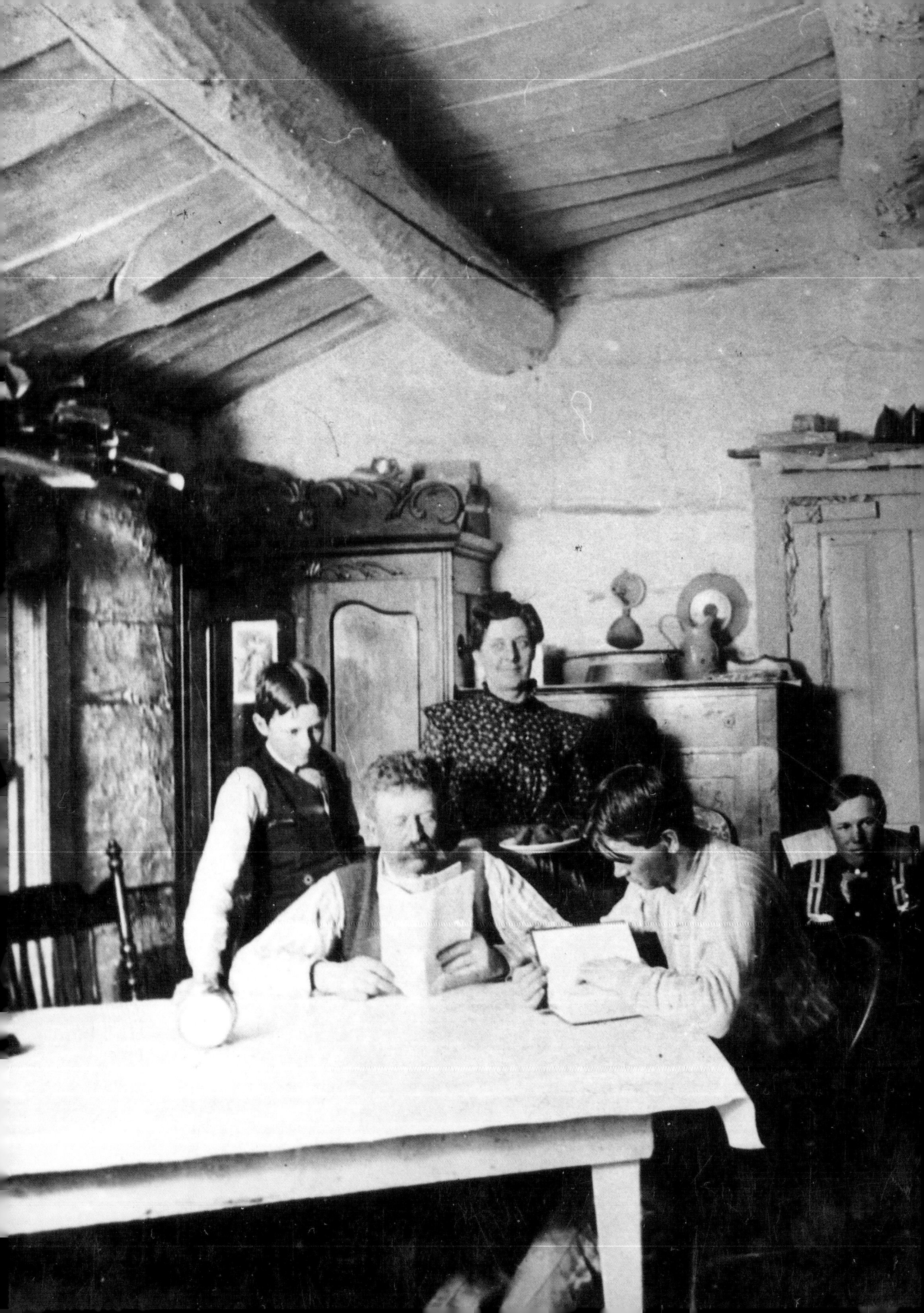

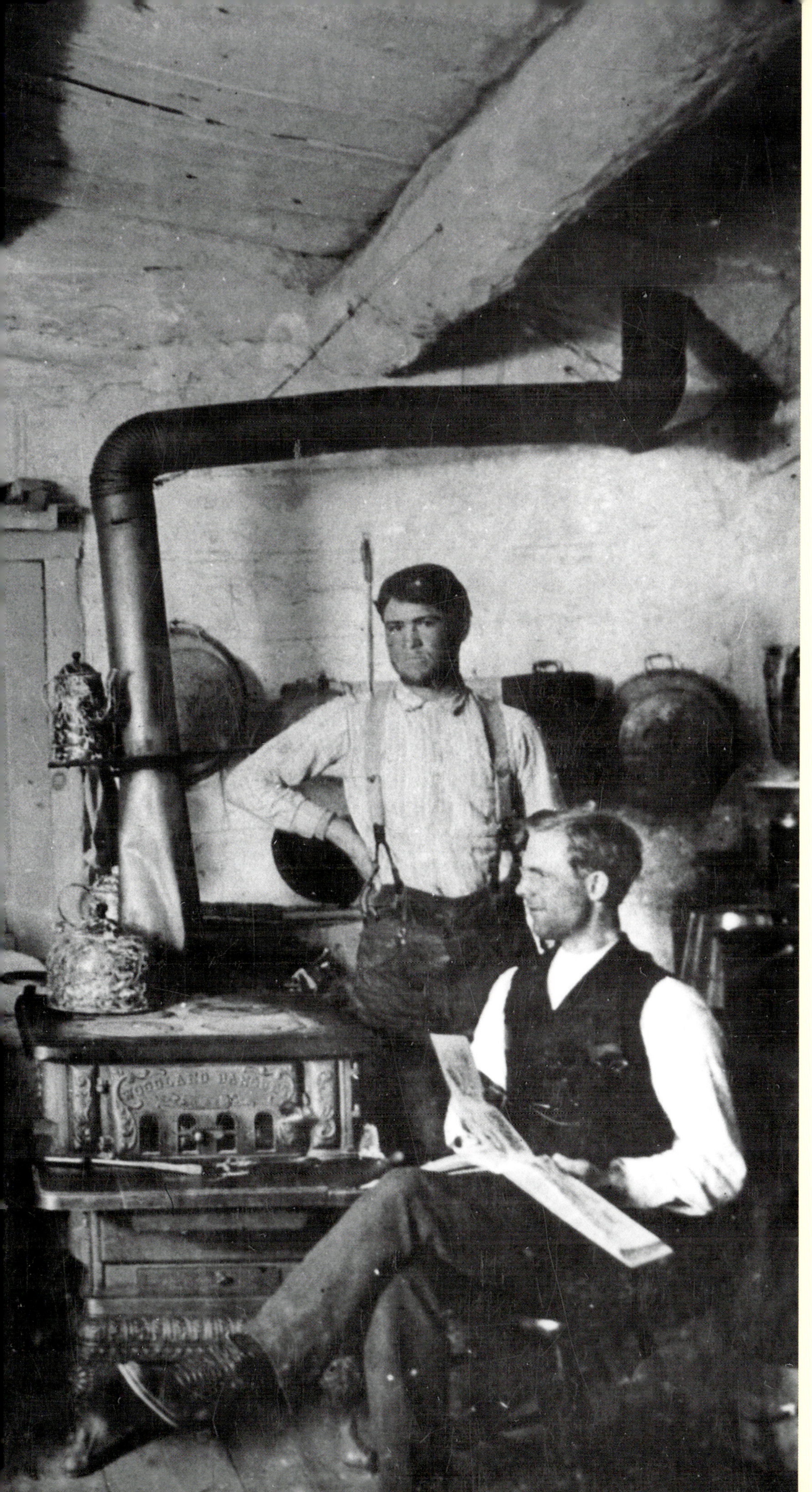

In this sod house in the Dakota Territory, photographed in 1885, the family lived, cooked, and ate in a space dominated by a cookstove, a rare luxury on the frontier.

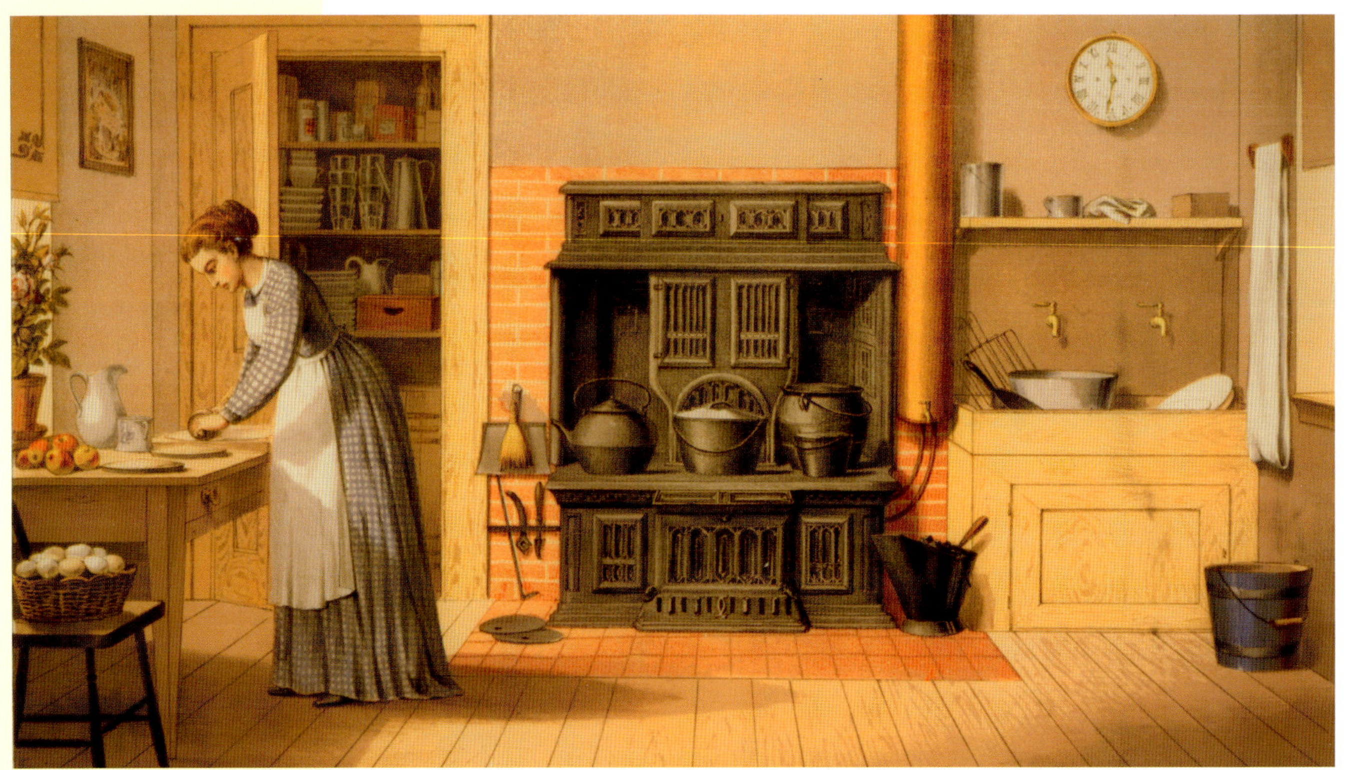

The ideal Victorian kitchen, as seen in this 1874 lithograph by Louis Prang, was a large space with a work table, stove, and sink along the walls, windows for plenty of light, and an adjacent pantry for storage. A clock, new to the kitchen in this period, enabled women to keep track of time while they were cooking.

## The Ideal Victorian Kitchen

The ideal mid-nineteenth-century kitchen was a large open room. *Miss Parloa's Kitchen Companion* (1887) recommended that it be fifteen by seventeen feet or sixteen by sixteen, larger than most kitchens of the 1950s and only slightly smaller than today's spacious kitchens.[10] The stove, a table or two, possibly a pie safe to keep baked goods fresh and flies away from meats, one or two wooden chairs, and perhaps a comfortable rocker were arranged around the perimeter. The sink, with or without running water, was often placed near a window and was as important to a well-equipped kitchen as the stove. The best kitchens were well lit from several windows, although basement kitchens with limited light were not uncommon, particularly in urban areas. The walls were painted a light color with a washable paint and, except for a prominent clock, were otherwise bare. Wrote one domestic adviser: "There should always be a clock in the kitchen, as indispensable to success in cooking, and regularity of meals."[11]

In the homes of well-to-do families such as the Davises, the kitchen was close to the dining room but separated by a hallway or a china closet that kept the cooking noises and smells from reaching the family. Nearby was a pantry, where staple provisions were stored along with pots, pans, and cooking utensils. There might be a closet as well for bowls, pitchers, dishes, and cleaning supplies. Also handy were the cellar stairs, for many perishable foods were stored in the cool basement. There was also an outside door for admitting provisions, garden produce, and visitors who might not be welcome to enter through the front door.

What set these kitchens apart from their predecessors were not only the stoves but the sheer number of pots, pans, and gadgetry. Many cookbooks from this period named close to a hundred items essential to the proper kitchen. They ranged from a wide assortment of specialty pots to patented ice-cream makers, jelly and pudding molds, egg coddlers, and potato mashers.

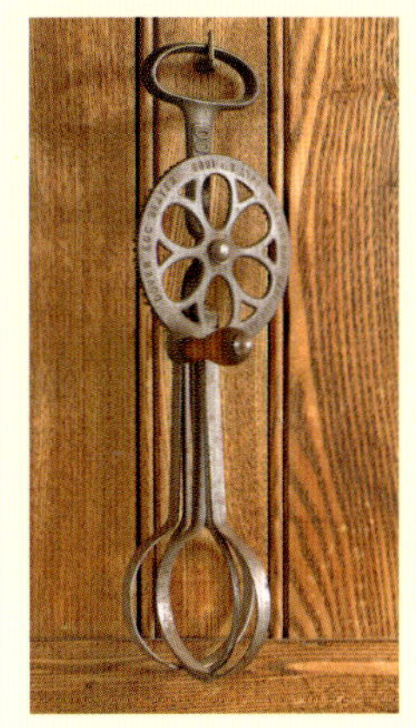

The rotary eggbeater, patented in 1857 and in wide use by 1869, was one of the most successful kitchen gadgets of its time. These beaters greatly simplified baking because eggs were used to leaven cakes and required extensive beating. In one of her cookbooks, Maria Parloa proclaimed, "It will do in five minutes the work that in former years took half an hour."[12] But although some of these utensils did save time, they also required a new level of care. In fact, the historian Ruth Schwartz Cowan has aptly pointed out the irony that from the eighteenth century to the present day new gadgets and technology have often meant "more work for mother."[13]

A Dover egg-beater should never be left to soak in water, as the oil will be washed out of the gears and the beater be hard to turn; or, if used again before it be dry, the oil and water will spatter into the beaten mixture. Use it with clean hands, and then the handle will require no washing. Wipe the wires with a damp cloth immediately after using, dry thoroughly, and keep it well oiled.

Mary Lincoln, *Mrs. Lincoln's Boston Cook Book*, 1884

Cooks embraced the Dover eggbeater as a wonderful time-saver. However, some of the time saved on beating ingredients now had to be devoted to cleaning.

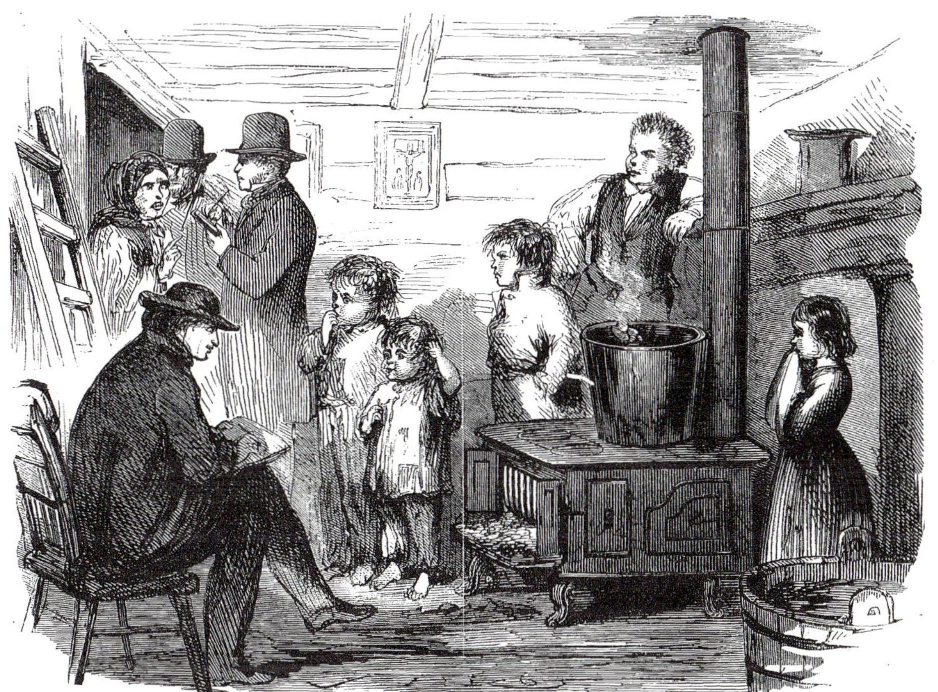

BACKGROUNDS OF CIVILIZATION.—ESTABLISHMENT OF MR. GLENNAN AND HIS FULL-HEADED FAMILY.

Many city households had kitchens that were less than ideal, often located in windowless, cramped basements. For the impoverished, a single room could serve as kitchen, sitting room, and bedroom. This 1860 engraving of a slum dwelling in the Dutch Hill section of New York City shows the kitchen of the Glennan family, presumably Irish immigrants.

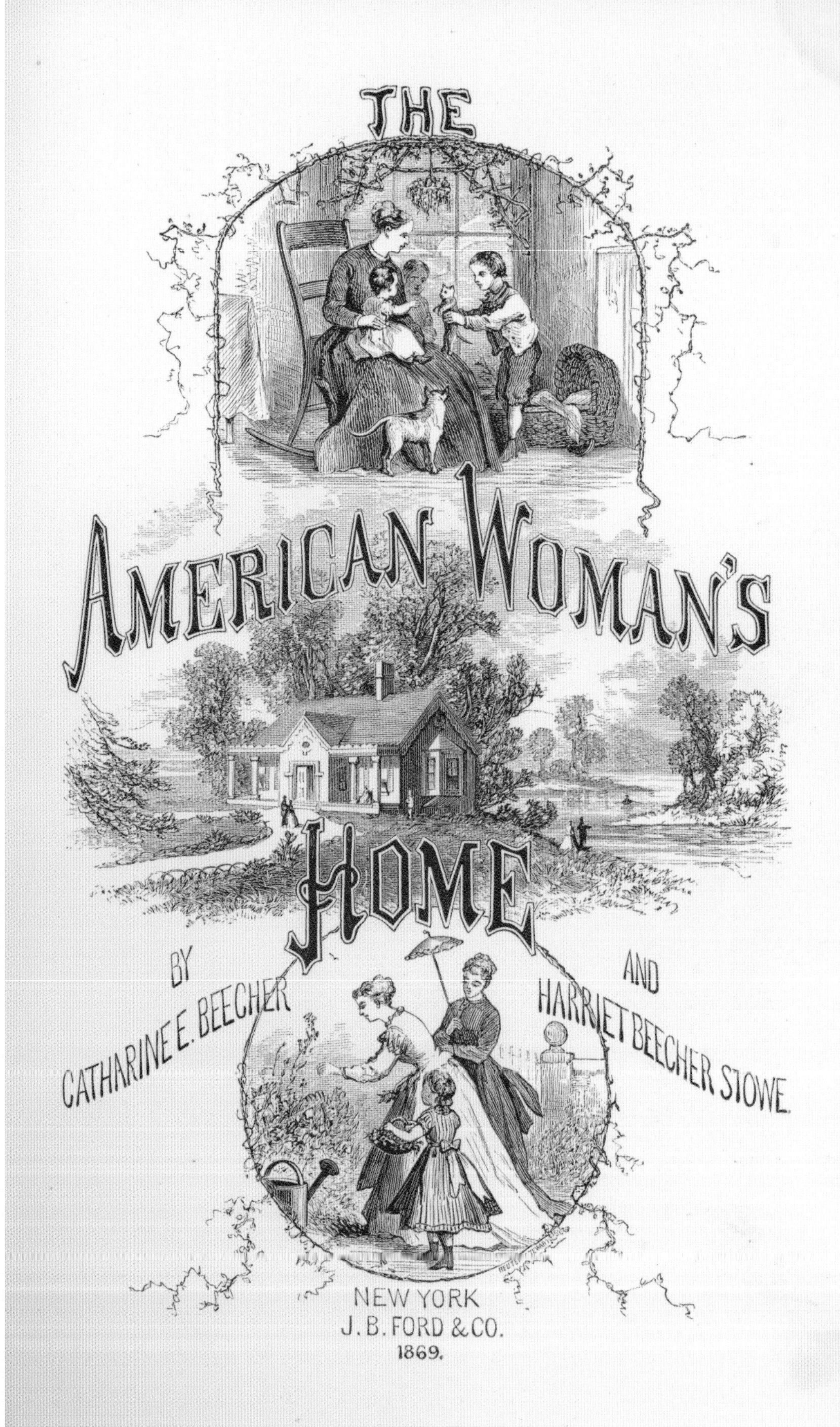


Domestic advice books proliferated in the nineteenth century. One of the most popular was *The American Woman's Home* by Catharine Beecher and Harriet Beecher Stowe. The authors counseled women on topics ranging from housekeeping, health and nutrition, child rearing, architecture, plumbing—even morality, education, and religion.

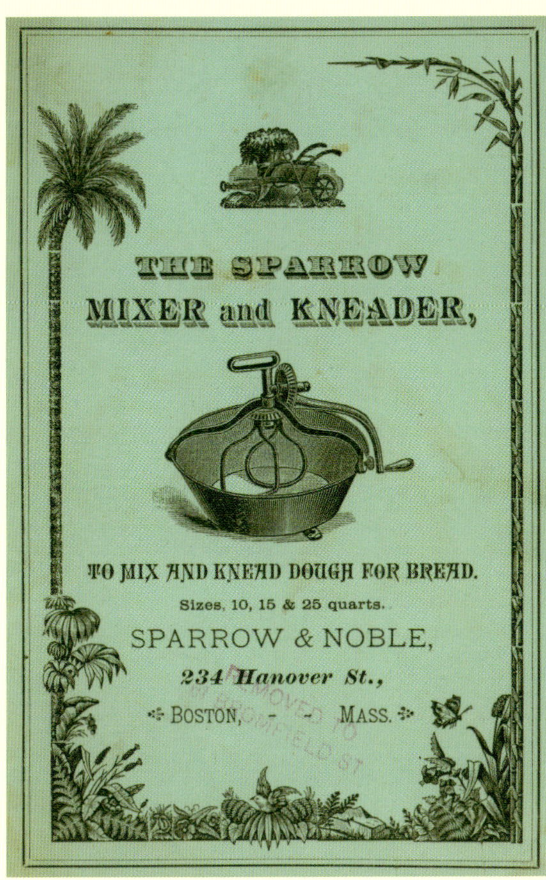


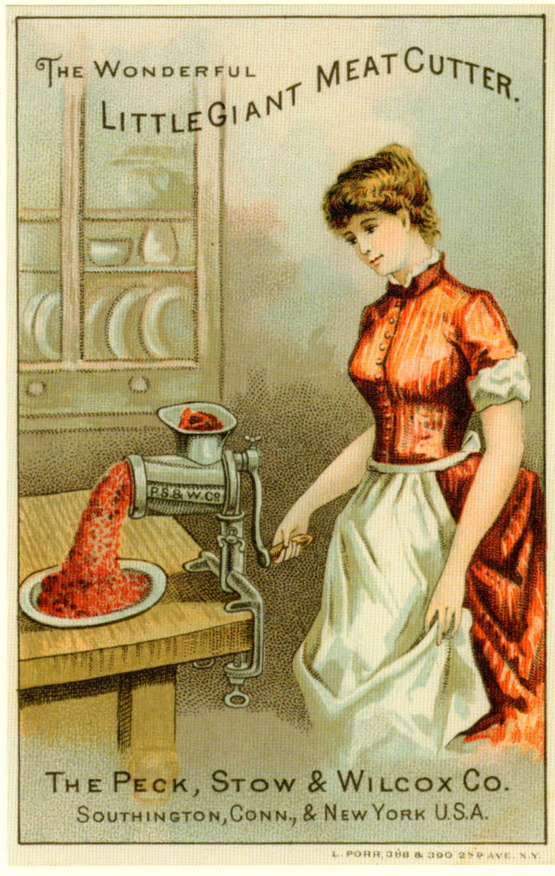


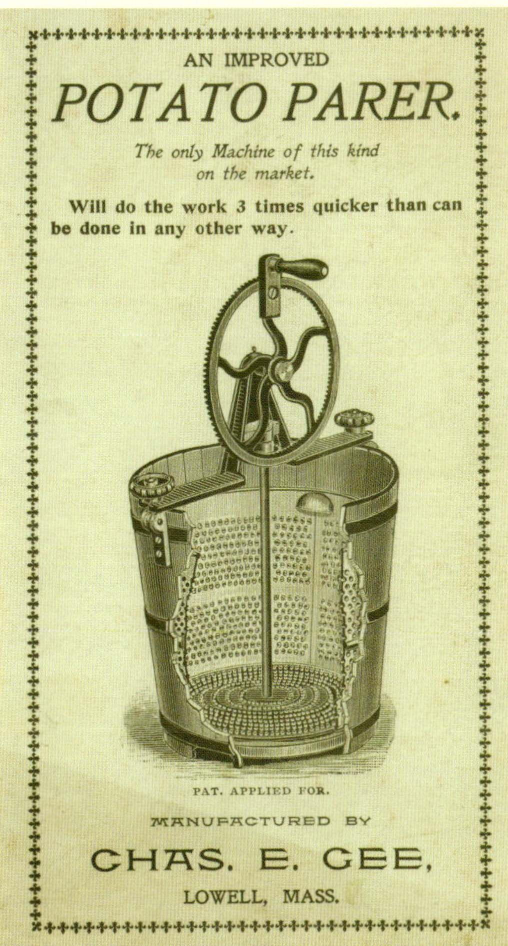


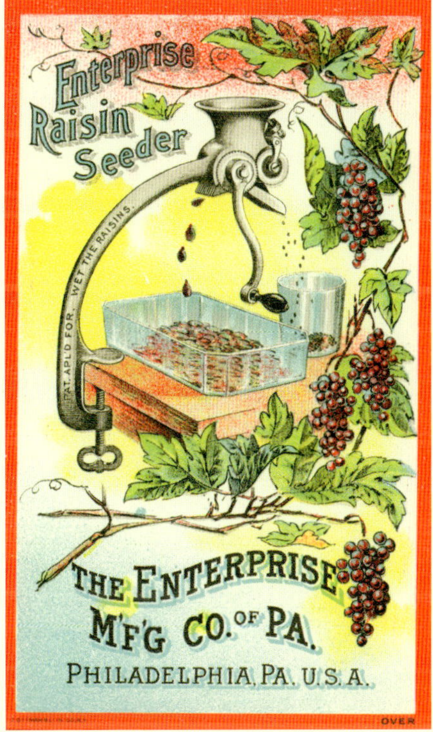


The Industrial Age produced a wealth of crank-driven gadgets aimed at reducing the amount of time women were confined to the kitchen. Similar items would be developed following the introduction of electricity to the kitchen, but they would come without the crank.

## Kitchen Work

Some women did not take readily to their role in the kitchen. In 1878 Hetty Morrison of Indianapolis wrote: "Not of my own free will did I enter upon a career of broiling, roasting, and baking." She complained, "I wish to say that I think two-thirds of cook book makers should be hanged without benefit of clergy." Morrison blamed men for demanding elaborate meals, commenting that left to their own devices, most women would be perfectly happy "with a few chocolate caramels and an occasional cup of tea."[14] Harriet Beecher Stowe shared Morrison's discontent. Despite coauthoring with her sister one of the most popular domestic advice books of the century, *The American Woman's Home*, Stowe was notorious in her family for her lax housekeeping. After a day spent in the kitchen, she wrote to her absent husband: "It is a dark, sloppy, rainy, muddy, disagreeable day, and I have been working hard (for me) all day in the kitchen, washing dishes, looking into closets, and seeing a great deal of that dark side of domestic life. . . . I am sick of the smell of sour milk, and sour meat, and sour everything."[15] For many women, the changes in family life, as young children left home to go to school and older ones along with their fathers left to go to work, and the increased expectations regarding the trappings of genteel style, created pressure and uncertainty.

> If you can offer an unexpected visitor nothing better than bread-and-butter and cold ham, he will enjoy the luncheon twice as much if the bread be sliced thinly and evenly, spread smoothly, each slice folded in the middle upon the buttered surface, and piled symmetrically; if the ham be also cut thin, scarcely thicker than a wafer, and garnished with parsley, cresses, or curled lettuce. Set on mustard and pickles; let the table-cloth and napkin be white and glossy; the glass clear, and plate shining clean; and add to these accessories to comfort a bright welcome, and, my word for it, you need fear no dissatisfaction on his part, however epicurean may be his tastes.
>
> Marion Harland, *Common Sense in the Household*, 1873

A recurrent theme of nineteenth-century cookbooks was to exhort women to try harder to understand the tasks involved in cooking. According to these books, housewives' unhappiness could be resolved if women would give the work the attention it deserved: "The great lesson to learn is that work well-done is robbed of its curse. The woman who is satisfied only with the highest perfection in her work, drops the drudge and becomes the artist."[16]

Middle-class women in the nineteenth century were faced with new standards of gentility that required an enormous amount of behind-the-scenes work.

In fact, women complained that the work was relentless, time-consuming, occasionally back-breaking, and even soul-destroying. In a letter to a cousin, one weary Minnesota farm wife described a particularly exhausting day during harvest time:

> *I got up before four, got breakfast . . . skimmed milk, churned, worked over the churning already on hand, did a large washing, baked 6 loaves of bread, & seven pumpkin pies, while I was baking put on the irons & did the ironing, got supper &c—besides washing all the dishes, making the beds*[,] *sweeping &c.—Mamie [a daughter] was not well so she didn't help me so much as usual. I was tired & lame enough at night, and feel miserable in consequence today.*[17]

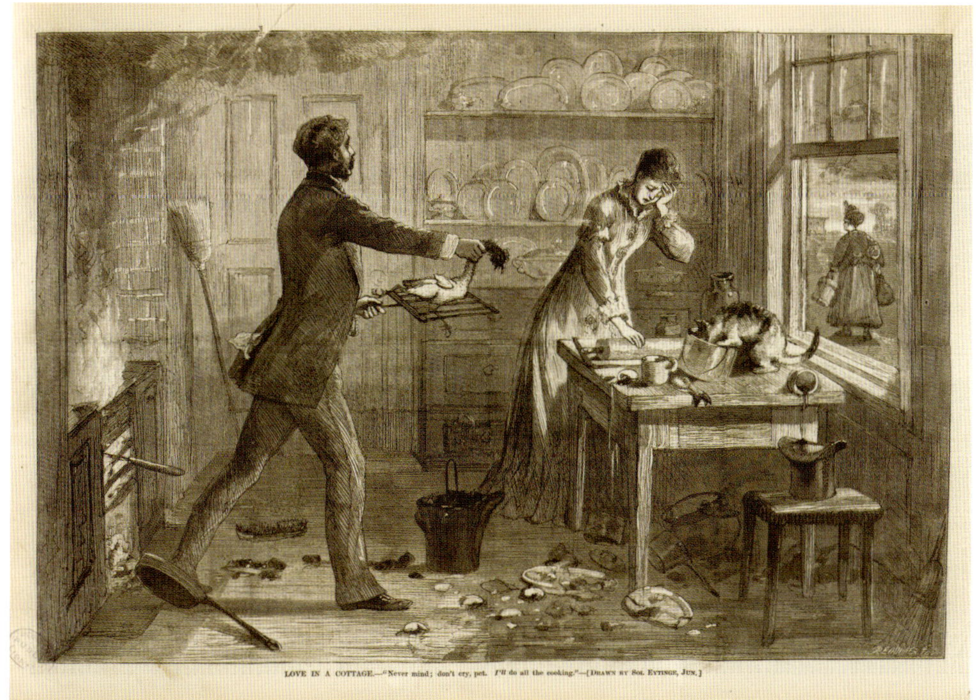


For some women, the departure of the cook was a disaster. Here, an anxious husband tries to soothe his wife by offering to take over the cooking. The disgusted cook is seen through the window, escaping with her bags.

A normal day in the kitchen started early, before anyone else was up. The housewife or hired cook began by brushing the ash from the stove and cleaning out the firebox, sifting the ashes so that any small cinders could be used again. She carried the water from the well or from the sink to fill the water tank and filled the firebox with wood or coal that had been brought in the night before. Then she would light the stove—not always an easy task. Domestic advice books frequently devoted several pages to the best way to light a stove. Above all, a cook had to learn the idiosyncrasies of her stove before lighting it became routine. Once the stove was lit and water was heating for coffee, the housewife would sweep the floor and begin to prepare breakfast.

> Become thoroughly acquainted with whatever stove you may have. If necessary, take it apart; learn how to clean it in the inside, to regulate the dampers for all the variations of wind, temperature, and fuel; and then learn how to make and keep a fire.
>
> Mary Lincoln, *Mrs. Lincoln's Boston Cook Book*, 1884

Meals, of course, were based on what was available, either fresh from the market or fields or stored in the root cellar through the winter. For a middle-class family, breakfast might include oatmeal, fried corn mush, toast, stewed meat, fried bacon with potatoes, and fresh or cooked fruit. In industrial regions of the country where family members found work away from home, the midday meal ceased to be the primary focus of the day. Lunch might include cold meats, pickled vegetables (chow chow and piccalilli were favorites), and a warm, sweet biscuit with fruit preserves. When women entertained over lunch, canned oysters, a new delicacy, were a favorite. Indeed, the *Presbyterian Cook Book* includes twelve oyster recipes, including oyster fritters, oyster soup, steamed oysters, oyster

Especially for women brought up cooking on a hearth, there was nothing straightforward about cooking on a cast-iron stove. Countless housekeeping manuals and cookbooks of the late nineteenth century provided advice about how to work on a stove.

pie, oyster patties, and oyster croquettes.[18] Dinner, when the entire family gathered, could begin with beef soup, followed by boiled pork with potatoes and cabbage and a dessert of doughnuts, bread pudding, or fruit.[19] No matter how poor or well to do the household, most cooks were careful to plan varied and economical meals and to make certain that little went to waste.

Cleaning up after any cooked meal was laborious, requiring sufficient hot water and care to save whatever was left that could be useful. Hot water could be obtained from a water tank attached to the cookstove or by heating water in kettles on top of the stove. The woman in charge of dirty dishes scraped bits of food into a slop pail, grease into a grease pot, and waste into a barrel. Those who lived in the country would take the slop pail out for the livestock. The grease would be saved or sold for making into soap and candles.[20] Tea leaves were saved to scatter on the floor to attract dust when sweeping.

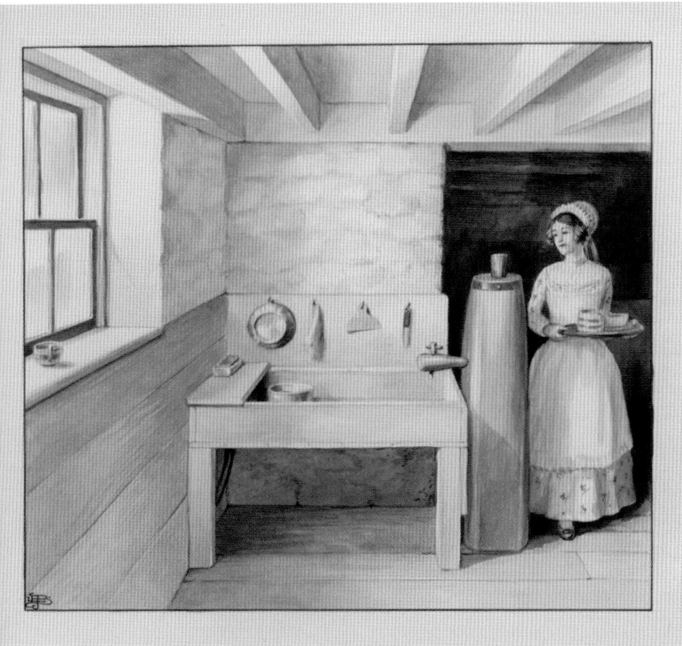

The sink was not a new feature in this period, but running water was. The 1850s Salem, Massachusetts, kitchen shown in this early-twentieth-century drawing had a sink hooked up to the town's aqueduct system. Salem was one of the first towns in New England to provide water to its residents.

Once the dishes were scraped, they were ready for washing in a dishpan filled with soap and hot water. If the dish cleaner followed the recommendations of the books (of course, many did not), she washed the dinner plates and glassware first, placing each piece to dry in a dish rack. Next, she washed the flatware, wiping it dry immediately to avoid rust or corrosion. Then she emptied the dishpan, carrying the water outside if she had no sink, filled it with fresh hot water and soap, and returned to the greasy platters and bowls, using a dishcloth set aside for them. Next she would attack the dirtiest pots and pans, changing the water as needed and occasionally using a wire pot scrubber to help remove any cooked-on foods.[21] When all the dishes and cookware were cleaned, the cook would rinse and dry the sink and wash the many dishcloths, hanging them near the stove to dry. Given the nature of the work, it is small wonder that at least one writer talked about the "terrors" of dishwashing.[22] Because of the effect of harsh, often homemade soaps, many cookbooks offered favorite remedies for sore and rough hands.

Once or twice a week, the cook or housewife would pour hot water and soda or lime down the sink's drain to keep it clean. If her kitchen had a refrigerator (what we today think of as an icebox, although it was known as a refrigerator at the time), she would inspect and clean it daily, using a special brush to clean out the drain. She needed to be diligent or

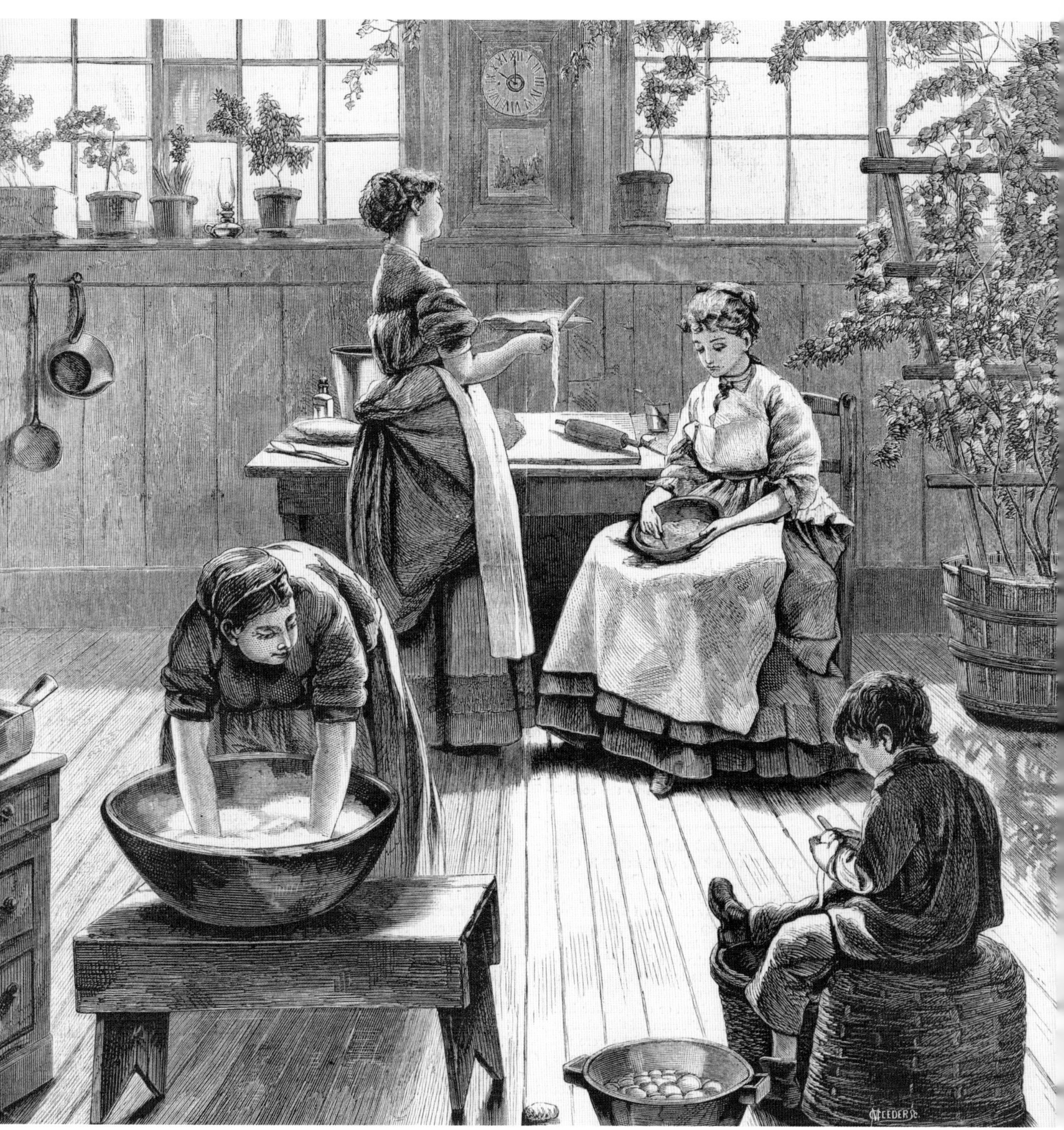

While kitchens of this period were places to gather, above all they were work spaces. Large windows provided light for a variety of chores. This illustration from the magazine *Hearth and Home* shows a New England kitchen in 1871.

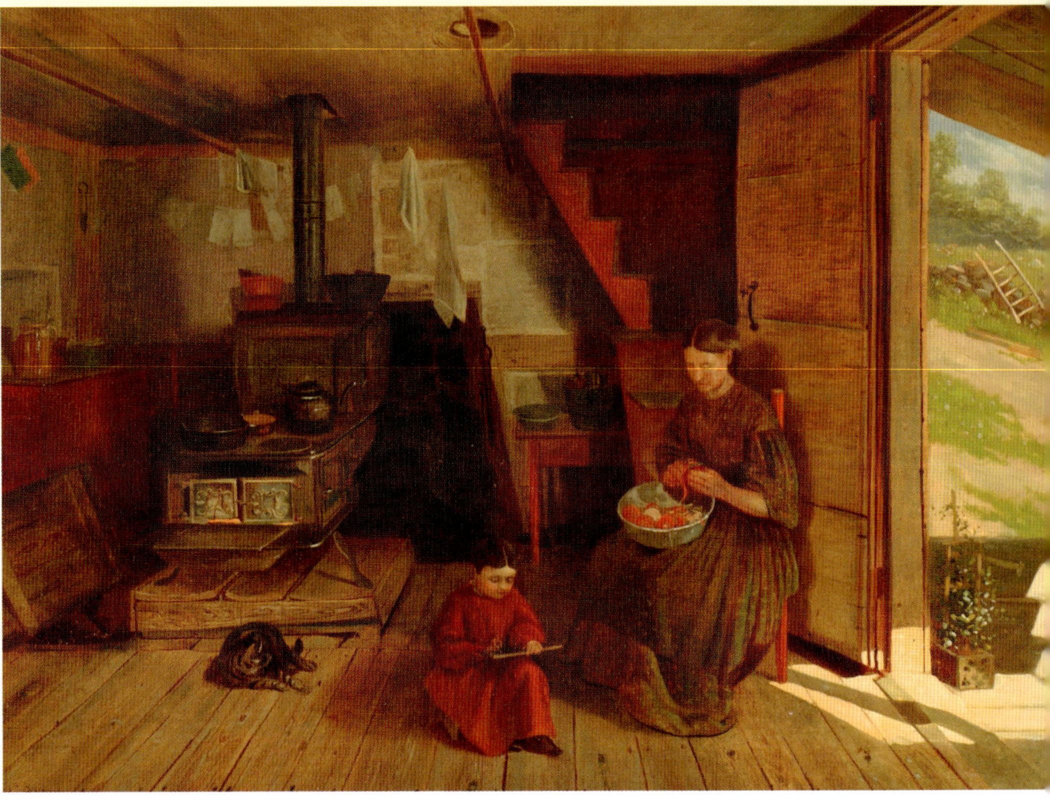

Cooking surfaces on early stoves remained awkwardly low because early cast-iron pots were too heavy to lift higher. The family who lived in this Adirondack shanty, painted by George Bacon Wood, Jr., about 1880, built a platform under their stove to raise it to a more comfortable working height. In the lower image, the cook stands upright to stir the simmering ingredients in her modern, relatively lightweight pots.

the cold foods would soon begin to smell sour. Another chore was disposing of the trash, which would be burned at the end of each day. Waste control was crucial for keeping down the relentless fly population.

The daily round of food preparation and cleanup was, for most women, done in combination with countless other ongoing tasks—looking after young children, making butter, doing laundry, scouring pantries, cleaning lamps, mending clothes, and tending the kitchen garden and orchard. Seasonally, women leached ashes into lye or potash and boiled lye and grease into soap. In summer and fall, they canned vegetables and made preserves. They stored fruits, vegetables, and meats in root cellars and smokehouses. During the winter these stored foods required careful monitoring. If one piece began to spoil, so would others nearby. Sprouts that appeared on the potatoes had to be removed. Moldy leaves on cabbages had to be taken off to keep the inside edible. Brines for pickled vegetables or meats had to be changed or refreshed from time to time. The well-being of many families depended on the housewives' ability to manage stored foods through the winter.

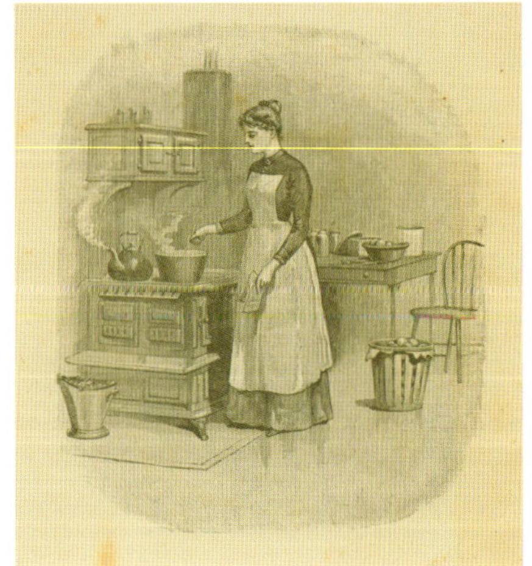

The most arduous seasonal task—butchering—took place in early winter. One Alabama woman described how she felt about it when she wrote to her absent husband in January 1833: "I will not weary you by recounting all my solitary troubles, you can well imagine them if you will but recall that hateful season to all housekeepers (the putting up of Pork)."[23] Although animals were occasionally slaughtered throughout the year, fresh meat spoiled quickly in warm weather and had to be consumed immediately by the family or shared with neighbors. Butchering was an operation in which men and women worked together. Men were responsible for slaughtering the animal. If it was a hog, they would kill it, scald it, scrape the bristles, remove the innards, and cut up the carcass. Then women cut the meat and made sausages, souse, and headcheese, rendered lard, and salted and smoked hams, bacon, and shoulders. To preserve the meat, they rubbed it with salt, sugar, and saltpeter, then packed it tightly in powdering tubs filled with salt for several weeks to draw out the liquid. After hours of salting meat, one plantation mistress complained, "All the skin was nearly off my hands."[24]

## Mock Turtle or Calf's Head Soup

Lay one large calf's head well cleaned and washed, and four pig's feet, in bottom of a large pot, and cover with a gallon of water; boil three hours, or until flesh will slip from bones; take out head, leaving the feet to be boiled steadily while the meat is cut from the head; select with care enough of the fatty portions in the top of the head and the cheeks to fill a tea-cup, and set aside to cool; remove brains to a saucer, and also set aside; chop the rest of the meat with the tongue very fine, season with salt, pepper, powdered marjoram and thyme, a tea-spoon of cloves, one of mace, half as much allspice and a grated nutmeg. When the flesh falls from the bones of the feet, take out bones, leaving the gelatinous meat; boil all together slowly, without removing the cover, for two hours more, take the soup from the fire and set it away until the next day. An hour before dinner set the stock over the fire, and when it boils strain carefully and drop in the meat reserved, which should have been cut, when cold, into small squares. Have these all ready as well as the force-meat balls, to prepare which rub the yolks of five hard-boiled eggs to a paste in a wedgewood mortar, or in a bowl with the back of a silver spoon, adding gradually the brains to moisten them, also a little butter and salt. Mix with these, two eggs beaten very light, flour the hands and make this paste into balls about the size of a pigeon's egg; throw them into the soup five minutes before taking it from the fire; stir in a large table-spoon browned flour rubbed smooth in a little cold water, and finish the seasoning by the addition of a glass and a half of sherry or Madeira wine, and the juice of a lemon. It should not boil more than half an hour on the second day. Serve with sliced lemons.

Estelle Woods Wilcox, *Buckeye Cookery and Practical Housekeeping*, 1877

Sarah Davis wrote to her husband after butchering pigs: "All that remains to be done are the two extremes of the animal." Mock turtle soup was one way to use calves' heads and pigs' feet.

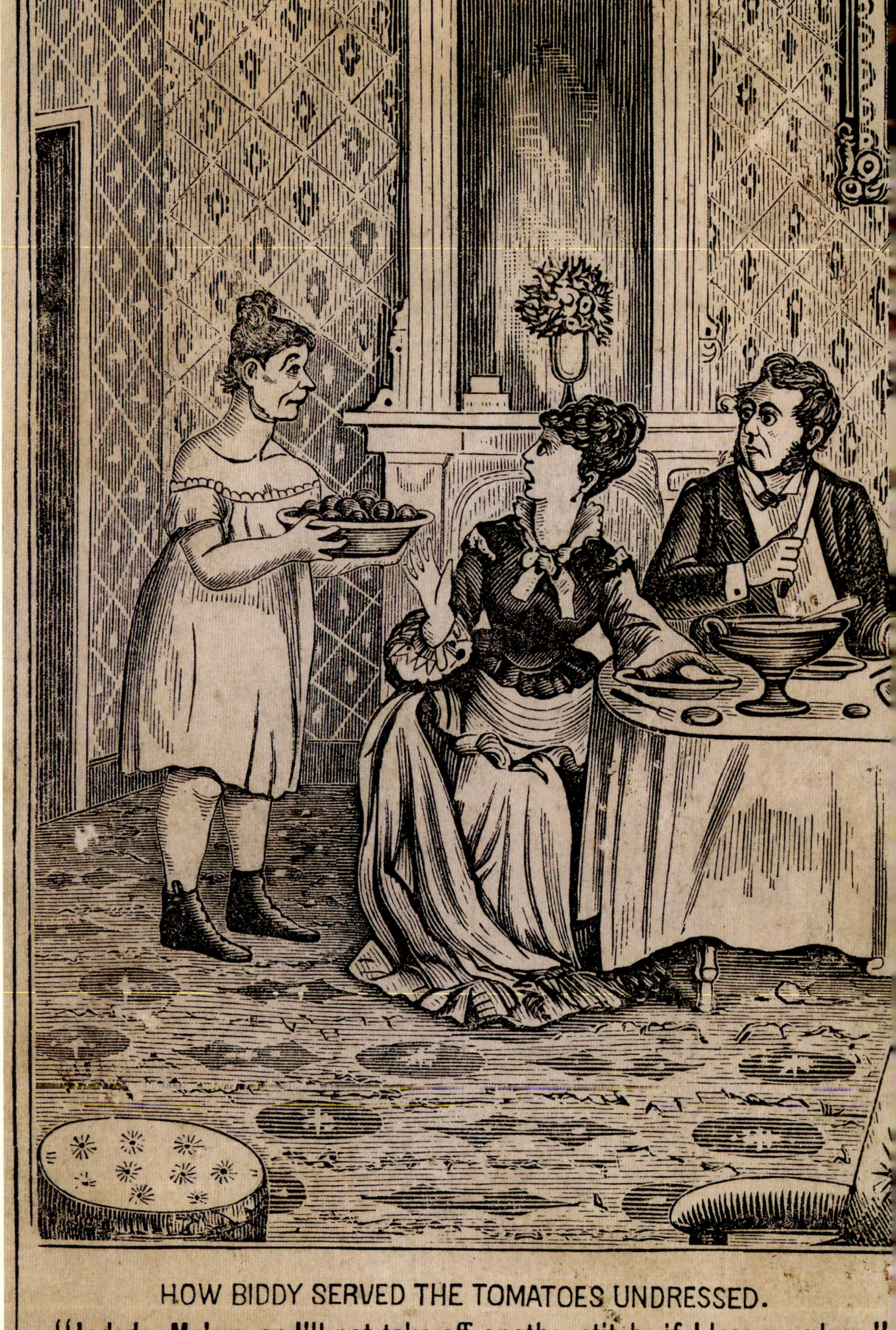


In the Northeast and Midwest, a large percentage of the servant population was Irish. Popular stories and images like the one on this trade card, published about 1880, used the misunderstandings between homeowners and their immiqrant Irish servants as a source of humor and ridicule, mocking the accents and ignorance of "Biddies" and "Bridgets."

## Servants

In the eighteenth and early nineteenth centuries, many women had household help. Like plantation owners in the South, some well-to-do families in northern cities and the rural countryside had a small number of enslaved workers until slavery in those places was abolished shortly after the Revolution. More commonly, families hired young women from the neighborhood as occasional help. This practice was gradually replaced in the nineteenth century by that of hiring strangers to "live in" and work as servants, with primary responsibility for cooking and cleaning. More often than not, those who hired servants were members of long-settled white families from wealthy or professional classes.[25] In her 1884 cookbook, Mary Lincoln estimated that three-quarters of all American women managed their households without full-time servants. She may have underestimated the numbers, but it seems clear that far fewer than half of all American households had servants.[26] Many families did have occasional help, employing someone part time whenever they could to do laundry and hiring people to help with cooking and cleaning only on special occasions.

> [Mrs. Brown] entertained her visitors during the first hour with her troubles with servants. The subject was an interesting one to them, for they were housekeepers and prepared to sympathize. They had also their own trials to relate and were eloquent upon their sufferings.
>
> Kate Sutherland, "Cooks," *Godey's Lady's Book and Magazine*, 1852

Given the small percentage of households with full-time servants, the prevalence of discussions of the "servant problem" in nineteenth-century women's magazines is surprising. Story after story suggests that the incessant topic of conversation in many middle-class parlors was the problem of finding good servants. Perhaps one reason was that even if a family could not hire help, complaining about servants made them feel part of a gentrified community. And, in truth, in many regions it often was difficult to find people to hire since women in the labor force had other options besides household work. In urban areas, unless they were African American, women could choose between domestic service and shop or factory work.[27]

Nineteenth-century women's magazines are filled with stories about the so-called "servant problem." The stories, of course, reflect the "sufferings" of the mistress, never those of the servant.

> The complaints made of Irish girls are numerous and loud . . . yet, in arrest of judgment . . . let us imagine our own daughters between the ages of sixteen and twenty-four, untaught and inexperienced in domestic affairs as they commonly are, shipped to a foreign shore to seek service in families. It may be questioned whether, as a whole, they would do much better. [These Irish] girls. . . are often the age of our own daughters, standing for themselves without mothers to guide them, in a foreign country, not only bravely supporting themselves, but sending home in every ship remittances to impoverished friends left behind. If our daughters did as much for us, would we not be proud of their energy and heroism?
>
> Catharine Beecher and Harriet Beecher Stowe, *The American Woman's Home*, 1869

In a passage that is unusually sympathetic for the time, authors Beecher and Stowe ask housewives to try to understand the lives of the recently immigrated Irish women working as servants in their households.

Since compensation for domestic service usually included room and board, there was an economic advantage to working in private homes over factories and shops.[28] The hours, however, were decidedly worse. Servants were generally allowed one evening off a week and every other Sunday afternoon. Otherwise, they were always on call. One domestic adviser believed that the favorable conditions of household servants outweighed the benefits of shop or factory work: "The employee in the private house has, as a rule, such wholesome accommodations, such excellent food, such good care in sickness, unattended by anxiety of mind concerning loss of wages, that these advantages and indulgences far outweigh any gain in other directions that the shop or factory may afford."[29]

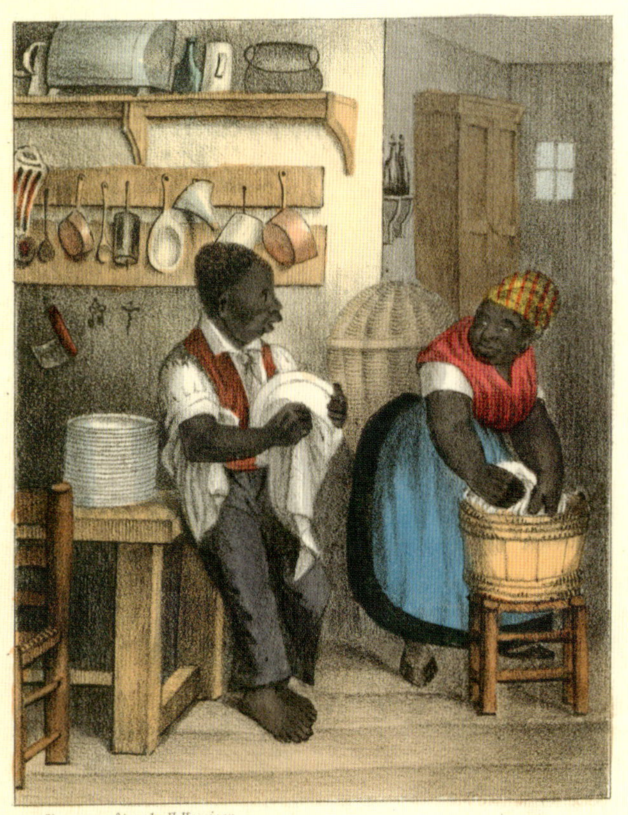


In this image, a couple is cleaning up companionably after a meal in their employer's well-equipped Philadelphia kitchen about 1833.

An anonymous writer painted a different picture when describing her thirty-year experience working as a servant. Instead of "excellent food," she found that "ladies sometimes feed meat to their dogs or cats in the dining-room when there is not enough meat for the girls in the kitchen." And instead of relief from "anxiety of mind concerning loss of wages," she complained that servants could be fired "without an hour's notice, and it may be raining pitchforks, and no reason is given."[30] Many also found that their employers were inconsistent about when and how often they paid their servants.

Rose Cohen, a Jewish immigrant, recalled her experience as a servant in the 1890s after working in a shop: "I realized that . . . at least [in the shop] I had not been alone. I had been a worker among other workers who looked upon me as an equal and a companion. . . . As a servant my . . . every hour was sold, night and day. I had to be constantly in the presence of people who looked down on me as an inferior."[31] Since most servants worked in households where there were no other servants, no doubt many would have agreed with the woman who recalled, "What I minded was the awful lonesomeness."[32]

In most households, the natural conflict between employer and employee was made worse by religious intolerance, ethnic prejudice, and racial bigotry. By the 1830s young white American women were finding work in factories and were less willing to serve as hired domestic workers. Instead, Irish, African American, German, or Chinese men and women went into domestic service, where cultural and class differences often led to employer-employee relationships fraught with tension and misunderstanding.

## *The Davis Household*

Sarah Davis's relationship with the women who worked in her kitchen was generally cordial, but she knew this was not the case in every household. "Everyone has their 'Katy'" was one of her mother's sayings, "Katy" apparently referring to a particularly vexing servant. According to Sarah, the phrase "signif[ied] that everybody had something to trouble them."[33] One reason for Sarah's good relations may have been that despite her wealth and social standing, she worked alongside her servants. In her letters, she talked about how her back ached from housecleaning, about seeding raisins to make loaf cake, the hardship of butchering season, making barrels of cider, and storing apples and potatoes for winter. She was determined that her own daughter and niece would be adept in domestic skills as well, writing, "I hope to teach both Sallie and Fanny enough of housekeeping to enable them to direct their servants, if they have any."[34]

Virtually all of the Davises' servants came from Ireland. In the 1850s Sarah retained several different women, including two who left to join a religious order. "My good girls are about to enter a Convent," she wrote to her brother-in-law. "One left me to prepare last week and Bridget goes next week. . . . To go into a Convent seems the height of an Irish girl's ambition."[35] By the time the new house was being built, Bridget Kelley and Mary Whalen, both from Ireland, were living in. Mary was apparently disagreeable and was let go in the winter of 1872–73. She was soon replaced by Katy Walsh. Another Irish woman, Ann—whom Sarah referred to in her letters variously as Ann, Anne, or Anna—occasionally lived in. Willie Fitzgerald also worked for the Davises and lived in. Sarah, unlike many of her contemporaries, tolerated her servants' Catholicism as well as their traditions. "Monday was observed by the Irish with the usual ceremonies of St. Patrick's day," Sarah wrote to her husband, "Anna was through with washing about eleven in the morning and all the servants went down to look at the Procession and Ann and Willie went to the Ball in the evening."[36]

Sarah Davis allowed her "girls" (she always called them "girls," not "servants" or "help") to entertain friends. On one occasion, when Thomas McGraw planned to visit Mary at dinnertime, Sarah sent to a neighbor for some recently slaughtered beef so that there would be enough for everyone to eat.[37] Another time she wrote: "Pat and Joe sat here for an hour or two to night and such laughter as came from the kitchen was quite amusing. Even the quiet Anne was heard to make a sound. Every thing seems serene to night—and the trio at the

### Chili Sauce

24 large ripe tomatoes, 8 green peppers, 8 onions, 5 cups vinegar, 8 tablespoons brown sugar, 1 tablespoon ground cinnamon, 2 tablespoons salt, ½ tablespoons mustard seeds, Celery cut fine, Tiny measures on tip of teaspoon 8 red peper if peppers are not strong enough

David Davis Family Papers

This recipe for chili sauce was handwritten by Sarah Davis's husband, Judge David Davis. Although professional men rarely entered the kitchen to do any sort of cooking, they were clearly interested in what appeared on their plates.

Even though Sarah Davis often worked behind the scenes with her servants (here she is shown reading a recipe with her cook Bridget Kelley) like many well-to-do women, she made sure the noises and smells from the kitchen were suitably removed from the rest of the house. A china pantry and back hallway separate the kitchen from the rooms in the front of the house. Two pantries, seen in the upper left, provided easy access to ingredients and kitchen equipment. A photograph of Sarah, taken toward the end of her life, is to the right.

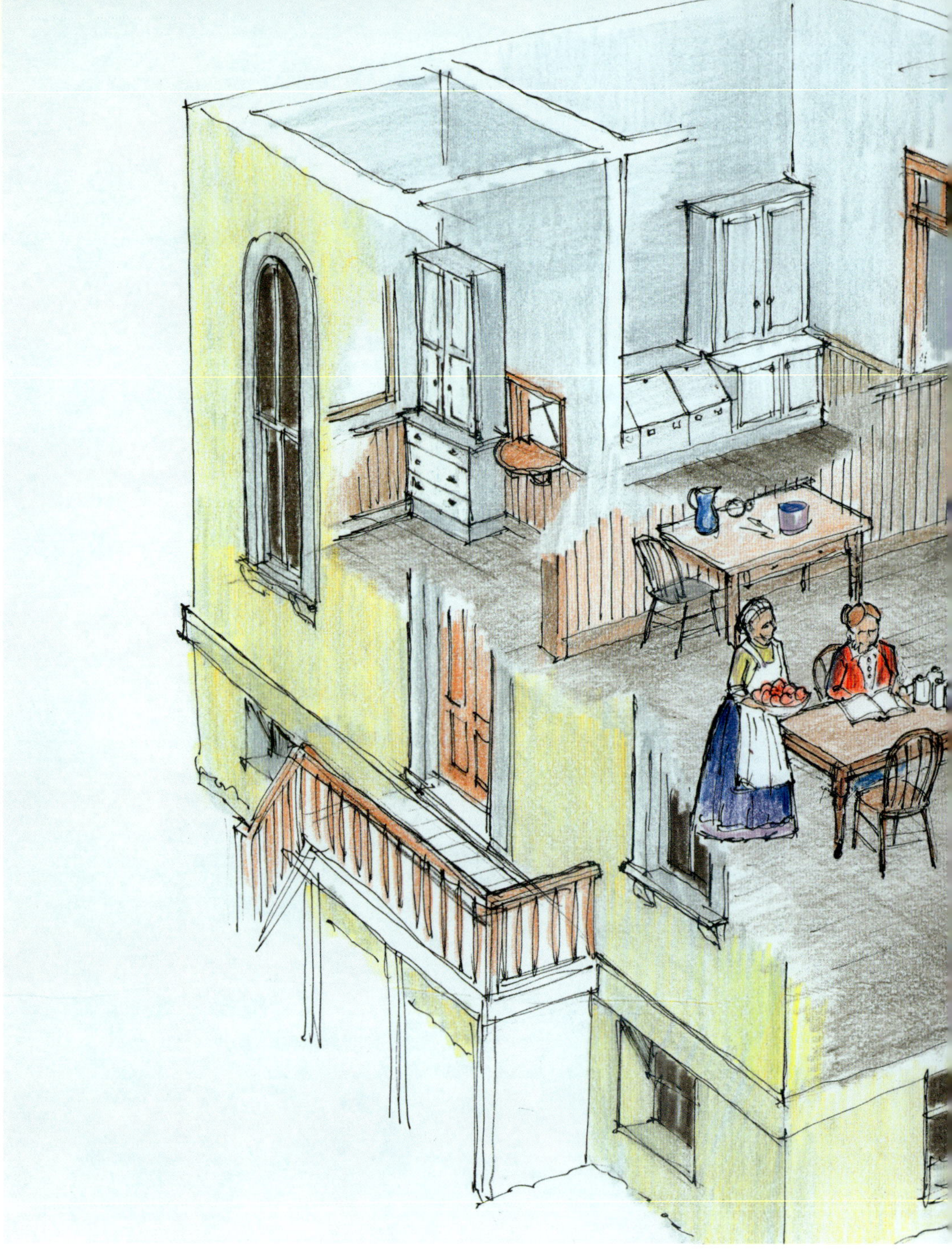

kitchen table are talking [about] a game of whist or some other equally attractive."[38] Clearly, the kitchen in the Davises' household served not only as a work site, but also as a center of social life for many, if not all, of the residents.

By working with her servants, understanding their recreational and religious needs, and providing them with a decent environment, Sarah Davis managed to avoid the problems that afflicted many of her class. Of course, only Sarah's description of her relations with her servants survives. In at least one instance, a cook, Bridget Kelley, was not entirely content. "I am surprised that Bridget should put on airs about wages," Sarah wrote in 1873.[39]

Whatever the relations between Sarah and her servants, the space they worked in was

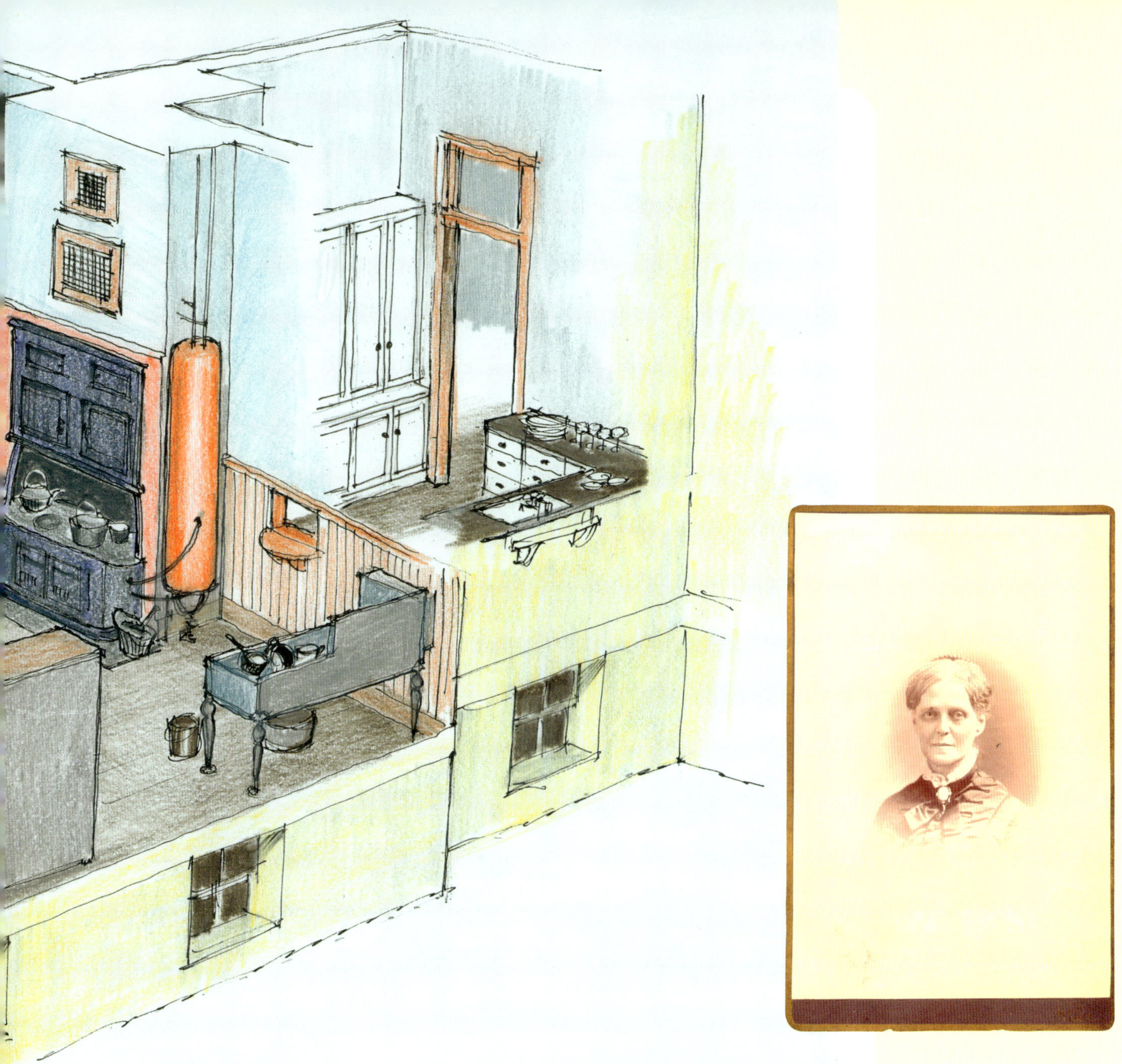

fundamentally different from that of earlier times. The main transformation in the nineteenth-century kitchen came from the introduction of the stove, a product of the Industrial Revolution that changed the nature of cooking, raising the work surface to an easier height and controlling the fire behind massive iron plates. The growth of industry and transportation networks provided new gadgets and new ingredients that broadened the types of cooking expected of women at the same time that it took husbands away from home and left women alone or supervising paid servants in their kitchens. And while businessmen tried to increase the efficiency of their workforce, a parallel concern for increasing efficiency in the kitchen paved the way for the modern kitchen of the next century.

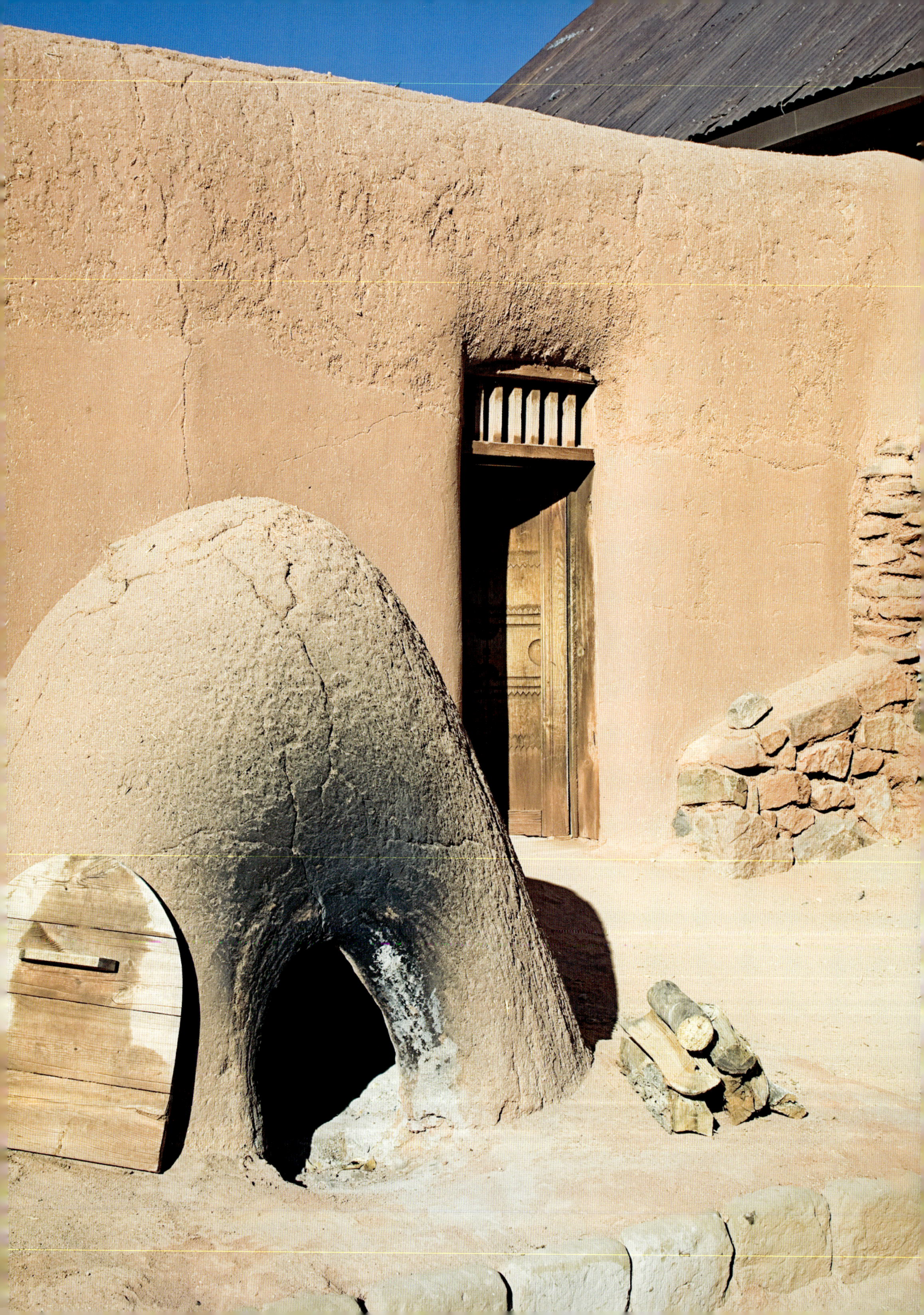

# KITCHENS ALONG THE RIO GRANDE

## {1821–1912}

### *Holy Week at El Rancho de las Golondrinas*

*Semana Santa* (Holy Week) was a busy time for the women of El Rancho de las Golondrinas, for there was much to be done to prepare for the feast that would mark the end of Lent.[1] This was a solemn time of year, a time of reflection and prayer. During this week of pageantry and celebration, religious observance took center stage, but food played a supporting role. Food stores would be running low by the end of Lent, and the celebration of Easter implied confidence in God's bounty. Preparations of traditional dishes would begin early in the week, when a member of a local religious sect known as the *Penitentes*, or Order of Brothers of Our Father Jesus of Nazareth, would bless the adobe *hornos* (outdoor bake ovens) by sprinkling them with salt, reciting prayers, and placing wooden crosses on the oven floors. Not until this occurred would the *hornos* be ready for the week's baking.[2]

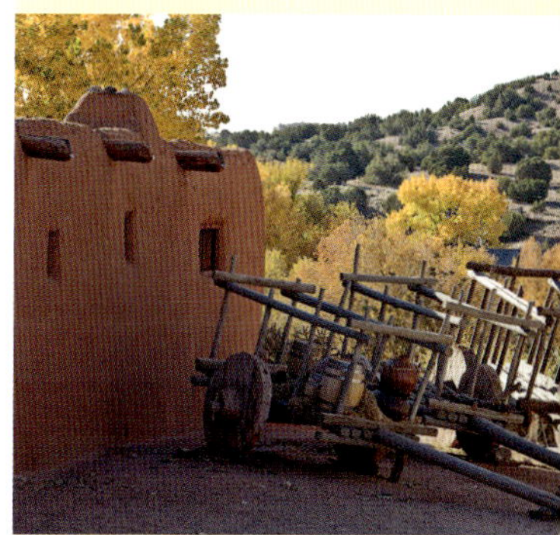

Today, El Rancho de las Golondrinas, fifteen miles south of Santa Fe, is a living history museum.

In 1850, around the time New Mexico became a U.S. territory, the occupants of El Rancho de las Golondrinas included don Manuel Baca y Delgado, his wife, doña Florencia Lucero, and the couple's three children. Two servants, a husband and wife, also lived at the hacienda with their three-year-old child.[3] A number of hired laborers worked in the adjacent fields; shepherds tended the sheep. As the last settlement before Santa Fe along the camino real, the royal road between Mexico and present-day northern New Mexico, the ranch was a frequent stopping place for merchants traveling with their wares between Chihuahua and Santa Fe. The Baca y Delgados, descendants of the area's earliest Spanish settlers, were among the wealthiest families in the region. Even so, compared to wealthy families in the United States, theirs was a hardscrabble existence.[4]

During *Semana Santa*, the women of Golondrinas would gather in the *cocina* (kitchen) and work together to prepare

> Prayer entered into every action or undertaking. Even in cooking, when starting to mix bread or any food, if you wanted it to come out specially good, the name of the Holy Trinity was invoked. A cross was marked on the bread dough before setting it away to rise.
>
> Cleofas Jaramillo, *Shadows of the Past (Sombras del Pasado)*, 1941

Spanish American families in New Mexico were inseparable from their faith, even in their cooking. As Fabiola Cabeza de Baca Gilbert wrote in *We Fed Them Cactus* (1954): "To the New Mexican of Spanish origin, his religion is his whole being."

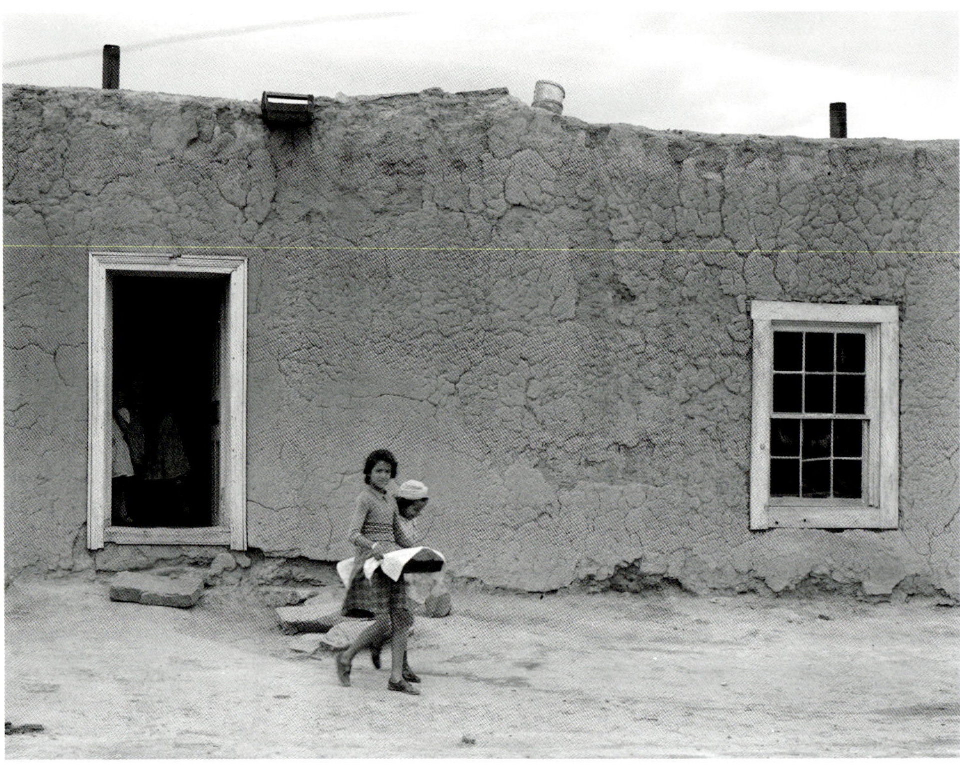

The tradition of sharing small gifts of food, called *charolitas*, persisted well into the twentieth century. Here, a young boy and girl carry a covered tray of special dishes to neighbors in the village of El Cerrito, New Mexico, in 1941.

*Bizcochitos* have been popular in New Mexico since at least the nineteenth century. The author of *Historic Cookery*, Fabiola Cabeza de Baca Gilbert, was a descendant of the owners of El Rancho de las Golondrinas.

meals for the celebrants and visitors, who would share the week's observance. Doña Florencia and her helpers baked breads, puddings, *molletes* (sweet rolls) and *bizcochitos* (sugar cookies seasoned with anise). Many of the baked goods were taken as gifts to neighbors on Holy Thursday and Good Friday. One of the favorite treats of the week was *panocha*, a pudding made from sprouted wheat and cooked for hours in the outdoor ovens.

Sprouting the wheat for *panocha* was itself a ritual that marked the season. The Golondrinas women would wash wheat kernels and place them in a canvas bag near the *fogón* (fireplace) for warmth, sprinkling the bag occasionally with water. Within two or three days the wheat would sprout and be ready to be dried and then taken to the family's mill nearby to be ground. The sprouted wheat was an apt symbol for Holy Week, suggesting the resurrection of Christ was at hand.

Holy Week culminated in a dance on Saturday night, and on Sunday the *hornos* were heated again to roast new spring lamb—the centerpiece of a feast that included the first meat that many had eaten since Lent began.

## *Bizcochitos* (Cookies)

1 c. sugar, 6 c. sifted flour, 2 c. lard, 3 t. baking powder, 1 t. anise seed, 1 t. salt, 2 eggs, 1/4 c. water

Cream lard with hand thoroughly; add sugar and anise seed. Beat eggs and add lard to mixture Blend until light and fluffy. Sift flour with baking powder and salt and add to first mixture. Add water and knead until well mixed. Roll 1/2 inch thick and cut into fancy shapes. Roll top of each cookie in a mixture of sugar and cinnamon—1 t. cinnamon to 1/2 c. sugar. Bake in a moderate oven until slightly brown.

Fabiola Cabeza de Baca Gilbert, *Historic Cookery*, 1939

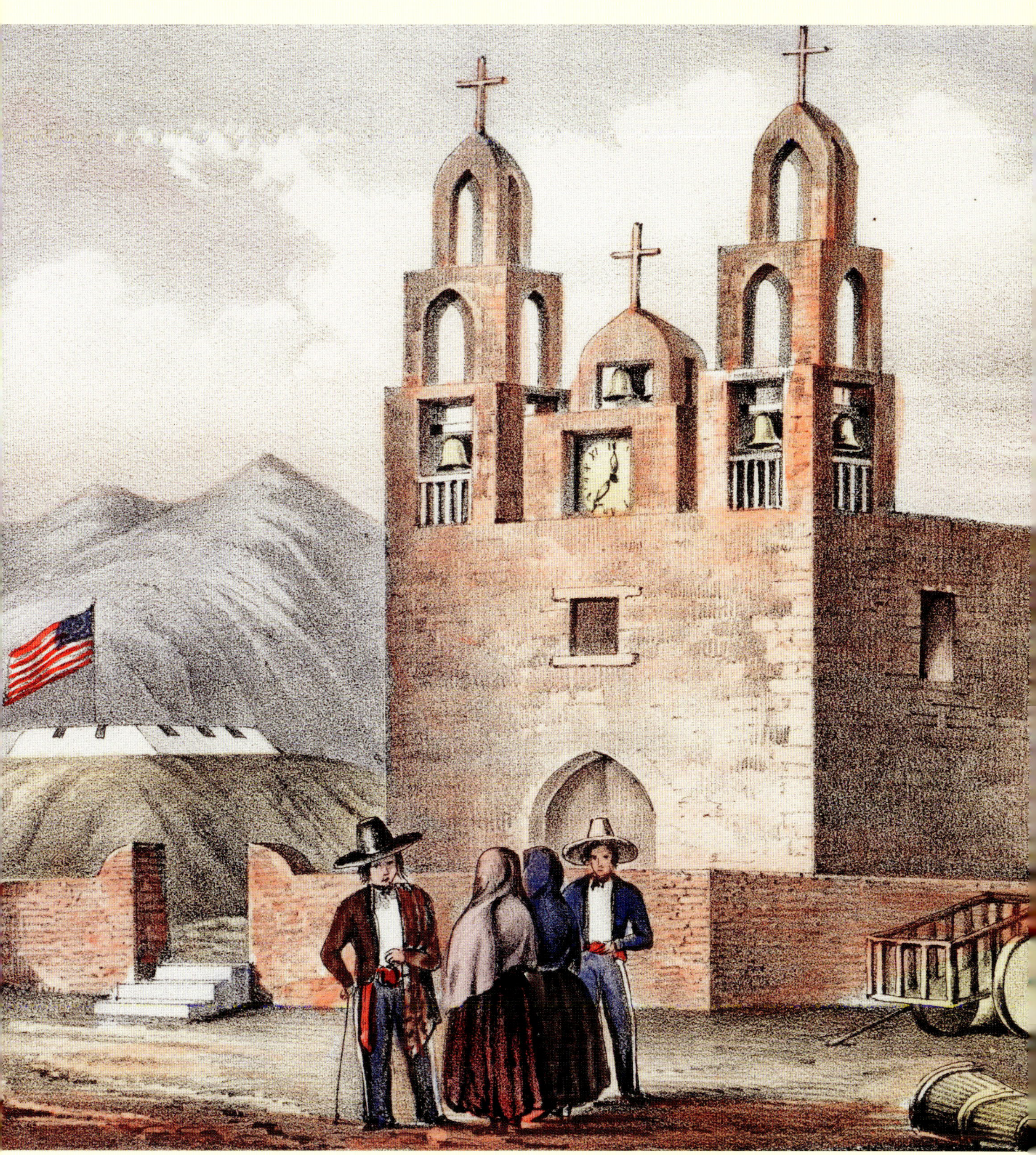

This church was among the most imposing structures in Santa Fe in the mid-nineteenth century. The image was recorded in 1848 as part of military reconnaissance for the United States Army.

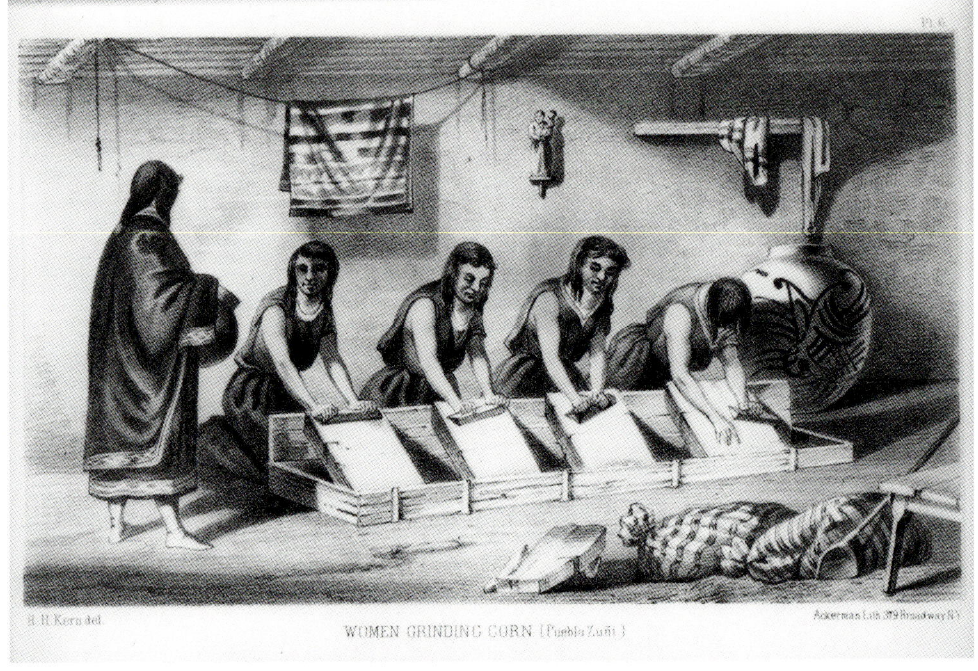


This 1853 lithograph shows a group of Zuni women grinding corn in fixed mealing troughs. To alleviate the monotony, the women would talk to one another or sing, sometimes accompanied by a fife player. The Zunis are one of a number of tribes that the Spanish called *Pueblos*.

This description of a typical meal suggests that in the 1880s Zunis not only continued to cook indigenous foods, such as corn, squash, bread, and jerked meat, but also made use of ingredients that had been introduced by the Spanish, like onions and peppers. Smithsonian anthropologist Frank Cushing's groundbreaking study of Zuni culture recorded not only the mythology, agricultural practices, and language of the Zuni people but also the mundane aspects of their lives, from what they wore to what they ate.

## *Native Cooking*

The Baca y Delgados lived in a region that the native population had occupied for millennia, where women had long processed and cooked the local foods. The region's first inhabitants were nomadic hunters. As early as 2000 B.C. they began cultivating corn, and by 1000 A.D., they had developed irrigation systems that enabled them to grow crops with surpluses that could be carried over from year to year. They lived in settled villages, usually comprising one large building with a multiplicity of rooms, most of which were occupied by individual families. By the sixteenth century, when the Spanish arrived in the region, an estimated sixty to one hundred thousand people, with diverse traditions and languages, lived in perhaps one hundred villages. The Spanish called these people "Pueblos," or town dwellers.[5]

Corn was the mainstay of the native diet. The Pueblos also cultivated squash and beans, gathered wild plants, domesticated dogs and turkeys, and hunted deer and rabbits. In the sixteenth century, watermelon and cantaloupes, introduced into Mexico by the Spanish, were brought north along native trade routes and cultivated even before the arrival of the Spaniards themselves.

During winter, breakfast is eaten at about ten o'clock. In summer, quite half the field work of the day is done before it is tasted—usually an hour later than in winter—and a luncheon intervenes between and as invariably consists of boiled corn or squash, *he'-wei* [wafer bread], either onions or red peppers roasted in hot ashes, and strips of the toughest jerked meat in the house. The meat must be, if perfected for the purposes which it served at luncheon, dipped in tallow or water, then broiled on a bed of coals until pliable.

Frank Hamilton Cushing, *Zuni Breadstuff*, 1884–1885

In the villages, women were responsible for preparing food. Much of their time was devoted to processing and grinding corn. Pedro de Castañeda, one of the first Spaniards to visit a native village, described their method. Writing in 1540, he explained that the natives used a separate, clean room for preparing corn, in which

> *they have a trough with three stones fixed in stiff clay. Three women go in here, each one having a stone, with which one of them breaks the corn, the next grinds it, and the third grinds it again. They take off their shoes, do up their hair, shake their clothes, and cover their heads before they enter the door. A man sits at the door playing on a fife while they grind, moving the stones to the music and singing together. They grind a large quantity at one time, because they make all their bread of meal soaked in warm water, like wafers.*[6]

While the music and singing no doubt helped pass the time, this was a laborious task. Ground corn was used principally to make tortillas, tamales, or various breads.

Cooking took place both outside and indoors in pits lined with clay. The women used earthenware pots or stone griddles, often placed over hot embers on three supporting stones. With the exception of benches built up along the walls, the Pueblo Indians had virtually no furniture. Preparing and eating meals took place on the floor. Until they adopted the Spanish practice of building chimneys, smoke from indoor cooking fires escaped through doors and windows.

Pueblo women adapted certain techniques from the Spanish settlers, such as the use of chimneys to carry away smoke. Here, a Zuni woman, photographed by Edward Curtis about 1903, is baking traditional bread.

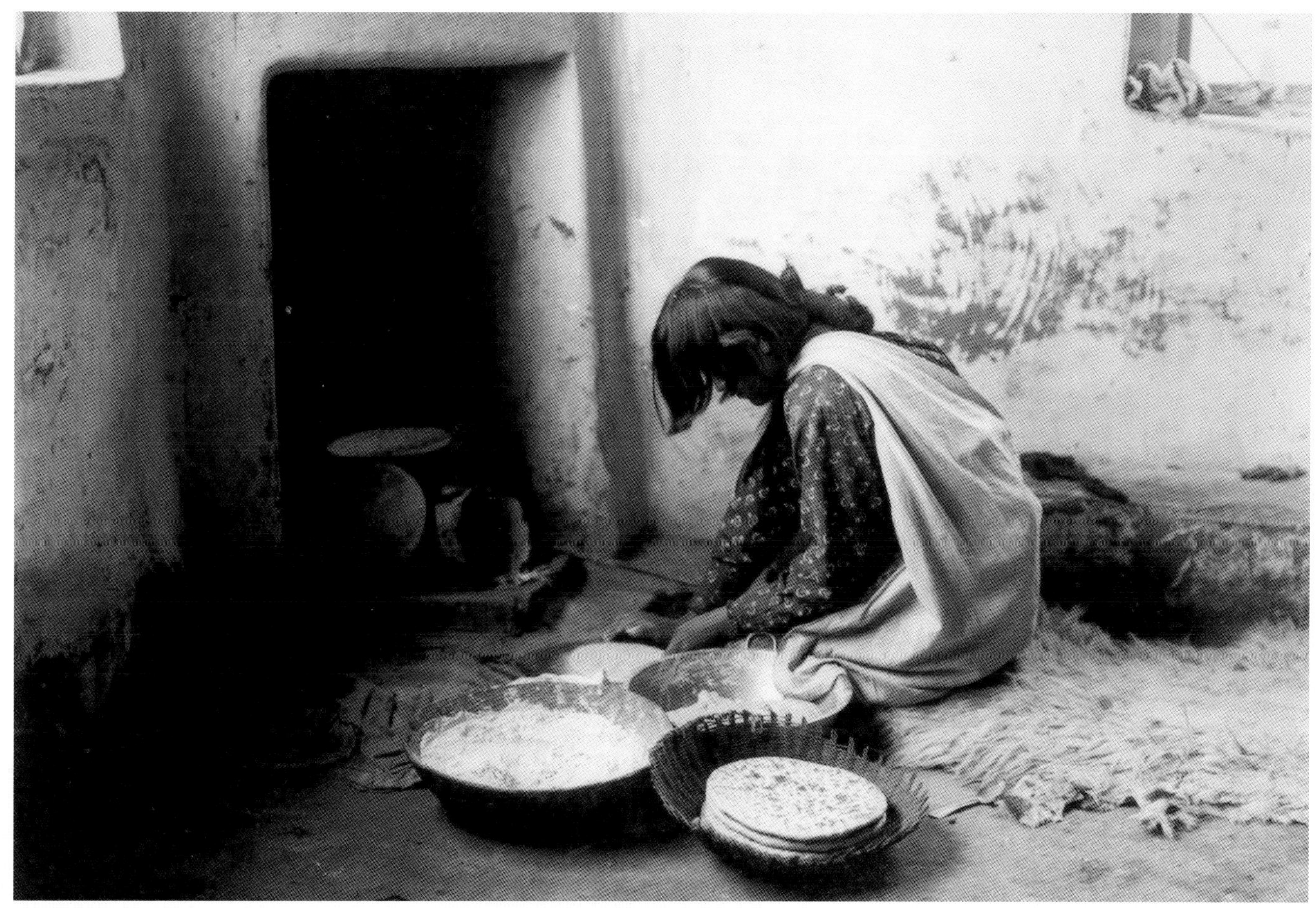

## *From Spanish Conquest to U. S. Dominion*

When don Juan de Oñate established a permanent Spanish colony in New Mexico in 1598, he initiated a long period of Spanish influence that affected the way native families lived in and used their cooking spaces. Their food came to reflect Spanish, Meso-American, and Native American influence, relying heavily on Spanish wheat and mutton, on chiles brought to the area from Mexico by Hispanic settlers and their Mexican servants, and on native corn, squashes, and beans.[7]

The Spanish who came into the region that is now northern New Mexico journeyed north from Mexico along the central mining corridor and crossed the Rio Grande at El Paso. They followed the river north in their relentless search for rich mineral deposits and precious metals as well as religious converts to furnish the labor force. Because so much of the local population was settled in villages, the Spanish viewed the natives as ideal candidates for conversion. Relations between Hispanic settlers and the Indian peoples were, at best, strained, culminating in the Pueblo Revolt of 1680 and the expulsion of the Spanish. Twelve years later the Spanish returned, with renewed determination to conquer and convert. This time, their presence had a far greater effect on the natives' way of life, including their way of cooking. Before long, natives were cultivating and eating chile, baking in *hornos*, and building chimneys.

The successful completion of the nearly one-thousand-mile journey from Independence, Missouri, to Santa Fe was cause for rifle-shooting celebration.

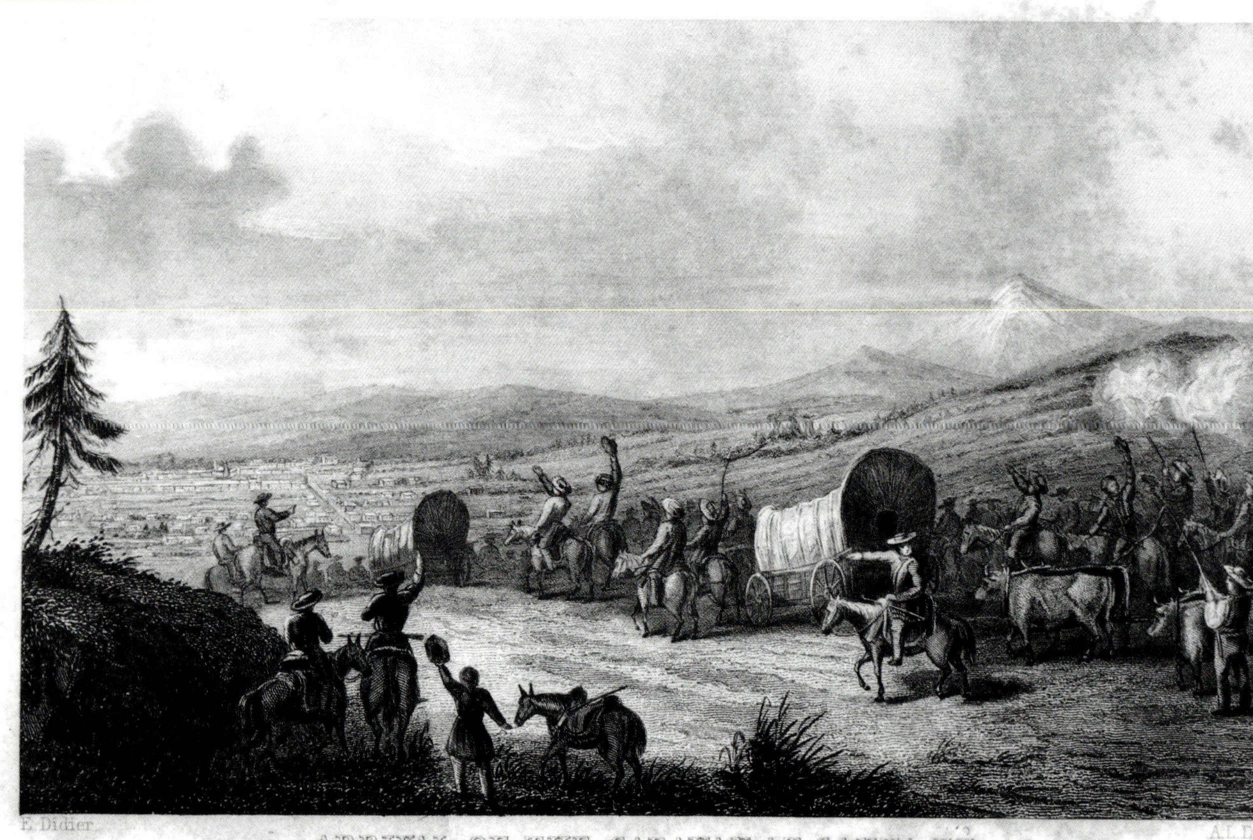

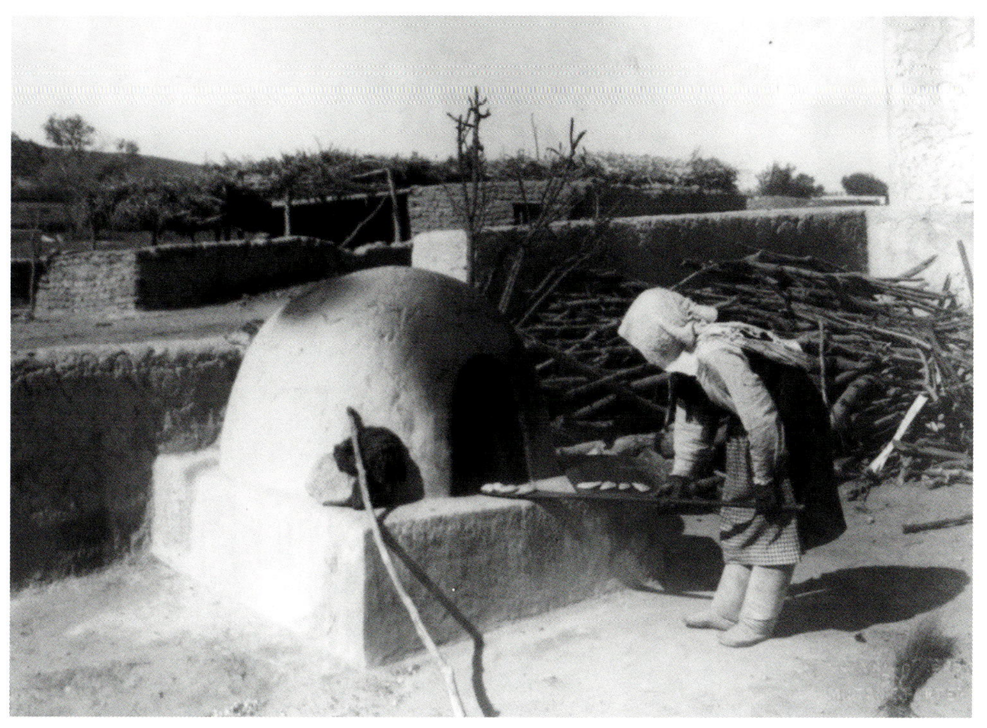

At the turn of the twentieth century, Pueblo villages like this one showed little American influence. Spanish influence was apparent in the widespread use of adobe ovens.

The region remained under Spanish rule until early in the nineteenth century. Following the Mexican War for Independence (1810–1821), the area that came to be New Mexico was controlled by Mexico. Once free of Spanish law, which had prohibited contact with traders from other countries, the Hispanic settlers in the region began to welcome Anglo merchants, who arrived with wagon loads of American goods brought in on the Santa Fe Trail from Missouri. These adventurers came with huge caravans carrying industrial goods—cottons, cast iron, tinware—that expanded the types of materials found in Spanish households. The trip was long, the risks were great, and the numbers of American traders who came to the region remained relatively small. Even so, the arrival of the traders whetted the appetites of New Mexicans for new goods, although few could afford to purchase them. After the Mexican-American War (1846–1848), the region once again came under new rule, this time by Anglo-Americans, whose religion, customs, language, and food preferences differed dramatically from those of the Indians and the Hispanic settlers. While U.S. governance quickly overtook the region's politics, the region's kitchens and food continued to follow the traditions of the native peoples and the Hispanic settlers for decades afterward.

> American immigration began to pour into the territory. The rich Spanish Dons, up to this time owners of the land for which their fathers had fought and bled, now found themselves against something they could not cope with. Transferred to a new sovereign of alien language and divers political views, the Spanish population, sensitive, proud, constantly fought to maintain its political and social equality.
>
> Cleofas Jaramillo, *Shadows of the Past (Sombras del Pasado)*, 1941

Hispanic families found their culture and their place in New Mexican society turned upside down after the region was made a U.S. territory.

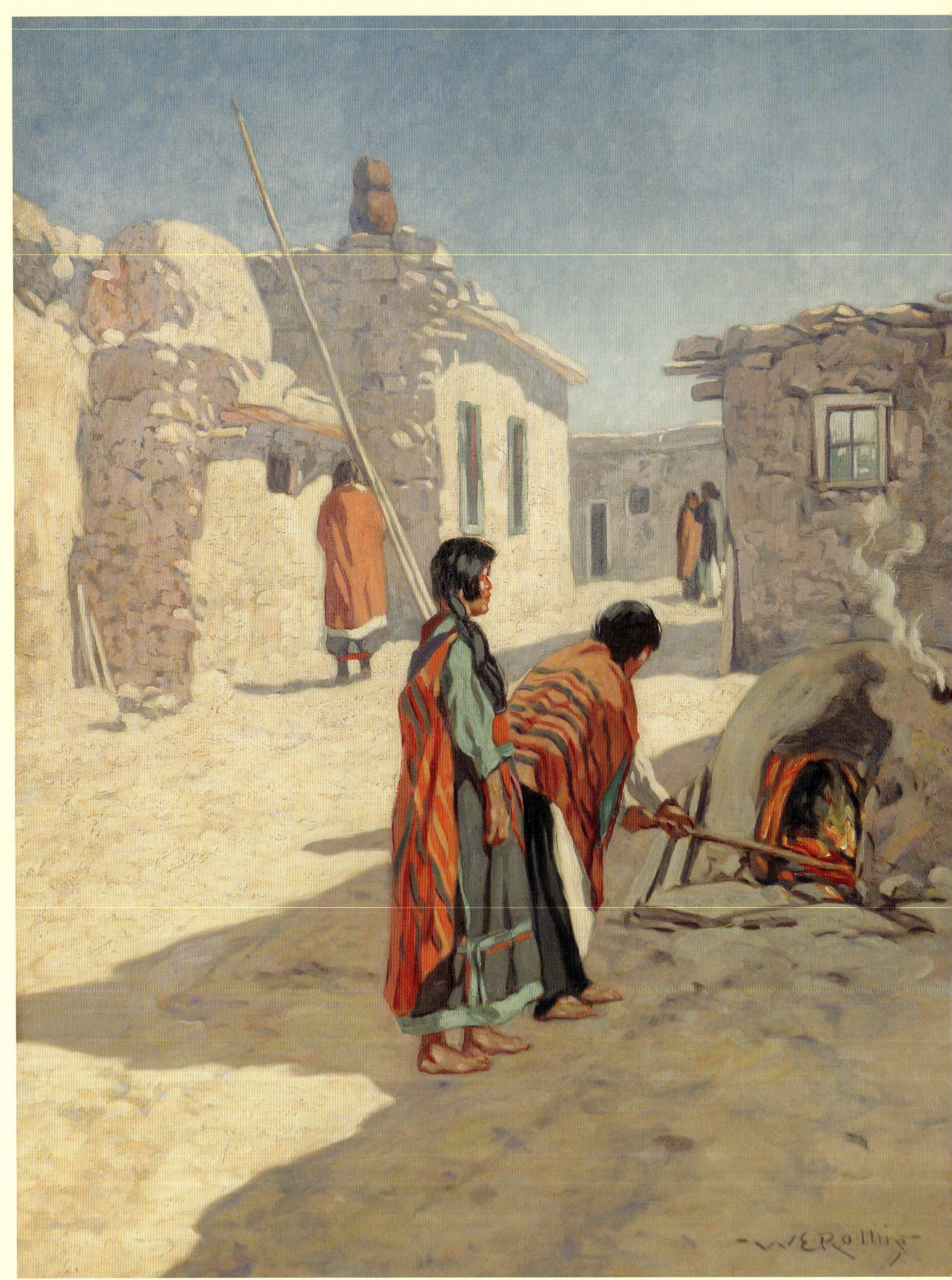
W.E.Rollins

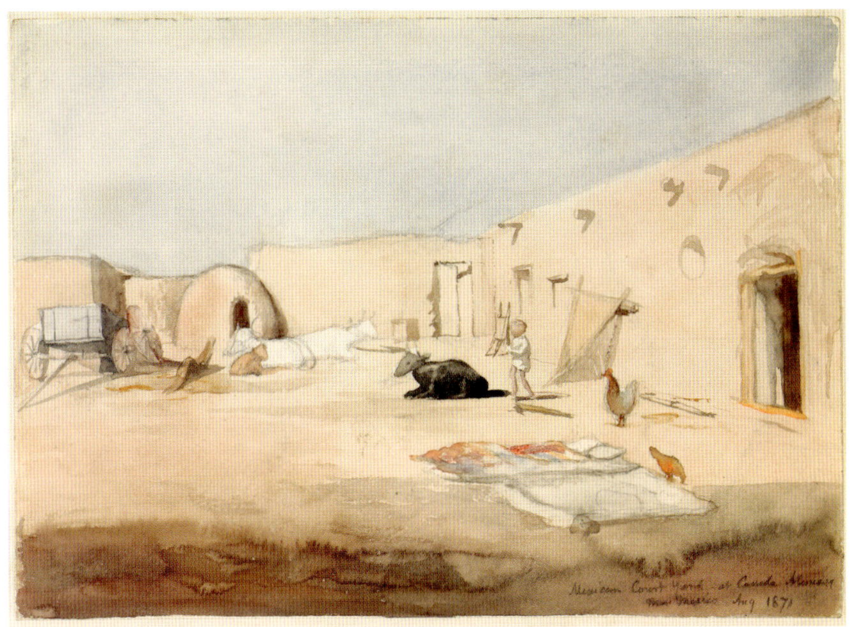

Vincent Colyer recorded a Hispanic family's courtyard in New Mexico in 1871. The courtyard, or *placita,* enclosed an *horno* as well as a few of the hacienda's cows and chickens.

## The Spanish Cocina in Nineteenth-Century New Mexico

Evidence about New Mexican kitchens in the nineteenth century is sparse, with few written records and even fewer pictorial ones. Letters and memoirs by American traders and soldiers describing an alien culture comprise most of the surviving documents. The kitchens themselves, housed in fragile adobe buildings, have all but disappeared. What survives from the period are archaeological artifacts, excavated and interpreted by archaeologists. Also remaining are oral traditions from Hispanic descendants who, early in the twentieth century, recalled the kitchens of their parents and grandparents. Even with the limited amount of information that survives, it is possible to develop a picture of what life was like for the Indian and Hispanic women who worked in the kitchens of the region.

The traditional Hispanic house in New Mexico was built of adobe bricks, one room added to the end of another over time. As families and households grew, the configuration of the rooms often grew to form an L-shaped structure, or eventually a four-sided one, with multiple rooms enclosing a courtyard. The enclosed building was particularly advantageous when Navajo, Comanche, and Apache raiders approached, as the single large exterior door could be barricaded and the building defended from the rooftop.

Lewis Garrard was seventeen when he traveled along the Santa Fe Trail to New Mexico. His memoir, published in 1850, described the alien culture he found on his arrival.

> In front of many dwellings is a mud oven, in shape like a cupping glass, in which is baked the whitest bread it has ever been my fortune to taste. No bolting cloths are here used; and those wanting white bread sift for themselves. The hard bread, *bischoche*, is light, porous and sweet—a perfect luxury with a cup of coffee by a mountain pine fire.
>
> Lewis Garrard, *Wah-to-yah*, 1850

Many Pueblo women learned Hispanic cooking techniques as servants in Hispanic households. By the early twentieth century, *hornos* and chimneys were commonplace in Pueblo villages like the one shown in this early twentieth-century painting, *Indian Home Life, Pueblo of Zuni*, by Warren Rollins.

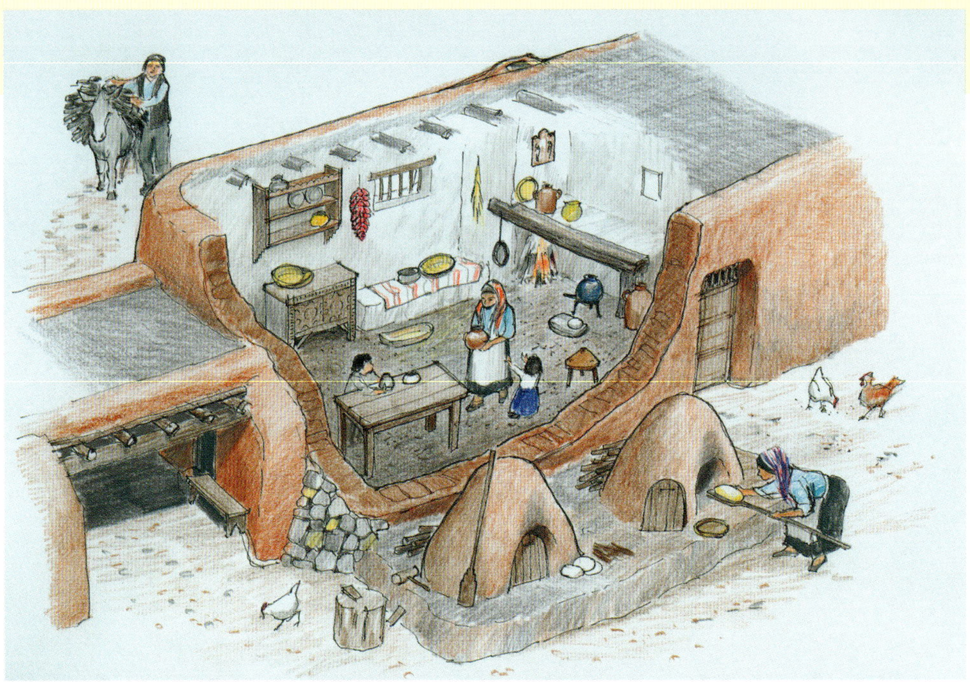

The kitchen at El Rancho de las Golondrinas was always a hub of activity.

The function of rooms in a Hispanic house varied according to the number of rooms. In a large house, one or two rooms might be used for storage, several as bedchambers, one as a parlor and dining room, and another as the kitchen. The largest complexes would include one room set aside for use as a chapel. Of course, the smaller the building, the more functions overlapped in a single room. In 1846 Susan Magoffin, an eighteen-year-old bride who traveled to the region along the Santa Fe Trail with her merchant husband, described the small house they rented. The four-room structure had a small sleeping chamber, a *cocina*, a storage room, and a large multipurpose room that served as "the reception room, parlour, dining-room, and in short the room of all work. This is a long room with dirt floor (as they all have) plank ceiling, and nicely white-washed sides."[8]

Even before entering the kitchen itself, travelers encountered one of the major features of New Mexican cookery—the large adobe bake oven outside, the *horno*. *Hornos* arrived in New Mexico with the Hispanic settlers, probably as early as Oñate's expedition in the late sixteenth century. The technology—the building up of a domed structure with bricks made of mud—may well have come from the Moors of northern Africa, who first settled in Spain in the eighth century. By the nineteenth century, *hornos* were a central feature of virtually every New Mexican household. In fact some households had two and even three *hornos* of varying sizes. The smallest required less fuel and could be used when only a small amount of baking was planned. For feast days, all of the *hornos* might be heated at once.

The upright corner fireplace at Golondrinas has a large projecting shelf over the hearth. Sometimes called "shepherds beds," these shelves were commonly used for storage.

The indoor *cocina* had a hearth dominated by an upright cone-shaped fireplace known as a *fogón de campana*. Although small, the fireplace was well-suited to generate the embers that were a critical part of cookery. These could be pulled out from the fireplace and placed along the dirt floor adjacent. Cedar logs brought on the backs of donkeys from the surrounding hills often served as the fuel for both *horno* and fireplace. Water had to be carried in from irrigation ditches, or in the case of the Baca y Delgados at Golondrinas, from nearby springs.

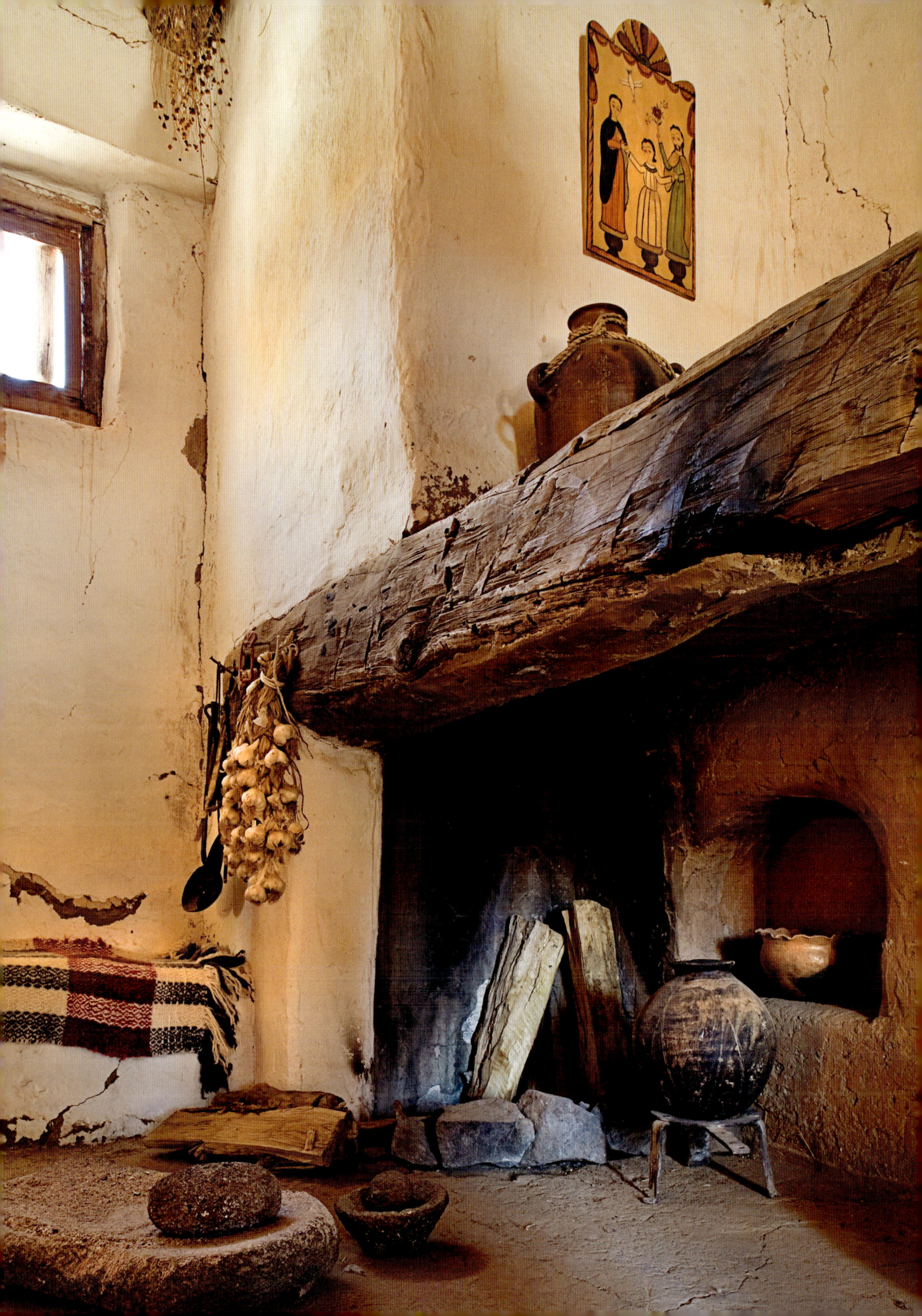

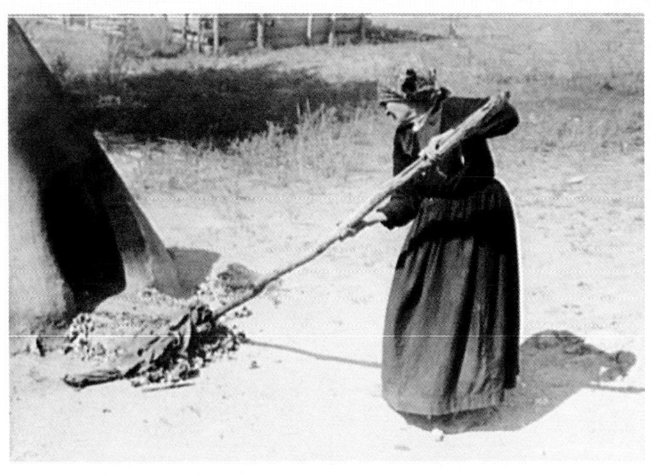
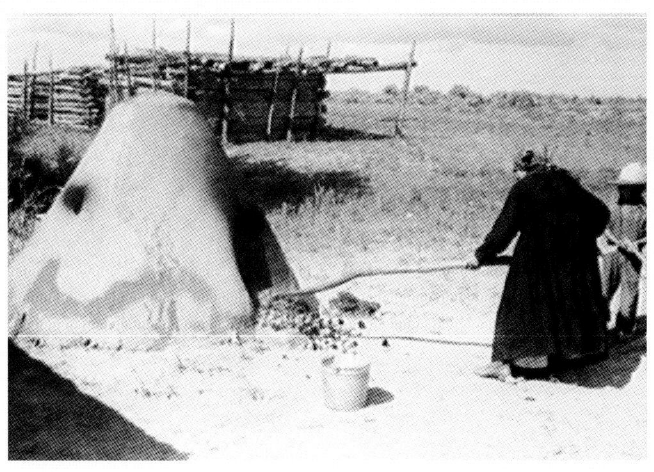
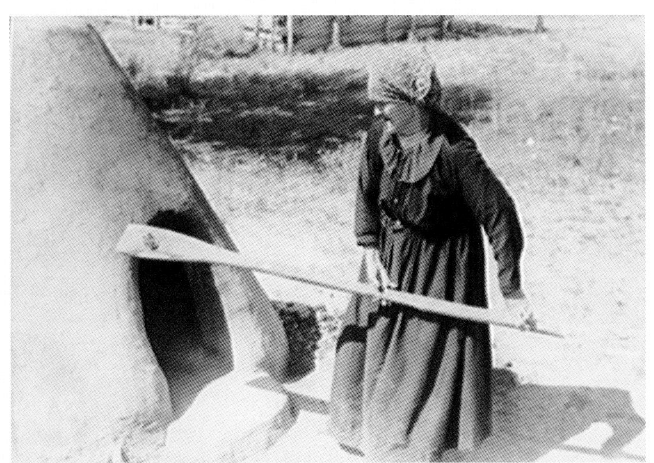
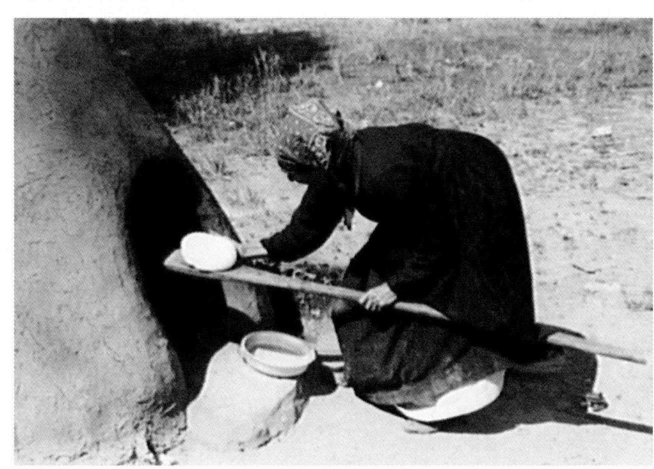
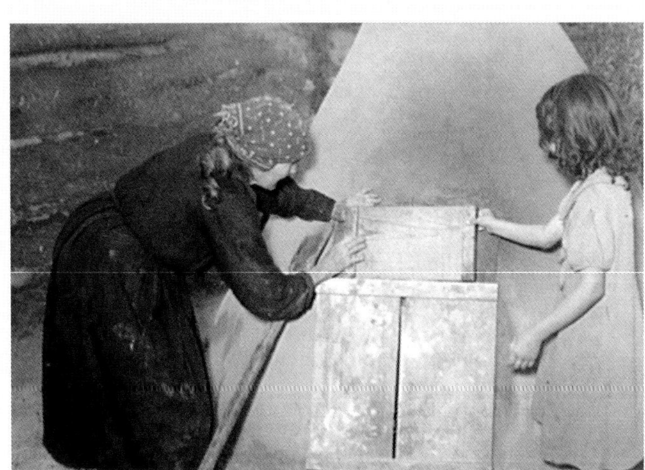
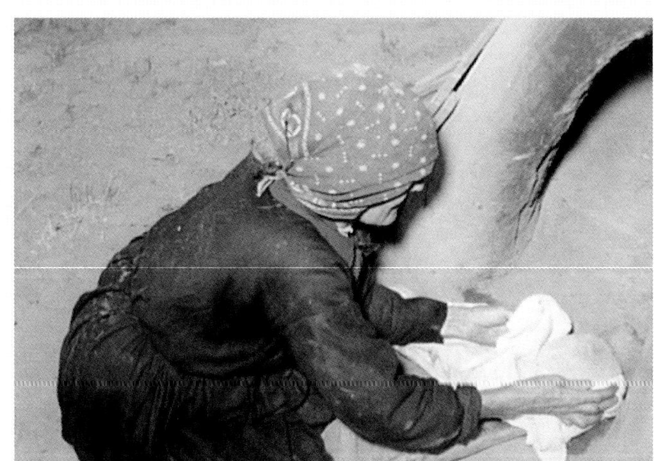

Whether baking in an *horno* or in a brick oven, the process is the same. First a fire is lit in the oven to heat it to baking temperature. After the fire has died down, the ash is raked out, and the oven floor cleaned off with a damp cloth (top row). The baker tests the heat of the oven several ways—one of which is to see how long it will take for a piece of wool to burn (middle left.) These images show a Hispanic woman outside of Taos in 1939.

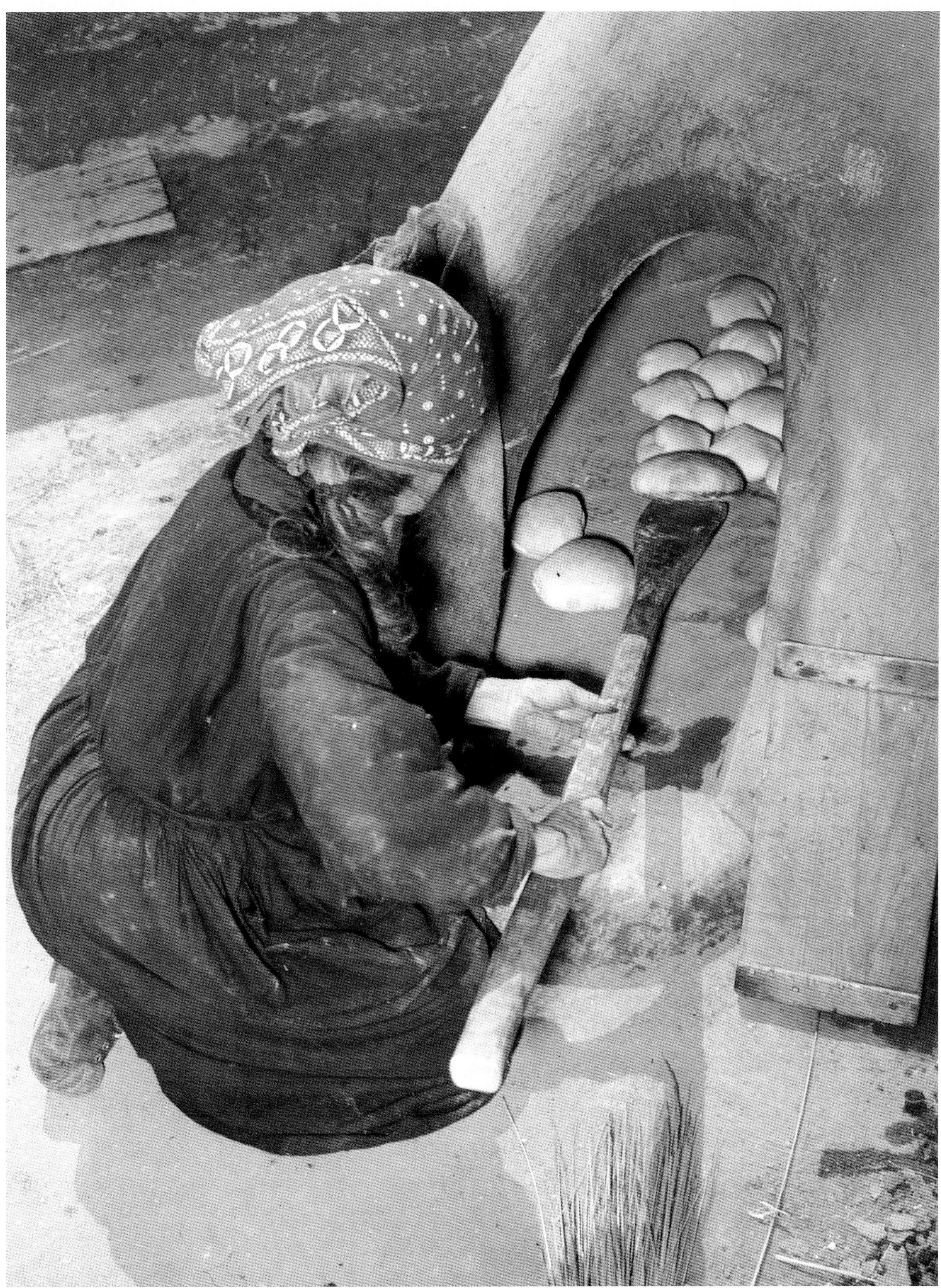

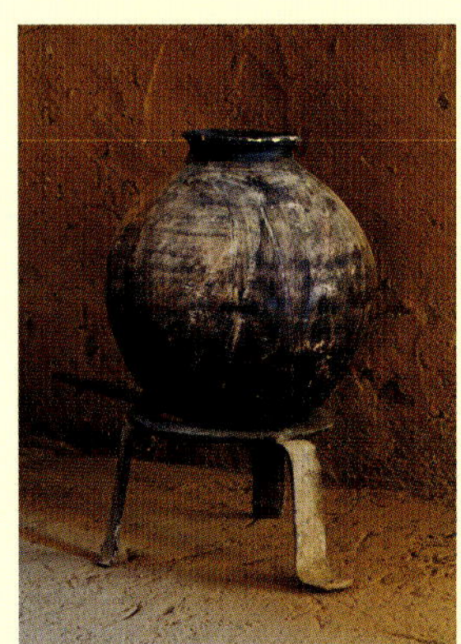

*Ollas* (clay pots)—sometimes placed on *tenemastes* (iron supports), sometimes on stones, and sometimes directly on the embers—were used for cooking. Hispanic families purchased these utilitarian vessels from local Pueblo potters. Another critical item in the New Mexican kitchen was the *comal* (griddle), whether of iron or earthenware, on which tortillas were cooked, a staple of the New Mexican diet. *Tinajas* (large pottery vessels) held food supplies. Until Anglo traders began making inroads into New Mexico, kitchen implements made of iron were rare. But soon metal kitchen tools made their way across the Santa Fe Trail, along with tableware from eastern factories. One archaeological dig in the region uncovered pottery shards almost certainly from ceramics brought in along the Santa Fe Trail. In his 1848 description of a military reconnaissance expedition through New Mexico, Lieutenant William Emory noted that the wine at one dinner he attended was served in "glass decanters, of Pittsburg manufacture."[9] After 1879 when the railroad made its way into the region, industrial goods, including kitchen equipment, became more widely available.

In many Hispanic households, young Navajo women, and occasionally women from other tribes, worked in the kitchens alongside the women of the Hispanic family. While some of these women were paid as servants, others were enslaved, having been captured by warring tribes and sold to Hispanic families. Spanish and later Mexican law required that enslaved natives be freed after serving for ten years. (After they were freed, formerly enslaved men and women were no longer welcomed back into their own tribes, and instead became members of the *genízaro,* an impoverished class of "de-tribalized" natives who made up a significant portion of New Mexico's population.)[10]

Traveling north from Mexico to New Mexico, George Ruxton and his companions were devastated when the ceramic *olla* in which they were preparing a long-delayed meal cracked over the flame and their food spilled away. Hispanos and natives alike must have occasionally experienced similar disasters when the pottery they cooked in succumbed to the flame.

[Our] combined efforts had produced an imposing pile of several yards of beef (for here the meat is cut into long strips and dried), onions, chiles, frijoles, sweet corn, eggs, &. An enormous olla was procured, and everything was bundled pell-mell into it, seasoned with pepper and salt and chile.

. . . Our appetites, ravenous with a fast of twenty-four hours, were in first-rate order, but we determined that the pot should be left on the fire until the savoury mess was perfectly cooked. It was within an hour or two of sunset, and we had not yet broken our fast. The olla simmered, and a savoury steam pervaded the air. The dragoons licked their lips, and their eyes watered—never had they had such a feast in perspective. . . . At length the moment arrived: my mozo [servant] . . . with guarded hands seized the top of the olla and lifted it from the ashes.

"Ave Maria Purissima [Holy Mary Most Pure]"! "Santissima Virgen [Most Holy Virgin]!" broke from the lips of the dragoons; "Mil carajos [A thousand curses]!" burst from the *heart* of the mozo; and I sank almost senseless to the ground. On lifting the pot the bottom fell out, and splash went everything into the blazing fire. Valgame Dios [God save me]! what a moment was that!

George Frederick Augustus Ruxton, *Adventures in Mexico and the Rocky Mountains,* 1848

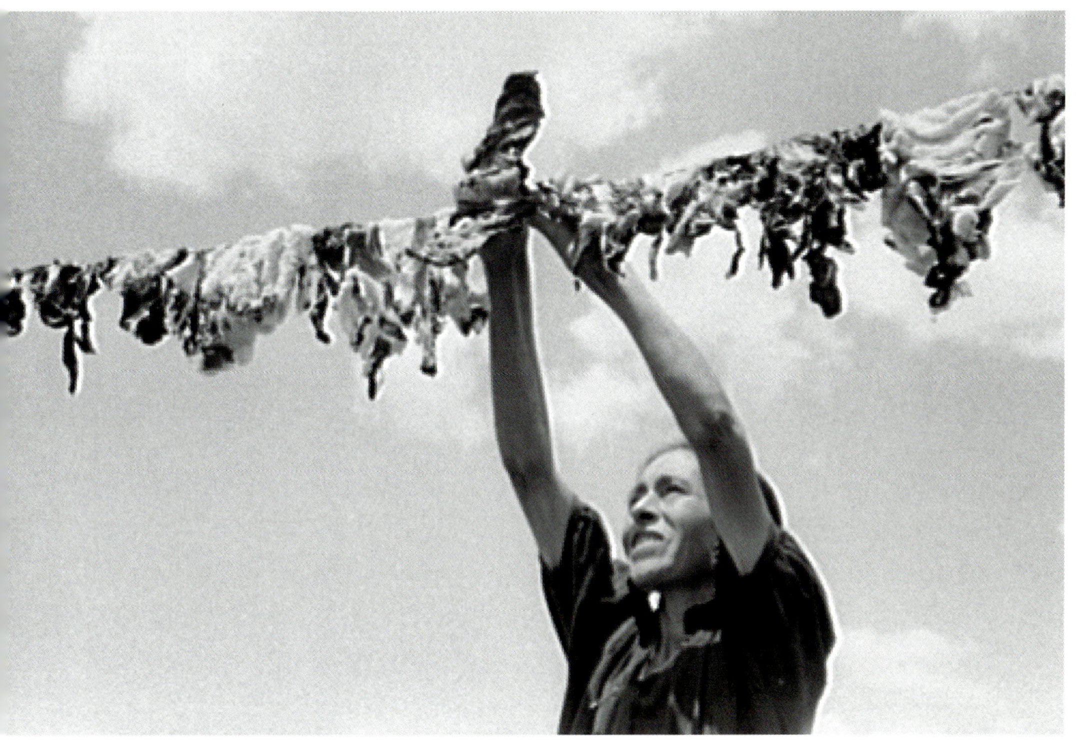

The hot dry weather in New Mexico made it possible to preserve meat by hanging it in the sun. This photograph taken in 1940 shows a woman from Chamisal, New Mexico, hanging meat.

## New Mexican Foodways

The food cooked in the fireplaces and *hornos* of New Mexico combined Spanish, Mexican, and Indian traditions. Hispanic settlers brought their own food traditions from Spain as well as those they acquired in Mexico, and adopted some of the foodways of the local population after they arrived. Native women, some of whom, when working as servants, had learned to cook traditional Hispanic foods, brought back some of these techniques and ingredients to their own villages.

> The extravagant use of red pepper . . . has become truly proverbial. It enters into nearly every dish at every meal . . . [and] is likewise ground into a sauce, and thus used even more abundantly than butter.
>
> Josiah Gregg, *The Commerce of the Prairies*, 1844

Corn remained at the center of the New Mexican diet, and its processing was a time-consuming affair that kept women tied to the kitchen. In the native tradition, the process required the use of heavy grinding stones or *metates*, and heavy stone rollers or *manos*. Susan Magoffin described her first encounter with grinding corn when a neighbor came to show her how it was done. She noted the way the woman was obliged to bend over "(on her knees all the time, a position most fatiguing to the back and indeed the whole frame) to rub the corn up and down . . . till it was ground to a paste." Magoffin commented, "What a deal of trouble it is too. I had not thought half the work."[11] In fact, grinding a sufficient amount of corn to feed even a small

Like many fellow travelers, Santa Fe trader Josiah Gregg commented on the pervasive use of chile in the food he found in New Mexico. Gregg's description of his experiences in New Mexico is one of the earliest accounts of the region by an American.

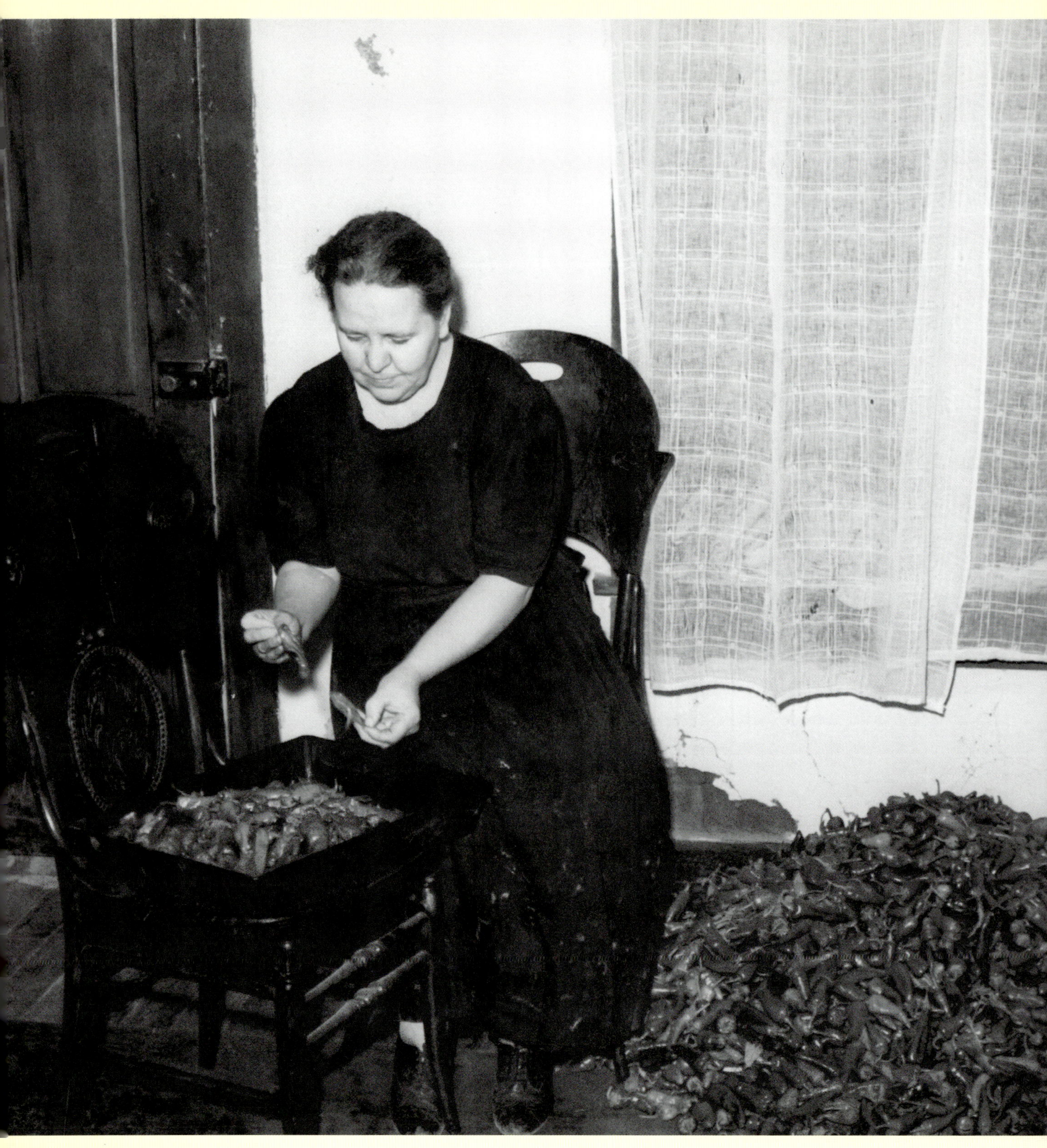

Although some Americans were slow to adapt to the fiery heat of chile peppers, by the early twentieth century chiles were a significant cash crop for southwestern farmers. Here a woman picks over her harvest in 1940.

household was hugely time-consuming and laborious. By some estimates, women may have spent as much as six to eight hours a day grinding corn and another two to three hours making tortillas.[12]

While Hispanic families quickly adopted the native tradition of eating corn, squash, and beans, they brought with them a variety of vegetables—onions, garlic, lettuce, cabbage, and carrots—and fruit such as peaches, apricots, pears, and grapes. Wheat was important, not only because many people of Spanish ancestry initially preferred wheat bread to corn tortillas, but because the Catholic Church required that its communion wafers be made of wheat. Because wheat, unlike corn, required a mill to be processed, it was expensive and was therefore most often used for special occasions. Spaniards also introduced sheep, goats, cattle, and poultry. Chickens provided meat and eggs, and sheep, goats, and cattle provided meat and milk, though much of the milk was processed into cheese. New Mexicans drank chocolate imported from Mexico when they could, or, less frequently, coffee. They also enjoyed wine, much of it produced in El Paso, and during feasts they drank a variety of alcoholic punches with spices—*mistelas* or *aguas frescas*. For sweetener there was imported sugar and corn syrup made locally from crushed corn stalks.[13]

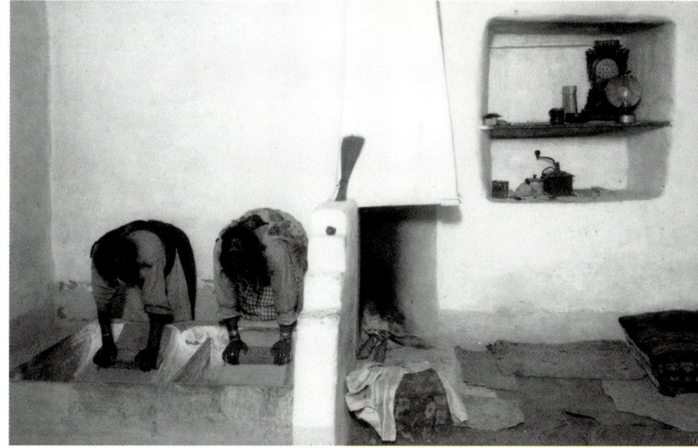

Pueblo women continued to use built-in mealing troughs and *metates* to grind corn into the twentieth century. Some Hispanic women adopted this method. Others used free-standing *metates* that were common in Mexico.

Chiles, a food commonly associated with the Southwest, were introduced to the region by the Spanish settlers who brought them from Mexico. By the nineteenth century chiles were not only an ever-present seasoning but the main vegetable eaten by New Mexicans. They were cultivated on every ranch, some picked while still green and the rest allowed to ripen. After they turned red,

## *Carne con Chile Colorado* (Meat with Red Chile)

Round steak cut in small cubes and browned in hot fat makes very good carne con chile. Boiling meats, however, impart a particular flavor which is not obtained otherwise. Avoid using meat with a great deal of fat. Genuine carne con chile must never have a greasy film.

1½ lbs. boiling meat, 1 t. salt, 2 T. fat, 1 t. oregano, 2 c. chile sauce, 1 clove chopped garlic or 8 T. powdered chile, 1 c. meat stock or tomatoes

Cook meat until tender but not too well done. Cut into small cubes. Fry in the fat until brown. Remove from fire. Add powdered chile or chile sauce. Season with salt, oregano, and garlic. Add meat stock or tomatoes. Cook for half an hour. If chile powder is used, increase the meat stock or tomatoes 1 cup.

Fabiola Cabeza de Baca Gilbert, *Historic Cookery*, 1939

Red chile sauce, Chile Colorado, was pervasive in the New Mexican diet. In *Commerce of the Prairies* (1844) Josiah Gregg described New Mexicans using tortillas instead of silverware to scoop up their meal, whether they were eating Chile Colorado or "chilly verde" (green chile).

they were hung and dried for use throughout the year. *Chile ristras*, strings of chiles, still common in New Mexico today, were part of the landscape of the region. Another important ingredient in the New Mexican diet, long eaten by native peoples, was the *piñon* (pine nut), gathered each year from *piñon* trees. Whole families traveled each fall to the hillsides, placing blankets beneath the trees and shaking them until the pine cones fell to the ground and the resinous nuts could be extracted.[14]

Both Hispanos and Pueblo Indians ate tortillas at every meal. Usually made of corn, the tortilla was New Mexicans' daily bread. It was often paired with a stew made of meat, likely mutton or goat rather than beef, and beans, vegetables, and the ever-present chile. *Posole* (boiled corn stew), made a frequent meal, and *torrejas* (egg fritters) replaced meat during Lent. For celebrations, New Mexicans ended the meal with a variety of sweets, such as *panocha* or *bizcochitos*. Susan Magoffin described a mouth-watering spiced boiled milk dish that ended one of her meals in the region.[15]

Not until the early twentieth century did canning became common in the region, in large part through the efforts of the Agricultural Extension Service of the U.S. Department of Agriculture. Before then, following native custom, foods were preserved by drying. Not only chiles, but corn, squashes, fruit, and meat were hung or placed out in the dry New Mexican sun and stored in *dispensas* (storage rooms) for use throughout the year.

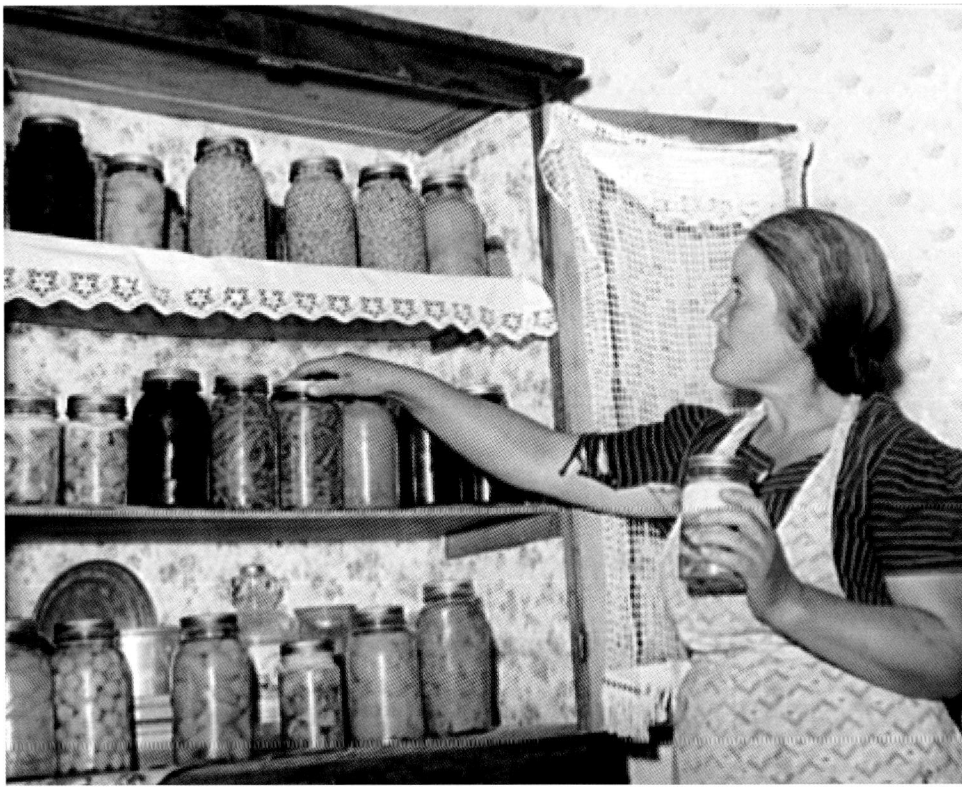

In the nineteenth century Hispanic women preserved food by hanging it to dry and storing it in rooms like the one on the far right, known as a *dispensa*, at El Rancho de las Golondrinas. Not until the twentieth century did New Mexican women start routinely canning their produce.

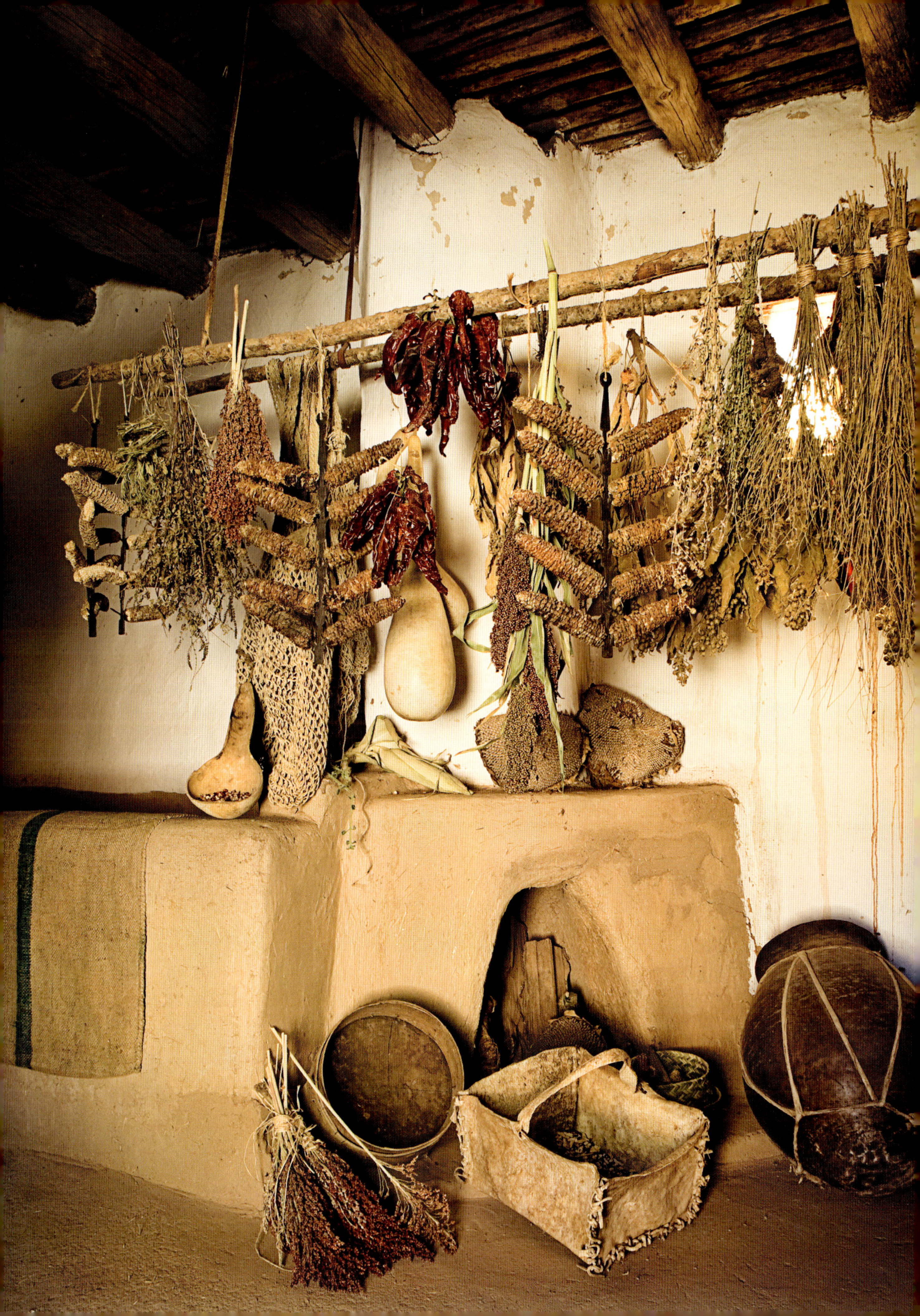

## United States Enters New Mexico

With the opening of the Santa Fe Trail, Americans slowly filtered into the region, some settling, more traveling to and fro with wagon loads of trade goods. The arrival of American soldiers during the Mexican-American War of 1846–48 created a new market for Hispanos, who supplied meat and grain to the army posts.[16] After the war, the region became a U.S. territory and attracted increasing numbers of Anglo-Americans, most of whom settled as farmers and created competition for scarce arable land.

Americans who traveled to the region commented on the food—the tortillas, and, of course, the chiles. Of his initial experience with chile, William Emory wrote, "The first mouthful brought the tears trickling down my cheeks, very much to the amusement of the spectators with their leather-lined throats."[17] Susan Magoffin wrote that the family she and her husband dined with soon after their arrival in the region made roasted corn and a fried egg for her when she was unable to eat the main course of *chile verde*.[18] But after a few months in the area, Magoffin raved about the food: "I shall have to make me a recipe book, to take home, the cooking in every thing is entirely different from ours, and some, indeed all of their dishes are so fine 'twould be a shame not to let my friends have a taste of them too."[19]

> That stove was the light of my eyes and the joy of my heart. It was made like two stair-steps. Each step was used for cooking. The oven heated nicely and many a savory roast did I bake in it. That stove was the envy of all my neighbors.
>
> Marian Russell, Tecolote, New Mexico, 1866.

Few cookstoves were available before the arrival of the train in New Mexico in 1879.

Women who moved from the States into the region and set up house with their husbands faced numerous challenges. Most came from middle-class backgrounds and were accustomed to kitchens with typical Victorian amenities—increasingly available gadgetry and of course, a cookstove. In 1851 Katie Bowen was one of the fortunate few who brought a cookstove with her when she moved from Maine with her soldier husband. At first she had no luck finding anyone who could set it up correctly. She complained, "brought a stove with us but have never been able to make it draw well." After months cooking in the small New Mexican fireplace in her new home, Bowen was delighted when her workmen finally got the stove properly installed. "Now [I] am independent for it works to a charm."[20] That same year, Harriett Shaw, the wife of a Baptist missionary, also moved to New Mexico. While she hoped to buy a cookstove, even more pressing was the need for cooking implements. Shaw noted that there were so few utensils "you can't cook but one thing at a time."[21] Even when American-made kitchen items were available, they were expensive. In 1869, after having to spend the exorbitant amount of $90 for a medium-sized cookstove, Sarah Wetter explained: "every article of merchandise here are extravagantly high. It is the transportation on the plains that makes them so."[22]

The arrival of the railroad in 1879 transformed Anglo and Hispanic households alike as prices dropped and the number of available consumer goods multiplied. Most Anglo-American women were quick to purchase utensils and cookstoves to make their kitchens as similar as possible to the ones they had left behind. Hispanic women took longer to adopt the new technology. At first, only wealthy Hispanos could afford cookstoves, but by the end of the nineteenth century more and more Hispanic families were installing them. In rural areas, however, it took far longer for cookstoves to become commonplace. A U.S. Department of Agriculture study written in 1897 noted that "in the families of people in moderate circumstances living in towns the stove and the table make their appearance." In the more remote countryside, "in the case of poorer class of Mexicans, one family, often large, usually occupies but a single room of less than 20 by 30 feet, . . . the cooking is done in an open fireplace, usually located in one corner of the room."[23]

It took even longer for cookstoves to become commonplace in the Pueblo villages. Even so, by 1902 anthropologist Matilda Coxe Stevenson, who had been studying the Zuni since 1879, noted that she had seen a number of changes among the tribe, including more and more families using stoves for heating and cooking. Perhaps more predictably, when Zuni women could afford to purchase flour, they no longer ground their own wheat. Stevenson wrote with regret, "Yeast powder bread baked in the stove is fast taking the place of bread prepared in the native manner."[24] Stevenson also noted that by this time Zunis were more

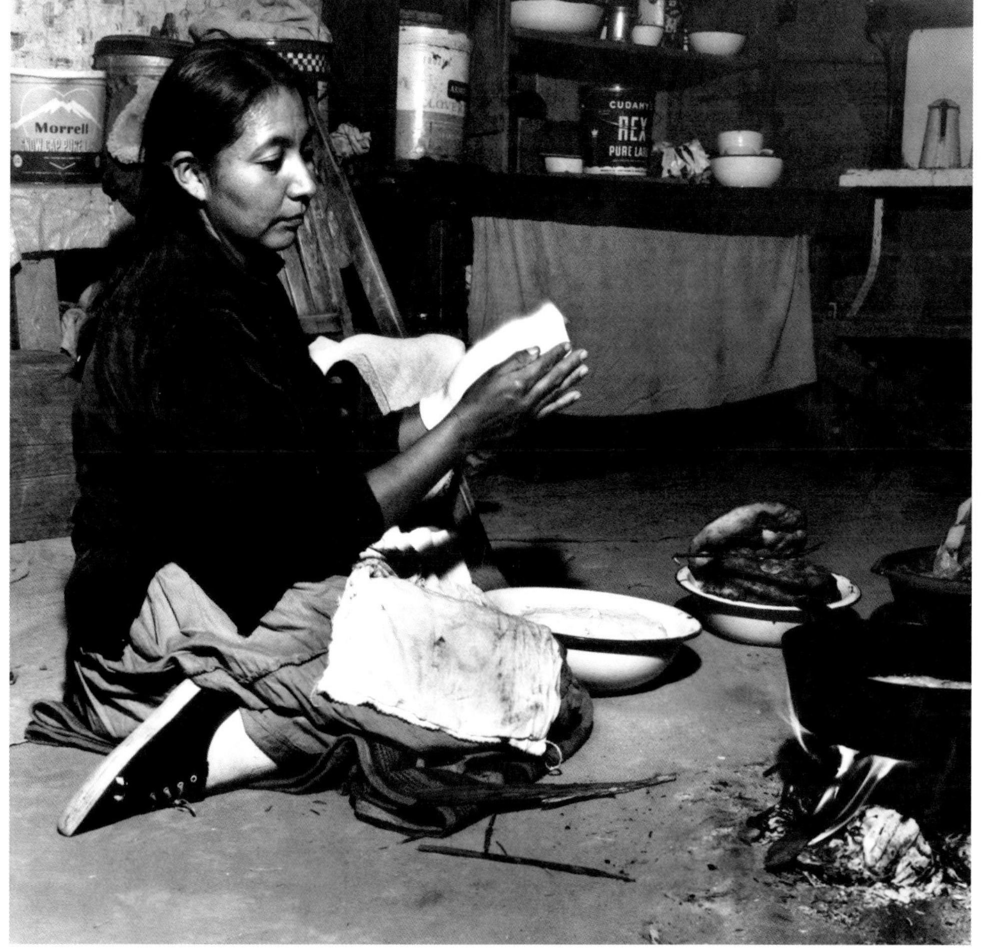


A people accustomed to working and eating on the floor saw little need for the raised work surfaces of Hispanic and Anglo kitchens and adopted them slowly. Here a Navajo woman, photographed around 1950, cooks and prepares food on the floor. The higher surfaces in her kitchen are used principally for storage.

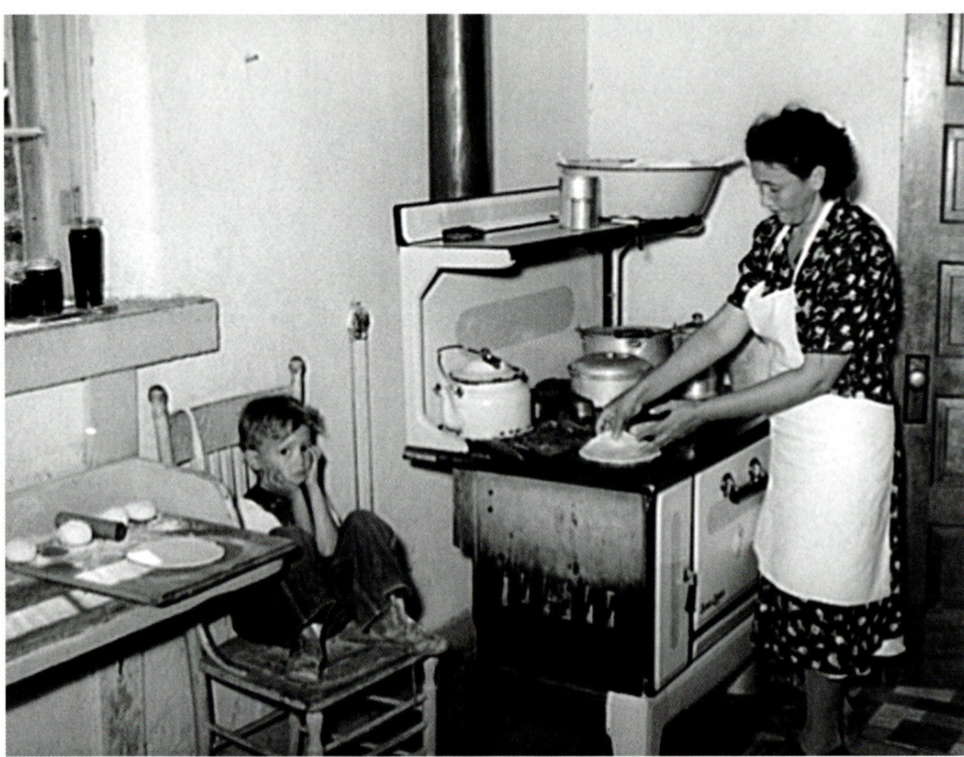

It took a long time for Hispanic women to adopt the cookstove, but once they did they quickly learned how to use it to make traditional New Mexican foods. In 1939 Ofelia Sandoval made tortillas while her son José Benito watched.

inclined to purchase manufactured ceramics than to make their own, and the result was a significant loss of skill, making the pottery they now produced suitable only for the tourist market.[25]

Yet even as native peoples adopted more and more commercially available American goods, they retained their traditional way of working and living with few pieces of furniture. In his study of Zuni and Hopi tribes, published in 1891, Victor Mindeleff noted that most natives made use of a raised bench around the edges of their rooms, perhaps supplemented only by a few stools: "Even the influence of the Americans has as yet failed to bring about the use of tables or bedsteads among the pueblo Indians. The floor answers all purposes of both these useful articles of furniture. The food dishes are placed directly upon it at meal times, and at night, blankets, rugs, and sheep skins that form the bed are spread upon it."[26]

> The recipes in *Historic Cookery* are a product of the past and present—an amalgamation of Indian, Spanish, Mexican, and American. They are typically New Mexican.
>
> Fabiola Cabeza de Baca Gilbert, *Historic Cookery*, 1939

Many of the women who began writing cookbooks in the 1930s were writing not only for their own people but also for the burgeoning tourist industry, which was slowly bringing economic growth to the region.

In the Southwest, as in other parts of the country, the early twentieth century saw a revived interest in the region's history and the history of the early (nonnative) settlers. In New Mexico, this meant not only a flowering of interest in Hispanic culture and art but also an increasing pride in the region's unique food heritage. Among the first to document the area's cuisine was an Anglo-American resident of Santa Fe. Alice Stevens Tipton's *The Original New Mexico Cookery* was published by the New Mexico State Land Office in 1916. Before long, Hispanas began to document their culture's food in a series of cookbooks. One was Fabiola

Cabeza de Baca Gilbert, a descendant of the family that owned El Rancho de las Golondrinas. She wrote books in Spanish and English, aiming the Spanish cookbooks for local women and the English ones for the increasing tourist market.[27]

By the 1930s ethnographers began to follow the anthropologists into the region. While the anthropologists had come to record information about the native population, the ethnographers focused instead on villages where Hispanic traditions were still largely intact. What they discovered, perhaps not surprisingly, was the centrality of the kitchen in the lives of Hispanic New Mexicans. At Cañon de Taos, one investigator noted:

> *Even though a house may have more than one entrance, that which passes through the kitchen is the one which is invariably used. It is in the kitchen that the greater part of the social life is spent. Visitors will be asked to sit down in the kitchen, for there the woman of the household spends most of the day preparing food and washing linen. When the men return from work they congregate in the kitchen and sit there talking both before and after the meal.*[28]

Whether formally, through published cookbooks, or informally through gatherings of family and visitors, in New Mexico the kitchen was not only the place where the blending of Mexican, Spanish, and native cultures was apparent in the people, equipment, and food, but the place where these converged to create a unique heritage.

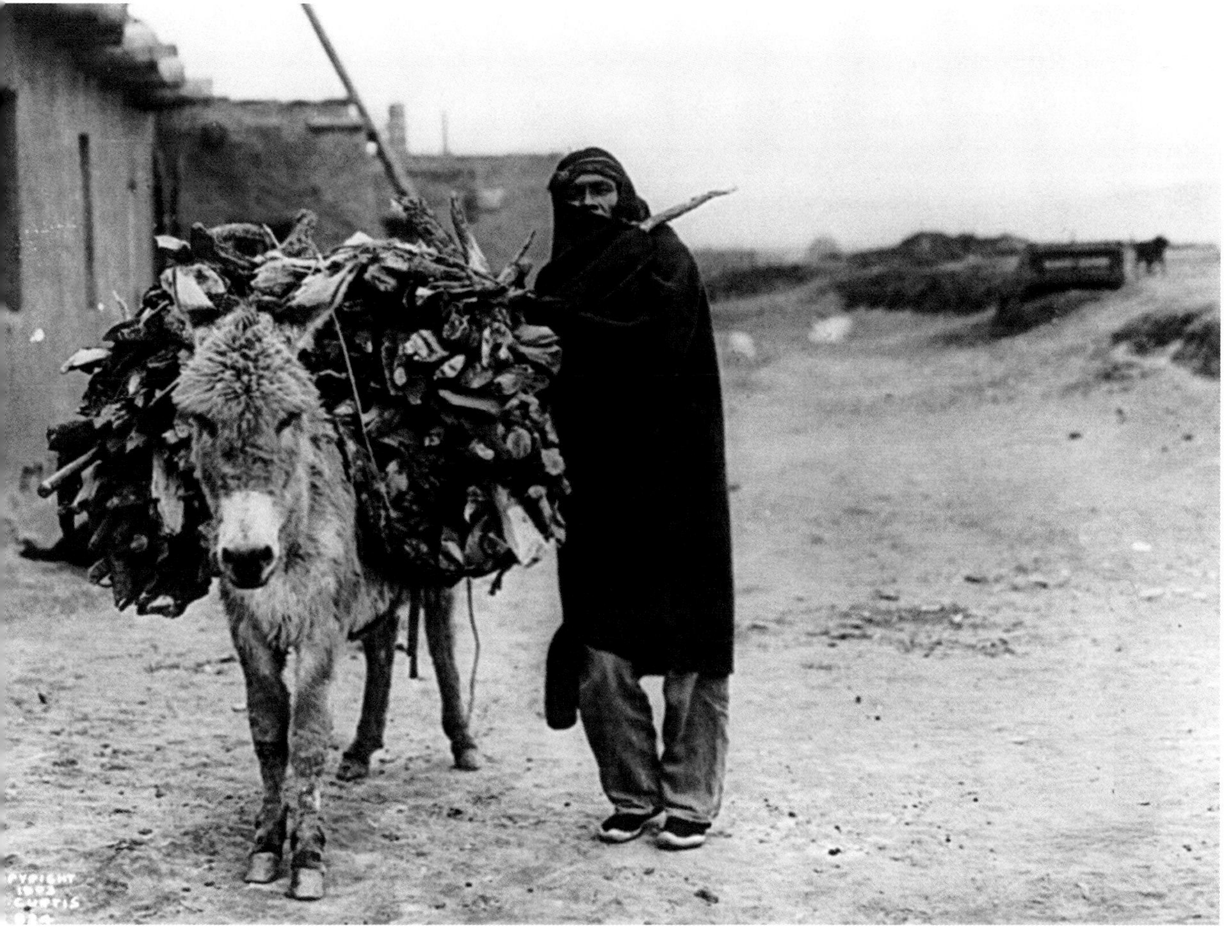

At one time the sight of donkeys or burros laden with firewood was commonplace in New Mexico around both Pueblo and Hispanic settlements. Edward Curtis photographed this fuel carrier in a Zuni village in 1903.

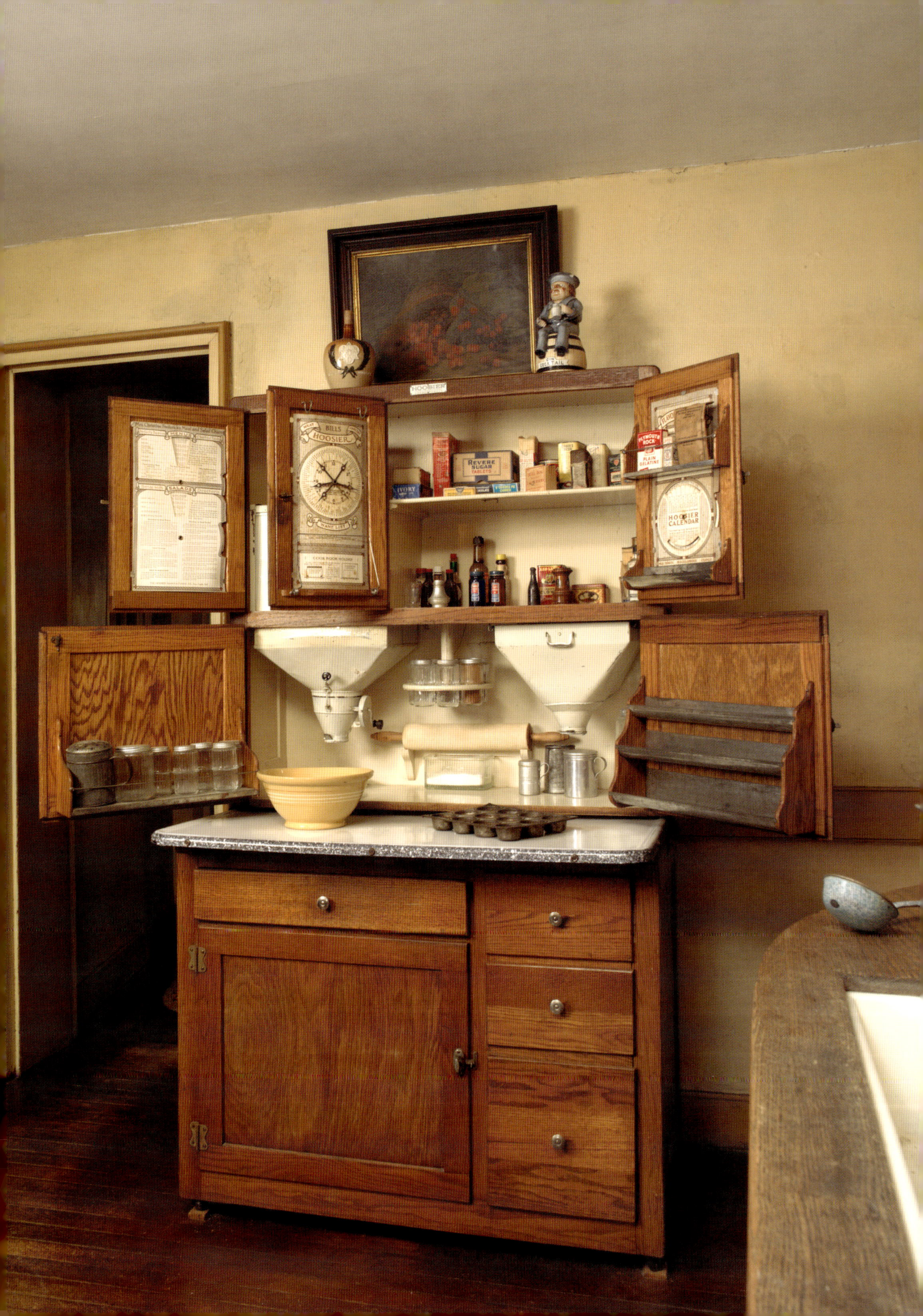
HOOSIER
BILLS
HOOSIER
REVERE
SUGAR
TABLETS
IVORY
PLYMOUTH
ROCK
PLAIN
GELATINE
HOOSIER
CALENDAR

# TOWARD THE MODERN KITCHEN

## {1890–1945}

### *Mollie Tucker's Hoosier Cabinet*

Mollie Tucker of Wiscasset, Maine, was no stranger to the kitchen.[1] Born in 1841, she began married life at the age of sixteen in relative comfort. However, when the family's fortunes dwindled, she resorted to various moneymaking schemes in order to stay in her home, known as Castle Tucker. She took in boarders and sold the pickles and preserves she made on her giant hotel range.[2]

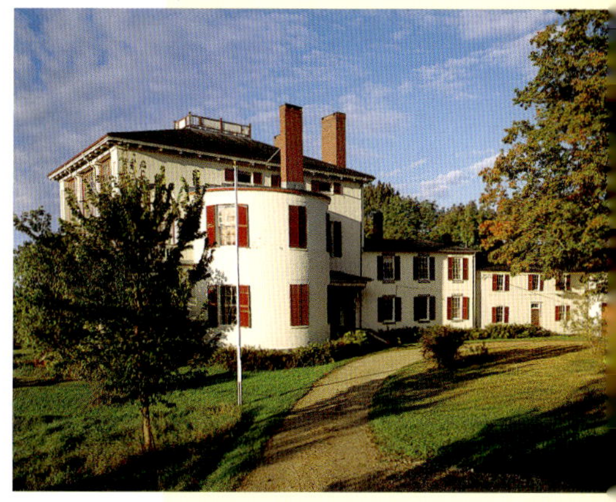

Castle Tucker, built in 1807, was extensively remodeled by Richard and Mollie Tucker when they purchased the home in 1858.

In 1906, having abandoned the boardinghouse idea, Mollie replaced the range with a smaller, more practical and fuel-efficient Empire Crawford cast-iron stove. A dramatic improvement came in 1915, when the house was equipped with electricity. It was then possible to have better lighting as well as small appliances, such as the electric toaster and waffle iron that had been billed as "modern servants."[3] At about the same time, the Tuckers tapped into the town water supply. All of these changes made the kitchen both more efficient and convenient. In 1921 Mollie acquired a new piece of furniture—a kitchen cabinet—that changed the way she had worked in the kitchen for more than sixty years. Her daughter Jane wrote to her brother, "All our money went into [the] kitchen cabinet and Ma wonders now how we ever got on without it—cuts all her work in half."[4]

Made by the Hoosier Manufacturing Company of New Castle, Indiana, the oak cabinet was fitted out for food preparation and storage with a flour sifter, a revolving spice rack and jars, cupboards, drawers, and a white enamel counter. The upper cabinet doors opened to reveal a cookbook holder, perpetual calendar, patented grocery list wheel with movable arrows, and "Mrs. Christine Frederick's Meal and Salad Charts," complete with nutrition information.

The Tuckers' kitchen cabinet was made by the Hoosier Manufacturing Company. Designed for efficiency, it featured a flour sifter, spice jar racks, and a sliding work surface.

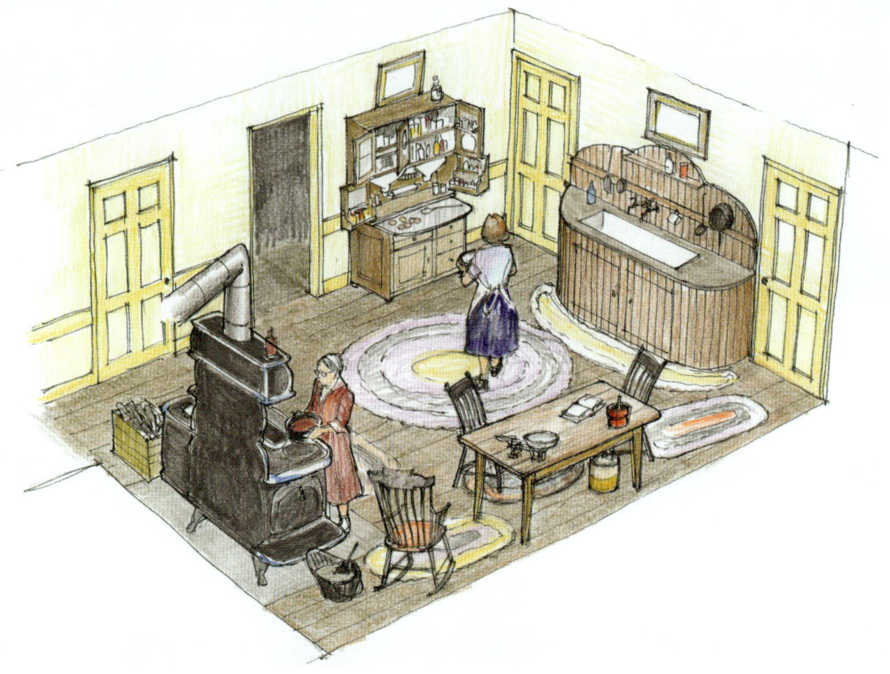

By 1921 the Tucker kitchen in Wiscasset, Maine, was old fashioned, but the addition of a new Hoosier cabinet improved its efficiency without costly renovations. That winter, eighty-year-old Mollie Tucker and her daughter Jane spent much of their time in the kitchen, closing off most of their large house to conserve heat.

The Hoosier cabinet appeared at the turn of the twentieth century and soon became an emblem of the mass-marketed efficient kitchen. In a competitive field, the Hoosier was the most recognized brand; two million cabinets were in use by 1920.[5] At a time when few households could afford servants, the Hoosier was advertised as, "the kitchen cabinet that saves miles of steps." It combined the traditional roles of the food pantry, tool cupboard, and work table. At first Mollie was skeptical, but Jane persisted, "I had a struggle to make her use all the things—but now she enjoys it all." The cabinet was particularly suited to eighty-year-old Mollie's needs. Jane claimed, "There is a wonderful saving of time & strength trotting back and forth for things." She raved about the metal-lined compartments: "The drawers keep the grains so sweet & dry, we notice the difference at once." The counter raised the standards of sanitation in the Tucker kitchen, "the porcelain table to mix & knead on seems so much healthier than the old board—it got mouldy & sour—for Ma couldn't keep it as clean as she used to—this she washes up in a second—like a dish." According to Jane, the cabinet turned kitchen work into child's play, "It's like playing house."[6]

## Hoosier Saves Steps

In it every staple food, every utensil, every movable adjunct to the preparation of meals—and the cleaning up after them—finds its logical place. Each is easy to get at—without walking, reaching, or stooping.

Hoosier Manufacturing Company advertisement, *The Saturday Evening Post*, September 11, 1920

The Hoosier Manufacturing Company advertised their cabinet aggressively, touting the years of scientific study that went into its design and the proclamations of more than two million users. In this ad, they describe the benefits of their cabinet and add that it is designed, "For the Good of All Womankind."

As advances in science and technology were transforming America, a new model of home life began to emerge, and kitchens like the Tuckers' were affected to varying degrees. Jane's letter about the Hoosier cabinet also mentioned that she had been pickling and smoking bacon and hams and had made forty pounds of sausage—certainly not the work of the modern woman in the magazine ads. But in kitchens across the United States, the Hoosier cabinet was a bridge between the old kitchen, with separate pantries, closets, and tables, and the modern kitchen, with integrated cabinets, counters, sink, stove, and refrigerator, which by the middle of the twentieth century had become the norm.

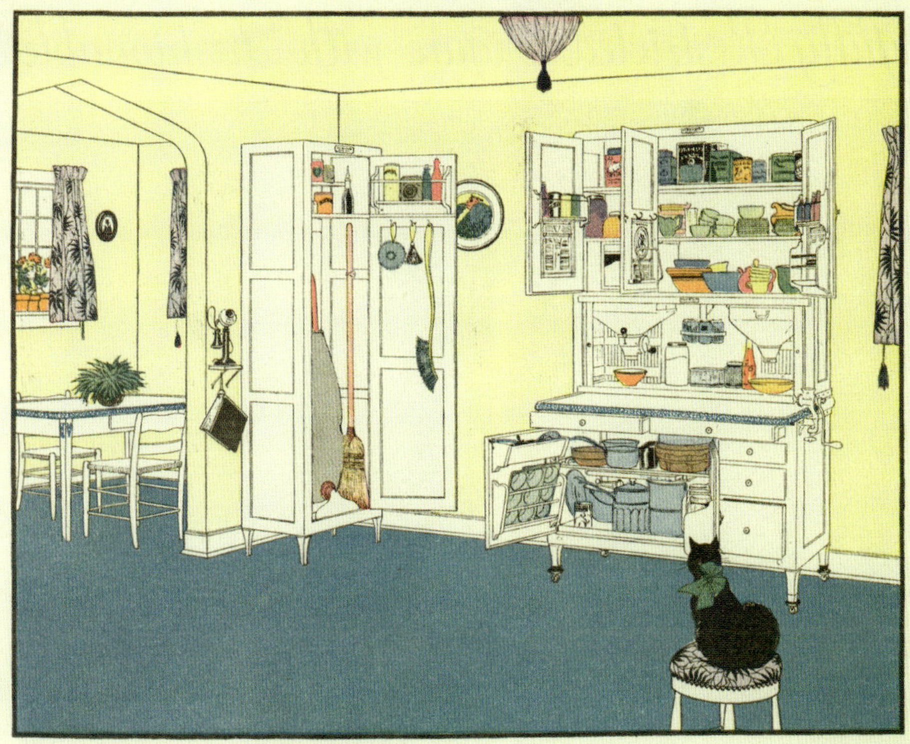



# *YOUR KITCHEN!*—FURNISHED AS COMPLETELY AND TASTEFULLY AS ANY OTHER ROOM

## —*how you can have it so with little trouble and expense*

BY LOIS M. WYSE, DIRECTOR HOOSIER TEST KITCHENS

K a home-loving woman what kind of a kitchen she would like and she will tell you with eager ısiasm of a room that's dainty, fresh, invit- where things shine immaculately clean and a of color cheers; a room which careful fur- ng has made well-ordered and convenient— sy, restful place to work!

room to dream about? To have some day— *ps?* Not at all! You can have just such a en—*now!*

### *A completely furnished kitchen —with Hoosier Kitchen Equipment*

no more planning and expense than you d ordinarily put into it, you can a kitchen furnished as com- ly and tastefully as any other in your home.

the test kitchens of the Hoosier ufacturing Company, domestic ce experts have designed equip- to make your kitchen the very you've dreamed of!

ie center of Hoosier equipment piece of furniture without which itchen can be completely modern e Hoosier Cabinet! Scientific ning in every least detail has e the Hoosier the most efficient ing center that can possibly be sed—with every imaginable facil- o make it a perfect working unit.

provide the extra storage space h every kitchen needs in addition to that afforded in the cabinet itself, Hoosier movable units in single and double size have been designed.

You may use these units as an extension of your cabinet on either side or in other suitable places in the room. But whatever the arrangement of Hoosier Cabinet and units, you have a charmingly furnished room, as uniform as if designed and built to your own special order—and so much more efficient and complete!

Another attractive feature of Hoosier Kitchen Equipment is the Breakfast Set of table and chairs. It is very dainty in white enamel, decorated with blue; yet is sturdy enough for practical needs. The table has a white porcelain-iron top; the chairs have cane seats.

HOOSIER DOUBLE CABINET UNIT—*provides extra storage space which every kitchen needs for utensils, dishes and food supplies. Very convenient for a bathroom cupboard. Also furnished as a single unit*

### *For a* COMPLETE KITCHEN *whether new or old*

Is your kitchen old and somewhat inconvenient, lacking the modern touch? You do not need to wait for new equipment. You can have a Hoosier kitchen *now*, with no fuss of remodeling and very little expense—surprisingly little for the completeness of it!

And do you know that in that new house you can have a Hoosier equipped kitchen, and it will be much more complete and handsome than with equipment of your own devising and building? Ask your architect to figure on Hoosier equipment.

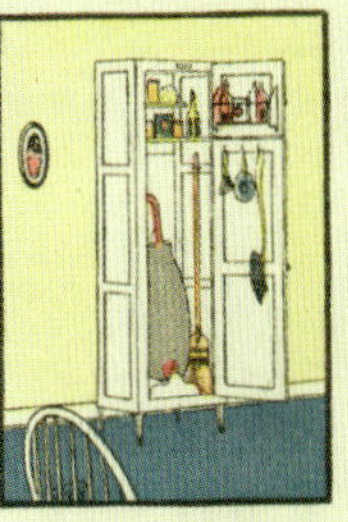

HOOSIER SINGLE CABINET UNIT—*Fitted to hold brooms, mops, vacuum, brushes and a score of little cleaning day necessities. May also be had as a double unit—in combination with the shelf unit*

### *Free to you! Our new book "Planning the modern kitchen"*

We have just published a new book on modern kitchens, giving plans and ideas which will make your own kitchen a more inviting, convenient room. This book is free to every woman who is interested. We hope you will send for it and also visit the Hoosier store in your town to see the complete Hoosier equipment. Fill out the coupon and we will mail book promptly.

The Hoosier Manufacturing Company
524 Leslie Street Newcastle, Indiana

The Hoosier Manufacturing Co.,
524 Leslie Street, Newcastle, Indiana.
British Address: Ideal Furniture Equipment,
No. 9 Preston St., Liverpool.
Please send me, free, your new booklet: "Planning the Modern Kitchen."

*Name*________________
*Address*________________
*City*________ *State*________

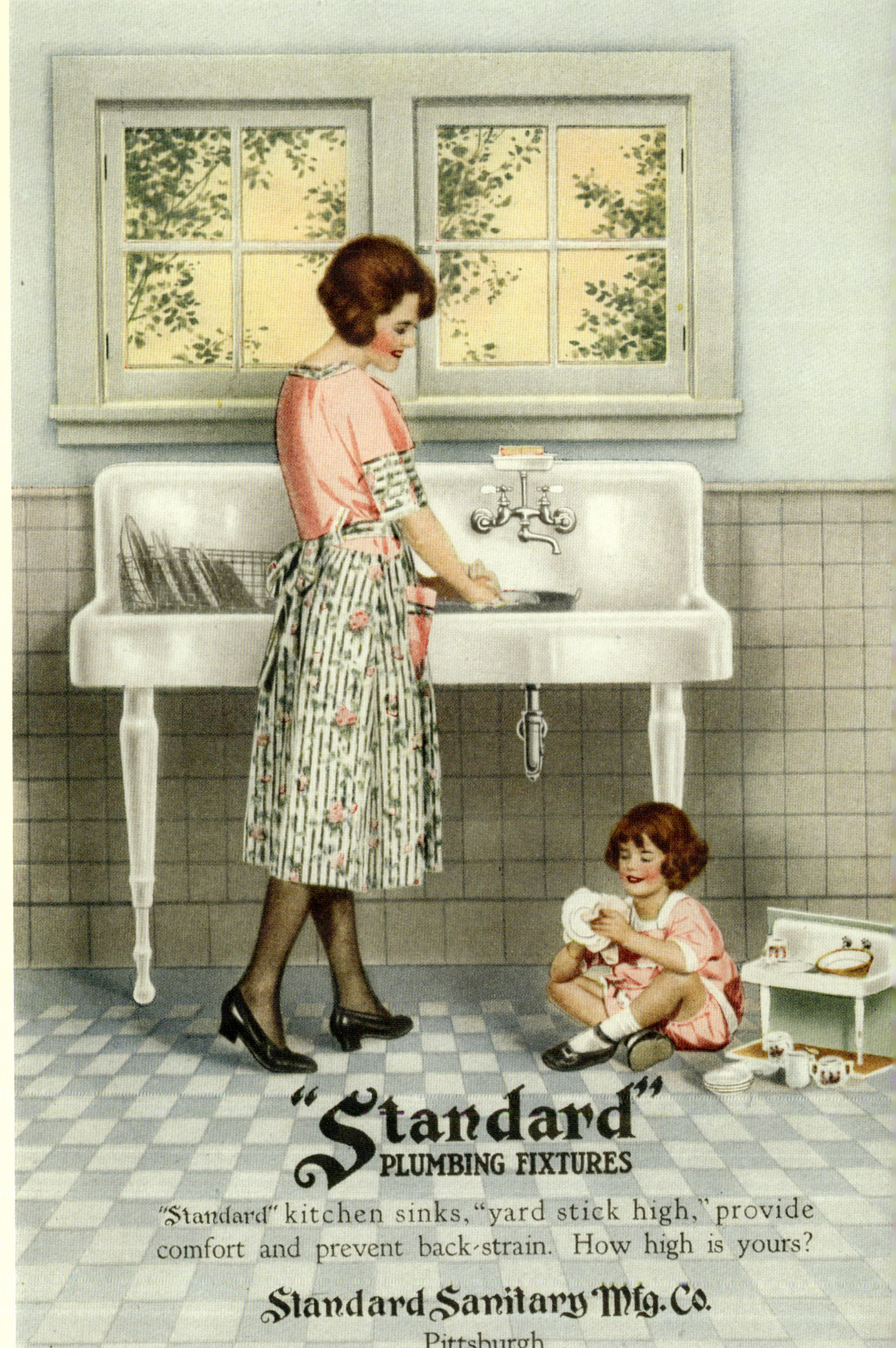


Companies such as this one advertised products that were both convenient and sanitary and appealed to mothers' concerns about hygiene and the health of their families. The kitchen in this 1922 image is depicted as clean enough for a child (and future homemaker) to play with her own toy sink on the floor.

## *Women's Work*

The number of servants in the United States dropped dramatically in the first decades of the twentieth century.[7] For many African American women, live-in or hourly domestic service continued to be the only opportunity for employment. Day work held several advantages over live-in service, including greater freedom and personal privacy. One former servant, Dolethia Otis of Washington, D.C., remembered: "The living-in jobs just kept you running; never stopped. Day or night . . . never a minute's peace. But when I went out days on my jobs, I'd get my work done and be gone . . . that's it. This work had a' end."[8]

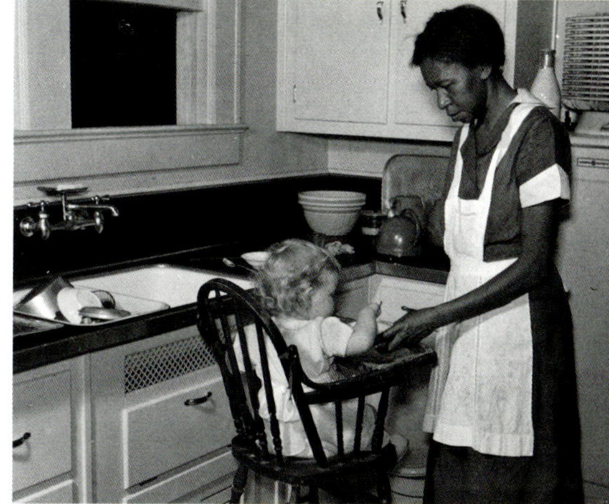

Photographed in the kitchen of her employer in Atlanta, Georgia, in 1939, this uniformed woman likely filled the roles of maid, cook, and nanny.

At the same time that fewer servants were available, middle-class kitchens became more automated, with running water, electric and gas fixtures and appliances, and better refrigeration. Housework was no longer portrayed in popular culture as a chore but as exacting work best done by a loving mother at home, giving new meaning to the traditional role of the housewife. While women were considered to be best suited to the task, they were not assumed to know much about food science or sanitation. They had to be trained—an attempt to elevate the status of this unpaid work by treating it as a skilled job. The one assumption that was rarely challenged was that housework was women's work, and no number of laborsaving devices relieved its emotional weight.[9] Furthermore, these tools created still more work by increasing expectations. According to the *Rural New Yorker* in 1900, "So many labor-saving devices have been common that woman's work should now be simpler, but with these improvements, our standard of comfort has been so greatly raised that the present-day housewife seems more overworked."[10] The modern kitchen may have made some tasks less physically demanding, but women worked just as many hours.[11]

### Monte Carlo Salad

Remove pulp from four large grape fruits, and drain. Add an equal quantity of finely cut celery, and apple cut in small pieces. Moisten with Mayonnaise, pile on a shallow salad dish, arrange around a border of lettuce leaves, and mask with Mayonnaise. Outline, using green Mayonnaise, four oblongs to represent playing cards, and denote spots on cards by canned pimentoes or truffles; pimentoes cut in shapes of hearts and diamonds, truffles cut in shapes of spades and clubs. Garnish with cold cooked carrot and turnip, shaped with a small round cutter to suggest gold and silver coin.

Fannie Farmer, *The Boston Cooking-School Cookbook*, 1911

Cookbooks encouraged women to use their creativity to disguise wholesome foods under a blanket of mayonnaise or white sauce and a layer of artful garnishes.

## The Efficient Kitchen

The ideal middle-class kitchen promoted by writers and advertisers was small (about nine by twelve feet) and arranged to maximize the housewife's time and energy. In 1915 Elna Harwood Wharton pointed out to *McCall's* readers that "we have to prepare and eat three meals a day, three hundred and sixty-five days a year; one thousand and ninety-five times we handle those dishes twice. Does it not seem important to get this enormous amount of work done with the fewest motions of either feet or hands?"[12] She recommended the thoughtful placement of stove, sink, work table, icebox, and cupboards, as well as adjusting the work surface to suit the height of the cook. Writing for *House Beautiful*, Isabel McDougall described the ideal kitchen of a woman of "slender means": "What she requires is a small, spotless space, conveniently planned, with the tools of her occupation all in easy reach—something on the lines of a Pullman-car kitchen, or a yacht's galley, or a laboratory—a place planned merely for one kind of work, which she leaves when that kind of work is done."[13]

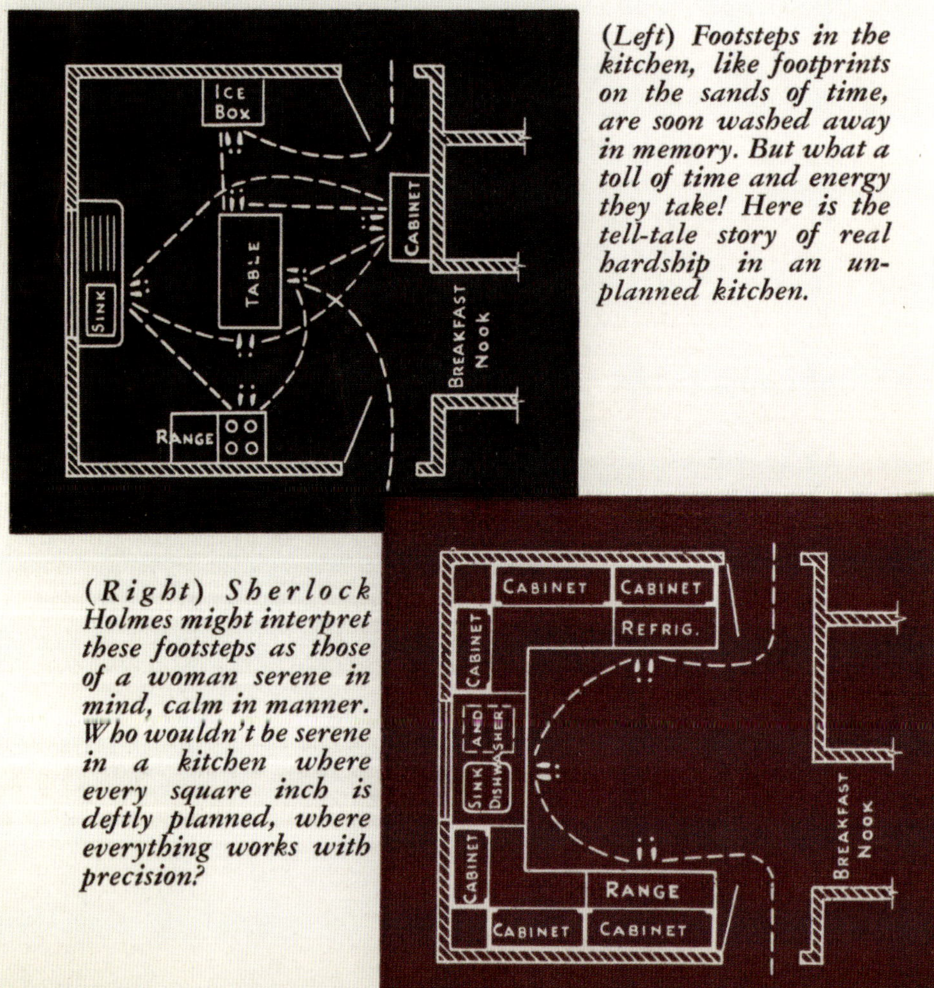


Telling women how many steps they wasted in poorly planned kitchens was a theme in advertising. Some women even used pedometers to test the efficiency of their work habits.

## *Life on the Farm*

In the first part of the twentieth century, some of the least modern households were in rural areas. Farm families were often isolated and lacked a steady income. Many were devastated by the effects of the Dust Bowl and the Great Depression. The kitchens were often large, busy rooms used for everything from family meals, to bathing, to bottle-feeding animals. Any cash that the farm generated was usually directed back into production rather than into the household, giving women fewer laborsaving conveniences than their urban and suburban peers. Farm women worked hard to care for their large households. Rubie Gillion of Michigan recalled, "I was one of seven [children], and there was always a hired girl in the house, and my grandmother lived with us in the winter, and a couple of hired men. So it made about fourteen at the table three times a day. You can imagine the amount of cooking that went on."[14]

Despite the rural electrification programs of the New Deal, by 1940 only a third of farm households were electrified.[15] Life without electricity more closely followed the seasons.

Even residents of the barnyard might seek the warmth of the stove, as did these piglets in Norfolk, Connecticut.

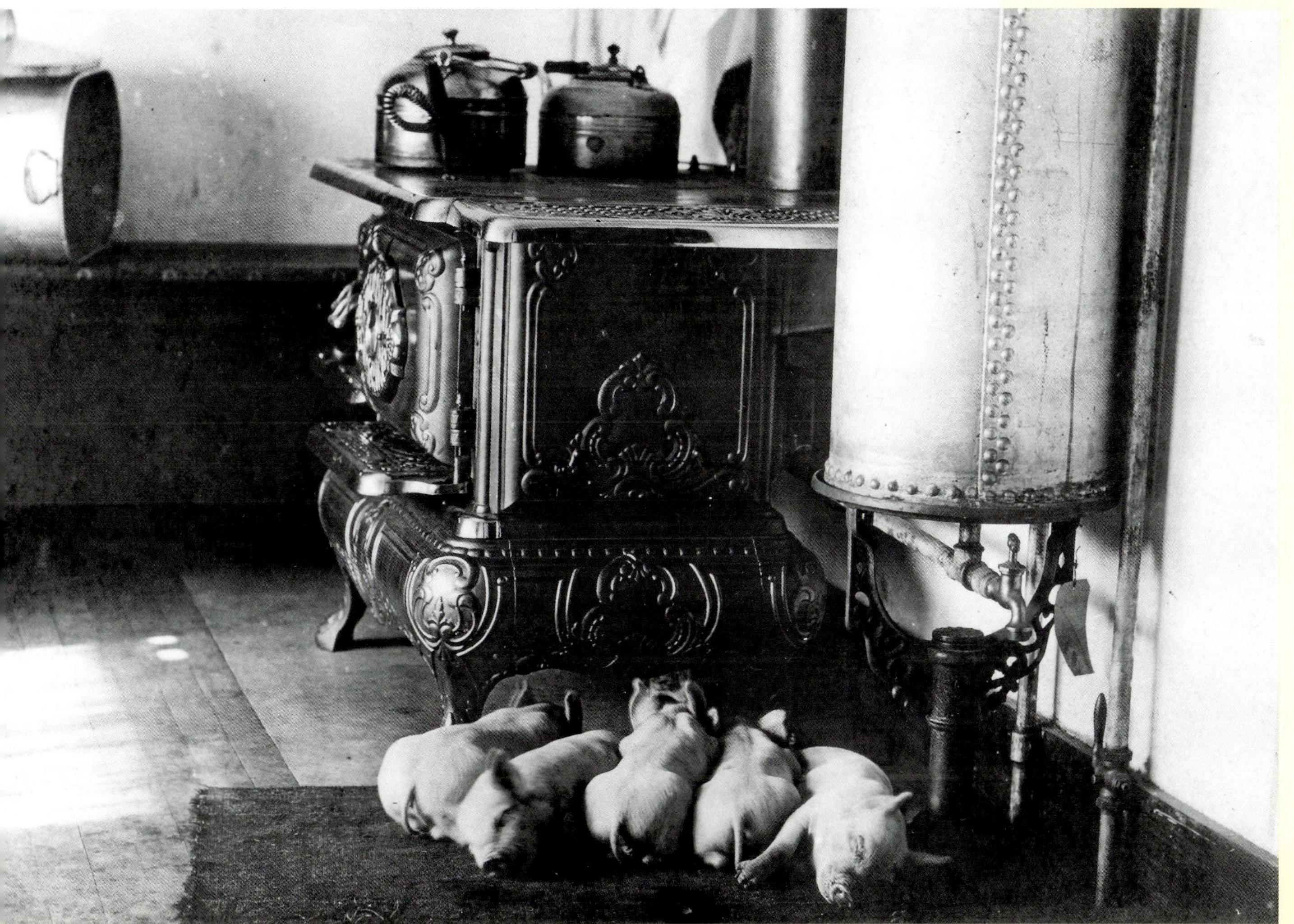

Many farm families set up "summer kitchens," moving the cookstove into the detached kitchen in late spring to keep insects, the heat of cooking, and messy, steamy chores like canning out of the house. Because iceboxes were not practical for families who lived far from a source of ice, springhouses and wells kept foods cool. Some produce—potatoes and apples, for instance—was buried or stored below ground in cellars; other foods had to be processed or consumed quickly. Women endured long hours of tedious work to process cream before it spoiled. Dorothy Personette of Oregon was optimistic: "With the dasher churn, I've counted up to a thousand strokes it took to bring butter. But you didn't think about that. You thought of poetry, or you tried to read, but you kept the old dasher going." Opal Becker of Indiana was despondent: "I sat there and I'd churn and cry, then I'd churn, then I'd cry." [16] Carrying water from cisterns, wells, and springs for cooking, cleaning, bathing, and gardening, as well as drinking for both people and animals was an arduous task that often fell to women. As late as 1945 three out of five farm households did not have a sink with a drain; any water carried in had to be carried out.[17]

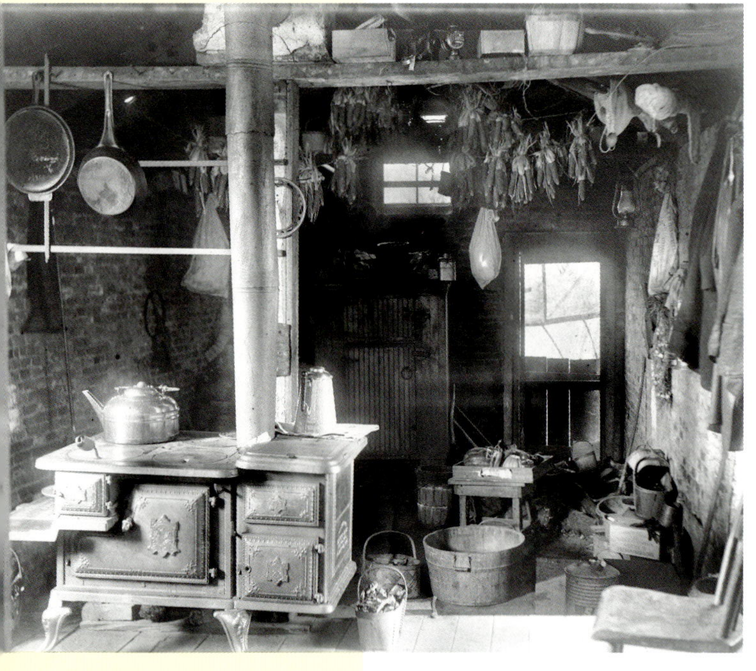

The Turville family of Wisconsin kept their farmhouse cool by removing the cookstove to the summer kitchen during the hottest months of the year.

Throughout the year, children rose early in the morning to help with the chores. Audrey Blackburn of Posey County, Indiana, remembered, "We girls always had to do the dishes and the kitchen work. That was just understood."[18] A 1915 study of rural education claimed that daughters were leaving farm life because of hardship: "Sometimes the drudgery of the farm is endured by the mother uncomplainingly, or even contentedly; but the daughter recoils from it with a growing discontent."[19] Historian Eleanor Arnold interviewed farm women and found that while many remembered the hardships, they also believed that laborsaving conveniences led to the deterioration of family values, neighborliness, and the spirit of cooperation.[20]

When prompted by an inquiry by the secretary of agriculture regarding ways that his department could better serve the domestic needs of farm women, many, including this woman from Georgia, described in detail the inconvenience created by inefficient kitchens.

> Women plod along in the same way, doing things as they were done years ago, and the kitchen and pantry show this more than any other place on the farm. The stove sits in one corner, the water bucket in another, the kitchen table in one, and the salt in the other. And the number of miles a woman races around the kitchen and dining room would leave a professional hiker far behind in a journey. But few women design a house. Most of them are not even consulted, and the buildinq qoes up to qive a pleasinq outward appearance or to suit the pocketbook. The shelves are often too high and narrow; the kitchen without a porch, and the steps out of proportion. Until farming folks can see and know things differently work will go on the same.
>
> *Domestic Needs of Farm Women*, 1915

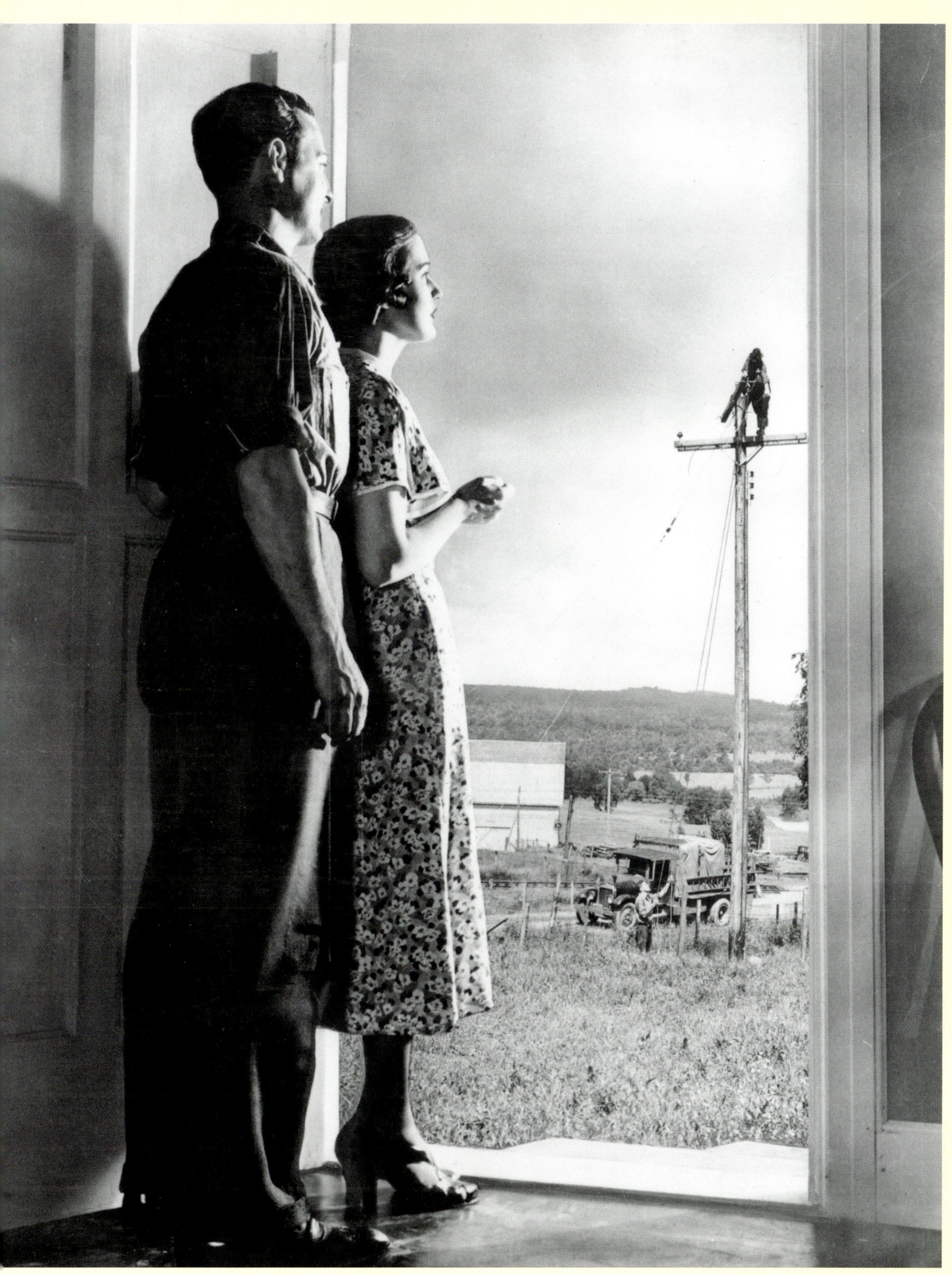

In an iconic image of progress, a young farm couple watches expectantly as power lines are installed along a country road in 1937.

## *Canning Homegrown Produce*

Whereas in urban areas working-class families lacked the land for gardening, the capital to buy large quantities of produce, and the time to can it, in the country canning was a seasonal chore that many women dreaded, "In summer, canning time came in the hottest weather, and bushel baskets emptied slowly. Hands and arms ached; the ever-present steam added to the other miseries. If there be a purgatory, canning in the country kitchen is a suggested pattern."[21]

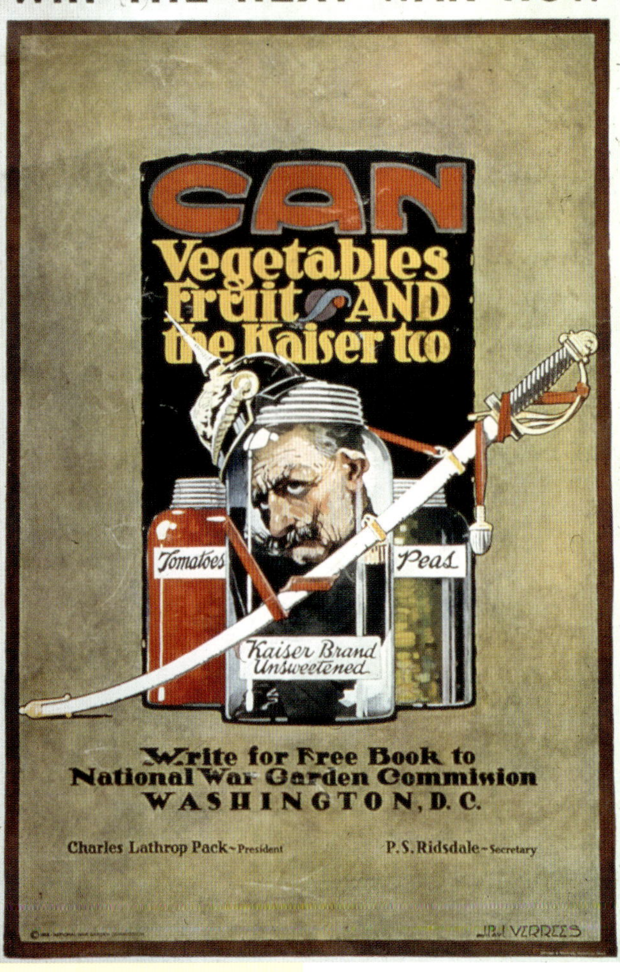


Propaganda posters like this one encouraged families to can foods at home during wartime.

Preserving foods in syrup or brine and packing them in jars and crocks was a centuries-old technique, but in 1858 John Mason patented a glass jar with a screw-on lid made of zinc that could be used at home. The relatively inexpensive, reusable jars were soon widely available. In the late nineteenth and early twentieth centuries, as a result of the increasing affordability of refined sugar and an improved understanding of safe canning methods, many households could can their own fruits and vegetables for use throughout the year. Canning clubs, often led by home economics instructors, were formed to help spread information and share resources.

With the entrance of the United States into World War I in 1917, home canning became a national priority, freeing commercial producers to support the war effort. The National War Garden Commission distributed information on gardening and canning produce. In 1917 almost twenty thousand women and girls in Oklahoma canned an estimated one million quarts of fruit and vegetables under the direction of fifty-three female county agents.[22]

Many women took pride in the results of their hard work. Women who canned in glass took advantage of the medium to show off uniformly sliced produce in harmonious colors. Rovertie Wills of Kentucky recalled, "I'd put [the jars] in colors, from light to dark, just because I liked the way it looked and I liked all my jams and stuff where I could find it."[23] Wills enjoyed showing off her collection to her daughter's boss and her children's teacher. Country fairs were more formal arenas for displaying canned goods, with judges awarding prizes based on such criteria as symmetry, consistency, clarity, color, and texture.[24]

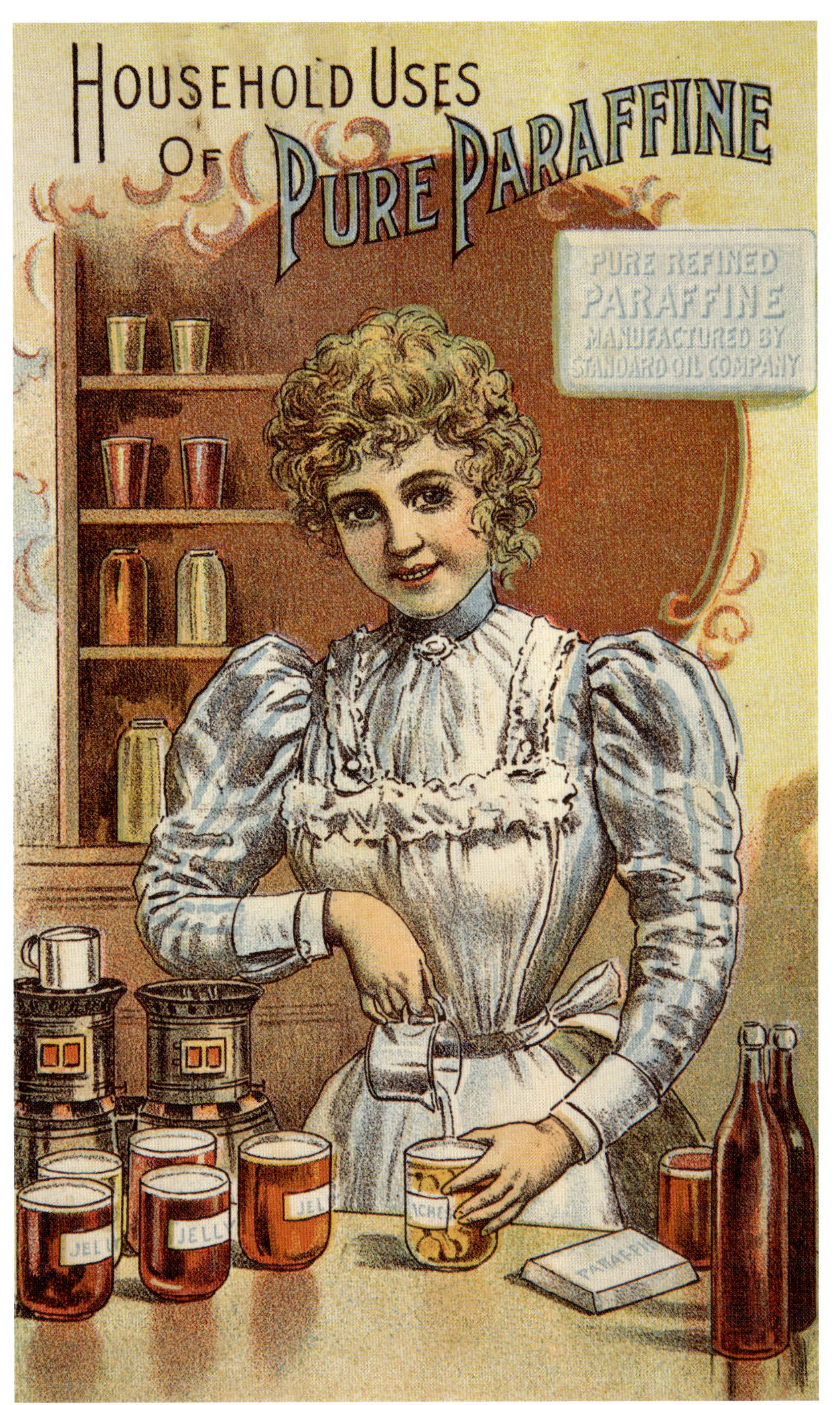


As canning became increasingly popular, industries appealed to home canners by offering products that improved and simplified the sealing of jars.

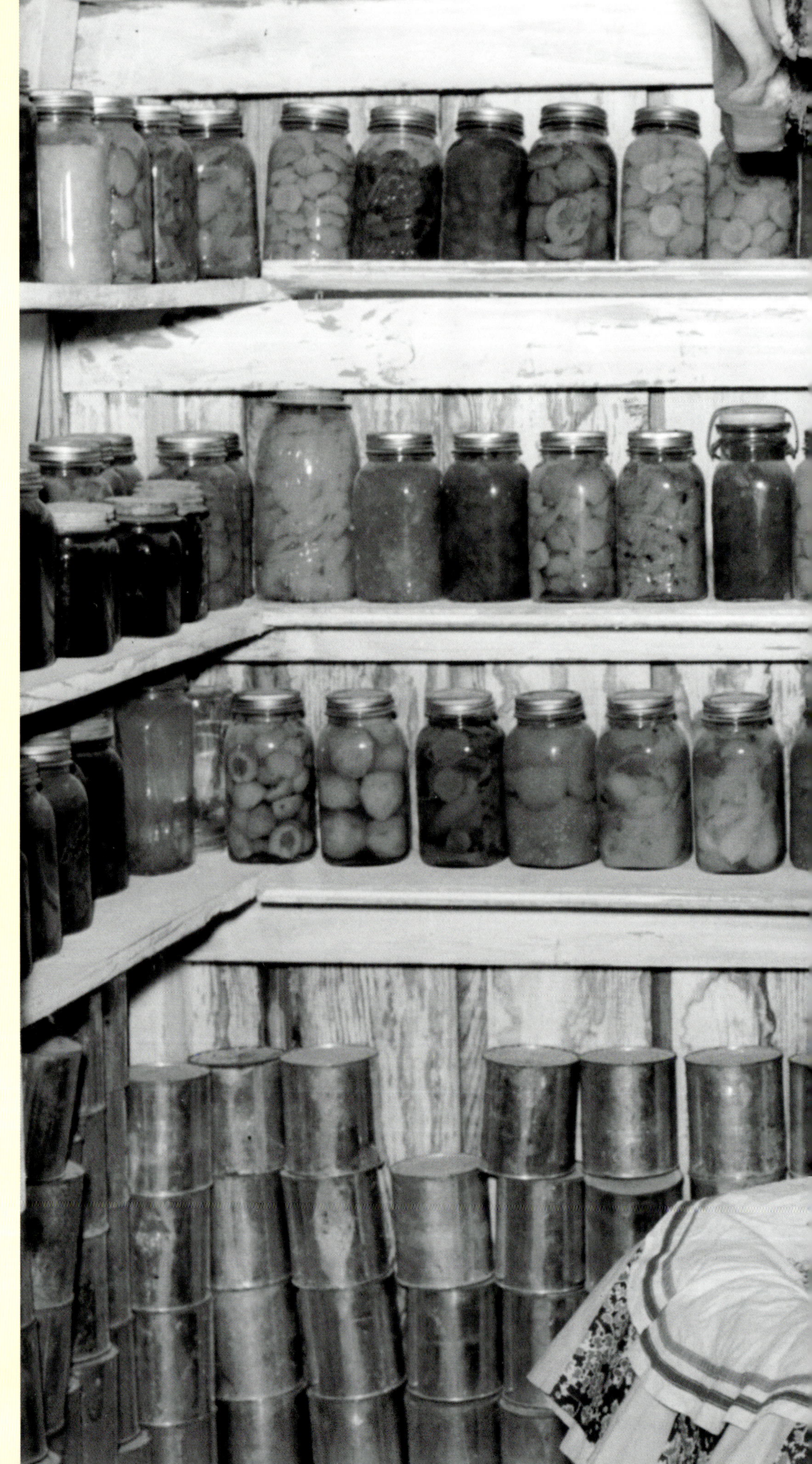

Photographed sorting dried peas in her smokehouse in Gee's Bend, Alabama, in 1939, Jorena Pettway had an impressive store of cans and jars of meat and produce, as well as hams hanging from the ceiling, all a testament to countless hours of hard work.

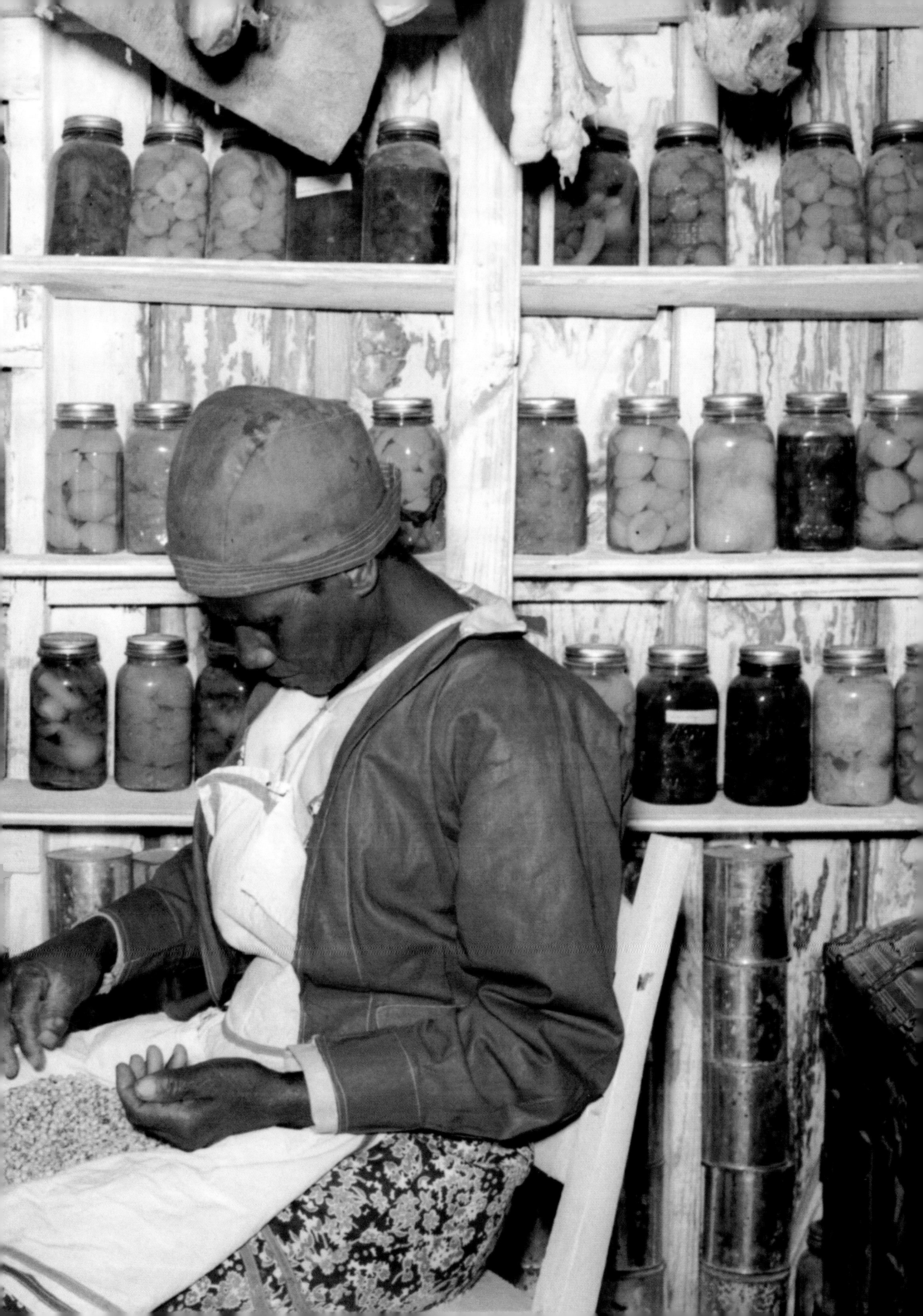

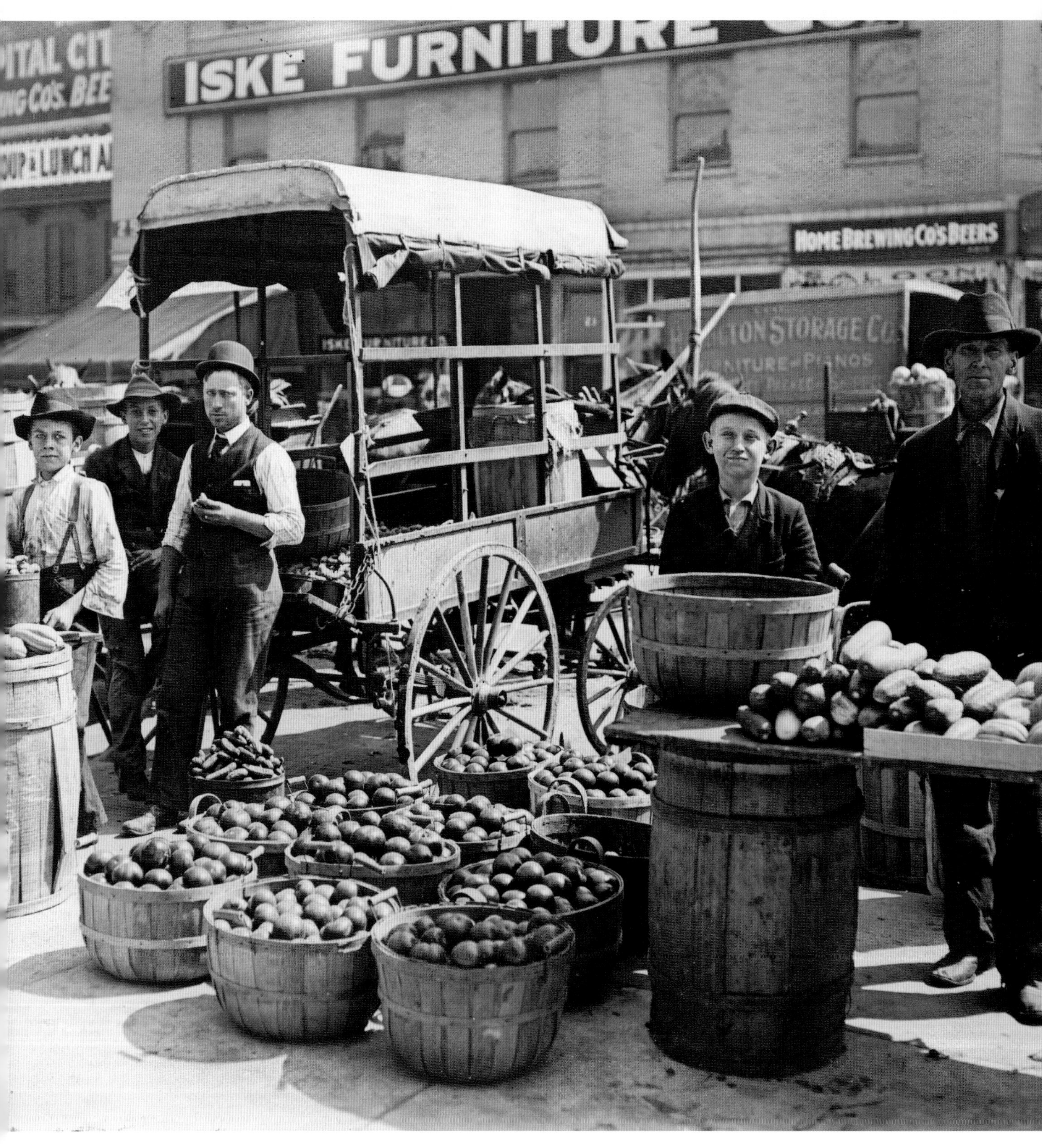


In urban areas, women could shop daily at markets such as this one in Indianapolis, photographed in 1908.

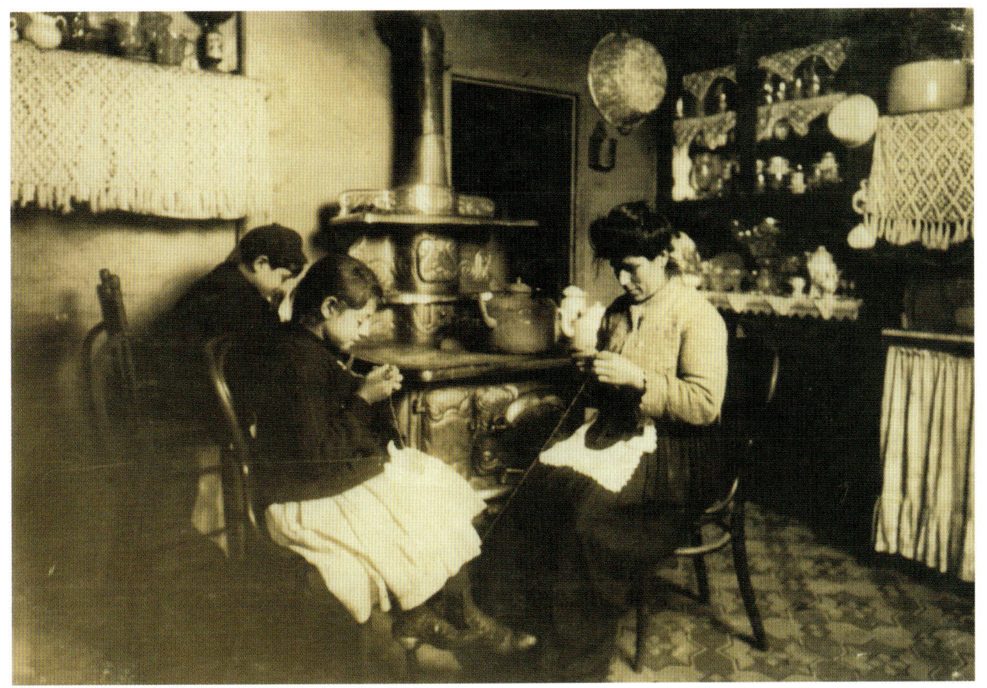

Working-class families sometimes used their kitchens for paid work, such as making hats or rolling cigars. Members of the Fazzino family, photographed in 1912, made Irish lace in the kitchen of their tenement apartment on East 149th Street in New York City.

## Urban Kitchens

The rhythm of housework was different in the city. There, working-class women, many of whom had outside jobs or did piecework at home, often did their marketing daily or bought prepared foods, eliminating some of the need to store, process, and preserve foods at home.[25] In crowded households, which sometimes included boarders, kitchens were used for visiting, bathing, sleeping, and working, leaving little room for preparing food or storing cookware. African Americans, millions of whom had migrated from the rural South to industrial cities such as New York, Detroit, and Chicago, as well as new immigrants faced the worst living conditions: crowded tenements sometimes devoid of running water and drains, with the kitchen stove often serving as the sole source of heat. Middle- and upper-class reformers tried to educate working-class women, especially immigrants, about nutrition, sanitation, and efficiency, but they had mixed success, often due to an imperfect understanding of the practical needs and preferences of the people they were trying to help.

### Matzos Charlotte with Apples

1 matzos, 2 tablespoons raisins, seeded, ¼ lb. suet, chopped fine, 1 tablespoon almonds, blanched and grated, 2 cups apples, sliced fine, ¼ cup sugar, ¼ teaspoon cin namon, 3 yolks, beaten, 3 whites of eggs, beaten stiff.

Soak matzos in water and press out dry; add the rest of the ingredients, mix thoroughly, fold in the beaten whites, last. Bake about 1 hour in moderate oven.

Lizzie Black Kander, *The Settlement Cookbook*, 1901

One of the most successful cookbooks of the twentieth century, first published in 1901, was *The Settlement Cookbook*, compiled by Lizzie Black Kander to benefit the Jewish Settlement House in Milwaukee. The recipes ranged from traditional New England creamed codfish, to matzos pudding, *schnecken* (cinnamon rolls), chop suey, and chile con carne.

## Home Economics

In the late nineteenth century, as part of an ongoing movement to validate women's work, cooking schools became increasingly popular. At the famous Boston Cooking-School, women studied food science and nutrition as well as basic cooking with Maria Parloa, Mary Lincoln, and Fannie Farmer. Ellen Swallow Richards, who had been trained at Vassar and the Massachusetts Institute of Technology, took the study of housekeeping to a new level. In a speech titled "The Relation of College Women to Progress in Domestic Science," she advised, "The woman who boils potatoes year after year, with no thought of the how or why, is a drudge, but the cook who can compute the calories of heat which a potato of given weight will yield, is no drudge."[26] Known as "the mother of home economics," Richards organized a meeting at Lake Placid, New York, in 1899 that helped define this new field dedicated to the study of the household and family, and she became the president of the American Home Economics Association.

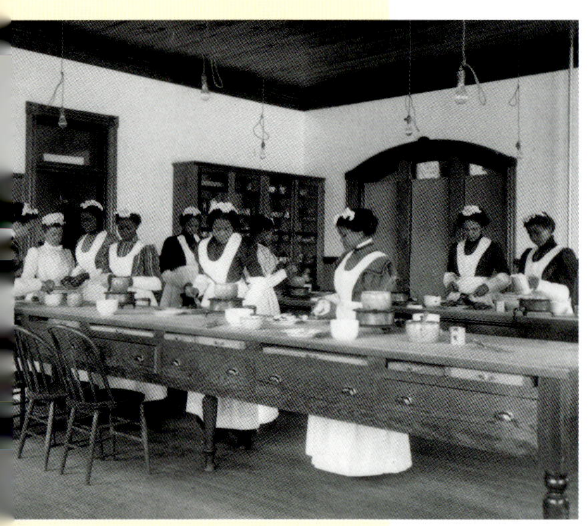

In the early twentieth century, home economics classes aimed to professionalize domestic tasks, like this cooking class at the Hampton Institute in Hampton, Virginia, about 1900.

Attracting women with a broad range of interests and goals, home economics offered careers as an alternative to marriage and motherhood at the same time that it supported these institutions. Many home economists worked as teachers or demonstrators. In 1914 the Smith-Lever Act created cooperative extension programs at land grant colleges and universities to help disseminate information about agriculture and home economics to families in both urban and rural communities.[27] Founded in 1919, the Farm Bureau was an independent organization that reached out with similar offerings. Because of their work load, isolation, and lack of basic conveniences, farm women were particularly receptive to these programs. Agents introduced them to the latest information and technology and taught them how to spruce up their kitchens with curtains and paint and to organize them for greater efficiency. One appreciative Kansas woman wrote: "The Farm Bureau has opened my eyes. . . . I am now accomplishing my work with more ease and pleasure than I ever thought possible, besides realizing I can be a better wife and mother than when worn and jaded by the necessary and unnecessary work I was doing."[28]

Other women resisted the introduction of urban, middle-class values. Jennie Williams of Wyoming recalled an all-day extension program: "After luncheon in this woman's home, they reorganized her kitchen. After they had all worked all afternoon, she looked it over and said, 'I'd druther have it the way I'd druther have it.'"[29] While many women welcomed instruction and the social aspects of club activity, they also felt the pressure to achieve higher standards of housekeeping.[30]

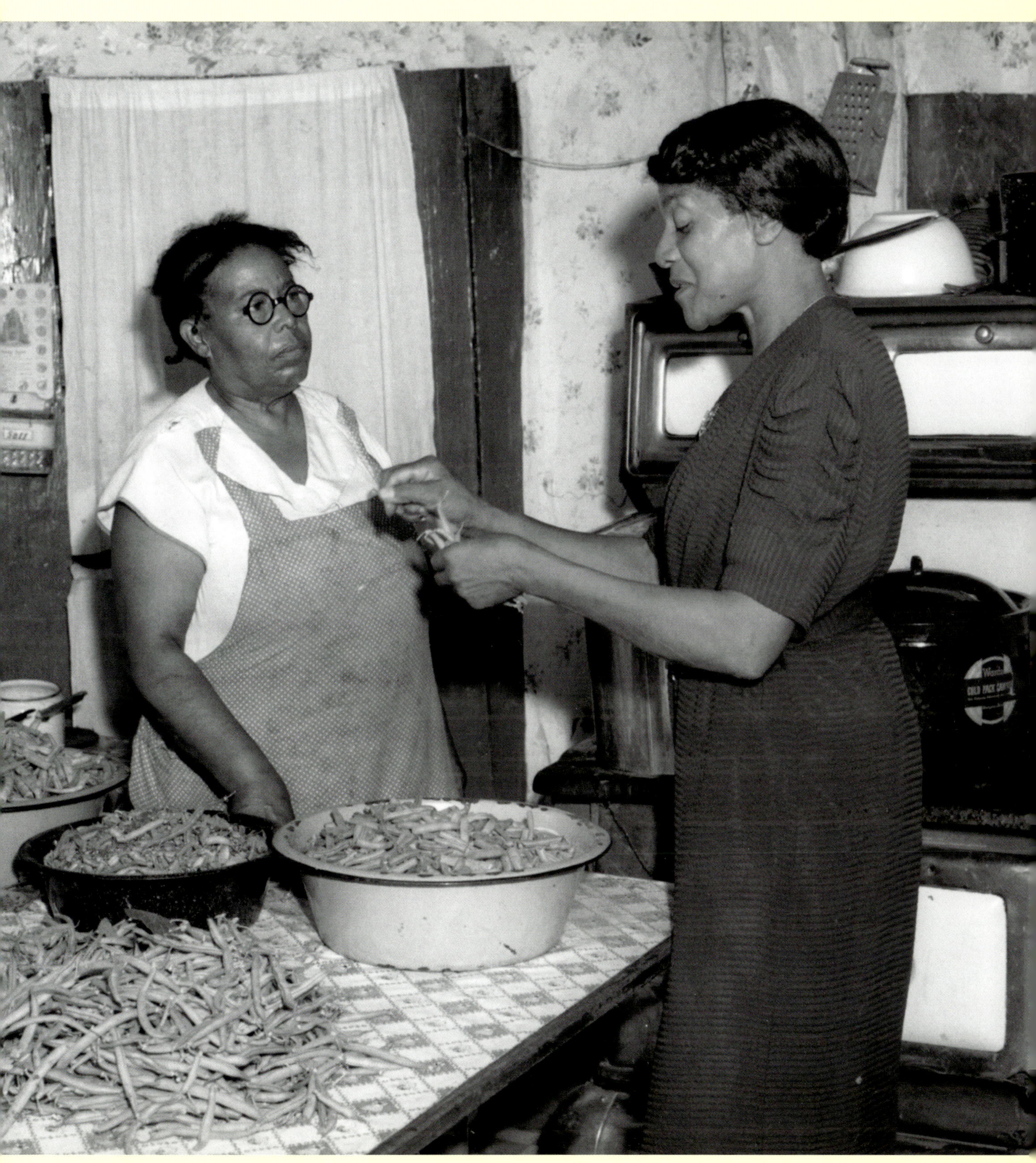

Like many women, Mrs. Smith may not have been completely receptive to the instruction provided by Miss Chappelle, a well-dressed Farm Security Administration home supervisor, on the proper techniques for canning beans in Saint Mary's County, Maryland, in 1940.

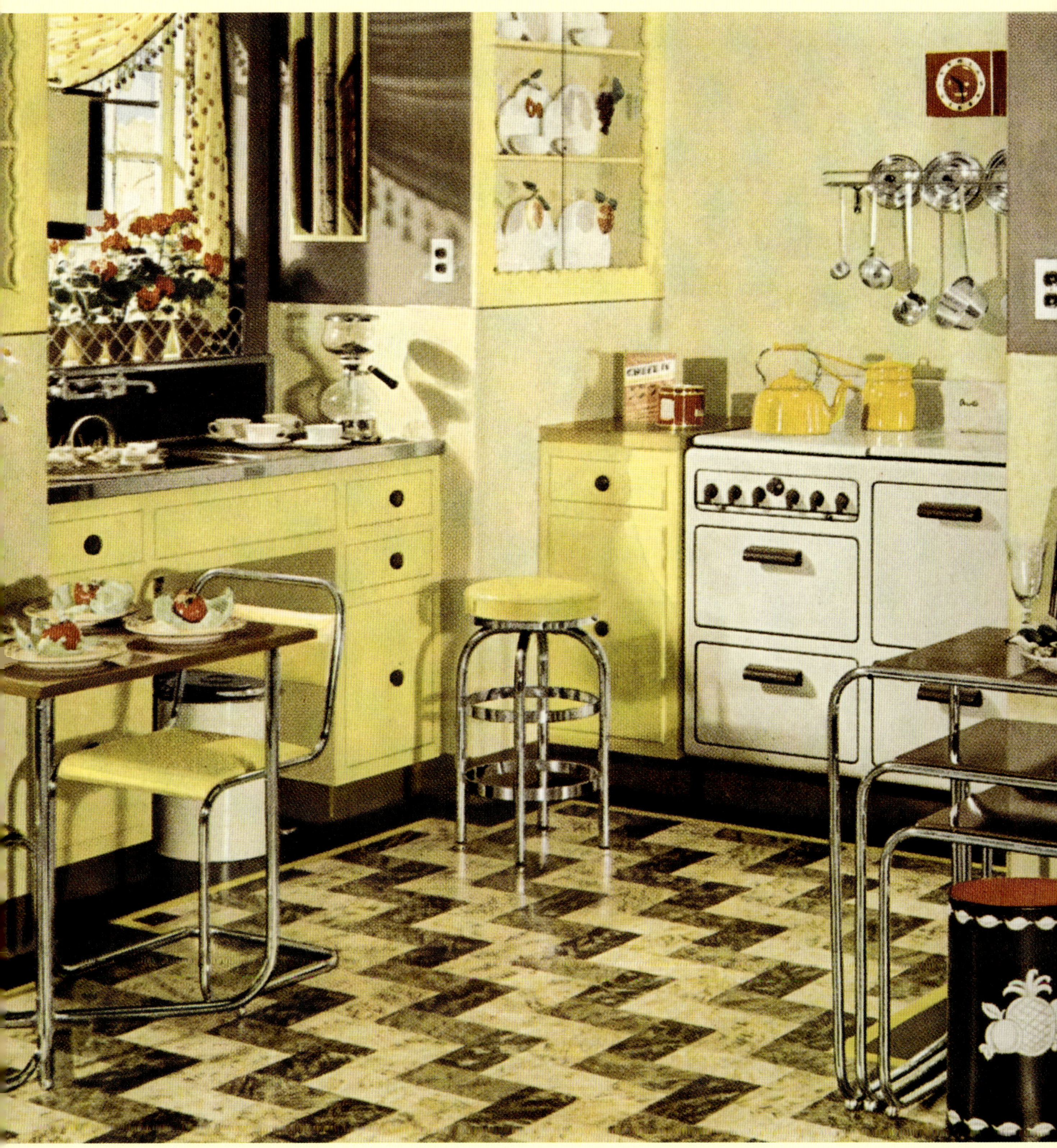

Popular magazines and manufacturers, like the linoleum company that produced this catalogue in 1936, encouraged women to decorate their kitchens with patterned curtains and potted plants in order to make kitchen work more appealing.

## Buying the Latest Kitchen

Outfitting the modern kitchen involved choosing from an array of mass-marketed products. Manufacturers promoted single-family housing units furnished with an array of consumer goods marketed to stay-at-home mothers. In 1934 the *American Gas Journal* reported that the executives of the Brooklyn Union Gas Company, "wanted women to stay at home, do more home cooking and build up the gas load with automatic gas appliances." The company used its demonstration kitchen as a stage for a theatrical presentation, "This, they figured, would introduce the thought that there IS drama in the business of homemaking."[31] Companies hired women (with an unspecified amount of expertise in home economics) as demonstrators to sell their products to other women, all the while promising to make housewives and families safer and happier. The ideal kitchen (not to mention the ideal housewife) was a vision exploited, if not manufactured, by business.[32]

These marketing efforts were generally successful, and many middle-class women began to reconsider the appearance of their kitchens. Margaret H. Clarke of the Hoosier Manufacturing Company wrote, "There was a time, not so long ago either, when the kitchen was considered the 'ugly duckling' of the house; today the woman of the home knows that she feels better, thinks better, works better, where things are orderly and beautiful and in no place does this hold true more than in the kitchen."[33] White enamel appliances, furnishings, and fixtures were popular in the first part of the twentieth century because they were both easy to clean and symbolically sanitary, a tremendous change from the large, black cast-iron appliances and wood surfaces of the nineteenth-century kitchen.[34] Once the basic elements were in place, women were encouraged to add a personal touch. In a book about home design, Jane, the fictional protagonist, consulted the Bureau of Home Economics for technical advice about her kitchen and then left the rest to fancy, "She would have dainty ruffled feminine curtains at the kitchen window. Her kitchen should have as dainty and feminine a look as a woman's boudoir." Words like "dainty" and "feminine" reinforced traditional gender roles associated with the kitchen. Jane was an ideal consumer: "She never expected to see the day when she would have everything she wished for the house. She really didn't want that day to come."[35]

While a concern for hygiene had mandated that kitchens in the early part of the century be fitted with easily cleaned white tile floors and walls, it was not long before women were clamoring for color.

It is not absolutely essential that our kitchens look like laboratories or hospital operating rooms. Professional good housekeepers and efficiency experts not withstanding, it is not even desirable.

Phyllis Ackerman, "Color in the Kitchen," *House Beautiful*, September 1922

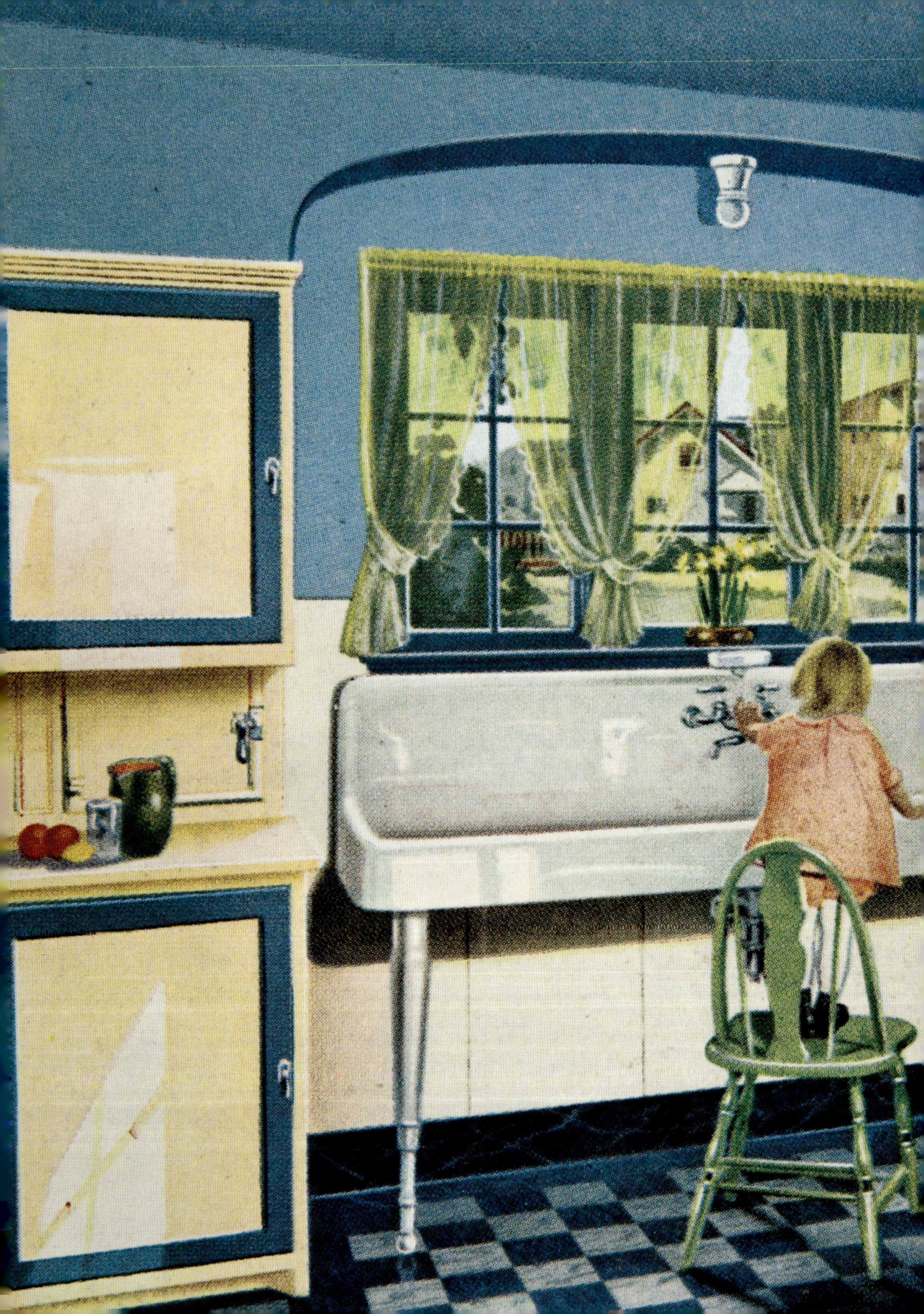

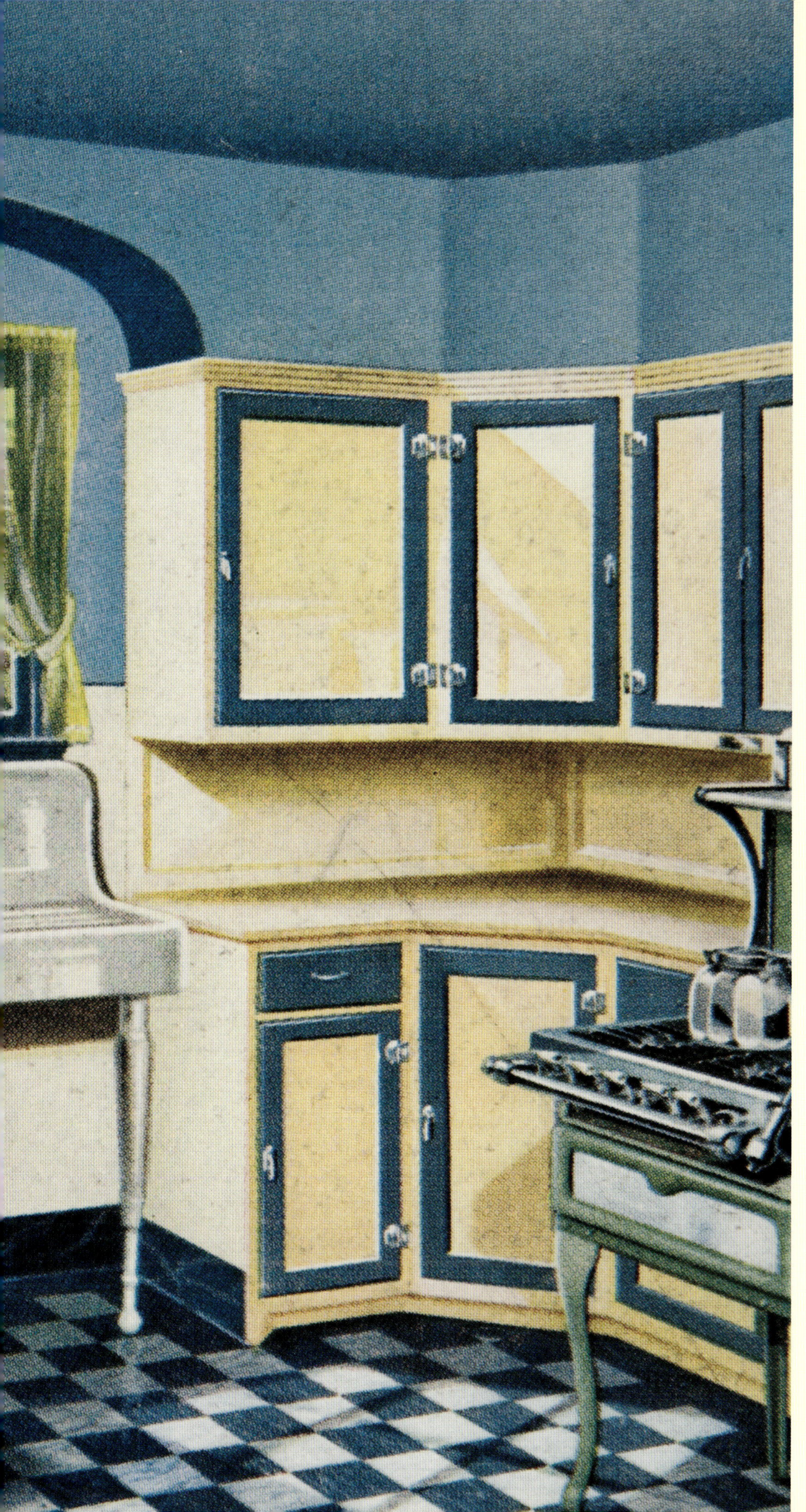

## *Efficiency Experts*

Following in the footsteps of Catharine Beecher and other authors of household advice, Christine Frederick helped develop the new efficient kitchen. Inspired by Frederick W. Taylor, the pioneer of industrial scientific management, Frederick applied "Taylorism" to the kitchen, publishing *Household Engineering: Scientific Management in the Home* in 1919. At her Applecroft Experiment Station on Long Island, New York, she performed time and motion studies of everyday tasks to eliminate wasteful steps and laid out ways to streamline housekeeping processes in exact detail. For example, her advice for washing dishes was: "Note, please, that my drainer is at my *left* and the dishes are stacked up to the *right*."[36] Housewives who followed precise directions for preparing food or cleaning up could expect consistent, predictable results. Frederick was also the household editor for *Ladies' Home Journal* and wrote and lectured widely. She envisioned women as household managers, workers, and, most important, consumers. She spoke to them directly, as in her Hoosier Manufacturing Company advertising leaflet, "You and Your Kitchen." *Selling Mrs. Consumer*, which she wrote in 1929, explained to manufacturers and advertisers how to market

Following the principles of "Taylorism," researchers at Christine Frederick's Applecroft Experiment Station used a stopwatch to record a time-motion study involving a woman using an eggbeater and a kitchen cabinet.

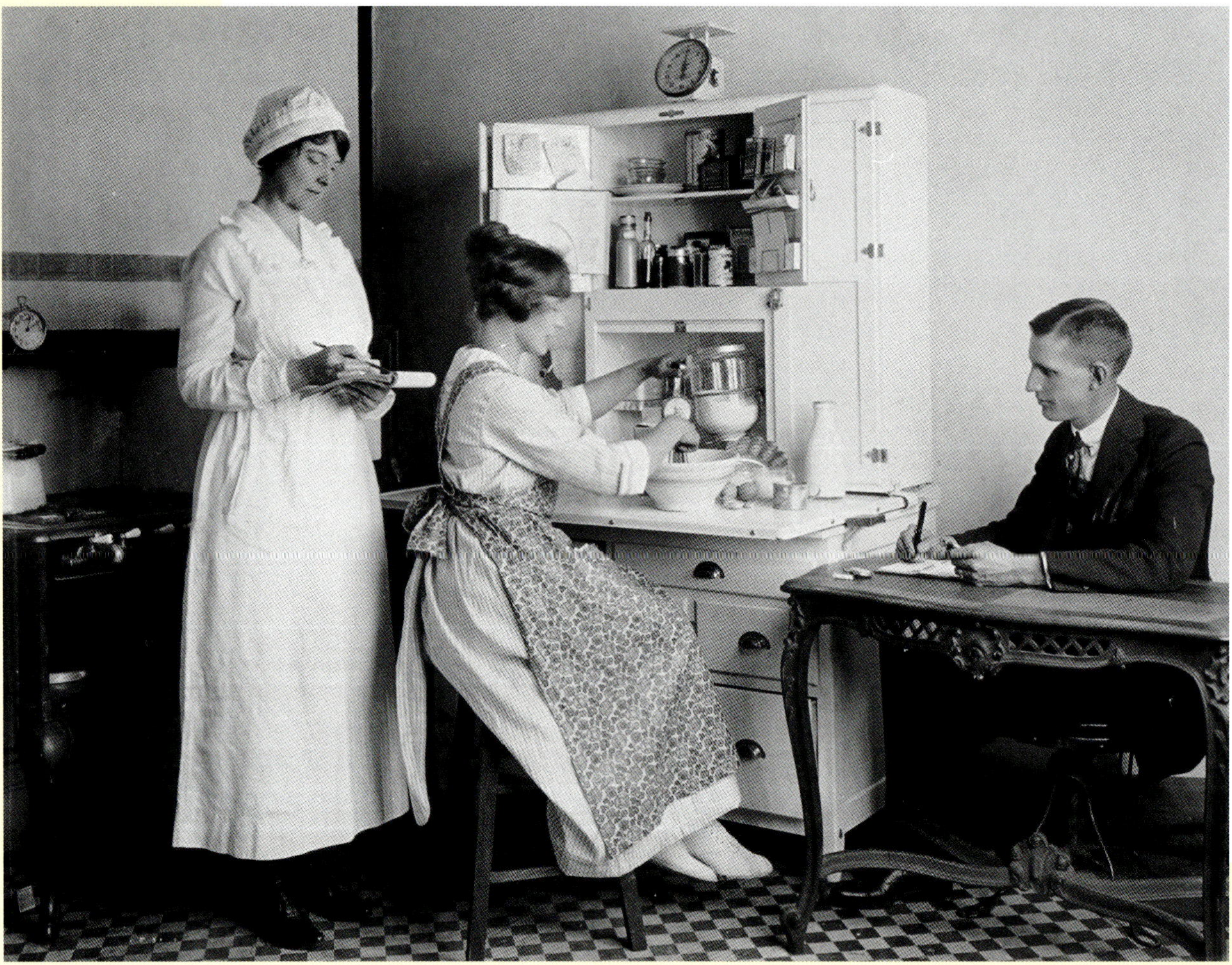

their products to women. Although she portrayed herself as an advocate for housewives, in effect she was a double agent: she used her influence to create markets then directed businesses toward consumers' weaknesses.[37]

The industrial engineer and psychologist Dr. Lillian Gilbreth was also an influential kitchen designer. She and her husband, Frank, were leaders of the scientific management movement and collaborated on a number of factory projects. After her husband's premature death, Gilbreth, a mother of twelve (*Cheaper by the Dozen* and *Belles on Their Toes* tell the Gilbreths' story), used the public interest in her family to restyle herself as an expert on domestic management. The sole breadwinner and not an accomplished cook, Gilbreth hired a servant to help run her large household while she designed ergonomic kitchens and published widely.[38] Her analytical mind attacked the most deceptively simple processes. In *Management in the Home: Happier Living through Saving Time and Energy* (1954), she explained how she reduced the task of making coffee from 14 transportations, 22 operations, 8 inspections, 2 storages, 1 delay, and 54 steps to 3 transportations, 6 operations, 2 inspections, 1 storage, 1 delay, and only 9 footsteps.[39]

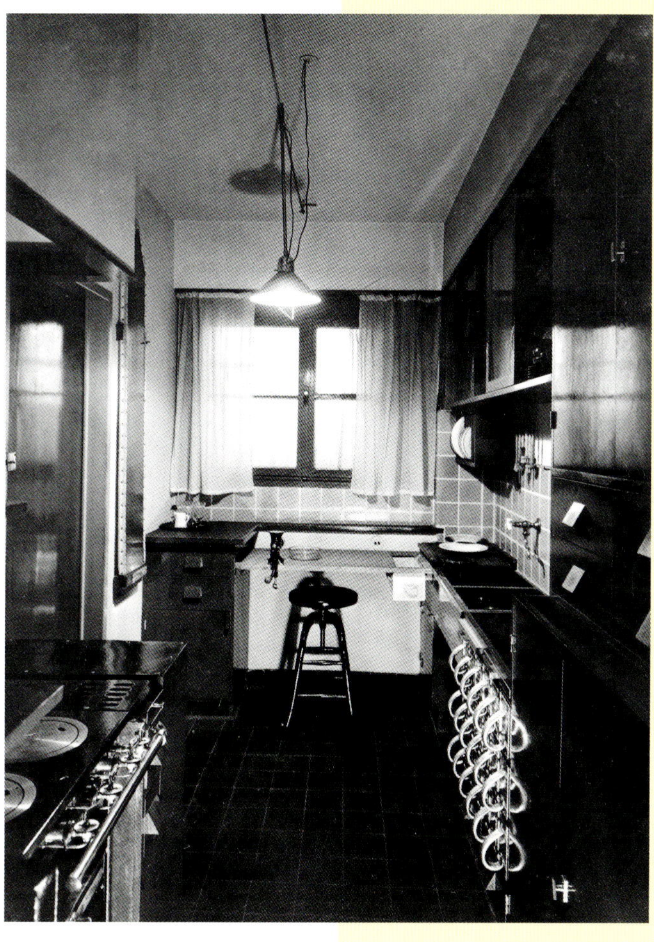

Margarete Schütte-Lihotzky's Frankfurt Kitchen, designed for a German housing project, contributed to an international dialogue on kitchen design.

The work of Frederick and Gilbreth had international significance. In 1926 Margarete (Grete) Schütte-Lihotzky, an Austrian architect, designed a compact kitchen based on principles of scientific management. Schütte-Lihotzky was familiar with Frederick's work, which had been translated into German and inspired a highly successful book by Erna Meyer, *Der neue Haushalt* (The New Household). Schütte-Lihotzky's Frankfurt Kitchen was efficient, tight, modular, and economical. Without consideration for the living patterns working-class families were accustomed to, the design isolated women's work space from the social area of the home. These prefabricated kitchens were installed in some ten thousand affordable housing units in Frankfurt and inspired apartment kitchens in Germany and beyond for decades.[40]

> We are not going to lose our homes nor our families, nor any of the sweetness and happiness that go with them. But we are going to lose our kitchens, as we have lost our laundries and bakeries. The cook-stove will follow the loom and wheel, the wool-carder and shears. We shall have homes that are places to live in and love in, to rest in and play in, to be alone in and to be together in; and they will not be confused and declassed by admixture with any industry whatever.
>
> Charlotte Perkins Gilman, *Women and Economics*, 1898

Charlotte Perkins Gilman was a radical reformer who imagined a day when women would be freed from kitchen work entirely. Along with other early feminists, she believed that one way to emancipate women from economic oppression was to develop "kitchenless houses."

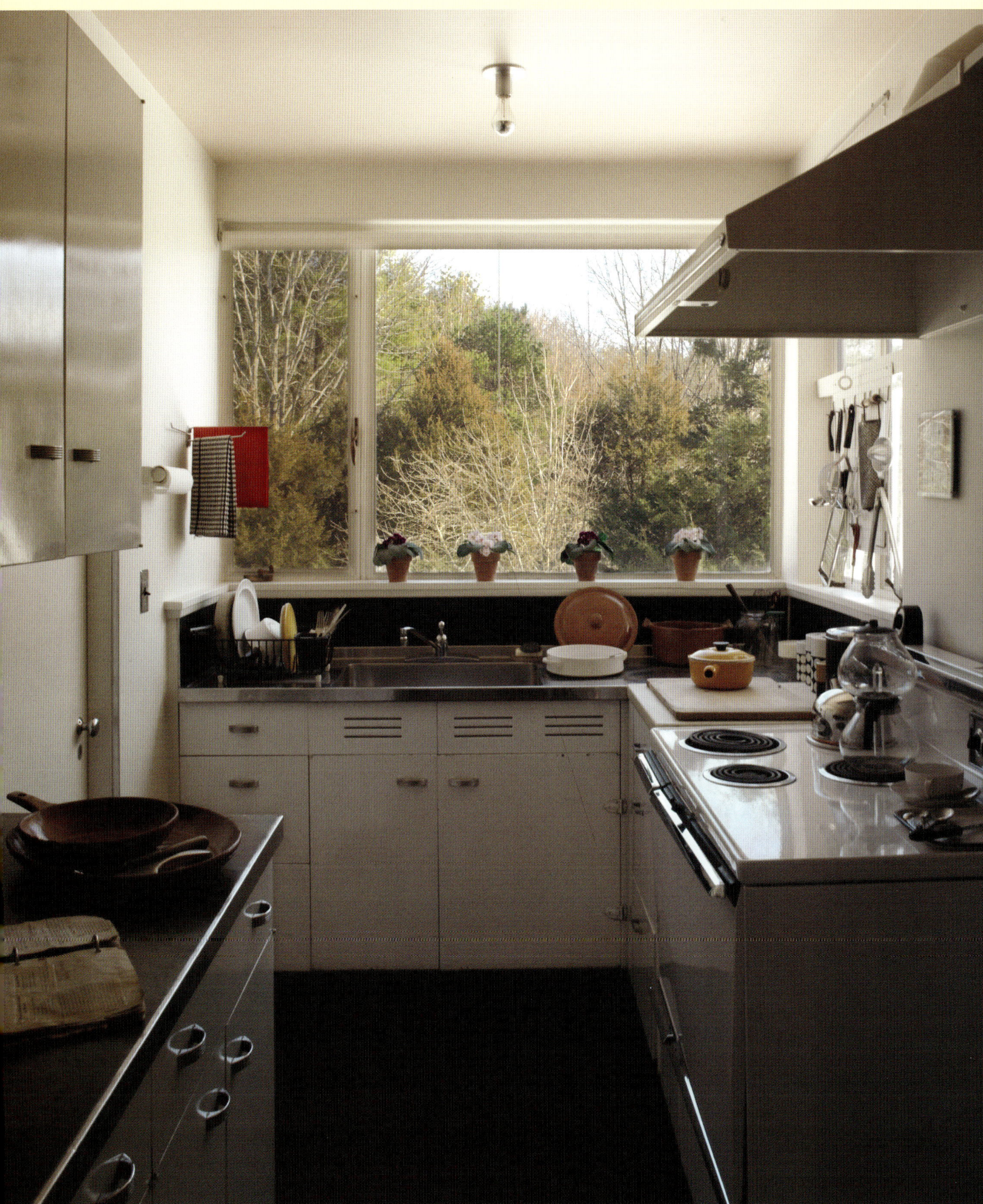

## The Gropius Kitchen

Walter Gropius, the architect and founder of the Bauhaus school of design in Germany, came to the United States with his wife, Ise, and their daughter, Ati, to teach at Harvard's Graduate School of Design. He may have known of the Frankfurt Kitchen when he designed his family's home in Lincoln, Massachusetts, in 1937.[41] Using modern design principles, Gropius made innovative use of light, space, and materials. The kitchen and pantry were at the back of the house, across a central hallway from the dining area and concealed by a curtain that could be closed to hide the preparations. The pantry, a buffer zone between the dining room and the kitchen, was used for dishwashing and storage and was separated from the cooking area by a swinging door that controlled odors and noise.[42] Both the kitchen and pantry were narrow, galleylike spaces designed, according to Ise, to avoid "wasting too many steps."[43] White metal cabinets and black continuous countertops gave both spaces the look of a laboratory. The dishwasher and garbage disposal were donated by the General Electric Company in hopes that their presence in this attention-grabbing house would promote sales.[44]

When Gropius designed the house, he assumed that a servant would be doing the cooking and cleaning. Not only was it customary for professional-class European households to have a maid, but Ise spent much of her time assisting her husband with his work.[45] According to Ati, her mother was "a bilingual secretary . . . with a million things to do. The last place she needed to be was in the kitchen."[46] Gertrud Ernst was their cook from 1939 until 1944.[47] Ati remembers "Gerdy" as "young and merry. . . . She became my bosom buddy and I spent many happy hours hiding out in her 'quarters': a little room and bath off the kitchen where we listened to spooky serial programs on the radio."[48] For Walter and Ise's frequent dinner parties, "the meal was organized down to the eighth of a teaspoon by sober recipes, often in German, that Isi researched and selected each morning."[49] During World War II many young women, including Gerdy, found work in factories, which had distinct advantages over domestic work. Ati mourned the loss of her companion, "cheery Gerdy left us to join the ranks of 'working women for the war effort'. It was a blow to us all."[50] Ise Gropius, who had always done the marketing, began cooking for the first time in her life. According to Ati, "All the delicate, gourmet recipes [Ise] had collected now lay in her own lap and were to be served impeccably on the dot of seven. In time she became a cook of great expertise but never one of joy, and the atmosphere of dogged desperation which I remember in the kitchen is, no doubt, partly the reason why I never became a cook."[51]

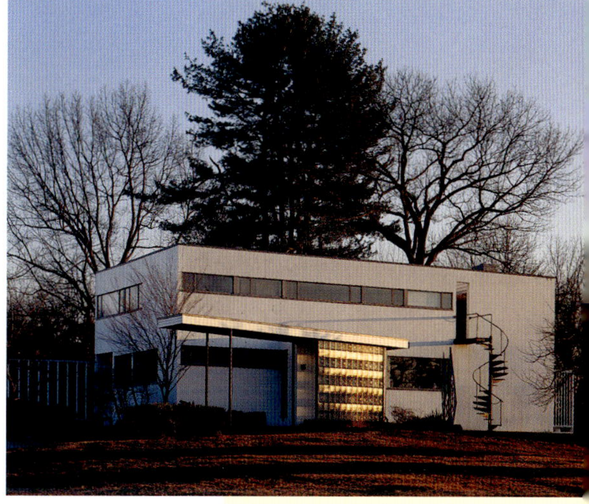

When designing their house, the Gropiuses carefully considered its placement in the landscape. Ise Gropius later wrote, "To work in the kitchen is particularly pleasant because of the large east window . . . which gives a sweeping view across the low lying wooded wetlands . . ."

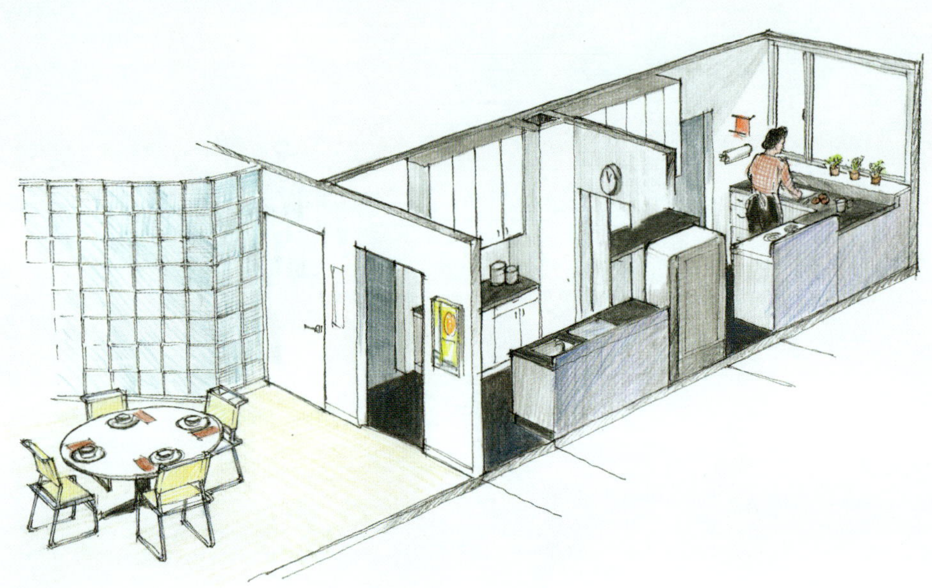

The side-by-side kitchen and pantry in the Gropius house in Lincoln, Massachusetts, are at the back corner of the house, isolating the noise and smells of cooking and providing direct access to the servant's quarters.

In retrospect, Ise decided that the design of the kitchen had been a "mistake." She had discovered that, "When many guests were entertained, as became the custom with the arrival of the cocktail party, we would have preferred a wide bar-like connection between the two rooms that would have enabled guests to serve themselves."[52] They made the best of the situation, however. When Ise cooked, Walter sometimes sat on a stool in a corner of the kitchen, out from underfoot but providing good company.[53] Walter helped Ati clean up after dinner, "Walter had become the steward of the dishwasher and allowed no one else in his after-dinner terrain in the pantry. I was the pots and pans washer in the kitchen."[54] The Gropius family managed to transform their efficient kitchen into a family space despite its inflexible design.

> A small kitchen is much more convenient than a large one, although even that has its drawbacks, as the whole family are inclined to congregate "where mother is." While this may be sociable and pleasant . . . there is such a thing as the room being too crowded for rapid work, and it is anything but agreeable to have every inch of available space around the cookstove occupied by irresponsible, hungry people, while the cook, tired and perhaps cross, must reach in between or over their heads to attend to things on the stove; or between their feet to see if the food in the oven is baking.
>
> Helen Laughlin, *Colman's Rural World*, 1900

The first half of the twentieth century saw the kitchen transformed from a wide-open room supported by pantries and cellars to a highly efficient space featuring built-in cabinets and countertops. However, real kitchens did not always function the way designers, educators, manufacturers, politicians, and feminists imagined, even in their own homes. After the Second World War, the ideal kitchen combined the best new features—compact, modular storage units, work surfaces, and appliances—with space for the family.

The new, highly efficient layouts may have simplified kitchen tasks, but they were far less sociable. Since the space no longer accommodated the family, women working in small kitchens were either isolated or crowded.

Ise Gropius learned to prepare meals after her cook, Gertrud Ernst, took a factory job. Despite the kitchen's small size, her husband, Walter, would sometimes keep her company while she worked.

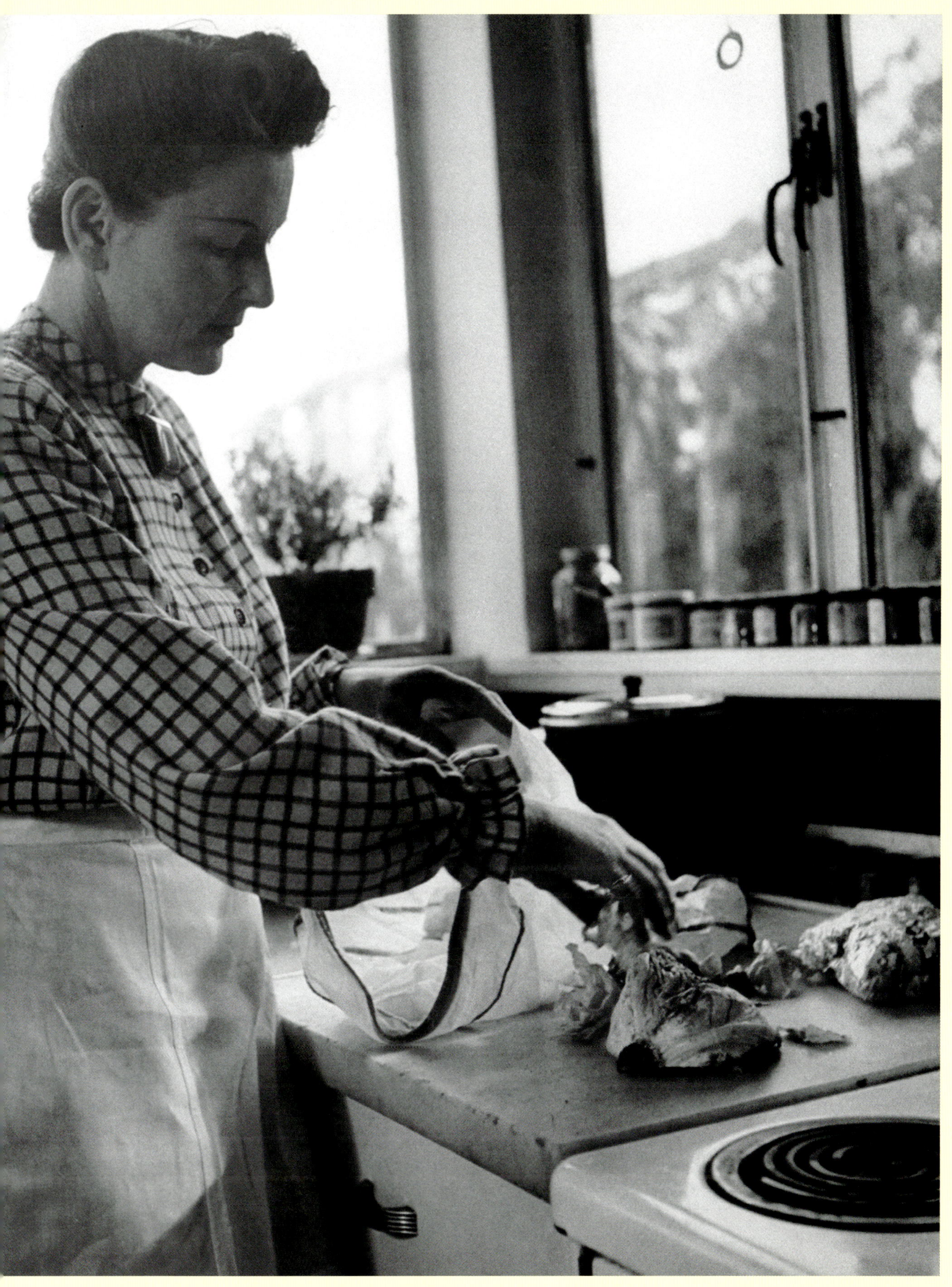

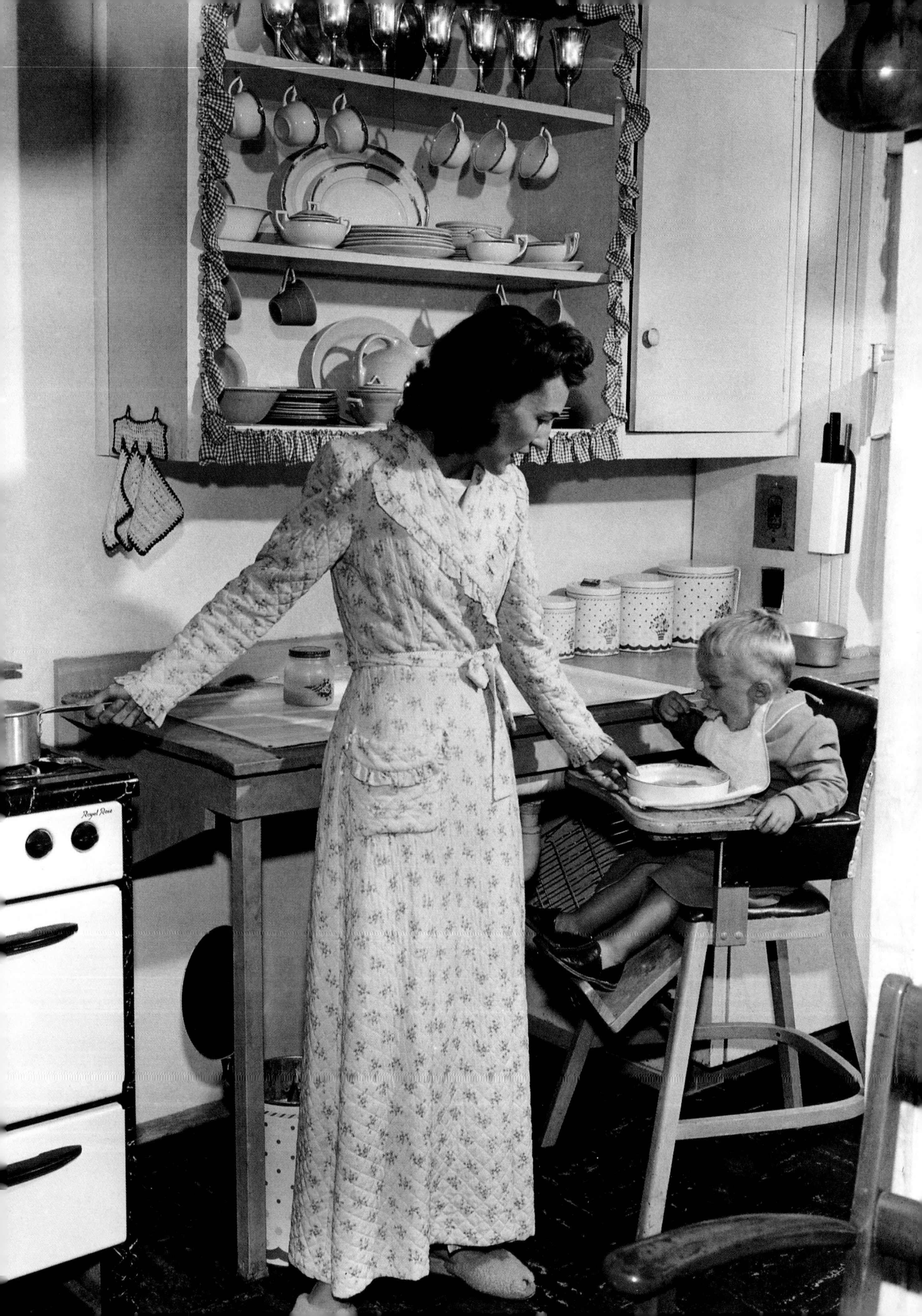
Royal Rose

# THE POSTWAR KITCHEN

{ 1945–present }

## *Two Levittown Kitchens*

On Easter weekend in 1958, Jack and Sally Sondesky moved into their brand-new home in Levittown, Pennsylvania, a planned community strategically situated between Philadelphia and Trenton, New Jersey. Like other "Jubilee" models in their neighborhood, the Sondeskys' house came with a fully equipped pink General Electric kitchen. The kitchen quickly became the center of home life for Sally, Jack, and later, their two children, Carol and Michael. Sally did all the cooking. The children did their homework and celebrated birthdays at the kitchen table, part of a gray dinette set that included vinyl-covered chairs with chrome legs. Sally enjoyed baking, especially during the Christmas season, when she and the children made dozens of cookies together.[1]

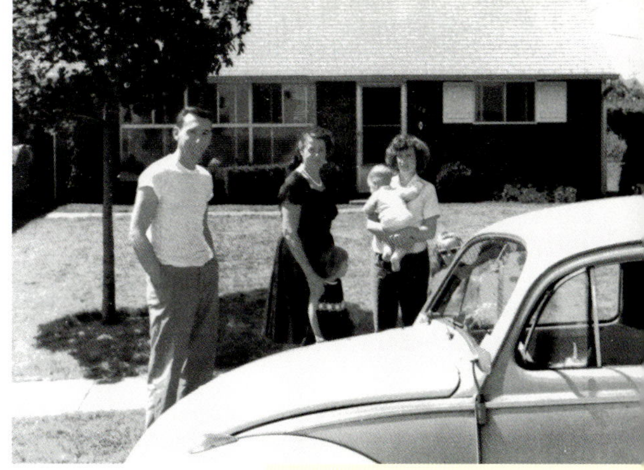

When Jack and Sally Sondesky moved to Levittown, Pennsylvania, in 1958, they joined thousands of Americans taking advantage of the space and amenities provided by new single-family suburban homes. The front of their "Jubilee" model is visible in this photograph of Sally with her children and friends.

Less than a year before the Sondeskys moved to Levittown, the Myers family had settled in another section of the rapidly growing suburb. Like many families, they wanted to take advantage of the space and amenities of the suburbs, but the Myerses' experience was marred by people who wanted to deny them this dream. William and Daisy Myers began moving in with their sons, William and Steven, and their infant daughter, Lynda, on August 13, 1957. They were relocating from an integrated community one mile from Levittown and were the first African American family to move into what had been an all-white suburb. Neighbors quickly learned of their arrival, and national press coverage followed. Crowds of onlookers, both curious and hostile, began congregating on their front lawn. Daisy Myers later wrote about first anxious days: "At times I thought I would go mad—the telephone, Lynda crying, telegrams arriving, friends coming and going. Groceries were brought in, gifts continued to arrive, flowers from the florist, cakes, cookies, candy, toys for the kids." In their kitchen

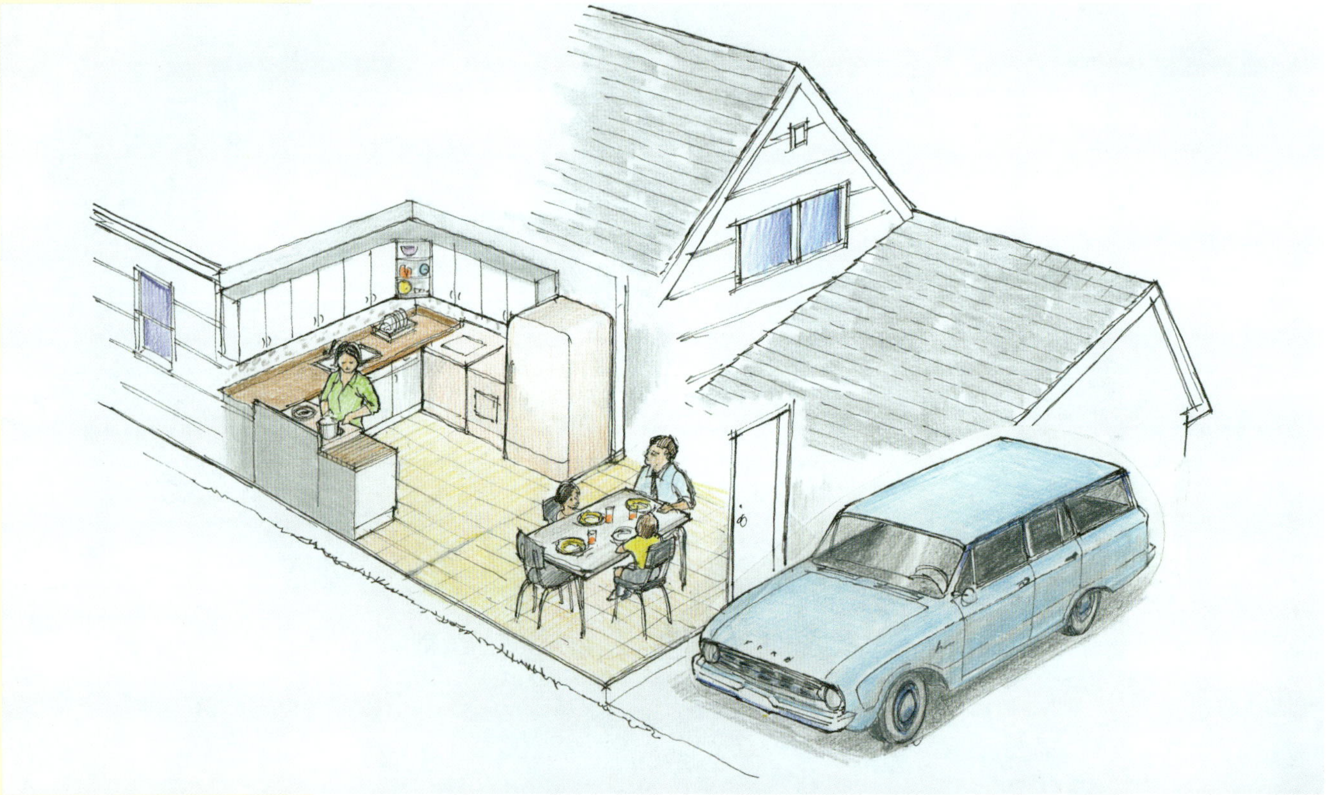

Levittown homes, like Jack and Sally Sondesky's "Jubilee" model, featured open floor plans and modern all-electric kitchens.

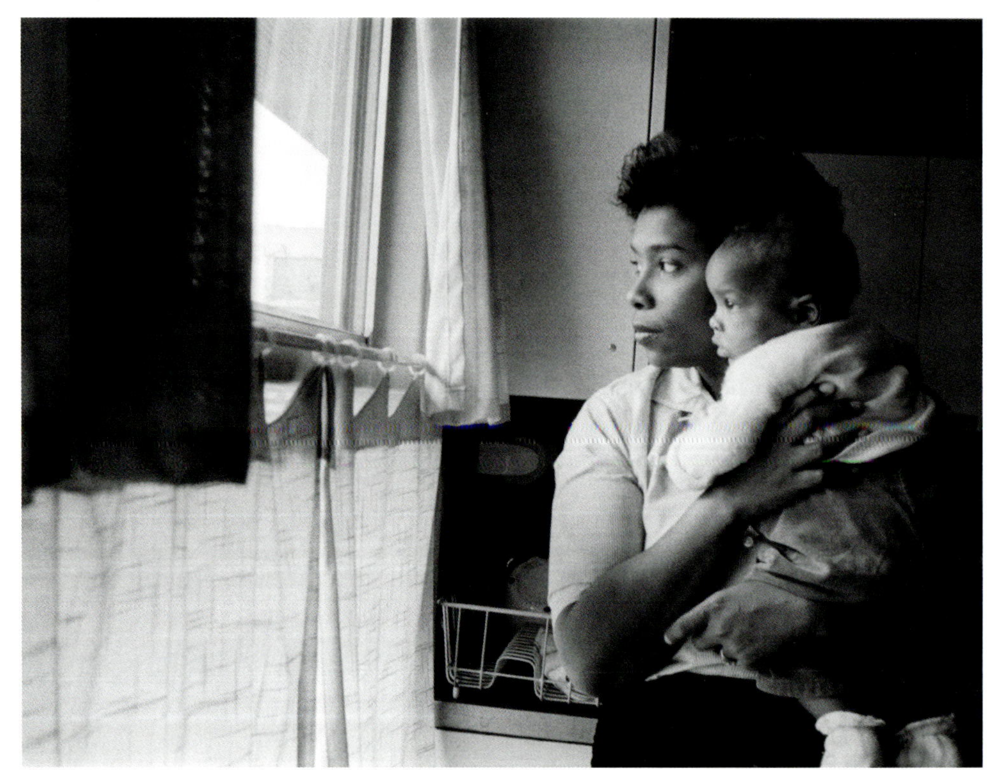

From her kitchen window, Daisy Myers could watch as crowds gathered on her front lawn to protest her family's move to all-white Levittown in 1957.

the Myerses tried to maintain some semblance of a daily routine, while also meeting there with friends and communicating with others on the telephone. For just over two months the Myerses and their supporters endured harassment and intimidation by other neighbors. Only after the state attorney general's office intervened on their behalf were they able to enjoy their new home.[2]

The middle-class suburban lifestyle was not the only one Americans experienced after World War II, but it became the most iconic. The basic design of the era's kitchens, in which communal space was created by open plans joining work and living areas, remains popular to this day. These kitchens, shaped by concerns for efficiency, became symbols of abundance and modernity. At the center of this open, efficient, communal space was the housewife, whose relationship to her kitchen was often complicated.

## "Food Fights for Freedom"

Less than a decade before the emergence of the 1950s suburban kitchen, kitchens functioned as a critical front in America's "Arsenal of Democracy." Only recently released from the hardship of the Great Depression, women once again found themselves carefully managing their family's food supply. Throughout the war, the government, food producers, and manufacturers reminded women of the patriotism behind their kitchen work and offered glimpses of the material goods that would result from their diligence.

Conservation was essential. The government asked families on the home front to make sacrifices so food could be sent to soldiers and allied civilians. In 1942 sugar became the first rationed food item, followed by coffee, meat, and canned foods (to save tin). A year later, ration books were issued to each man, woman, and child. Stamps of different colors and values allowed families to purchase only limited amounts of rationed items. Women carefully planned meals to make the best use of available products. Meat rationing proved one of the greatest challenges, for meat had long been a staple of the American diet, while vegetarian dishes (except macaroni and cheese) were rarely served.[3] Wartime cookbooks taught women how to stretch meat rations and offered recipes for curried eggs, baked soy beans, and baked bean loaf.[4] Other types of conservation activities, such as saving fats, which could be made into glycerin for explosives, were promoted as necessary kitchen duties.

> Since in wartime we cannot buy as much food as we did, nor as much food as we would like, we must either "dig or diet," that is, we must either produce and preserve most of our own food supplies or do without.
>
> *New York State College of Home Economics Bulletin 578, 1943*

As the need for conserving the nation's food supply increased, university extension agencies worked to educate Americans about how to modify their diets and preserve produce grown in Victory Gardens.

Preservation of foods grown in home gardens provided greater variety in American diets and eased reliance on rationed canned products. Gardening and canning efforts ranged from small plots and a few jars to large gardens with substantial produce.[5] Sheril Jankovsky Cunning of Long Beach, California, remembered, "Everybody grew a Victory Garden. We had

"We'll have lots to eat this winter, won't we Mother?"

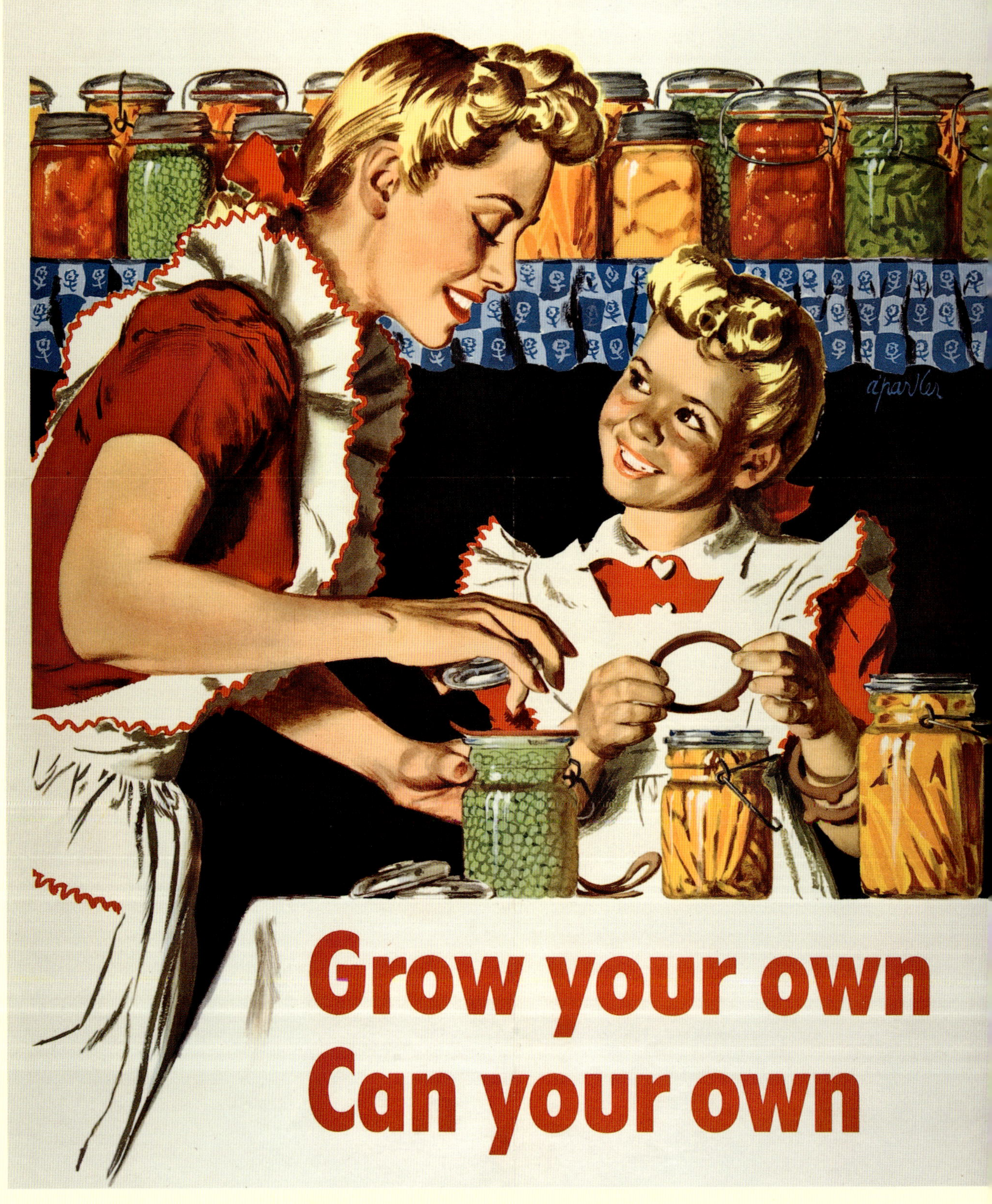

the most miserable, hard-as-cement, three-by-five foot plot of ground, and grew radishes and carrots as our contribution to the war. But radishes weren't anybody's mainstay, and our carrots never got bigger than an inch. Yet we all wanted to do our part for the war."[6] Women working in the many manufacturing plants that opened to them during the war fought on two fronts, in the factory and in the kitchen.[7]

Kitchens changed little during the war, and many predated the Great Depression. Manufacturers regularly reminded Americans of the rewards their sacrifices would reap after the war's conclusion. Because factories formerly producing refrigerators were now producing tanks and other weapons of war, there were no new durable goods to advertise. To keep their brands fresh in the minds of future consumers, companies published advertisements showing how they were contributing to the war effort, encouraging the sale of war bonds, or offering examples of the new and improved products they hoped to sell after the war was over. An ad from Republic Steel claimed, "When a peacetime dawn dispels the dusk of war, the American housewife will find a new joy in the kitchen of tomorrow. It will be bright, cheerful, efficient—because steel, and especially stainless steel, will make it so."[8] Thus they simultaneously offered encouragement in the face of sacrifice while tantalizing consumers longing to spend their growing savings.

## The Suburbs

The wartime economy, with near full employment for men, jobs for many women, and many durable goods unavailable, laid the foundation for massive postwar developments like Levittown and their sparkling kitchens. Using the money they saved during the war, American consumers eagerly purchased new homes and appliances, many of them for the kitchen, that had been off the market or unaffordable.[9] These suburban homes and the consumer goods that filled them became icons of the postwar lifestyle.

Although suburban development began in the nineteenth century, by the 1930s and 1940s, planned communities like Greenbelt, Maryland, and William Levitt's Long Island development, Strathmore-at-Manhasset, were made possible by applying experimental mass-production techniques to house construction.[10] As veterans reunited with loved ones and started families, they encountered a severe housing shortage. Although the GI Bill and other federal programs provided low-interest mortgages with minimal down payments to many veterans, they found few homes for sale.[11] William Levitt responded to this situation by planning and developing three Levittowns. Between 1947 and 1964 his company built 17,447 houses in New York, 17,311 in Pennsylvania, and 12,000 in New Jersey, all intended for working- and middle-class families. Many residents of Levittown, Pennsylvania, worked in a newly opened steel mill nearby.

From the beginning, critics condemned suburbs for being homogeneous communities of conformity. In Levittown, most houses sold for similar prices and appealed to young

World War II posters like this one reminded women that they fought the war from their kitchens. In 1943 Americans preserved 4.1 billion jars of food; more than half of the preserved produce was grown in Victory Gardens.

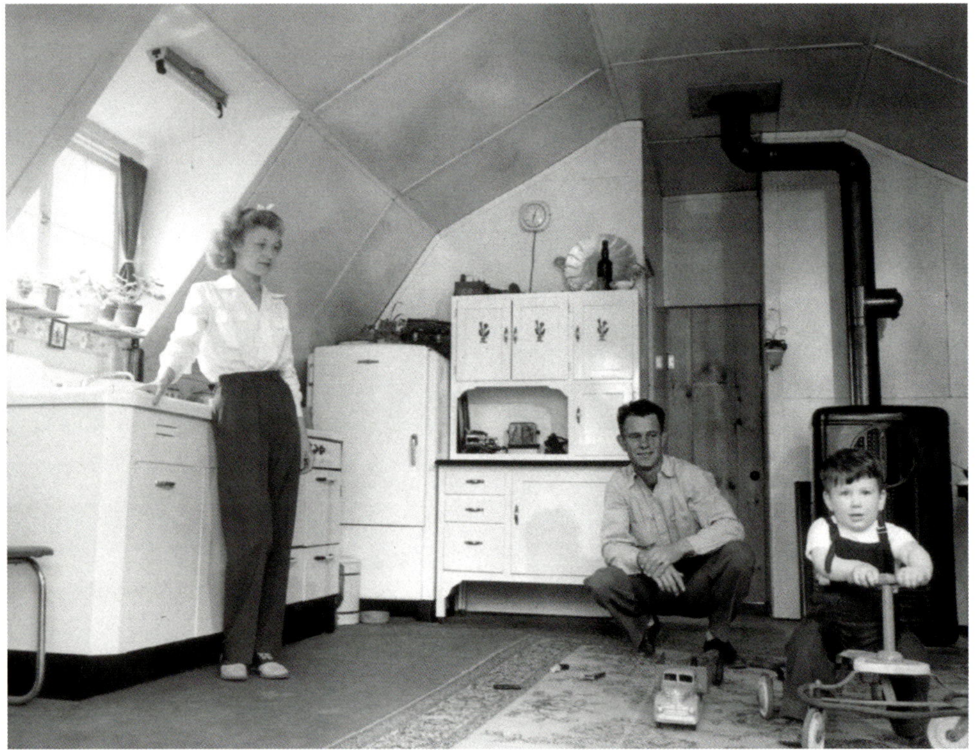

The shortage of housing immediately after World War II led families to live in spaces previously unimaginable. Quonset huts, like this one in Connecticut, built during the war to house soldiers, became starter homes for young families after soldiers came home.

families seeking starter homes; therefore, the majority of residents came from similar social classes, age groups, and life stages.[12] Levitt refused to sell homes to African Americans, claiming that "as a Jew, I have no room in my mind or heart for racial prejudice. But . . . I have come to know that if we sell one house to a Negro family, then ninety to ninety-five percent of our white customers will not buy into the community. . . . As a company, our position is simply this: we can solve a housing problem, or we can try to solve a racial problem. But we cannot combine the two."[13] Levitt's position reflected the policies of the Federal Housing Administration, which encouraged builders to target specific ethnic or class groups.[14] This did not stop original Levittown purchasers from selling to African Americans, as in the Myerses' case, but even after the Myerses settled into their new home, few other black families moved to Levittown. There was, however, some ethnic and religious diversity, as significant numbers of Catholics and Jews bought homes in the community.[15]

> Some housewives, researchers found, preferred a relaxed, homey kitchen with room for toddlers to play and neighbors to chat over coffee. Others wanted a room of gleaming efficiency which they could clean up and clear out quickly.
>
> "Planning Your New Kitchen," *Small Homes Guide*, 1953–1954

After World War II, Cornell University's Housing Research Center conducted extensive research on kitchen design, including its sociological, psychological, and technological aspects. The study's results were discussed widely in 1950s builder's guides and design publications.

Levittown homes offered amenities that were new to many homeowners, especially the General Electric kitchens Levitt prominently featured in his advertising. Many families relocating to the suburbs left crowded urban tenements, often shared with their parents or other extended family. Their previous kitchens were typically hodgepodges of technology not nearly as well integrated as the efficient and visually unified kitchens of Levittown.

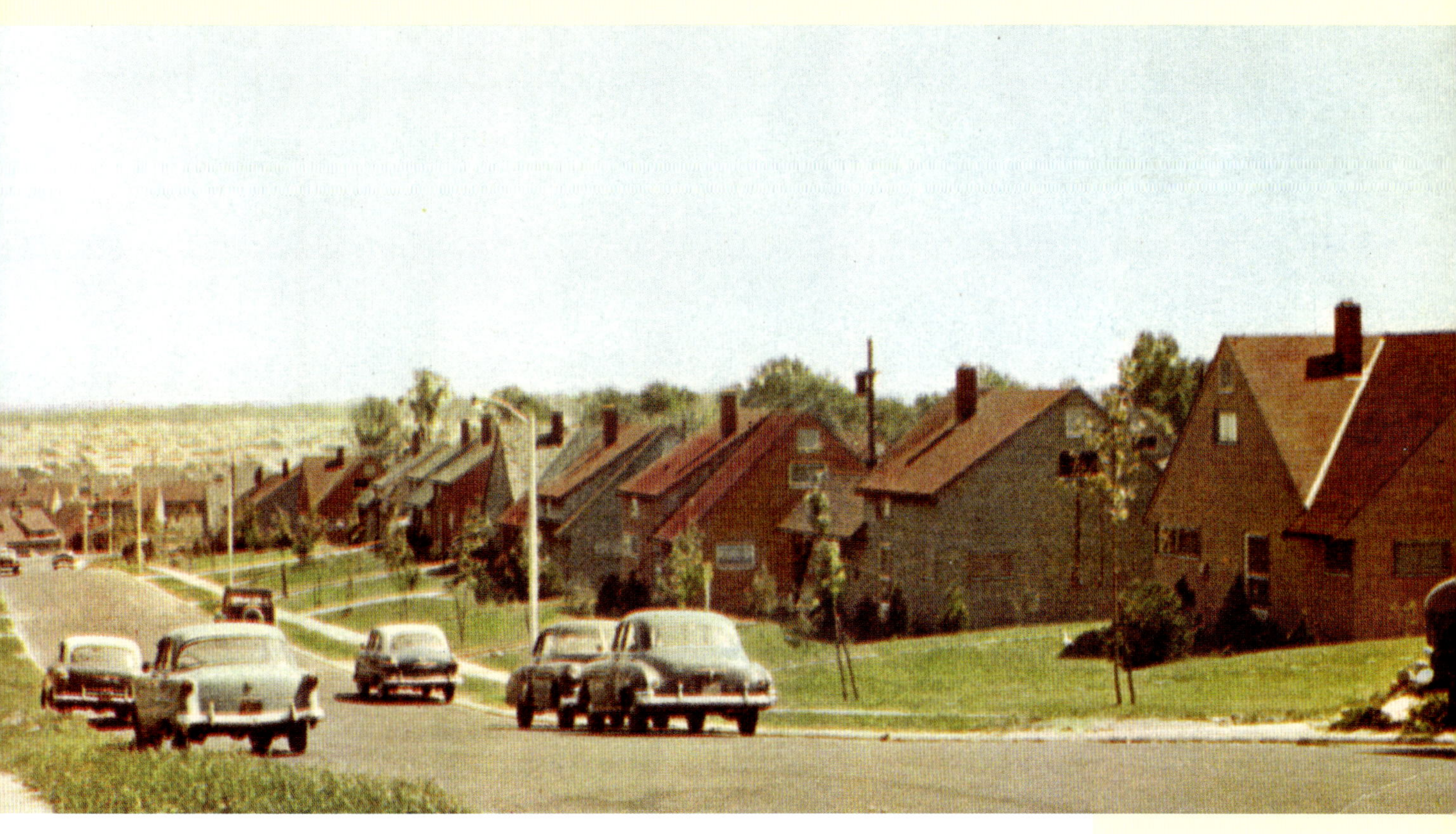

Cele Roberts, who moved to Levittown, New York, with her husband in 1949 remembered, "Everything you dreamed about was there, everything was working, brand-new, no cockroaches."[16] Although the suburban kitchens may have been more modern in design and technology, they remained all-purpose spaces where families worked and lived.

William Levitt is often remembered for creating what many see as a bland suburban landscape, but his company's design of the middle-class kitchen has had lasting influence.

Despite the improved kitchen amenities, life in the suburbs created challenges for former urbanites when it came to making dinner. Women accustomed to food markets within walking distance found that in Levittown they needed a car to get to the nearest supermarket. Levitt placed the Shop-a-Rama Shopping Center on the outskirts of Levittown so that its supermarket and other stores would also attract shoppers from nearby communities. At the time, it was the largest shopping center east of the Mississippi and served as a Main Street of sorts for Levittown. Naturally, the shopping center was surrounded by a massive parking lot. Because not all women could drive or had a second car to take to do their marketing while their husbands were at work, carpool arrangements among neighbors were common.[17]

The shift of population from city to suburb was significant. During the 1950s, in the twenty largest metropolitan areas, city populations remained stable, while their suburbs expanded by 45 percent. However, nonveterans, African Americans, and others who did not benefit from government mortgage assistance were more likely to remain in older homes, where kitchen upgrades occurred slowly. Even so, consumer spending on household furnishings and appliances soared, and the percentage of American families who owned a mechanical refrigerator jumped from 44 to 80 percent between 1940 and 1950.[18]

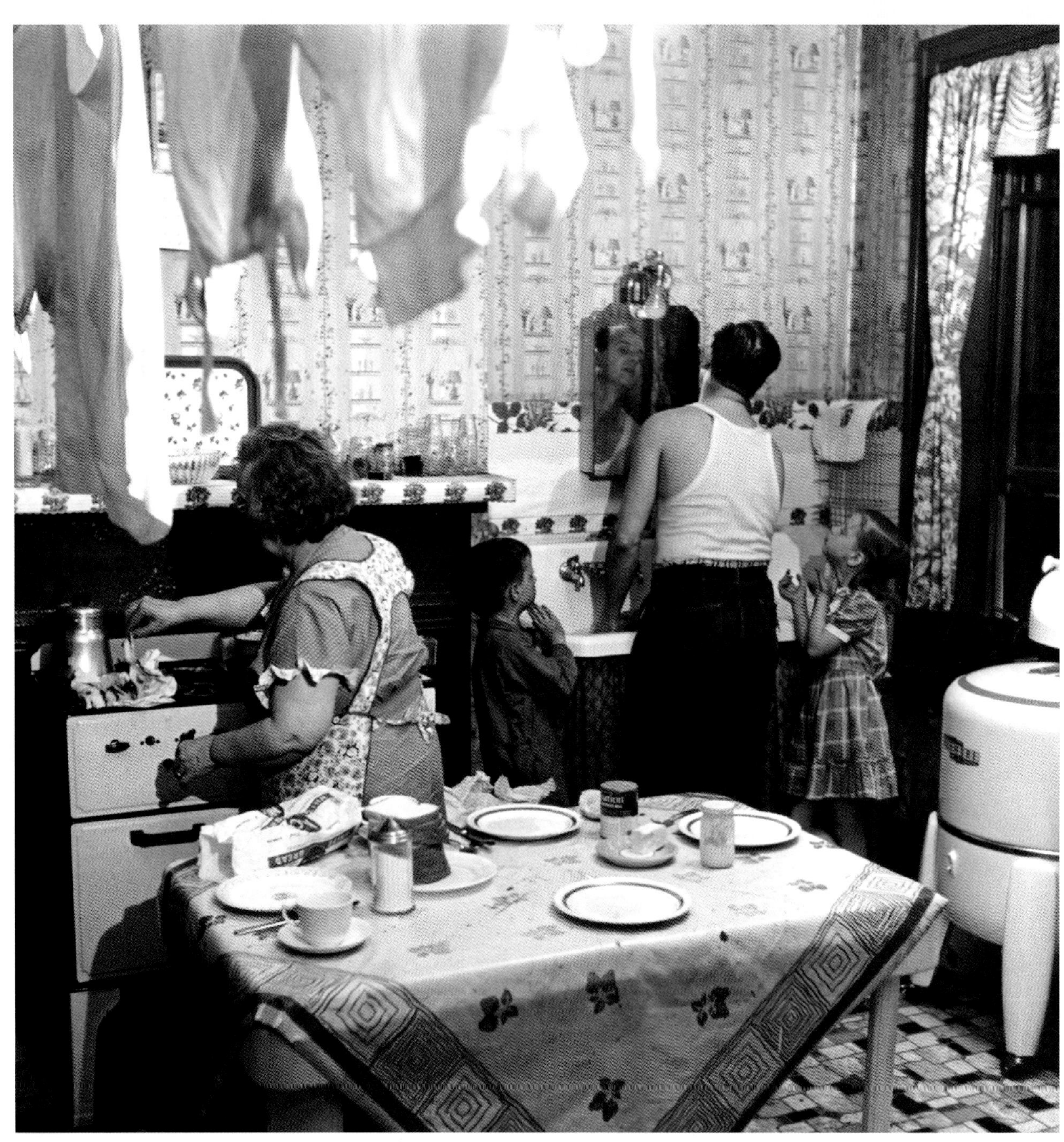

For many urban families, like the Rochnas of Pittsburgh, Pennsylvania, photographed in 1950, kitchens contained a mixture of new and old technology and functioned as the hub of family activity.

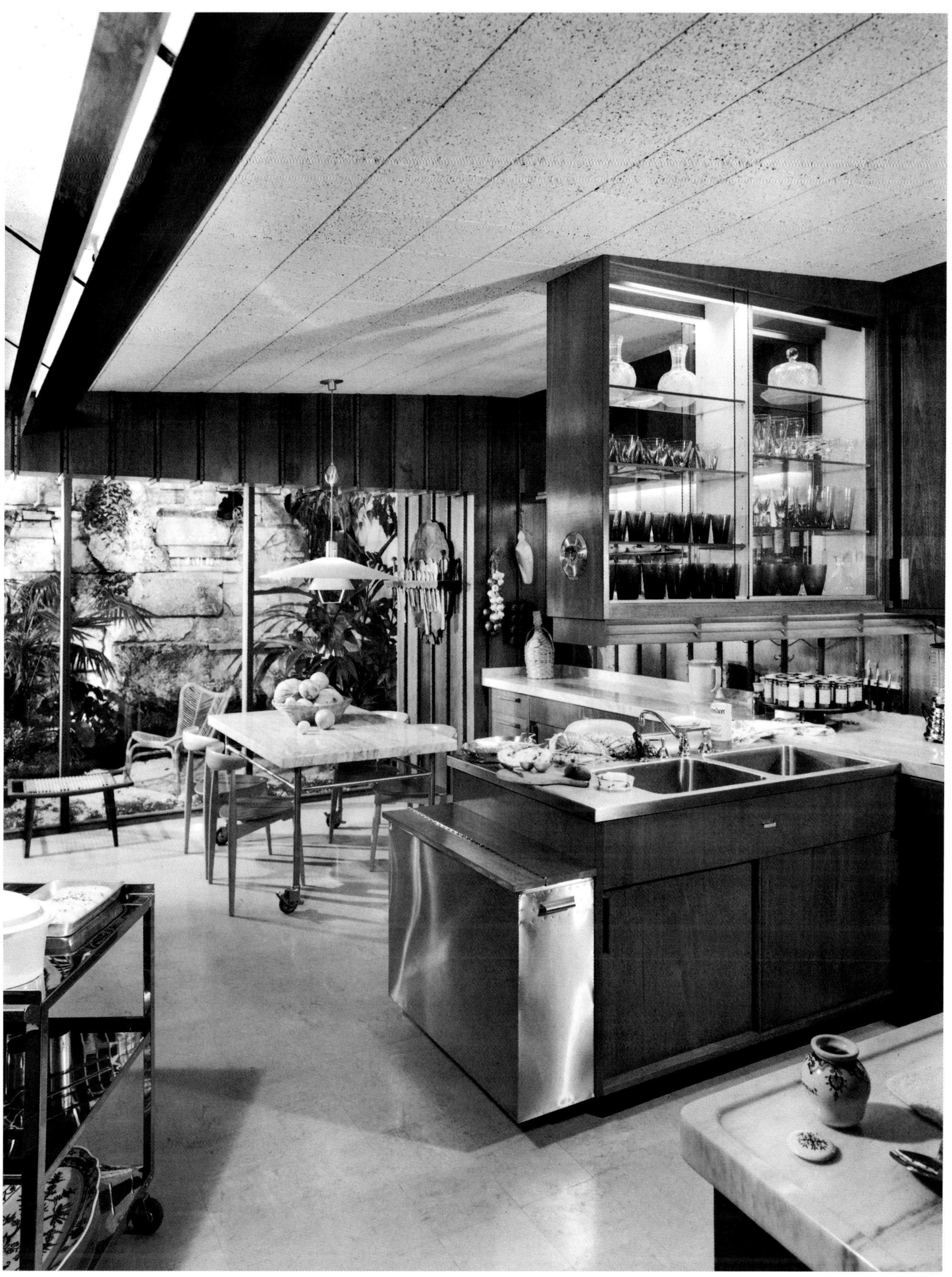

The "Pace Setter" kitchen, featured in a 1954 issue of *House Beautiful,* combined efficiency with attractiveness. Many postwar homes were built without separate dining rooms; instead open plans facilitated casual entertaining and easy interaction between people in the kitchen and those in the adjacent dining area.

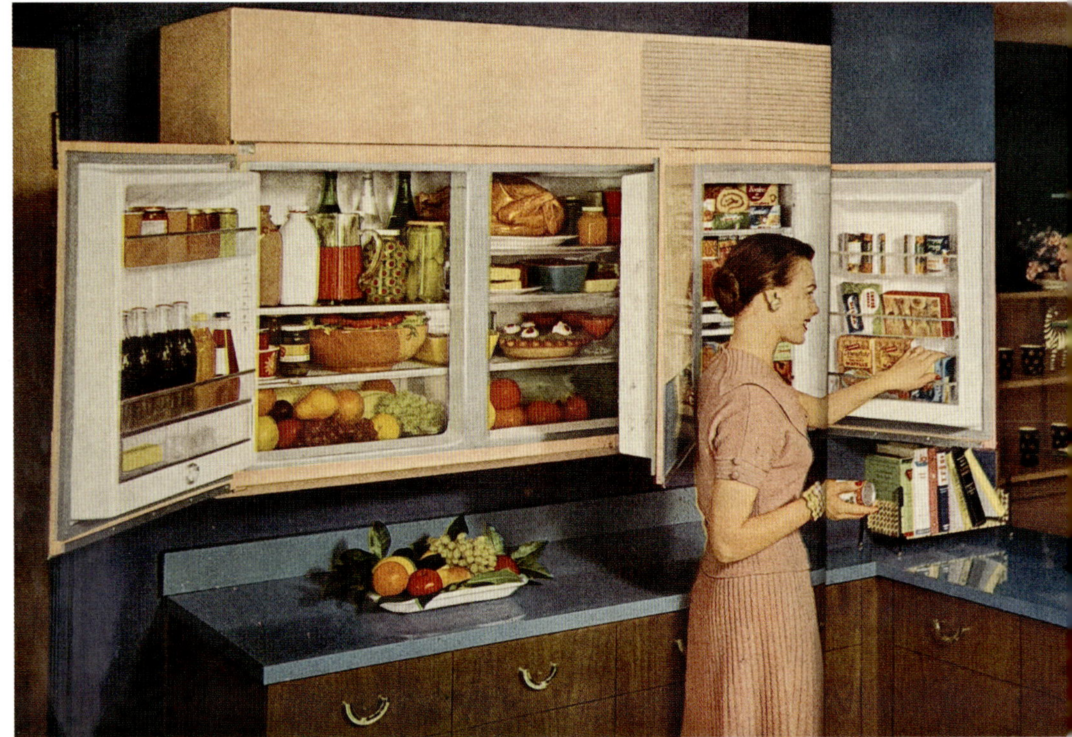

In the postwar period, manufacturers introduced kitchen appliances in new colors and designs in an effort to entice families to replace their old appliances before it was actually necessary. Even though many of the new models, like this 1955 General Electric wall refrigerator, were mechanically and stylistically innovative, they often failed to meet consumer desires.

## *The Ideal Postwar Kitchen*

By the time the war ended, housewives had already been fed a steady diet of optimistic visions of the postwar kitchen. *McCall's* magazine asked readers in 1943 to choose between a "Tried-and-True" kitchen, with a streamlined style and built-in metal cabinets, and the "Day after Tomorrow" kitchen, which featured an oven and horizontal refrigerator with glass doors and a sink operated by foot pedals.[19] Manufacturers created more "Kitchens of the Future" throughout the 1950s to test design and appliance concepts on consumers. These proposed kitchens and those that actually materialized continued to draw on the efficiency movement of the early twentieth century.

After years of being pushed farther to the back of the house and isolated from the family activities of those who employed servants, the kitchen in new postwar houses was reintegrated into everyday life. Levitt placed the kitchen and adjoining dining room in the front of early "Levittowner" models, just to the left of the front door, where they were clearly intended to be part of the home's public space.[20] His later designs returned the kitchen to the back of the house but continued to incorporate one of the most significant features of postwar kitchen design—the open plan. In many open plans, kitchen, dining area, and living room flowed from one to the next with no walls.[21] "The Kitchen Opens Up," a 1953

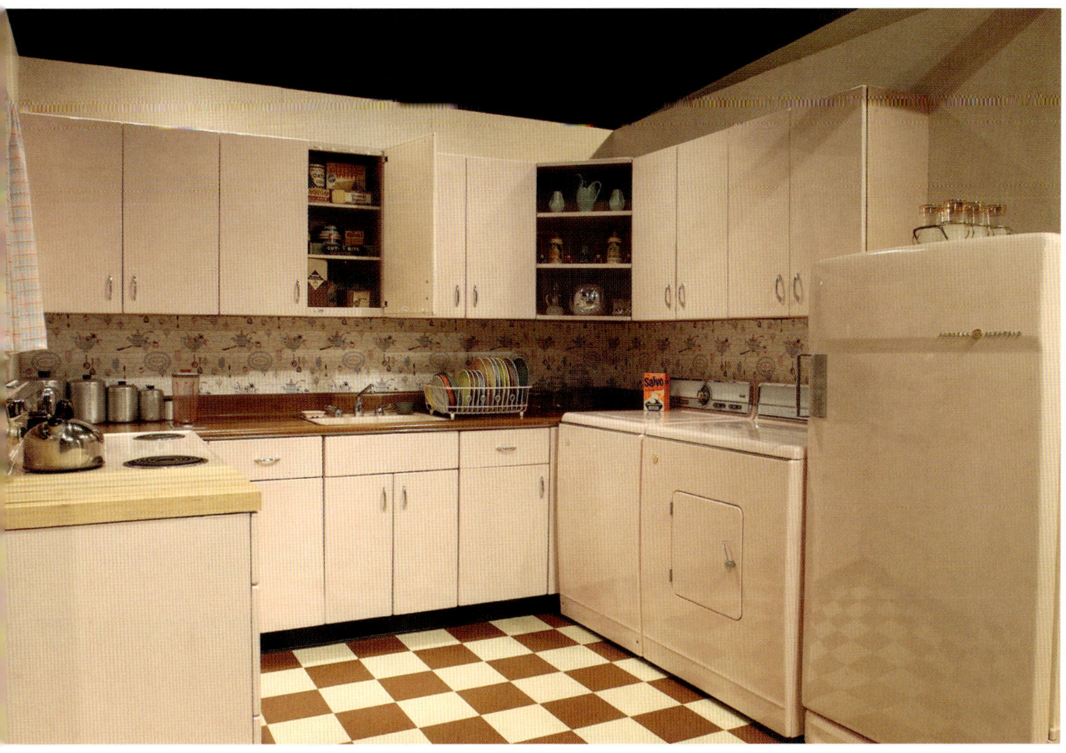

Sally Sondesky thought her kitchen had "an excellent setup" and found it very efficient. It included a General Electric "Push-Button" range, a refrigerator with "lazy Susan" shelves, and a washer and dryer. This photograph shows the Sondesky kitchen installed at the State Museum of Pennsylvania.

article in *House and Home*, explained that the average housewife "wants a command post, not a foxhole. She wants to talk to people while working, watch her children playing indoors or outdoors, keep an eye on the front door."[22] This plan made relatively small suburban homes seem larger. Promotional material created by Tracy Stainless Steel Kitchens, whose products were featured in Levittown, reminded customers that "today your kitchen is more than a busy center for household duties—it is a center for special occasions, a gathering place for snacks, lunches, refreshments, and conviviality."

In the postwar period, color was "in." Because kitchens were visible from adjoining rooms, some suggested that their color palettes match dining and living rooms.[23] Manufacturers saw the advantages of selling color appliances that families would feel compelled to buy as a matched set.[24] Companies also attempted, unsuccessfully, to introduce new styles and colors regularly as a way to entice consumers to replace appliances more often, just as car companies introduced new models each year.[25] Sally Sondesky was not fond of the color of her new kitchen, but when the appliances needed sprucing up, she repainted them with another layer of pink paint.[26]

The Sondesky kitchen illustrates the popularity of built-in cabinets and the unified look of postwar kitchens. By the 1930s the streamlined kitchen, in which the range and coun-

In 1943 *McCall's* magazine held a contest to find out "What Women Want in Their Kitchens of Tomorrow." Although many participants were intrigued by the futuristic "Day after Tomorrow" kitchen, they overwhelmingly preferred the "Tried-and-True" model, which for many represented their idea of the ideal kitchen.

The Tried-and-True kitchen will be my choice because it's the very one I've dreamed planned and even loved through several years of carrying water and lighting kerosene lamps in an ugly ramshackle old house.

Mary Davis Gillies,
*What Women Want in Their Kitchens of Tomorrow, A Report on the Kitchen of Tomorrow Contest Conducted by* McCall's *Magazine*, 1944

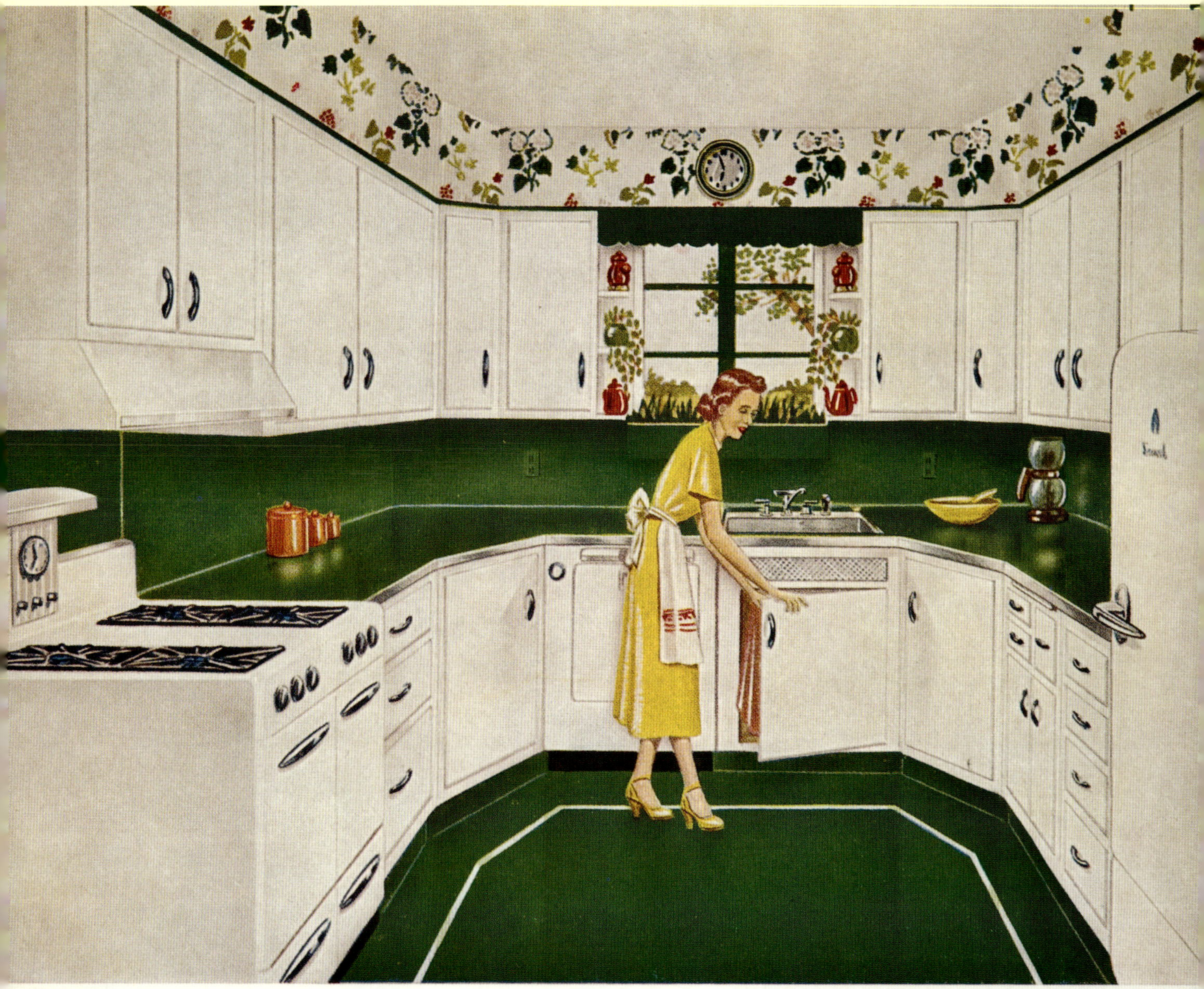

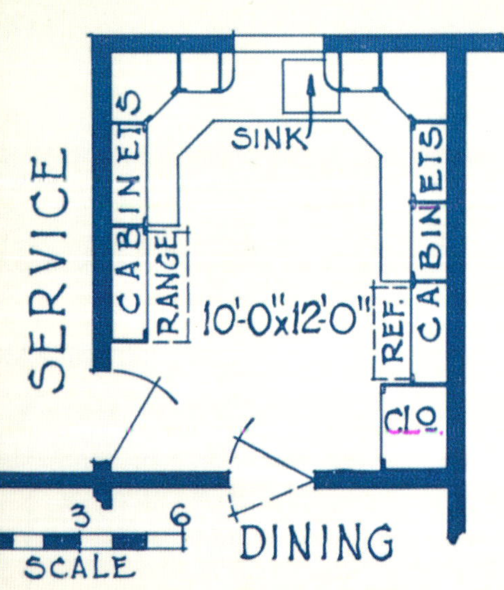


## TYPICAL "U" DESIGN

Rich, full-bodied colors emphasize the efficiency and satisfaction which can be expected in a kitchen with this simple "U" arrangement of the refrigerator, sink and range. Note that the sink is under a window at the bottom of the "U." This is an example of how the rich, full-bodied colors now being used so extensively in living rooms, dining rooms and bedrooms is being applied to kitchens. One of the special features here is the ventilating hood over the range.

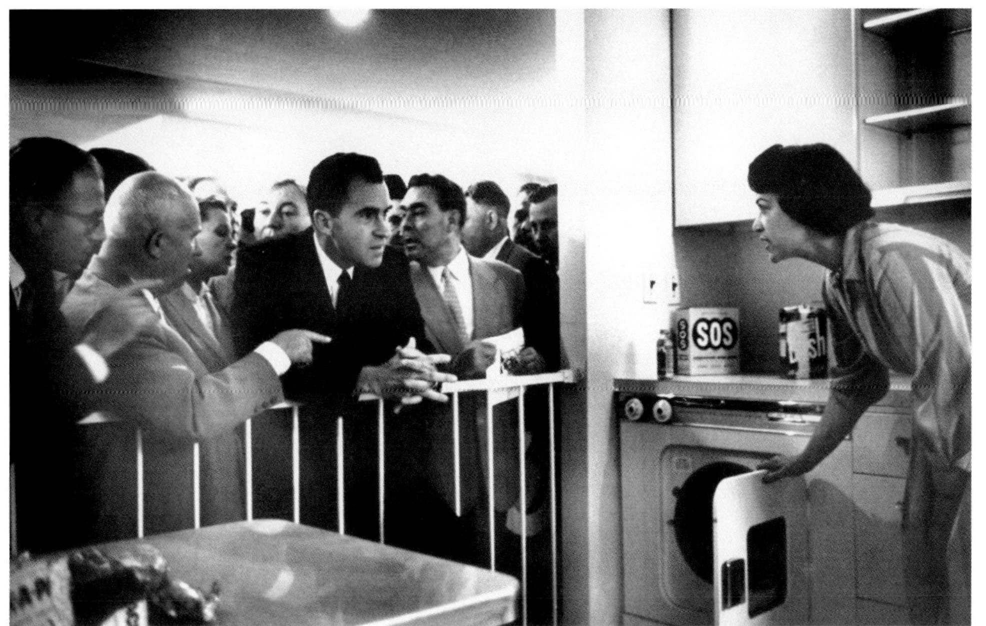


The U.S. Trade and Cultural Fair opened in Moscow in 1959 as part of a cultural exchange between the United States and the Soviet Union. Vice President Richard Nixon and Soviet Premier Nikita Khrushchev debated the relative merits of communism and capitalism in the exhibition's model kitchen. This event highlighted the modern kitchen's importance as a symbol of American prosperity and political superiority.

ters shared a uniform height and built-in cabinets replaced the pantry, had been established by kitchen designers and continued to be popular in the postwar era.[27] Because all the appliances in Levittown kitchens were preselected and included in the mortgage, new owners were not able to choose their own or bring in hand-me-down appliances, which encouraged Americans to see the kitchen as a unit.[28]

Kitchen gadgets and small appliances had been plentiful since the widespread availability of electricity, but like most postwar consumer goods, the number of products available and their popularity soared. Manufacturers touted them as the newest and best way to make kitchen work faster and more efficient. In the Sondesky kitchen, a built-in NuTone mixer/blender/knife sharpener combined multiple tasks into one easily stored appliance, but the family used it only to make milkshakes.

Plastics also made an impact on the postwar kitchen, especially on leftover food storage. Saran Wrap hit the market for home use in 1953, and the sandwich bag was invented in 1957. Earl Silas Tupper invented Tupperware in 1942 and had some early success selling these unbreakable, airtight, and attractive containers in department stores and other retail outlets. However, the product's iconic status was made possible through the work of saleswoman Brownie Wise, who pioneered the Tupperware Party; by 1951 this became the company's sole method of sales.[29] One catalogue described Tupperware as "the answer to the Housewife's demand for efficiency [and] economy . . . [and] the woman's demand for beauty"—a perfect fit in kitchens that were beginning to be thought of as fashionable as well as functional.[30]

The open plan, in addition to fostering sociability, also reflected the influence of earlier efficiency studies. Some kitchen designers considered the U-shaped layout, in which the work triangle consists of a sink along the back wall with the range on one adjacent wall and the refrigerator on the opposite side, to be the most efficient plan.

## Housework and Cooking

Efficient electric kitchens and new appliances changed some of the ways women did housework but not the amount of time it required, now that the work was theirs alone. The number of families with servants had already diminished significantly by the Great Depression, and following World War II the decline continued. Only the well to do continued to hire domestics, most of whom were day workers. As African Americans slowly gained access to jobs once closed to them, especially during the war, they left domestic service for more desirable positions.[31] New laborsaving appliances continued to be introduced; advertisements for these products touted that these "electric servants" would bring housewives more leisure. Although the amount of time spent preparing food, cleaning the house, and doing laundry decreased, more time was now spent shopping (and driving to more distant markets), caring for children, and managing the household, resulting in only a small net reduction in total time spent keeping house.[32]

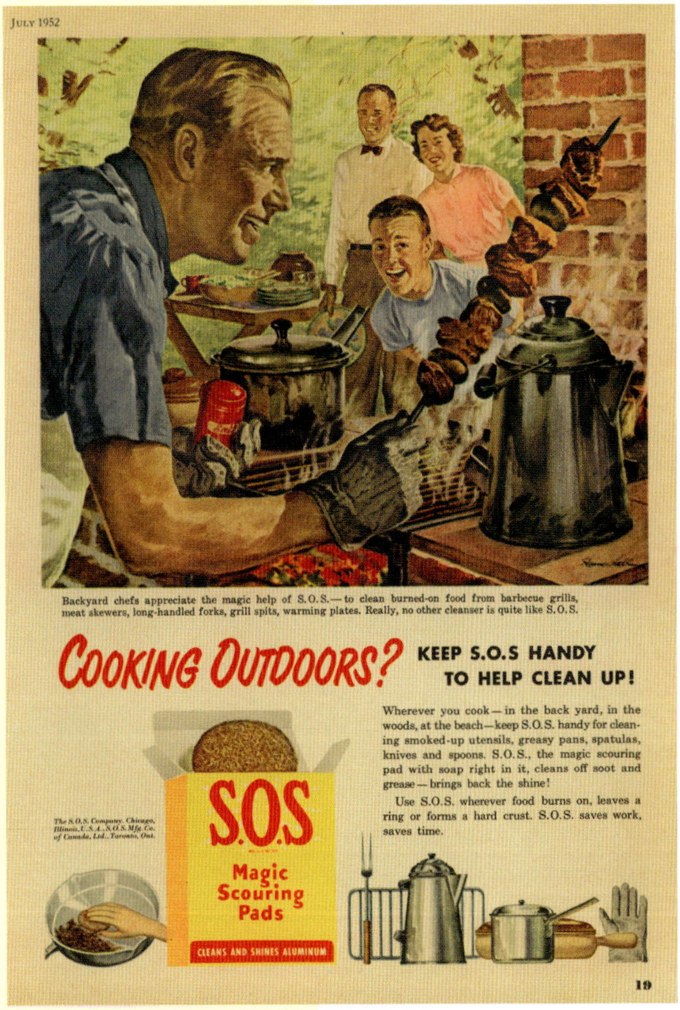

Men generally avoided the demands of housework. The move to the suburbs meant that many men now had longer commutes. Newly middle-class husbands were more likely to entertain their business associates, creating additional demands on their wives to prepare food for dinner parties and other social occasions. However, the growing popularity of the backyard barbecue, made possible by the patios and backyards of suburbia, began to engage more men in food preparation. Cookbooks highlighted the grill as the place for men to practice their "natural" affinity for cooking meat and working with fire. Men working in the kitchen, however, were portrayed in numerous, often contradictory ways: as weekend cooks, natural gourmets with adventurous palates, or as totally inept and untidy buffoons unable to boil water or find the breadbox.[33]

The popular stereotype of the postwar housewife depicts women as submissive family-focused domestics, but the reality was far more complex.[34] For some, discontent lay beneath the surface. In 1963 Betty Friedan published *The Feminine Mystique*, in which she described the

The popularity of the barbecue grill reflects the postwar era's more casual approach to dining and entertaining. As in this image, husbands were encouraged to handle the preparation of meat, while wives provided salads, side dishes, and desserts.

Tupperware provided more than convenient storage for leftovers. For suburban women who spent much of their time at home, Tupperware parties offered social outlets and ways to earn money while maintaining their roles as homemakers.

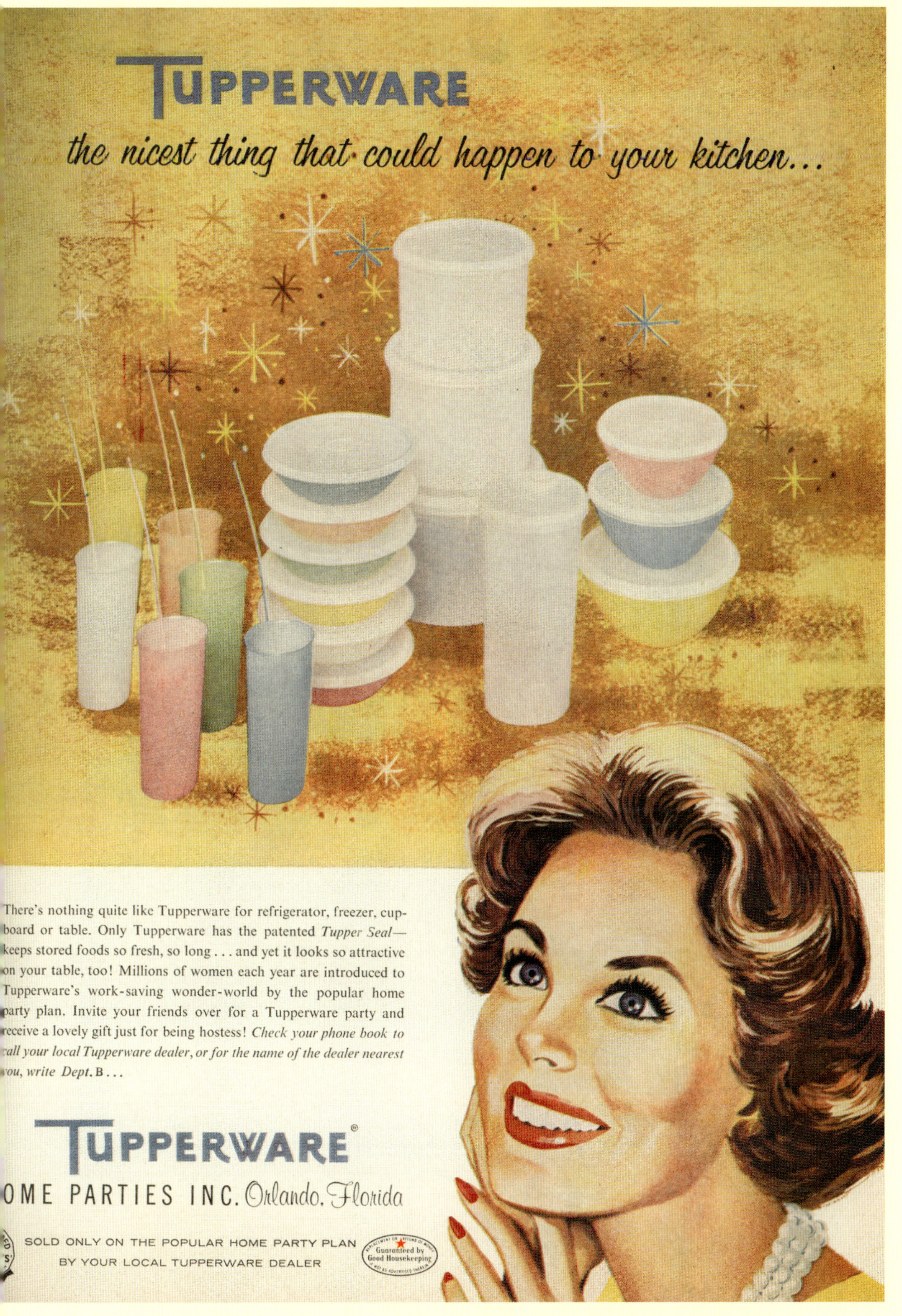

TUPPERWARE
the nicest thing that could happen to your kitchen...
There's nothing quite like Tupperware for refrigerator, freezer, cupboard or table. Only Tupperware has the patented *Tupper Seal*—keeps stored foods so fresh, so long . . . and yet it looks so attractive on your table, too! Millions of women each year are introduced to Tupperware's work-saving wonder-world by the popular home party plan. Invite your friends over for a Tupperware party and receive a lovely gift just for being hostess! *Check your phone book to all your local Tupperware dealer, or for the name of the dealer nearest ou, write Dept.* B . . .
TUPPERWARE®
OME PARTIES INC. Orlando, Florida
SOLD ONLY ON THE POPULAR HOME PARTY PLAN
BY YOUR LOCAL TUPPERWARE DEALER
Guaranteed by Good Housekeeping

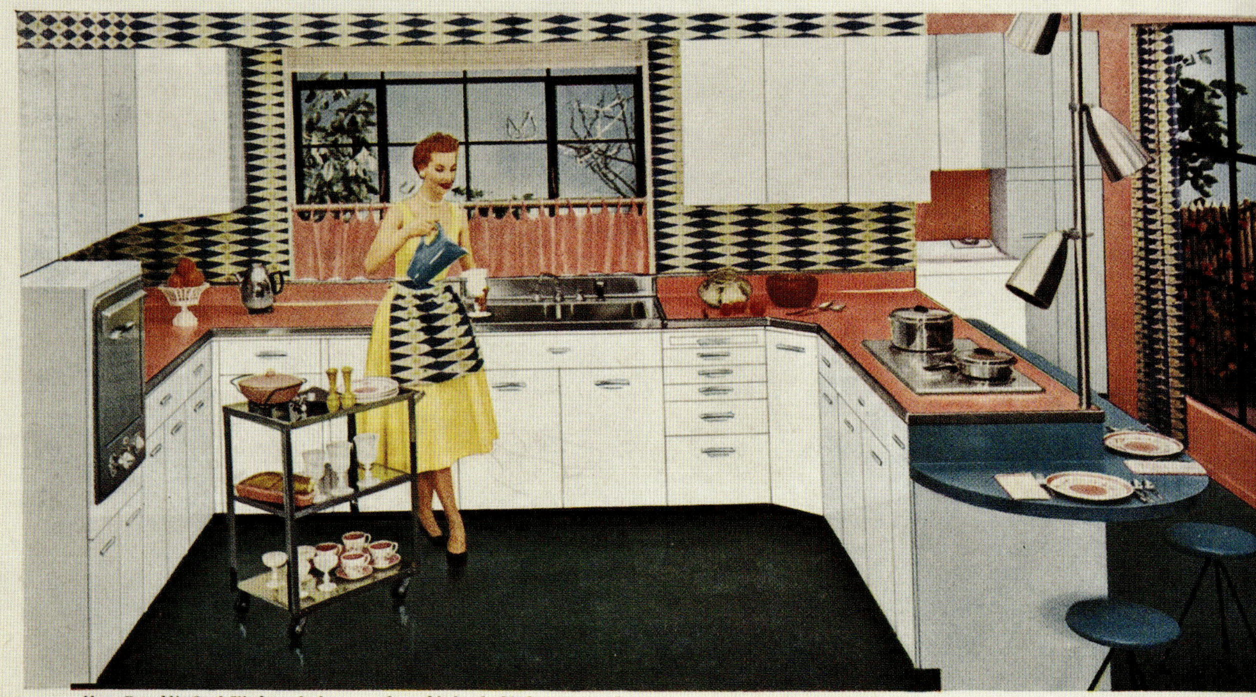

*Your Republic Steel Kitchens dealer can adapt this lovely kitchen to your home.*

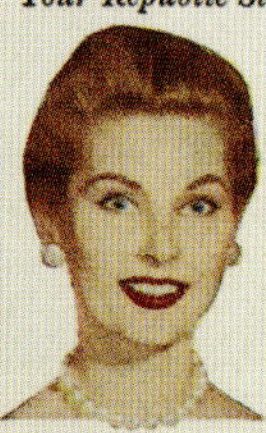

STEP INTO MY

# Take-it-easy Kitchen

**...and you'll find a wonderful new world of efficiency and charm!**

What makes this Republic kitchen so "easy to take"? First, the plan, which helps you organize your energy. Everything where you want it, when you want it, as you like it. Second, the line of modern cabinets, so varied in size and features you can make your kitchen fit *you.* Third, counter tops of practical coved Formica on durable steel. Fourth, accessories that ease your kitchen chores. Fifth, color accent on counters and walls—and beautiful fresh-white Perma Finish Enamel that lives happily ever after in any surroundings. Sixth, the low cost of a Republic Steel Kitchen. Here's "beauty and the budget" at its best!

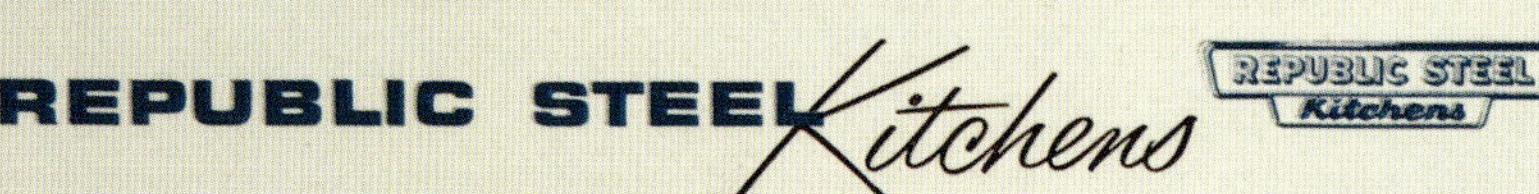


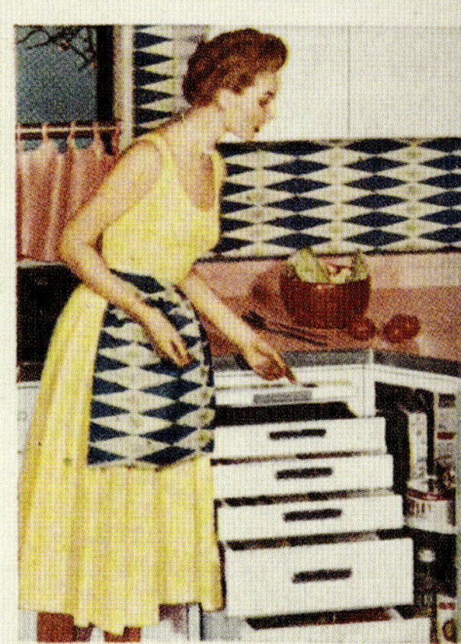

**YOU'LL FIND A "COZY CORNER."** This l
susan cabinet corners every inch of spa
swings around at fingertip beckoni
Republic turns the trick, too, with th
clever shallow drawers—just the park
space for cutlery, silverware and line

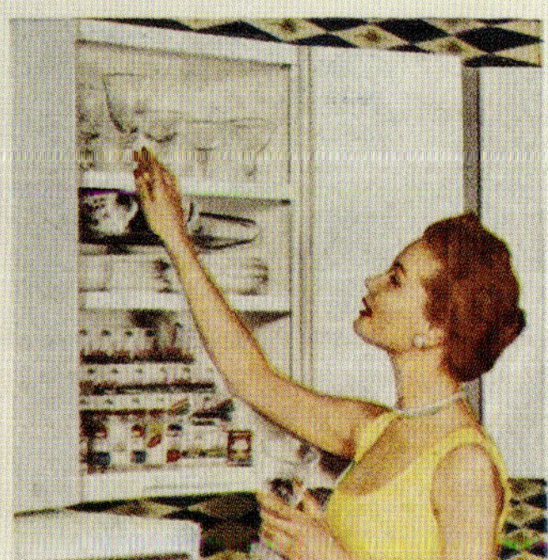

**YOU'LL FIND THE "HEIGHT OF CONVENIENCE"!** See how Republic's adjustable shelves cater to your own height, put everything within your "comfort reach." More take-it-easy touches are apparent in this spice shelf and handy cup rack.

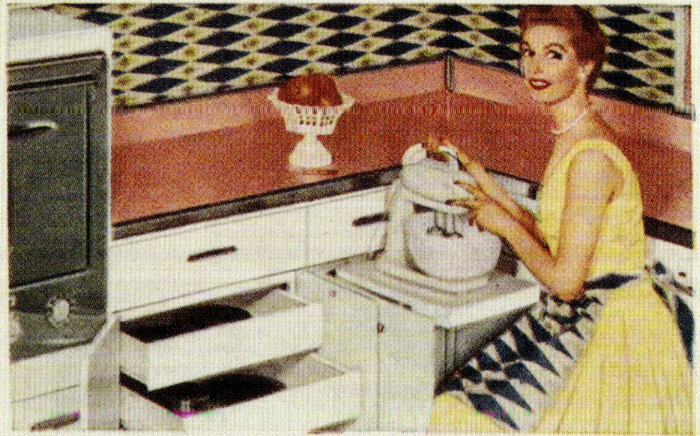

**YOU'LL FIND SOME DELIGHTFUL "INNER SECRETS!"** Just open the door, pull up the shelf, and presto! your mixer pops into sight and into use. Flick the release, wave your hand, and it does a disappearing act right under your counter. And, hidden behind the doors of the adjoining cabinet are not just shelves, but *inner drawers* that slide out magically on quiet nylon glides. Supernatural? Nope—just *super!*

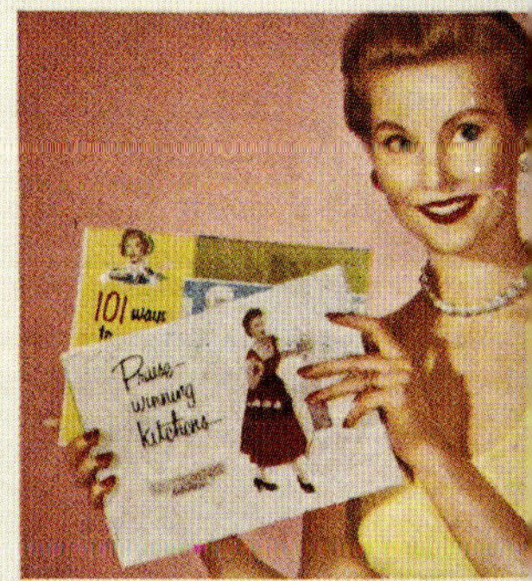


**NEW PLANNING BOOKS:** For remodeli
"101 Ways To Make Awkward Kitch
Behave"; for new homes, "Praise-Winn
Kitchens." Send 25c for one, 40c for b
with your address to Republic Steel, Be
Division, 1050 Belden, Canton 5, O

frustration of suburban housewives who felt trapped by domesticity and the cultural forces that encouraged their repression. One of Friedan's many examples illustrated how educated women gave up careers for kitchens:

> *A friend of mine, an able writer turned full-time housewife, had her suburban dream house designed by an architect to her own specifications. . . . The house . . . was almost literally one big kitchen. . . . there wasn't any place where she could get out of the kitchen, away from her children, during the working hours. The gorgeous mahogany and stainless steel of her custom-built kitchen cabinets and electric appliances were indeed a dream, but when I saw that house, I wondered where, if she ever wanted to write again, she would put her typewriter.*[35]

Friedan's book resonated with many housebound women and provided a seed for the feminist movement, but the experiences she described were not shared by all women of the decade. Women had been working outside of their own homes before their famous contribution to the World War II work force, especially those who were single, immigrants, or African Americans, or from working-class families. In the 1950s and 1960s many middle-class women went back to work after their children started school, and the number of jobs in the "pink collar" sector (such as clerical work) increased. Women's wages, as minimal as they often were, contributed to the family's ability to purchase the cars, refrigerators, and televisions that so many Americans desired.[36]

With more women working and kitchen technology constantly improving, new trends in cooking emerged. Postwar Americans experienced an abundance of foods, recipes, appliances, and cooking advice, in sharp contrast to prior years of shortages and making do. The increased production and promotion of convenience foods, the publication of a record number of cookbooks, and the growing sophistication of American taste began a long-term shift in cooking and eating habits.

Packaged and processed foods had been on the market for years, but after World War II they were used increasingly in different and inventive combinations. Manufacturers promoted these products as modern shortcuts for busy homemakers that would help them escape their kitchens to spend more time pursuing leisure activities. Advertisers and food writers encouraged women to transform well-established convenience foods, such as canned fruits, vegetables, soups, and JELL-O, into salads and casseroles. In her *Can-Opener Cook-*

A twenty-four-year-old housewife from Trenton, New Jersey, recently moved to Levittown, described her day to interviewers for a 1959 study on working-class housewives. Despite the presence of electric appliances, the relentless schedule of her day was not much different from that of an eighteenth- or nineteenth-century woman.

> Well, naturally, I get up first, make breakfast for my husband and put a load of clothes in my washer while breakfast cooks. Then I wake him up, give him his breakfast and he's off to work. Then I make breakfast for the children. After the children eat I dress them and they go out to play. Then I hang the clothes up and clean lightly through the house. In between times I do the dishes—that's understood, of course. Then I make lunch for the children and myself and I bring them in, clean them up, and they eat. I send them out to play when they're done and I do the dishes, bring the clothes in, and iron them. When I'm done ironing it's usually time to make supper, or at least start preparing it. Sometimes I have time to watch a TV story for half an hour or so. Then my husband comes home and we have our meals. Then I do the dishes again.
>
> A Levittown housewife,
> in *Workingman's Wife: Her Personality, World, and Life Style*, 1959

For women with limited time or patience for kitchen work, products promising to save time and effort were likely to have considerable appeal.

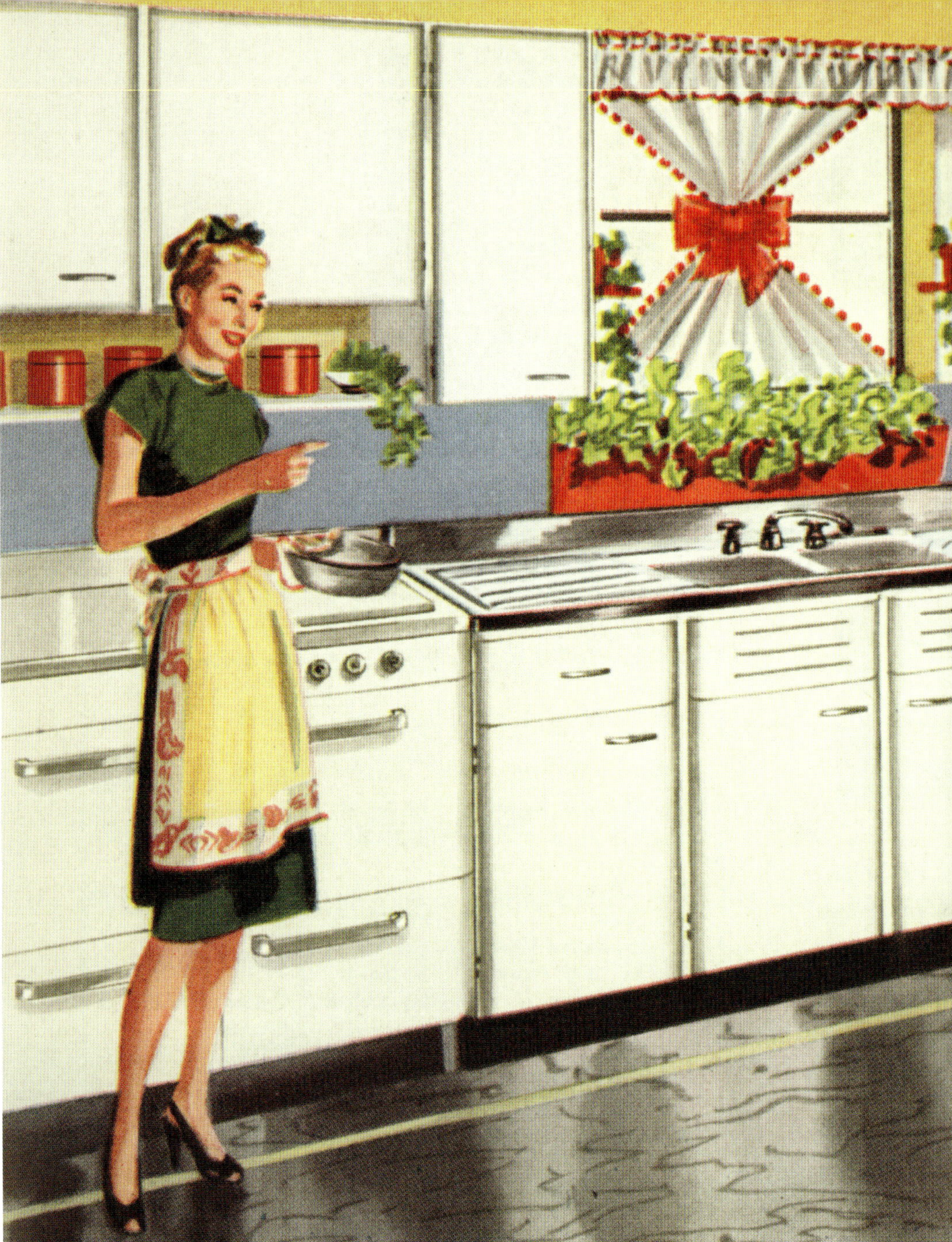

While the reality of women's lives in the postwar years was rich and varied, images like this one from a 1947 Kitchen Maid catalogue abounded in popular magazine advertisements and television programs, suggesting that ideal women spent their days with their children in harmonious, spotless surroundings.

*book* (1951), Poppy Cannon celebrated the variety of canned products by creating recipes she believed turned plain products into gourmet meals by adding extra seasonings and occasionally "a splotch of wine." Peg Bracken's bestselling tribute to the harried housewife with no interest in lingering in the kitchen, *The I Hate to Cook Book* (1960), offered recipes for everyday dishes, many of which used a combination of fresh and convenience foods. Anticipating Betty Friedan's critique of suburban domestic culture, Bracken responded to the idealistic expectations that American culture and cookbook authors created for women in the kitchen.[37]

Frozen convenience foods became increasingly common and diverse in the postwar period. Clarence Birdseye's 1925 patent on the process of quick-freezing seafood, vege-

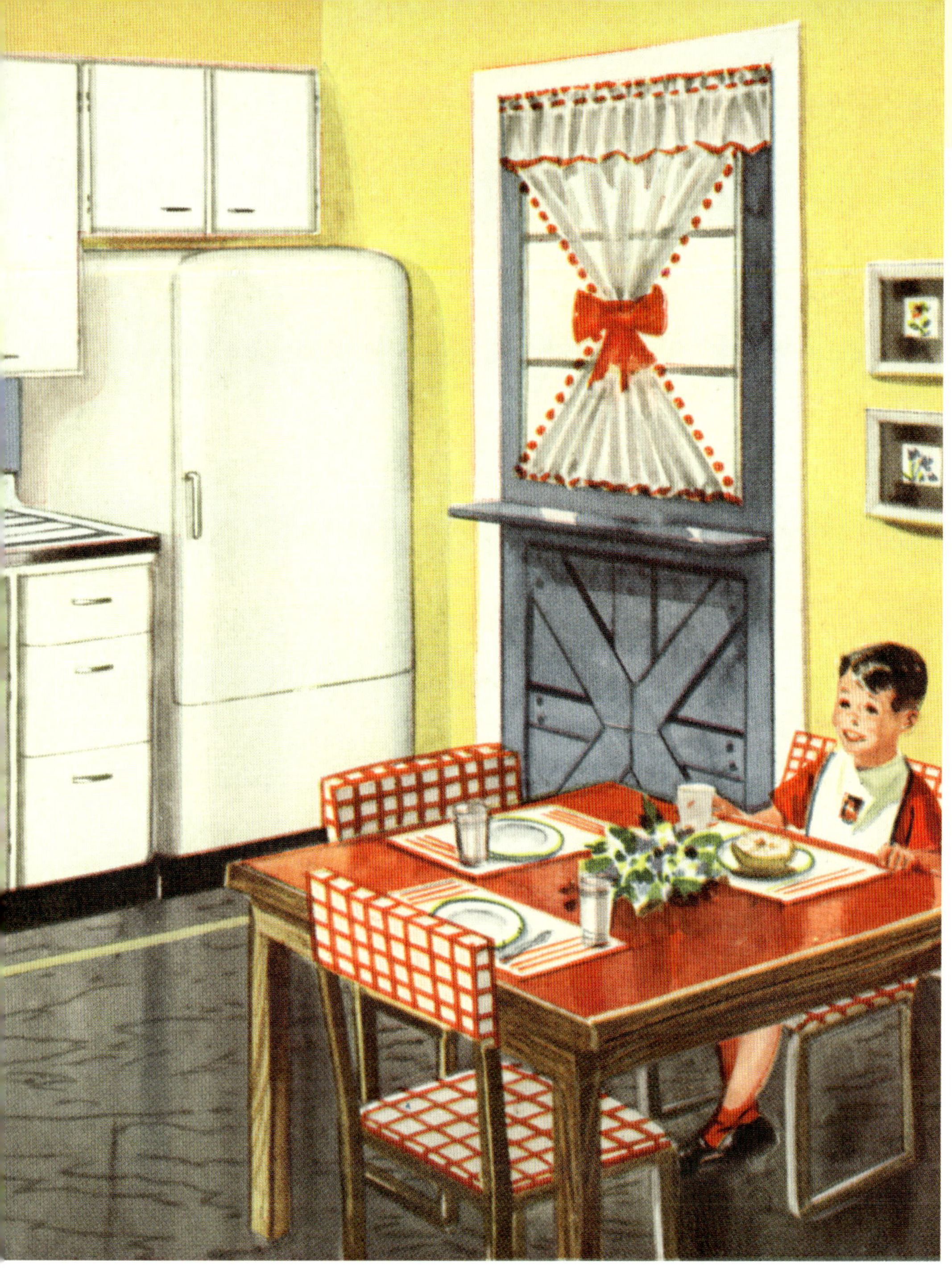

Women found Peg Bracken's irreverent approach to everyday cooking refreshing, given the pervasive depiction of the happy homemaker in postwar cookbooks and popular culture.

tables, and fruits inaugurated the frozen food industry, but until the late 1940s few grocers had frozen food cases to sell these products, and consumers lacked adequate space to store them.[38] Sales of home freezers broke records in the late 1940s and early 1950s, and the shift toward supermarket shopping expanded the industry's market to include middle- and working-class consumers.[39] Orange juice concentrate and fish sticks were two of the early successes. By the late 1950s the frozen food industry had grown enough to seek new markets, for instance, by packaging frozen okra, turnip greens, and other "Southern" vegetables to attract African American consumers.[40]

> Add the flour, salt, paprika, and mushrooms, stir, and let it cook five minutes while you light a cigarette and stare sullenly at the sink.
>
> Peg Bracken, recipe for "Skid Road Stroganoff," *The I Hate to Cook Book*, 1960

The success of Swanson's TV Dinners has been credited to the company's decision to link its frozen meal with television, a new, modern, and popular medium. Television's popularity also inspired cereal-based snack mixes that families could easily consume while watching their favorite programs.

Self-contained frozen meals had also been available prior to the war, but Swanson's TV Dinners, introduced in 1953, were the first successful products of this type. The original dinner included turkey, gravy, dressing, whipped sweet potatoes, and peas, a typically labor-intensive meal associated with holidays and good times, now made quick and easy.[41] Frozen dinners were promoted as convenient meals but rarely replaced home-cooked dinners. More often, they served as alternatives when parents left the kids with the baby-sitter or when the man of the house was left to fend for himself.[42]

Convenience products also transformed baking during the 1950s as companies perfected cake mix formulas and established marketing campaigns to encourage housewives to try them. The home-baked layer cake was seen as the sign of a housewife's skill; cake mixes offered guaranteed success, and the time saved could be dedicated to expressing one's creativity through frosting and decorating. However, two icons of the 1950s, the Pillsbury Bake-Off, and *Betty Crocker's Picture Cookbook*, indicate that the cake mix did not replace baking from scratch. In 1949 Pillsbury held its first Grand National Recipe and Baking Contest. Contestants were required to use at least one-half cup of Pillsbury's Best Family Flour but could use no mixes. The incredible success of the Pillsbury Bake-Off suggests that women continued to take pride in their homemade baked goods, while the competition provided the recognition homemakers craved.[43]

In 1950 another flour company, General Mills, published *Betty Crocker's Picture Cook Book*, which quickly became a best-seller. The most revolutionary aspect of the book was its visual method of instruction, which used photographs of hands demonstrating each step in the recipe. For suburban women who had moved some distance from their families, Betty Crocker served as a substitute mother who educated a new generation of home bakers.[44] As one might expect from a cookbook published by a flour company, recipes for cakes, cookies, and desserts significantly outnumbered those for meat and other entrées.

Despite the prevalence of convenience foods and shortcut cooking that sacrificed freshness for speed and ease, some Americans began taking greater interest in gourmet cooking

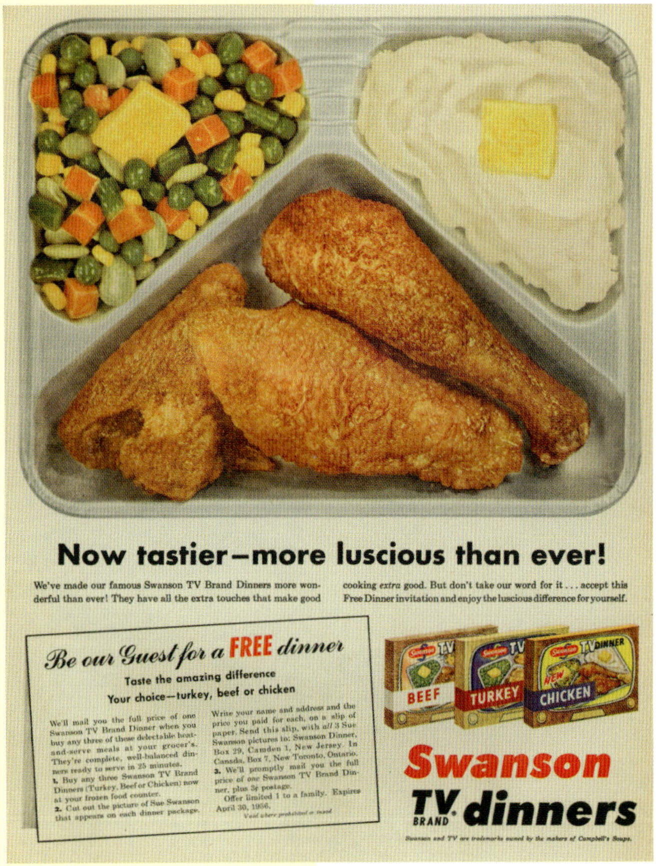

Manufacturers of frozen and other packaged foods hoped to entice busy housewives to use their products as replacements for time-consuming home cooking. However, many women were suspicious of such products, and the lack of effort they required led to feelings of guilt.

My children yearned for the gourmet delights of T.V. dinners. I knew that to give the children T. V. dinners was to neglect them. A mother is supposed to cook. . . . So it was rarely, and quietly, that I allowed the baby-sitter to feed them those neat packages. I hoped that in delegating the betrayal they would remember me for the home cooking, and the baby-sitter for the ersatz stuff.

Caroline Urvater, "Thoughts for Food," in *Through the Kitchen Window: Women Explore the Intimate Meanings of Food and Cooking*, 1997

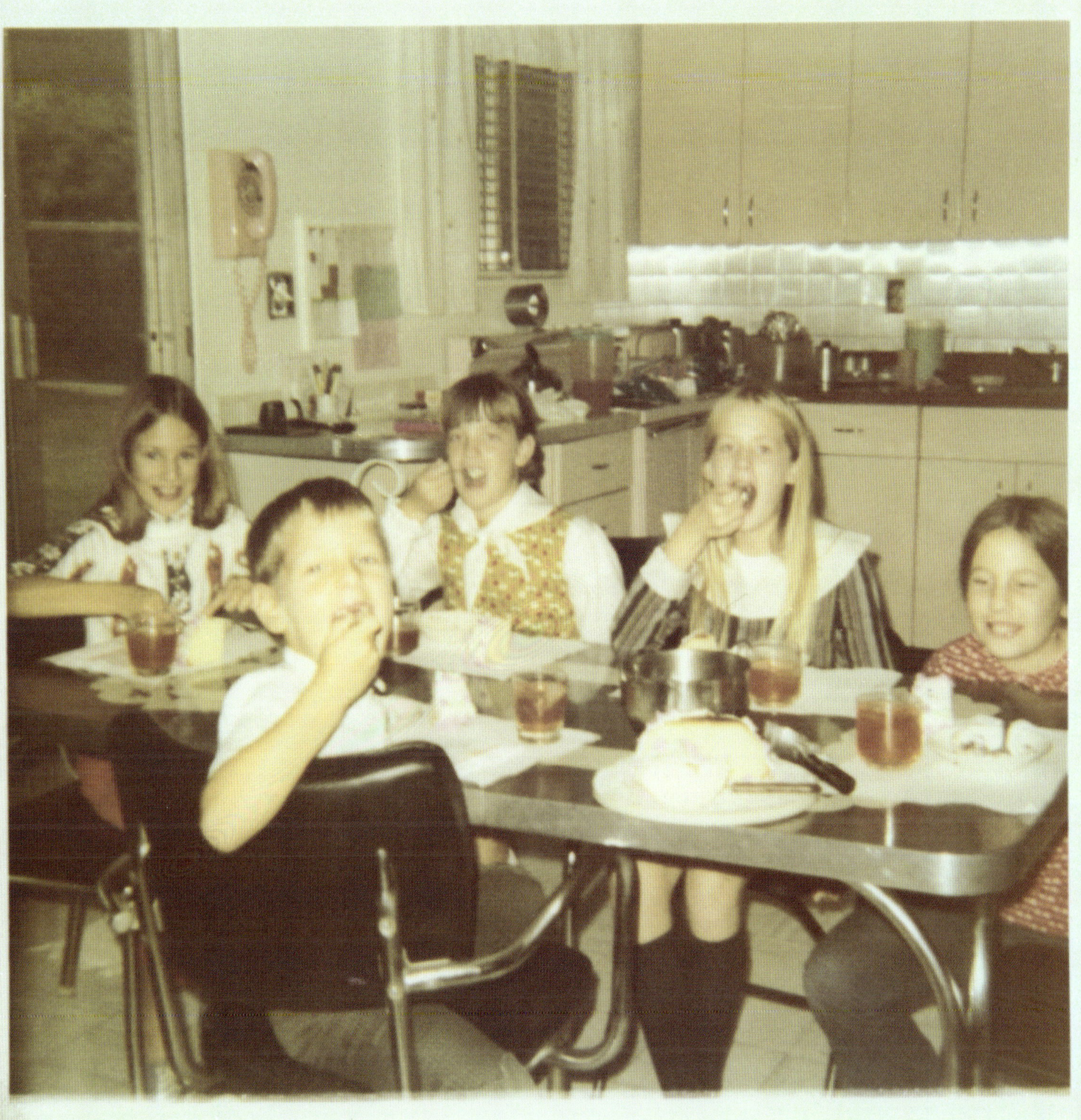

Sally Sondesky always made fancy cakes, sometimes shaped like dolls or ducks, for her children's birthday parties, which were celebrated at the kitchen table.

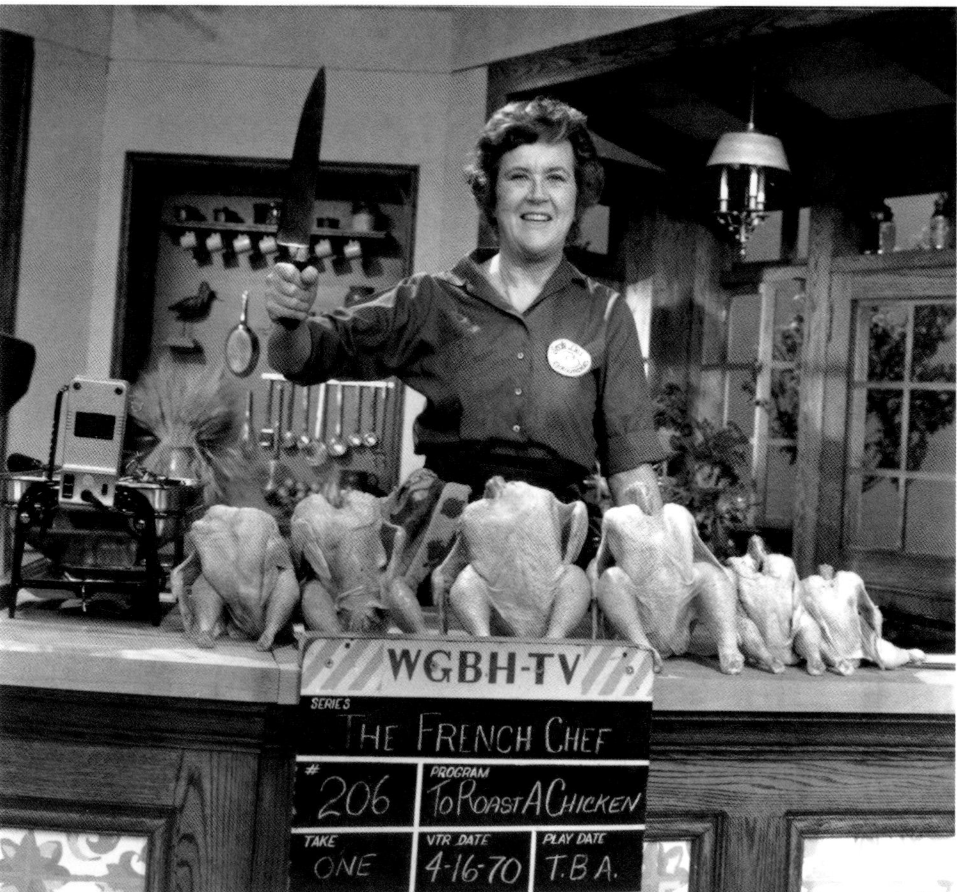


The pilot episode of Julia Child's program, *The French Chef*, aired on Boston's public television network in 1962. Viewers were enchanted by Julia's humor and her down-to-earth approach to preparing French classics.

and ethnic cuisines. Curiosity about French cuisine, in particular, increased, in part due to the presence of a French chef in the Kennedy White House. Julia Child's popular cookbook and television show demonstrated that many women (and men) were interested in more than packaged food cuisine. In the introduction to *Mastering the Art of French Cooking*, Child and her coauthors made it clear who their audience was:

> *This is a book for the servantless American cook who can be unconcerned on occasion with budgets, waistlines, time schedules, children's meals, the parent-chauffeur-den-mother syndrome, or anything else which might interfere with the enjoyment of producing something wonderful to eat. Written for those who love to cook, the recipes are as detailed as we have felt they should be so the reader will know exactly what is involved and how to go about it.*[45]

Those who were willing to follow the book's clear and detailed instructions found that preparing French cuisine at home was within their reach. Child and her coauthors created master recipes using ingredients that could be found in any supermarket to teach cooks the basic techniques of French cooking. Child's experience as a cooking teacher translated well to television and contributed to the success of her program, *The French Chef*, which gained a wide following, even among viewers who never attempted to duplicate the dishes in their own kitchens.[46]

Other foreign flavors began emerging in middle-class kitchens. Soldiers fighting overseas had opportunities to experience new cuisines and brought their newly educated palates home.[47] However, many of the "ethnic" recipes published in postwar cookbooks were far from authentic. For example, recipes for "Chicken India" and "Indonesian Drumsticks" in Poppy Cannon's *Frozen-Foods Cookbook* included only tiny amounts of the garlic and ginger that would customarily be included in dishes from these regions. Other cookbook writers provided more authentic recipes, but even those who modified ethnic flavors paved the way for more experimentation, which continued into the latter half of the century.[48]

Despite all the cookbooks and advice, when it came to making dinner, what mattered was personal taste. One participant in a study of the preferences of middle- and working-class families indicated, "We love plain foods. No burgundy sauces for us. Roast beef is our favorite. I never read the menus in magazines or cook any fancy dishes. I just make sure the food isn't boring."[49] Women believed in serving meals their families enjoyed even when the repertory was limited. According to popular media and published cookbooks, convenience foods seem to have dominated postwar kitchens, but in reality, everyday meals combined packaged food with food cooked from scratch.[50]

## Kitchens after the 1950s

Apart from the near universal presence of the microwave, the basic design of today's kitchen has changed little from the kitchen of the 1950s. Colors, styles, scale, and materials have changed according to fads and fashion, but the desire for efficiency and unified kitchen design remains. As in the postwar period, the ideal kitchen is part of an open plan and the center of household activity. People continue to eat, pay bills, do homework, visit with friends and neighbors, and even entertain while cooking.

The most dramatic change in the kitchen over the past half century may be the trend toward the kitchen as a less gendered space. In the complex family dynamic of the early twenty-first century, in which both parents commonly work outside the home and many children live in single-parent households, men are preparing family meals at an increasing rate.[51] A recent national survey by Leo J. Shapiro & Associates of Chicago found that nearly 20 percent of men do all the cooking in their households, and considerably more do at least some of the cooking.[52]

Greater awareness of national and global issues affecting food has changed the way many Americans cook. Health foods are nothing new; in the late nineteenth century, John Harvey Kellogg promoted a vegetarian diet that ultimately led to the invention of breakfast cereals. The health food movement of the 1960s and 1970s was motivated by environmental concerns, such as the use of DDT and other pesticides, and

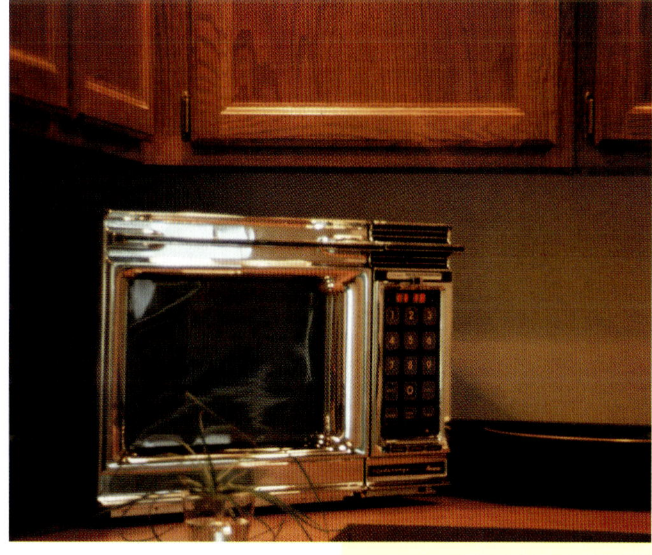

Amana introduced the first countertop microwave oven in 1967. By the late 1970s and early 1980s microwaves were in enough homes to prompt publication of many cookbooks that showed how to use the microwave as a substitute for the regular stove. By the early 1990s the use of microwaves had not resulted in a new kind of cookery. However, they were popular for reheating leftovers and warming packaged frozen meals.

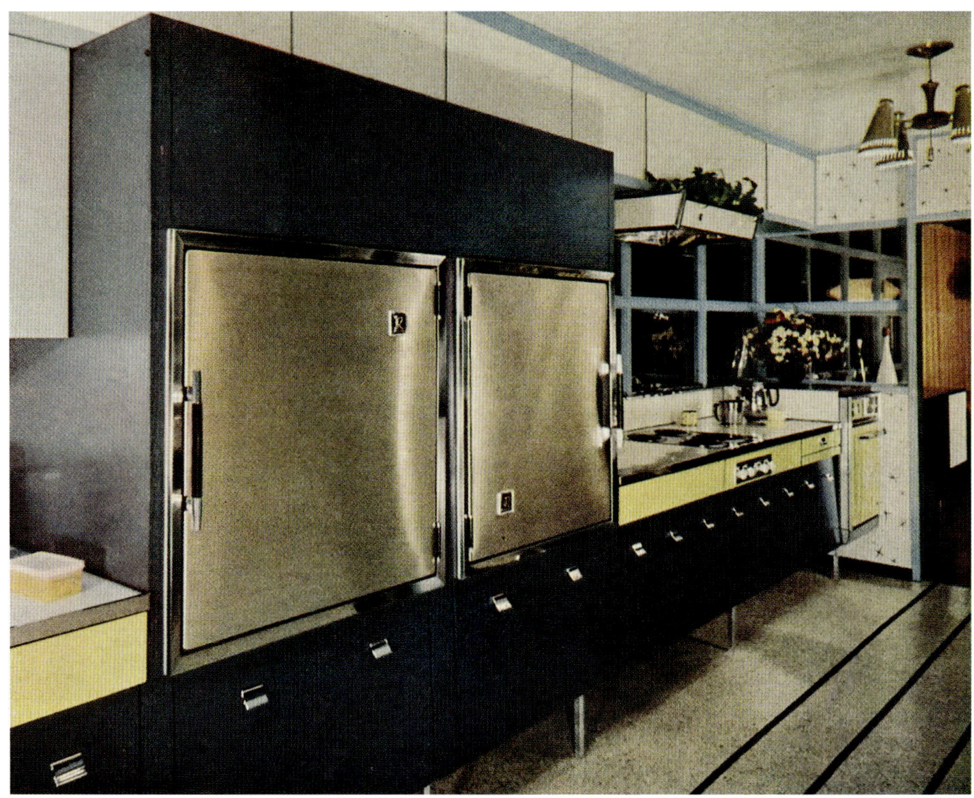

As this 1959 advertisement for a stylish built-in refrigerator demonstrates, stainless steel appliances and sleek high-tech design, common in twenty-first-century kitchens, were also present in kitchen designs of the postwar era.

the control by large corporations and agribusinesses of the nation's food supply.[53] Organic farming, food co-ops, natural foods supermarkets, community-supported agriculture (CSA) programs, and the Slow Food movement all grew out of the desire to get closer to the source of one's meal.[54]

From the relatively tame offerings of Poppy Cannon's recipes to Julia Child's more sophisticated *boeuf bourguignon*, Americans incrementally embraced new cuisines and more authentic versions of them. Increased travel, the continued proliferation of cookbooks, celebrity chefs, and cooking programs on television, as well as new immigration patterns have made American cooking more diverse and adventurous. By the end of the century, tortilla chips and salsa had become the chip and dip of choice, and wasabi could be found in many a spice rack.

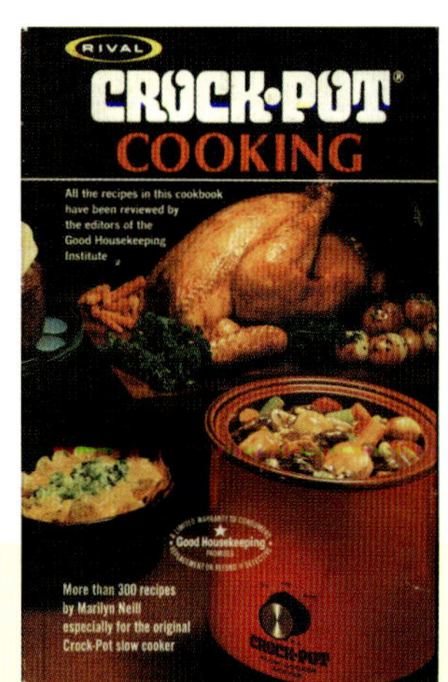


One of many small appliances marketed in the 1970s, a decade when two-income households became increasingly common and necessary, Rival's Crock-Pot reintroduced the traditional one-pot meal that would "Cook all day while the Cook's away."

Americans continue to embrace the convenient meal. New technology has led to an even greater abundance of packaged foods from shelf-stable dairy products to fortified foods with added nutrients, usually based on the nutritional fads of the moment.[55] Peanut-butter-and-jelly sandwiches can be bought premade (with the crusts removed) in the frozen food sec-

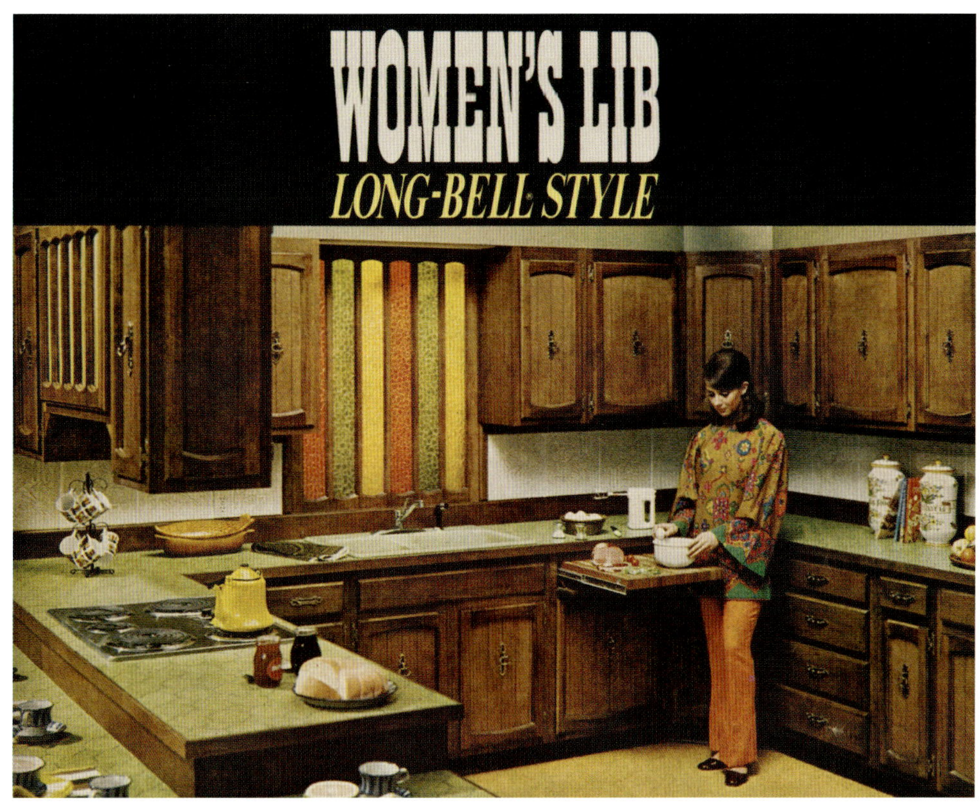


The copy for this 1972 advertisment claims that "Liberation begins on the home front," implying that, even once liberated, women will still find themselves confined to the kitchen.

tion. Commuters can eat yogurt from a tube or sip soup from a cup designed to fit into their cars' cupholders. Such products allow Americans to spend even less time preparing meals and more time working or pursuing leisure activities.

While some see the family kitchen as the center of all that is right and good in America, others see the collapse of the American family played out in the kitchen and at the dinner table. As Cameron Stracher observed in the *Wall Street Journal*, "We are a nation of take-outers and drive throughers, eating our meals on the go, dining by ourselves and laughing alone. The family dinner has become an endangered species, the victim of our own ingenuity and productivity."[56] Although there are germs of truth to be found in these statements, in fact, most families report that they regularly cook meals from scratch. A recent survey found that between 1998 and 2005 there was significant increase in the number of adolescents who regularly eat with their parents.[57] While people are actually increasingly sitting down together to eat, the fear that the collapse of the American family can be seen in the way people use their kitchens suggests the importance of the room in the American psyche.

As early as 1952, Americans were recognizing that kitchens once again were becoming communal spaces like those experienced by previous generations.

> In the old-time kitchen there was space for the baby in the cradle and the toddler at play while his mother cooked, washed or did other jobs. The family gathered there for meals and work—school children at their lessons, old folks helping with lighter chores or just enjoying a comfortable chair by the cookstove. The old kitchen was the busiest, most-used room in the house, and it was shared by the whole family. This is the new as well as old idea in kitchens.
>
> Helen C. Douglas, *Small Homes Guide*, 1952

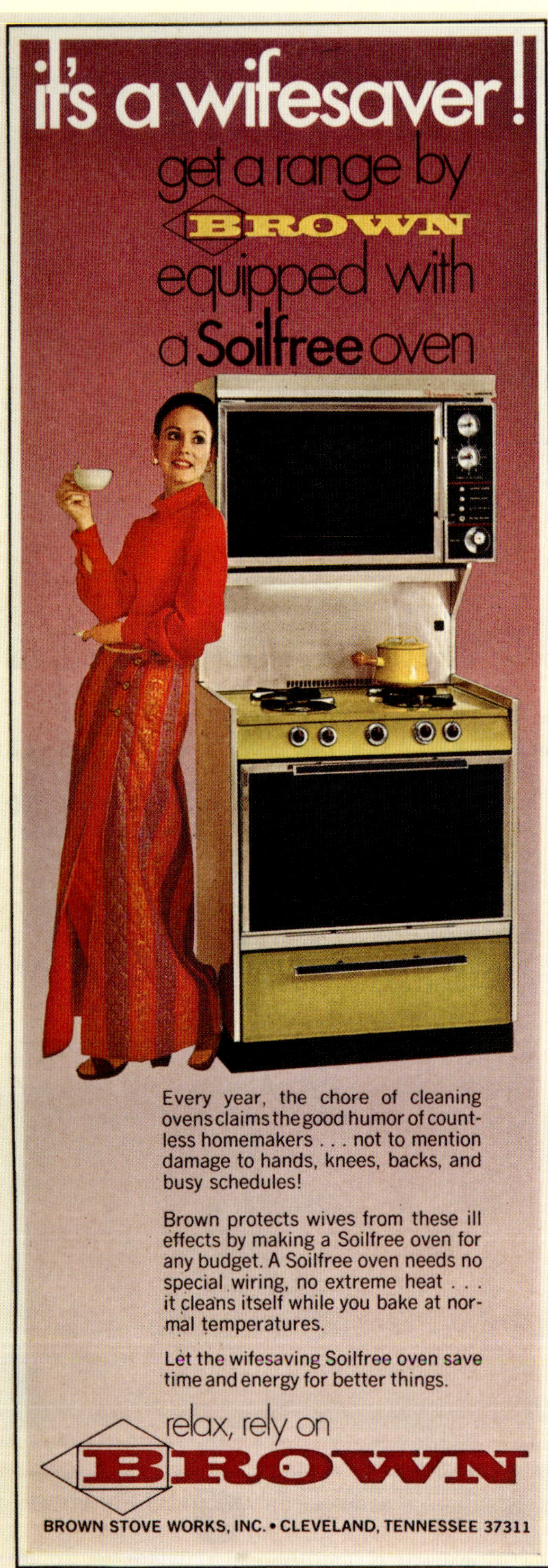
it's a wifesaver!
get a range by
BROWN
equipped with
a Soilfree oven
Every year, the chore of cleaning ovens claims the good humor of countless homemakers . . . not to mention damage to hands, knees, backs, and busy schedules!
Brown protects wives from these ill effects by making a Soilfree oven for any budget. A Soilfree oven needs no special wiring, no extreme heat . . . it cleans itself while you bake at normal temperatures.
Let the wifesaving Soilfree oven save time and energy for better things.
relax, rely on
BROWN
BROWN STOVE WORKS, INC. • CLEVELAND, TENNESSEE 37311

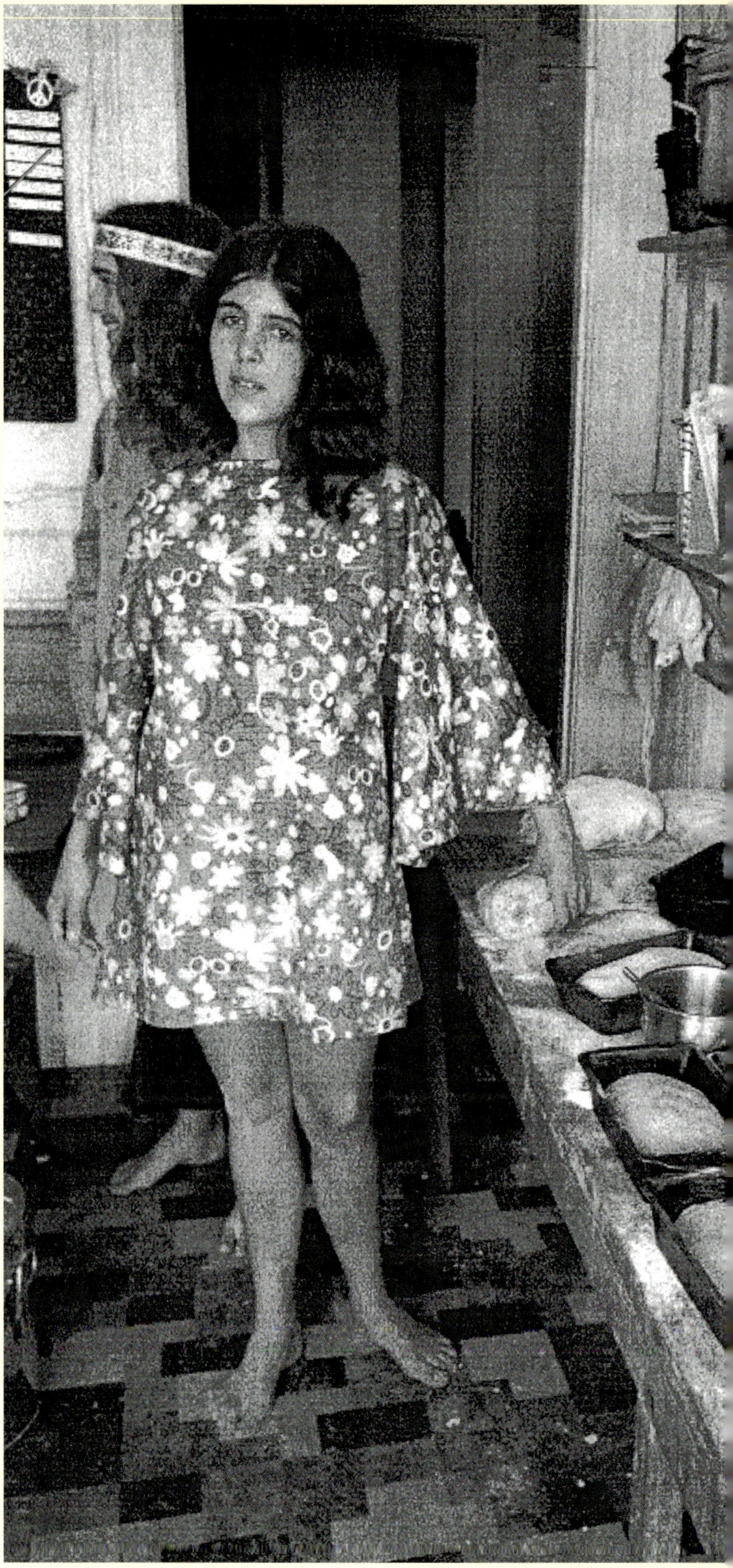

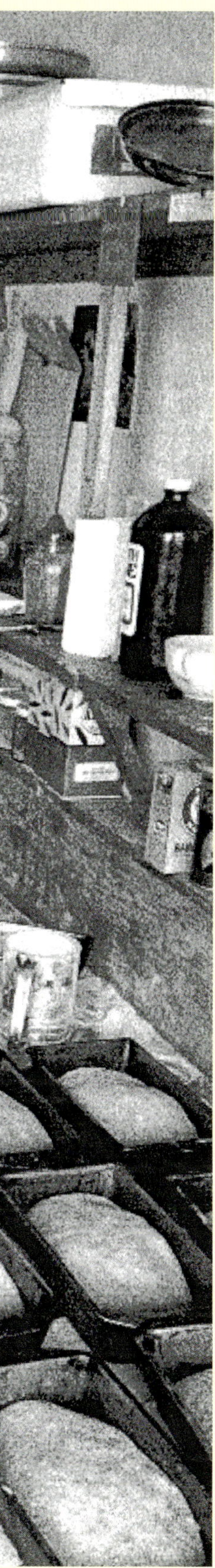

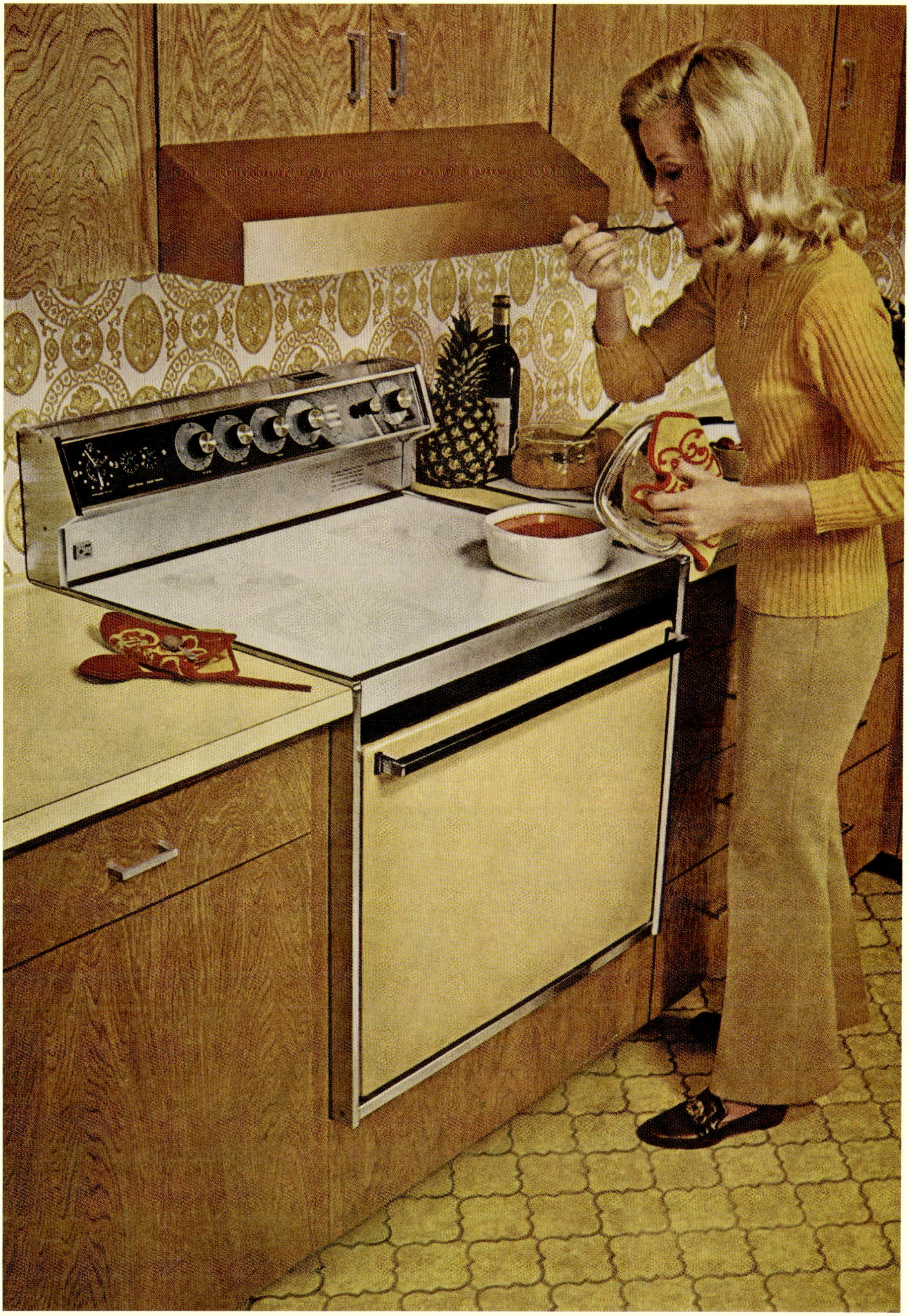

Popular imagery in the late twentieth century continued to depict women as the primary users of the kitchen, now equipped with self-cleaning ovens and cooktops that could be easily wiped down. However, many young ideologues continued to look for alternatives to the single-family kitchen. In 1969 Dennis Stock photographed members of Messiah's World (center image), an urban commune in San Francisco, where the kitchen was a shared work site.

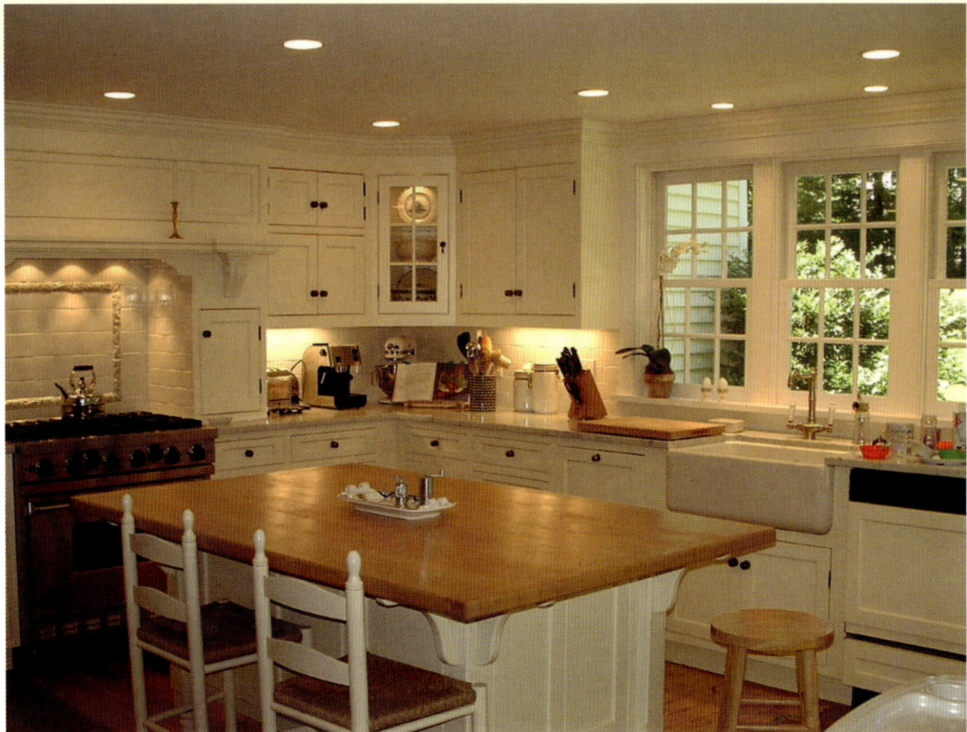

The kitchen island, which slowly gained in popularity throughout the second half of the twentieth century, has become a place for family and friends to gather. As a workspace for food preparation and as a focal point of social activity, the island hearkens back to the hearth and kitchens of earlier centuries.

In his 1956 essay, "Coon Tree," E. B. White reflected on the merits of two stoves used in his Maine kitchen, one electric and one a cast-iron, wood-burning stove. If forced to choose, White favored the wood stove despite the labor required to maintain and operate it. Among the stove's virtues are "the quality of its heat, the scope of its talents, the warmth of its nature (the place where you dry the sneakers, the place where the small dog crawls underneath to take the chill off, the companionable sound it gives forth on cool nights in fall and on zero mornings in winter)."[58] White's reflections, written at a time when efficient electric kitchens were promoted as standard equipment, offer a reminder that America's kitchens are complex, often contradictory places. The nostalgic tone in which he describes the cast-iron stove's merits reflect the ideal sentiment many associate with the kitchen, but the equipment White lauds is far from what people of his time considered part of the ideal kitchen. Although the kitchen helps people fulfill their basic daily need to eat, its significance is far greater than providing physical sustenance.

For better or worse, women have been and continue to be associated with the kitchen. Today, for some, the kitchen is still a place of relentless drudgery. Yet increasingly, thanks to modern technology and the weakening of traditional gender roles, those who are able to choose freely when and what to cook are finding the kitchen a place for creativity and release from the stress of the outside world.

More than any room in the house, the kitchen shapes and reflects cultural identity. From an early age, we observe the roles men and women play in the kitchen, we experiment with both new and old technology, and we eat foods that reflect our heritage and beliefs. As our lives change, so do our kitchens. The growth and contraction of families, financial security or insecurity, and changes in health or belief systems are but a few of the things that affect how we relate to kitchens. Regardless of whether we love or hate the kitchen, it is hard to deny its ability to reveal the complexities of American culture.

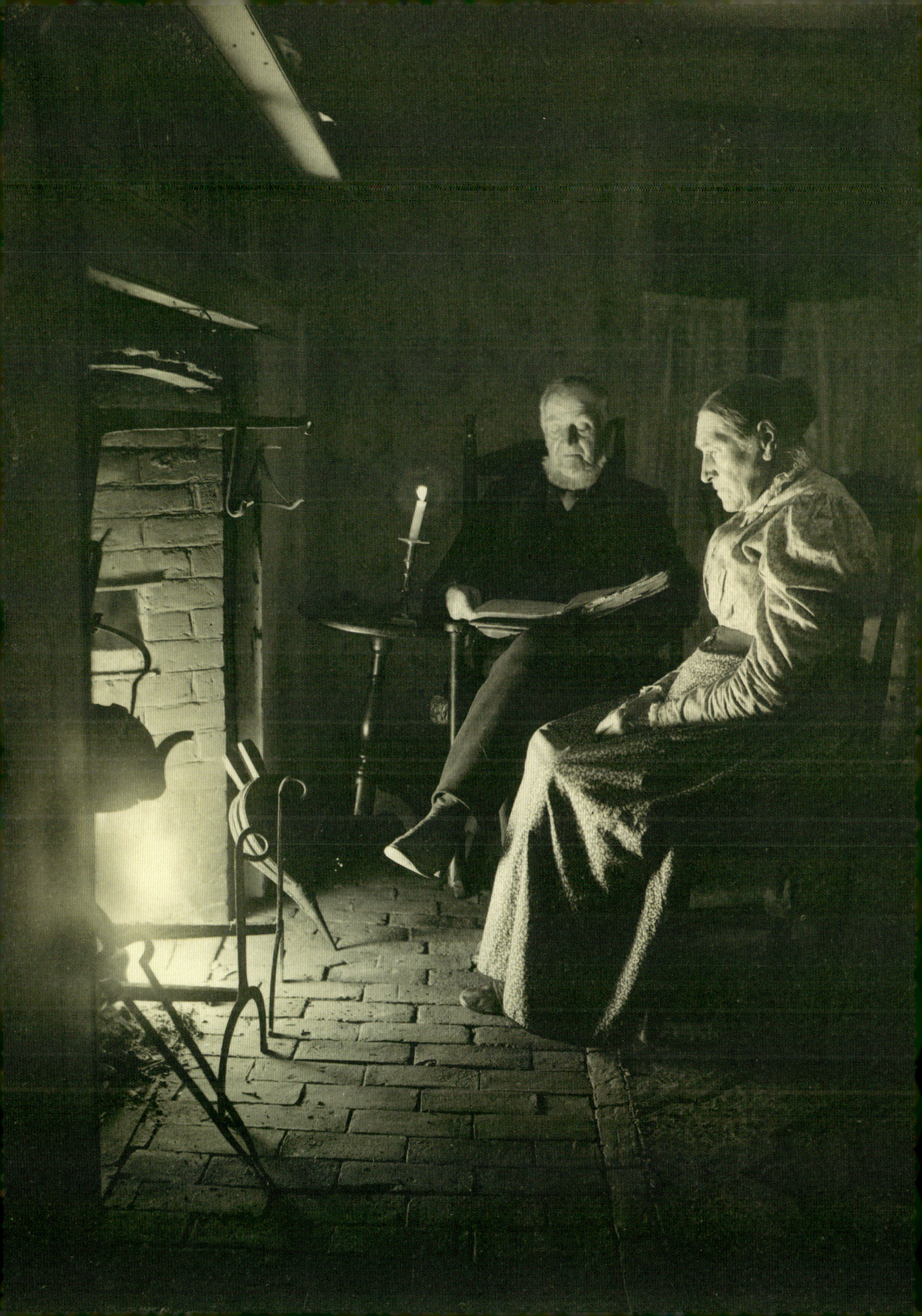

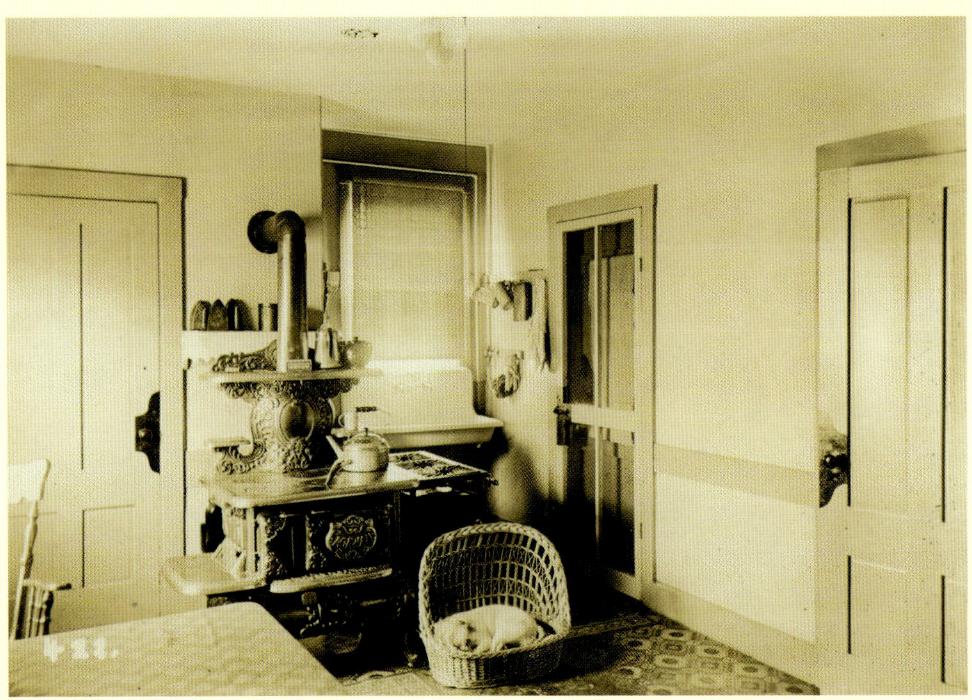

We have two stoves in our kitchen here in Maine—a big black iron stove that burns wood and a small white electric stove that draws its strength from the Bangor Hydro-Electric Company. We use both. One represents the past, the other represents the future. If we had to give up one in favor of the other and cook on just one stove, there isn't the slightest question in anybody's mind in my household which is the one we'd keep. It would be the big black Home Crawford 8-20, made by Walker & Pratt, with its woodbox that has to be filled with wood, its water tank that has to be replenished with water, its ashpan that has to be emptied of ashes, its flue pipe that has to be renewed when it gets rusty, its grates that need freeing when they get clogged, and all its other foibles and deficiencies. We would choose this stove because of the quality of its heat, the scope of its talents, the warmth of its nature (the place where you dry the sneakers, the place where the small dog crawls underneath to take the chill off, the companionable sound it gives forth on cool nights in fall and on zero mornings in winter). The electric stove is useful in its own way, and makes a good complementary unit, but it is as cold and aseptic as a doctor's examining table, and I can't imagine our kitchen if it were the core of our activity.

E. B. White, "Coon Tree," 1956

Above: The kitchen of the Carlisle house, Newport, Rhode Island, about 1914.

# ENDNOTES

## THE KITCHEN IN AMERICAN LIFE

1. E. B. White, "Coon Tree," *The Points of My Compass: Letters from the East, the West, the North, the South* (New York: Harper & Row, 1962), 70. Originally published in *The New Yorker* in 1956.
2. Ibid., 71.
3. Elizabeth Erhlich, *Miriam's Kitchen: A Memoir* (New York: Viking, 1997), xii.
4. Ibid.
5. Pearl Bailey, *Pearl's Kitchen* (New York: Harcourt Brace Jovanovich, 1973), 21.
6. Ruth Reichl, *Tender at the Bone: Growing Up at the Table* (New York: Broadway Books, 1998), 7.
7. Louise DeSalvo, *Crazy in the Kitchen: Food, Feuds, and Forgiveness in an Italian American Family* (New York: Bloomsbury, 2004), 10.
8. Quoted in Caroline L. Hunt, *The Life of Ellen H. Richards* (Boston: Whitcomb & Barrows, 1912).
9. For an overview of American Indian foods and cookery, see Linda Murray Berzok, *American Indian Food* (Westport, Conn.: Greenwood Press, 2005).
10. Lori Rackl, "Broiling Hot: Rising Interest Rates and Cooling Home Sales Have Yet to Put a Damper on Americans' Stampede to Remodel," *Chicago Sun-Times*, August 6, 2006. Rackl also cites an estimate by *Kitchen and Bath Business's* Market Forecaster that Americans would spend nearly $80 billion on kitchen remodeling in 2006, 21 percent more than they spent in 2005.
11. Brett Buckner, "Kitchen Neglect in Alabama Noticed as Dining Out Grows," Associated Press, July 23, 2006.
12. Margaret E. Beck, "Dinner Preparation in the Modern United States," *British Food Journal* 109, no. 7 (2007): 531–47.
13. The study is cited in A. Elizabeth Sloan, "What, When, and Where America Eats," *Food Technology* 62, no. 1 (January 2008): 20.
14. " 'Convenience' Foods Save Little Time for Working Families at Dinner," ScienceDaily.com, August 13, 2007.
15. Results of a National Survey of 450 households, statistically projectable to all U.S. households, conducted in June 2007, by Leo J. Shapiro & Associates, and communicated to Nancy Carlisle by telephone.
16. Maureen Jenkins, "Real Men Can Stand the Heat: More Guys Step Up to the Stove These Days—and Like It," *Chicago Sun-Times*, August 10, 2006.
17. In the wake of the September 11, 2001, terrorist attacks, more than forty new shelter magazines were launched, as people turned to their homes for comfort and solace. Carol Lloyd, "Shelter Shocked," *SF Gate, San Francisco Chronicle*, March 23, 2004.
18. Quoted in Bill Saporito, "Inside the New American Home," *Time Magazine*, October 14, 2002.
19. Quoted in ibid.
20. Quoted in Karl Greenberg, "Chasing Viking," *Brandweek*, August 8, 2003.
21. This benefit of cell phone use was described by George Rosenbaum of Leo J. Shapiro & Associates in a telephone conversation on May 16, 2007.
22. "An Unexpected Kitchen: The George Foreman Grill, Story Note from The Kitchen Sisters," NPR's *Morning Edition*, October 8, 2004.
23. Crystal Marra, Kitchen Questionnaire (2007), America's Kitchens Research Files, Historic New England.
24. The Sintros family is part of a close-knit Greek community centered on the Greek Orthodox church in Lawrence, Massachusetts. While some families in their community have two kitchens, others do not. In Brooklyn, New York, and elsewhere around the country, Italian families with two kitchens are not uncommon. The Sintros kitchen eventually found its way into the collection of Historic New England.

## THE NEW ENGLAND HEARTH (1720–1840)

1. The Coffin Family Papers (hereafter cited as CFP) in the Historic New England Library and Archives contain account books documenting the family's farming, tanning, and household activities, as well as letters, financial records, and legal documents.
2. For three generations, a Coffin son brought his wife to live in his father's house. According to a history of Newbury, "During the latter part of his [Joseph Coffin's] life his son Joshua, born Jan. 9, 1731, occupied one-half of the house." This suggests that the housekeeping was divided rather than shared. John J. Currier, *"Ould Newbury": Historical and Biographical Sketches* (Boston, 1896), 171.
3. Sarah Anna Emery, *Reminiscences of a Nonagenarian* (Newburyport, Mass., 1879), 289. Similarly, in the late eighteenth century, Sarah Emery lived with her father and mother in one half of a house; her widowed grandmother and aunt and uncle occupied the other half. Although Emery's mother and aunt would sit and sew together in the afternoon, they had a formal arrangement when it came to sharing milk, and they evidently did not dine together regularly, as Emery specifically mentions that when her father returned from a long journey, "Grandma'am, Aunt Sarah and Uncle Enoch joined us at supper." (Ibid., 6, 7, 23).
4. CFP, box 2, folder 32.
5. "*Honored Sir*, 'Tis in your power to make my life (as to outward circumstances) either Happy or Miserable, & I am sure 'twould be with the Greatest Regrett I should do anything to Render your life uneasy. I don't ask you to give me house or land at present, although I d'ont think in that case I should be unreasonable (considering my family Increases so fast), but at present I only ask Leave to build a Bedroom chimney on my own cost for our present comfort. Which, when you have properly weighed the affair & Considered what you have done for Bro. David & Paul . . . I C'ant suppose you will single me out from the rest of your Children as an object of your Displeasure. Since I don't know as either of them have done more to merit your favor, I now Intreat you, S$^{r}$, in this Request to treat me only as a son, whose happiness so much Depends on your approbation & afection. I am, S$^{r}$, with all Due Reverence & Duty. Your Dependent son, Joshua Coffin." This letter, dated September 27, 1764, is quoted in Currier, "*Ould Newbury*," 171. The location of the original letter is unknown.
6. Many years later, this space was described by Caleb Huse, who knew the Coffin kitchen as a boy in the 1840s. Caleb Huse to Marjorie Huse, December 27, 1901, quoted in "The Coffin House in the Early Nineteenth Century," *Old-Time New England* 27, no. 2 (October 1936): 70.
7. CFP, box 4, Account Book 3, unnumbered page, "An account of some things which my daughter Jane had of me."
8. The word "dowry" was not used in this sense until the mid-nineteenth century. See Jane C. Nylander, *Our Own Snug Fireside: Images of the New England Home, 1760–1860* (New York: Alfred A. Knopf, 1994), 59. Joseph Coffin's daughter Susanna was married in 1757 and Sarah in 1759. For comparison, he gave his son David a "house & Expense upon it" worth £858. CFP, box 1, folder 13.

9. Among the household goods likely used in the kitchen were two brass kettles (one valued at more than £5), a dish kettle, two iron pots, bails for the pots, three skillets (one described as "belmetle"), two skillet frames, a gridiron, a spit, a fender, a large pair of andirons, a flesh fork, a pudding pan, a fire shovel, a pair of bellows, a box iron, two basins, a chafing dish, four porringers, two candlesticks, eight platters, and a dozen plates. "An account of some things which my daughter Jane had of me." CFP, box 4, Account Book 3, unnumbered page.
10. CFP, box 1, folder 13. It is not clear how long before 1771 Joseph Coffin gave his daughters shares of the enslaved girl or indeed whether she ever lived in his household. Joseph's father, Nathaniel Coffin, gave an enslaved African American man named Jack to his son Edmund (CFP, box 4, Account Book 2, 70, and the page facing 180). See Joshua Coffin, *A Sketch of the History of Newbury, Newburyport, and West Newbury, from 1635 to 1845* (Boston, 1845), 337.
11. African American slaves made up 2.5 percent of the population of Essex County, Massachusetts, by 1764. Daniel Vickers, *Farmers and Fishermen: Two Centuries of Work in Essex County, Massachusetts, 1630–1850* (Chapel Hill: University of North Carolina Press, 1994), 230. See also William Dillon Pierson, *Black Yankees* (Amherst: University of Massachusetts Press, 1988); and Joanne Pope Melish, *Disowning Slavery: Gradual Emancipation and "Race" in New England, 1780–1860* (Ithaca, N.Y.: Cornell University Press, 1998).
12. January 1, 1742, Essex County Probate Records, vol. 325, book 25, 119–20, cited in Andrea Constantine Hawkes, "'To Brass Iron pewter Wooden & other Ware for housewifery': A Comparative Study of the Coffin House Kitchen and 466 Colonial Kitchens in Essex County, Massachusetts, 1699–1760," unpublished report (2006), Historic New England Library and Archives, 53.
13. Coffin, *Sketch of the History of Newbury*, 337.
14. CFP, box 2, folder 32, Sarah Bartlett Coffin account book, no page number. See Carol Lasser, "Mistress, Maid and Market: The Transformation of Domestic Service in New England, 1790–1870" (PhD diss., Harvard University, 1982); and Lawrence Towner, *A Good Master Well Served: Masters and Servants in Colonial Massachusetts, 1620–1750* (New York: Garland, 1998).
15. See Laurel Thatcher Ulrich, *Good Wives: Image and Reality in the Lives of Women in Northern New England, 1650–1750* (New York: Vintage, 1980); and Nylander, *Our Own Snug Fireside*.
16. Emery, *Reminiscences*, 10.
17. Lucy Larcom, *A New England Girlhood, Outlined from Memory* (Boston, 1889), 21–22.
18. The full description reads as follows: "The fire places have no Jambs (as ours have) But the Backs run flush with the walls, and the Hearth is of Tyles and is as farr out into the Room at the Ends as before the fire, w[ch] is Generally Five foot in the Low'r rooms, and the peice over where the mantle tree should be is made as ours with Joyners work, and as I suppose is fasten'd to iron rodds inside." Sarah Kemble Knight, *The Journal of Madam Knight* (Boston: David R. Godine, 1972), 29.
19. Howard S. Russell, *A Long, Deep Furrow: Three Centuries of Farming in New England* (Hanover, N.H.: University Press of New England, 1982), 97, cited in Priscilla J. Brewer, *From Fireplace to Cookstove: Technology and the Domestic Ideal in America* (Syracuse, N.Y.: Syracuse University Press, 2000), 28.
20. Elizabeth Boyd, "Fireplaces and Stoves in Colonial New Mexico," *El Palacio* 65 (December 1958): 219.
21. James L. Garvin to Rosemary Brandau, May 20, 1992, New Hampshire Division of Historical Resources files. Many thanks to James L. Garvin for sharing his extensive files on stew stoves. See also Betty Crowe Leviner, "The Stew Stove at the Governor's Palace, Williamsburg, Virginia," unpublished report (2004), Colonial Williamsburg Foundation; and Patrick Dunne and Charles L. Mackie, "In Pursuit of the *Potager*," *Historic Preservation* 42 (November/December 1990): 58–61.
22. The stew stove was installed in 1809, after James Hemings, who was trained in France, had gained his freedom on the condition that he instruct his brother, Peter. Fossett and Hern were trained at the President's House by the chef Honoré Julien and the maître d'hôtel Étienne Lemaire. Damon Lee Fowler, ed., *Dining at Monticello: In Good Taste and Abundance* (Charlottesville, Va.: Thomas Jefferson Memorial Foundation, 2005), 21, 24, 40.
23. Benjamin Thompson, a loyalist who left the colonies during the Revolutionary War, is best known for redesigning the traditional English fireplace and chimney for more efficient heating. This change was nearly universally adopted over time, partly due to the scarcity and expense of firewood. In recognition of his work, Thompson was elected a count of the Holy Roman Empire, choosing the name of his first wife's hometown of Rumford (now Concord), New Hampshire, for his title.
24. Rumford recommended kitchen design to gentlemen "and even to ladies" as an "amusing occupation." [Benjamin Thompson], *Collected Works of Count Rumford*, ed. Sanborn C. Brown, 5 vols. (Cambridge, Mass.: Belknap Press of Harvard University Press, 1968–70), 3:89.
25. *New-Hampshire Gazette*, December 16, 1786, 3.
26. *Boston Weekly News-Letter*, November 25, 1742.
27. "Sometimes a turkey or a goose was depended before the fire by a strong string hitched to a nail in the ceiling." Emery, *Reminiscences*, 32.
28. Larcom recalled that the Thanksgiving turkey was roasted in a "tin-kitchen" and "the business of turning the spit being usually delegated to some of us, small folk, who were only too willing to burn our faces in honor of the annual festival." *A New England Girlhood*, 22. For more information on tin kitchens, see Frank G. White, "Reflections on a Tin Kitchen," *Chronicle of the Early American Industries Association* 36 (September 1983): 45–48, 61.
29. An ad running in the *Pennsylvania Gazette* on September 15, 1743, noted that Henry Clarke had for sale "several Turnspit Dogs, and Wheels, for Roasting Meat, at Thirty-five Shillings each Dog and Wheel," *Pennsylvania Gazette*, September 15, 1743, 3. Mary Anne Hines, Gordon Marshall, and William Woys Weaver, *The Larder Invaded: Reflections on Three Centuries of Philadelphia Food and Drink* (Philadelphia: Library Company of Philadelphia and Historical Society of Pennsylvania, 1987), 18.
30. For lists of expenses of feeding an average family, see *New-England Weekly Journal*, November 25, 1728, 2 and *New-England Weekly Journal*, December 2, 1728, 1. See also Sarah F. McMahon, "A Comfortable Subsistence: The Changing Composition of Diet in Rural New England, 1620–1840," *William and Mary Quarterly*, 3rd ser., 42 (1985): 26–65.
31. Emery, *Reminiscences*, 7. Some families, including the Coffins, had rooms devoted to processing dairy products within their homes. A 1785 document refers to a room close to the two kitchens as the "Buttery." CFP, box 2, folder 31. Caleb Huse's reminiscence of his 1840s childhood described the space as the "dairy-room, always as clean and sweet as possible." "The Coffin House in the Early Nineteenth Century," 71.
32. Sarah Josepha Hale recommended that "if the family have a real desire of keeping [Sunday] for that which it was evidently intended, rest for worldly care, as well as for moral and religious improvement," people who baked only once a week should choose Saturday, as a meat and pudding could be prepared for the following day. Hale, *The Good Housekeeper, or The Way to Live Well and to be Well While We Live* (Boston, 1839), 109.
33. Emery recalled that "wheat flour was somewhat of a luxury; a housekeeper felt rich with a bushel or two on hand, and it was made to last a long time." *Reminiscences*, 23–24.

34. Ruth Henshaw Bascom, July 22, 1830, quoted in Nylander, *Our Own Snug Fireside*, 189.
35. Emery, *Reminiscences*, 312.

## KITCHENS IN THE PLANTATION SOUTH (1830-1860)

1. The "Big House" at Green Hill appears to have been built in two stages. The original dining room was probably the east room at the front of the house, under which the basement kitchen was located, with evidence of a staircase leading to the dining room above. There is an original walkway leading directly from the detached kitchen to the exterior door of this dining room as well as to the exterior door of the basement kitchen. When the ell was added, the dining room was likely moved to the west front room of the house, which has elaborate display cabinets and sliding shelves. Access to the two kitchens was then made from an exterior door and a basement staircase, both located in the new center hall created between the new and old sections of the house.
2. Marion Harland [Mary Virginia Terhune], *Marion Harland's Autobiography: The Story of a Long Life* (New York: Harper and Brothers, 1910), 111.
3. 1850 U.S. Census, Schedule 4, Production of Agriculture during the Year Ending June 1, 1850, vol. 1, Agricultural Census, Campbell County, Virginia, 1850, Special Census Reel 1850–1880, Collection of the Library of Virginia.
4. Robert A. Lancaster, Jr., *Historic Virginia Homes and Churches* (Philadephia: J.B. Lippincott, 1915), 422. A number of slaves listed in Pannill's will have last names that may refer to their occupations (particularly as some of these last names are not capitalized), for example, Aaron Cooper, Wilson Miller, Ryal Carpenter, Wirt Gardiner, Richard Cook. Campbell County, Va., Probate Records, Will Book 12, 577–84.
5. For examples, see Keith C. Barton, "'Good Cooks and Washers': Slave Hiring, Domestic Labor, and the Market in Bourbon County, Kentucky," *Journal of American History* 84, no. 2 (September 1997): 436–60.
6. Travelers in the South like Durand de Dauphine, who visited Virginia in 1686, often remarked on the presence of detached kitchens. Quoted in Dell Upton, "Early Vernacular Architecture in Southeastern Virginia" (PhD diss., Brown University, 1979), 174, cited in Donald W. Linebaugh. "'All the Annoyances and Inconveniences of the Country': Environmental Factors in the Development of Outbuildings in the Colonial Chesapeake," *Winterthur Portfolio* 29, no. 1 (1994): 1.
7. White families who did not own slaves also emulated the "Big House and kitchen" arrangement, as in the photo of the Ephraim Bumgarner cabin on page 53. This may reflect the plantation arrangement, or it may reflect a desire to separate living and work space. It is also possible that the term *big* was used in the antiquated Scottish or northern English sense of "to live in" or "dwell." Michael Ann Williams, *Homeplace: The Social Use and Meaning of the Folk Dwelling in Southwestern North Carolina* (Athens: University of Georgia Press, 1991), 38–45.
8. Robert Beverley, *The History and Present State of Virginia*, ed. Louis B. Wright (1705; repr., Chapel Hill: University of North Carolina Press, 1947), 289–90, quoted in Dell Upton, "Vernacular Domestic Architecture in Eighteenth-Century Virginia," *Winterthur Portfolio* 17, no. 2/3 (Summer–Autumn 1982): 102.
9. John Michael Vlach, *Back of the Big House: The Architecture of Plantation Slavery* (Chapel Hill: University of North Carolina Press, 1993), 43. See also Cary Carson, "Segregation in Vernacular Buildings," *Vernacular Architecture* 7 (1976): 24–29; Carson, "Doing History with Material Culture," in *Material Culture and the Study of American Life*, ed. Ian M. G. Quimby (New York: W. W. Norton, 1978), 41–64; and Cary Carson, Norman F. Barka, William M. Kelso, Garry Wheeler Stone, and Dell Upton, "Impermanent Architecture in the Southern American Colonies," *Winterthur Portfolio* 16, no. 2/3 (1981): 135–78.
10. Mary Jones to Mrs. Mary S. Mallard, November 17, 1865, quoted in *The Children of Pride: Selected Letters of the Family of the Rev. Dr. Charles Colcock Jones from the Years 1860–1868*, ed. Robert Mason Myers (New Haven, Conn.: Yale University Press, 1984), 570. Harriet Martineau's statement that mistresses "are as they and their husbands declare, as much slaves as their negroes" is quoted in Deborah Gray White, *Ar'n't I a Woman? Female Slaves in the Plantation South* (New York: W. W. Norton, 1999), 51.
11. Elizabeth Fox-Genovese, *Within the Plantation Household: Black and White Women of the Old South* (Chapel Hill: University of North Carolina Press, 1988), 100 and 118.
12. Mary Withers to Ann Eliza Withers, 1831, quoted in Catherine Clinton, *The Plantation Mistress: Woman's World in the Old South* (New York: Pantheon, 1982), 19. Dolly Burge is quoted in Kristen E. Wood, *Masterful Women: Slaveholding Widows from the American Revolution through the Civil War* (Chapel Hill: University of North Carolina Press, 2004), 173.
13. Harland, *Marion Harland's Autobiography*, 111.
14. Caroline Howard Gilman, *The Lady's Annual Register and Housewife's Memorandum Book for 1838* (Boston, 1837), 28, quoted in Marli F. Weiner, *Mistresses and Slaves: Plantation Women in South Carolina, 1830–80* (Urbana: University of Illinois Press, 1998), 39.
15. Caroline E. Merrick, *Old Times in Dixie Land: A Southern Matron's Memories* (New York: Grafton Press, 1901), 17; Fox-Genovese, *Within the Plantation Household*, 142.
16. Charles Joyner, "The World of the Plantation Slaves," in *Before Freedom Came: African-American Life in the Antebellum South*, ed. Edward D. C. Campbell, Drew Gilpin Faust, and Kym S. Rice (Charlottesville: University Press of Virginia, 1991), 56–57.
17. Emmaline Heard, in *Georgia Narratives*, Federal Writers' Project, WPA Slave Narratives Project, vol. 4, pt. 2, 150. Transcriptions of the interviews conducted as part of the Slave Narratives Project have been published online as part of the Library of Congress's "American Memory" Web site "Born in Slavery: Slave Narratives from the Federal Writers' Project, 1936–1938," http://memory.loc.gov/ammem/snhtml/snhome.html.
18. Cornelia Andrews, in *North Carolina Narratives*, Federal Writers' Project, WPA Slave Narratives Project, vol. 11, pt. 1, 29–30; Lucy Chase's frustration with Mary Jane's refusal to clean the molasses jug is quoted in *Dear Ones at Home: Letters from Contraband Camps*, ed. Henry L. Swint (Nashville, Tenn.: Vanderbilt University Press, 1966), 63.
19. Lizzie Johnson, in *Arkansas Narratives*, Federal Writers' Project, WPA Slave Narratives Project, vol. 2, pt. 4, 102.
20. Mark P. Leone and Gladys-Marie Fry, "Conjuring in the Big House Kitchen: An Interpretation of African American Belief Systems Based on the Use of Archaeology and Folklore Sources," *Journal of American Folklore* 112 (Summer 1999): 372–403.
21. Eliza Bruce to her husband, James C. Bruce, February 10, 1838, Bruce Family Papers, MS 2692, Special Collections, University of Virginia Library. In 1838 the Bruces lived at Tarover Plantation on the Dan River in Halifax County, Virginia. The word *servant* frequently served as a euphemism for slave.
22. Keziah Goodwyn Hopkins Brevard, *A Plantation Mistress on the Eve of the Civil War: The Diary of Keziah Goodwyn Hopkins Brevard, 1860–1861*, ed. John Hammond Moore (Columbia: University of South Carolina Press, 1993), 64 (December 29, 1860).
23. Easter Wells, in *Oklahoma Narratives*, Federal Writers' Project, WPA Slave Narratives Project, vol. 13, 317.
24. Ellen Betts, in *Texas Narratives*, Federal Writers' Project, WPA Slave Narratives Project, vol. 16, pt. 1, 75.
25. Lucy McCullough, in *Georgia Narratives*, Federal Writers' Project, WPA

Slave Narratives Project, vol. 4, pt. 3, 67–68. See also Fox-Genovese, *Within the Plantation Household*, 158–59.
26. Charles Gayarre, "A Louisiana Sugar Plantation of the Old Regime," *Harper's New Monthly Magazine*, March 1887, 620.
27. Frederick Douglass, "The Church and Prejudice," in *Frederick Douglass: Selected Speeches and Writings*, ed. Philip S. Foner (Chicago: Lawrence Hill Books, 1999), 3.
28. M.M. Manring, *Slave in a Box: The Strange Career of Aunt Jemima* (Charlottesville: University Press of Virginia, 1998).
29. Malvina Gist Waring, 1865, quoted in Faust, *Mothers of Invention*, 78.
30. Lucy Chase, 1863, in Swint, *Dear Ones at Home*, 65. Sarah Frances Hicks Williams, December 10, 1853, quoted in James C. Bonner, "Plantation Experiences of a New York Woman," *North Carolina Historical Review* 33 (July 1956): 396–97.
31. For more on food in the South, see Sam Bowers Hilliard, *Hog Meat and Hoecake: Food Supply in the Old South, 1840–1860* (Carbondale: Southern Illinois University Press, 1972) and Joe Gray Taylor, *Eating, Drinking, and Visiting in the South: An Informal History* (Baton Rouge: Louisiana State University Press, 1982).
32. William Howard Russell, *My Diary North and South*, vol. 1 (London, 1863), 400–1, quoted in Eugene D. Genovese, *Roll, Jordan, Roll: The World the Slaves Made* (New York: Pantheon, 1974), 541.
33. Brevard, *A Plantation Mistress on the Eve of the Civil War*, 28 (August 30, 1860).
34. Frederick Law Olmsted, *A Journey in the Back Country* (1860; repr., Williamstown, Mass.: Corner House Publishers, 1972), 161–62.
35. Foby, "Management of Servants," *Southern Cultivator*, August 1853, 226.
36. Stacy Gibbons Moore, "Established and Well Cultivated: Afro-American Foodways in Early Virginia," *Virginia Cavalcade* 39 (Autumn 1989): 75–79. See also Jessica B. Harris, *Iron Pots and Wooden Spoons: Africa's Gifts to New World Cooking* (New York: Atheneum, 1989).
37. Moore, "Established and Well Cultivated," 80–81.
38. Lucy Chase, 1863, quoted in Swint, *Dear Ones at Home*, 65. In the following paragraph, Lucy wrote of *The Virginia Housewife*: "When every receipt calls its roll of ingredients, we are obliged to answer, 'Absent without leave.'"
39. John W. Blassingame, ed., *Slave Testimony: Two Centuries of Letters, Speeches, Interviews, and Autobiographies* (Baton Rouge: Louisiana State University Press, 1977), 652; Benjamin Johnson, in *Georgia Narratives*, Federal Writers' Project, WPA Slave Narratives Project, vol. 4, pt. 2, 322.
40. Amanda Jackson, in *Georgia Narratives*, Federal Writers' Project, WPA Slave Narratives Project, vol. 4, pt. 2, 289–90.
41. Booker T. Washington, *Up from Slavery: An Autobiography* (New York: Doubleday, Page, 1904), 9.
42. Lina Hunter, in *Georgia Narratives*, Federal Writers' Project, WPA Slave Narratives Project, vol. 4, pt. 2, 254–55.
43. Robert Shepherd, in *Georgia Narratives*, Federal Writers' Project, WPA Slave Narratives Project, vol. 4, pt. 3, 249.
44. Frederick Douglass, *My Bondage and My Freedom* (New York, 1857), 75.
45. Julia Brown (Aunt Sally), in *Georgia Narratives*, Federal Writers' Project, WPA Slave Narratives Project, vol. 4, pt. 1, 147.
46. See Emma Slade Prescott, Reminiscences, and Charlotte Ravenel diary, quoted in Faust, *Mothers of Invention*, 77. See [Fannie Caison] to M. B. Murchison, 1866, quoted in Weiner, *Mistresses and Slaves*, 212. See also Charlotte Ravenel, March 11, 1865, in *Two Diaries from Middle St. John's, Berkeley, SC, February–May 1865: Journals Kept by Susan R. Jervey and Miss Charlotte St. J. Ravenel* (Pinopolis, S.C.: St. John's Hunting Club, 1921), 37.
47. Sarah P. Payne to Mary (M. Clendenin), 1865, quoted in William A. Blair, "Barbarians at Fredericksburg's Gate: The Impact of the Union Army on Civilians," in *The Fredericksburg Campaign: Decision on the Rappahannock*, ed. Gary W. Gallagher (Chapel Hill: University of North Carolina Press, 1995), 162–63.

## COOKSTOVES AND SERVANTS (1850-1890)

1. Sarah W. Davis (SWD) to David Davis (DD), Bloomington, Ill., January 21, 1872. David Davis Family Papers, Abraham Lincoln Presidential Library, Springfield, Illinois. Unless otherwise noted, all subsequent letters from Sarah Davis are in the holdings of the Abraham Lincoln Presidential Library.
2. The most important work on the history of the cookstove in America is Priscilla J. Brewer, *From Fireplace to Cookstove: Technology and the Domestic Ideal in America* (Syracuse, N.Y.: Syracuse University Press, 2000). On fuel use, see 28, 70.
3. Quoted in Jacqueline B. Williams, *The Way We Ate: Pacific Northwest Cooking, 1843–1900* (Pullman: Washington State University Press, 1996), 47.
4. Denison Olmstead, "Observations on the Use of Anthracite Coal" (1837), quoted in Brewer, *From Fireplace to Cookstove*, 96.
5. Nathaniel Hawthorne, "Fire Worship," *Mosses from an Old Manse* (1843; repr., Boston, 1882), 167–68.
6. Sarah Orne Jewett, *A Country Doctor* (1884; repr., Somersworth, N.H.: New England History Press, 1984), 21.
7. Frances A. Breckenridge, *Recollections of a New England Town* (Meriden, Conn., 1899), 143–44. See also Brewer, *From Fireplace to Cookstove*, 88.
8. Maria Parloa, *Miss Parloa's New Cook Book* (New York, 1882), 64.
9. Mary Johnson Bailey Lincoln, *Mrs. Lincoln's Boston Cook Book* (Boston, 1884), 5.
10. Maria Parloa, *Miss Parloa's Kitchen Companion*, 20th ed. (Boston, 1887) 11; Les Christie, "Honey, I stretched the house—again," *CNNMoney.com*, July 25, 2006, http://money.cnn.com/2006/07/24/real_estate/home_stretching/index.htm.
11. Catharine Beecher, *Miss Beecher's Domestic Receipt Book*, 3rd ed. (New York, 1850), 254.
12. Parloa, *Miss Parloa's New Cook Book*, 77.
13. Ruth Schwartz Cowan, *More Work for Mother: The Ironies of Household Technology from the Open Hearth to the Microwave* (New York: Basic Books, 1983).
14. Hetty A. Morrison, *My Summer in the Kitchen* (Indianapolis, 1878), 9.
15. Harriet Beecher Stowe to Calvin Stowe, Cincinnati, June 16, 1845, in *Life of Harriet Beecher Stowe*, ed. Charles Edward Stowe (Boston, 1889), 63–64.
16. Estelle Woods Wilcox, *Buckeye Cookery and Practical Housekeeping* (Minneapolis, 1877), 332.
17. Mary E. Carpenter, Rochester, Minn., 1871, quoted in Marjorie Kreidberg, *Food on the Frontier: Minnesota Cooking from 1850 to 1900 with Selected Recipes* (St. Paul: Minnesota Historical Society Press, 1975), 7.
18. *Presbyterian Cook Book*, by the Ladies of the First Presbyterian Church, Dayton, Ohio (Dayton, 1873), 17–20.
19. Wilcox, *Buckeye Cookery*, 299–300.
20. Susan Strasser, *Waste and Want* (New York: Henry Holt, 1999), 23, 29.
21. Catharine Beecher's *Treatise on Domestic Economy*, rev. ed. (New York, 1851) includes a section "Rules for Washing Dishes," 318–19.
22. Lincoln, *Mrs. Lincoln's Boston Cook Book*, 447.
23. Susanna Clay to Clement Clay, January 24, 1833, quoted in Catherine Clinton, *The Plantation Mistress: Woman's World in the Old South* (New York: Pantheon, 1982), 23. Although writing about her childhood in Virginia in the early twentieth century, Edna Lewis beautifully described the hog killing process, practically unchanged since the antebellum period. See Edna Lewis, *The Taste of Country Cooking* (New York: Alfred A. Knopf, 1987), 181–85.
24. Rebecca Wyche to Thomas Wyche, January 15, 1836, quoted in Clinton, *Plantation Mistress*, 24.
25. In 1855, 19 percent of homeowners in Providence, Rhode Island, and Buffalo, New York, had full-time live-in help. See Faye Dudden,

*Serving Women: Household Service in Nineteenth-Century America* (Middletown, Conn.: Wesleyan University Press, 1983), 78.

26. Lincoln, *Mrs. Lincoln's Boston Cook Book*, vi–vii.
27. For the African American experience as domestics, see Elizabeth Clark-Lewis, *Living In, Living Out: African American Domestics in Washington, D.C., 1910–1940* (Washington, D.C.: Smithsonian Institution Press, 1994).
28. Employers of African American women preferred that they not live in. For African American mothers this was an advantage, as they could get home to see their families at night. See David M. Katzman, *Seven Days a Week: Women and Domestic Service in Industrializing America* (New York: Oxford University Press, 1978), 90–91.
29. Catherine Selden, "The Women of Today. II: The Tyranny of the Kitchen," *North American Review*, October 1893, 432.
30 "The Experiences of a 'Hired Girl,'" *Outlook*, April 6, 1912, 778–80.
31. Rose Cohen, *Out of the Shadow* (New York, 1918), 180–81.
32. Helen Campbell, *Prisoners of Poverty: Women Wage-Workers, Their Trades and Their Lives* (Boston, 1887), 226.
33. Sarah W. Davis (SWD) to David Davis (DD), Bloomington, Ill., March 21, 1852.
34. SWD to DD, Bloomington, Ill., March 16, 1872.
35. SWD to Daniel Rogers Williams, Bloomington, Ill., June 18, 1859, Samuel Chapman Armstrong Collection, Williams College Archives and Special Collections, Williamstown, Mass.
36. SWD to DD, Bloomington, Ill., March 20, 1872.
37. SWD to DD, Bloomington, Ill., March 16, 1872.
38. SWD to DD, Bloomington, Ill., December 13, 1871.
39. SWD to DD, Bloomington, Ill., April 14, 1873.

## KITCHENS ALONG THE RIO GRANDE (1821-1912)

1. El Rancho de las Golondrinas (the Ranch of the Swallows), fifteen miles south of Santa Fe, was first settled in the eighteenth century and was owned by descendants of the original settlers until early in the twentieth century. By the mid-twentieth century, when many of the buildings had fallen into disrepair or ruin, new owners decided to repair and rebuild and turn the ranch into a museum. Today, El Rancho de las Golondrinas is a living history museum devoted to telling the story of the region's Spanish colonial culture and heritage.
2. This chapter is largely based on the thoroughly researched work of historian Cheryl Foote, whose unpublished manuscript, "The Kitchens of New Mexico" (2007), is in the Historic New England Library and Archives. The imagined scene at Golondrinas is based on the writings of Cleofas Jaramillo, who recorded her childhood reminiscences in the 1940s. To date, no period description of a mid-nineteenth-century celebration of Holy Week has been discovered. Cleofas M. Jaramillo, *Shadows of the Past (Sombras del Pasado)* (1941; repr., Santa Fe, N.M.: Ancient City Press, 1972), 67–72.
3. The 1850 census for La Cienega lists the family of servants living at the hacienda but does not indicate any tribal affiliation, or even whether the family was Indian.
4. In the wake of the Mexican-American War (1846–1848), New Mexico was under the control of the United States, but it was not until the passage of the Compromise of 1850 in September of that year that New Mexico, along with Arizona and part of Utah, officially became a U.S. territory.
5. Foote, "The Kitchens of New Mexico," 1–2; Ramón A. Gutiérrez, *When Jesus Came, the Corn Mothers Went Away: Marriage, Sexuality, and Power in New Mexico, 1500–1846* (Stanford, Calif.: Stanford University Press, 1991), xx–xxi.
6. George Parker Winship, *The Journey of Coronado, 1540–1542* (1922; repr., New York: Greenwood Press, 1969), 101, cited in Foote, "The Kitchens of New Mexico," 4.
7. Foote argues that the appropriate spelling of chile is with an *e* rather than an *i* in "What's in [the spelling] of a Name? Chile, Chili?" *Food History News* 17, no. 2 (2005), 1, 7–8. In New Mexico, the Spanish-speaking nonnative populace is often referred to as *Hispanic* rather than by the earlier term *Spanish-American*, which some people still prefer. "Latino" is not widely used to refer to people who trace their ancestors back to the Spanish colonial period.
8. Stella M. Drumm, ed., *Down the Santa Fé Trail and into Mexico: The Diary of Susan Shelby Magoffin 1846–1847* (New Haven, Conn.: Yale University Press, 1926), 103–4.
9. James L. Moore, Guadalupe Martínez, Linda Mick-O'Hara, Mollie S. Toll, and Macy Mensel, "Life Along the Santa Fe Trail: From the Hispanic Perspective," in *Archaeology in Your Backyard: Proceedings of the Santa Fe Symposium*, ed. Charles M. Haecker and Nancy Ford (Santa Fe: City of Santa Fe, 1999), 85. W.H. Emory, *Lt. Emory Reports*, ed. Ross Calvin (Albuquerque: University of New Mexico, 1951), 68; both cited in Foote, "The Kitchens of New Mexico," 36.
10. Gutiérrez, *When Jesus Came*, 149–51.
11. *Down the Santa Fé Trail and Into Mexico*, 167–68.
12. Elizabeth M. Brumfel, "Weaving and Cooking: Women's Production in Aztec Mexico," in *Engendering Archaeology: Women and Prehistory*, ed. Joan M. Gero and Margaret W. Conkey (Oxford: Basil Blackwell, 1991), 238, cited in Foote, "The Kitchens of New Mexico," 79, note 67.
13. Cheryl Foote, "Southwestern Regional Cookery," in *The Oxford Encyclopedia of Food and Drink in America*, ed. Andrew F. Smith (Oxford: Oxford University Press, 2004), 2:480–83.
14. Foote, "The Kitchens of New Mexico," 49.
15. *Down the Santa Fé Trail and Into Mexico*, 135.
16. Foote, "The Kitchens of New Mexico," 38, 52.
17. Emory, *Lt. Emory Reports*, 68, cited in Foote, 37.
18. *Down the Santa Fé Trail and Into Mexico*, 94.
19. Ibid., 209.
20. Katie Bowen, letters, January 1, 1852, May 28, 1852, typescripts in Arrott Collection, New Mexico Highlands University Library, Las Vegas, New Mexico. Cited in Foote, "The Kitchens of New Mexico," 53.
21. Harriett Shaw letters, January 26, 1852, and February 22, 1852, Dorothy Woodward Collection, New Mexico State Records Center and Archives, Santa Fe, New Mexico, cited in Foote, "The Kitchens of New Mexico," 53.
22. Sarah Wetter, June 18, 1869, and June 21, 1869, Henry Wetter Collection, Museum of New Mexico, Santa Fe. Cited in Foote, "The Kitchens of New Mexico," 53.
23. Arthur Goss, *Dietary Studies in New Mexico in 1895*, U.S. Department of Agriculture Bulletin No. 40 (Washington, D.C.: Government Printing Office, 1897), 5–7, cited in Foote, "The Kitchens of New Mexico," 55.
24. Matilda Coxe Stevenson, "The Zuni Indians: Their Mythology, Esoteric Fraternities, and Ceremonies," *Twenty-Third Annual Report of the Bureau of American Ethnology to the Secretary of the Smithsonian Institution, 1901–1902* (Washington, D.C.: Government Printing Office, 1904), 380, cited in Foote, "The Kitchens of New Mexico," 58.
25. Stevenson, "The Zuni Indians," 381, cited in Foote, "The Kitchens of New Mexico," 58.
26. Victor Mindeleff, *A Study of Pueblo Architecture in Tusayan and Cibola* (1891; repr., Washington, D.C.: Smithsonian Institution Press, 1989), 214.
27. Cheryl Foote, "New Mexico Recipes in Print," typescript, 7–12.
28. A. Goubad and Michael Pijoan, "Food and Culture. A Nutritional Study of Cañon de Taos" (Albuquerque, N.M.: United Pueblos Agency, n.d.), 24, cited in Foote, "The Kitchens of New Mexico," 62.

## TOWARD THE MODERN KITCHEN (1890-1945)

1. "Mollie" was Mary Geraldine Armstrong Tucker (1841–1922). For more information about Mollie's life in the kitchen, see Abigail Carroll, "Mollie Tucker's Kitchen," unpublished report (2005), Historic New England Library and Archives.
2. Castle Tucker is one of Historic New England's historic house museums and is open to the public. Although the Tucker family referred to this stove as their "hotel range," unlike the Davis family's built-in range, the Tuckers' was not built into the wall.
3. See, for example, Hotpoint Electric Heating Company, *Home Book of Electricity* (Ontario, Calif.: Hotpoint Electric Heating Co., 1915), 18.
4. Jane Tucker to Richard Tucker, January 17, 1921, Tucker Family Papers, Historic New England Library and Archives.
5. Philip D. Kennedy, *Hoosier Cabinets* (Indianapolis, 1989), 8.
6. All quotes are from Jane Tucker to Richard Tucker, January 17, 1921.
7. The number of persons employed in household service dropped from 1,851,000 in 1910 to 1,411,000 in 1920, while the number of households rose from 20.3 million to 24.4 million. Ruth Schwartz Cowan, "The Industrial Revolution in the Home," in *The Social Shaping of Technology: How the Refrigerator Got Its Hum*, ed. Donald MacKenzie and Judy Wajcman (Milton Keynes, U.K., and Philadelphia: Open University Press, 1985), 187.
8. Quoted in Elizabeth Clark-Lewis, *Living In, Living Out: African American Domestics in Washington, D.C., 1910–1940* (Washington, D.C.: Smithsonian Institution Press, 1994), 147.
9. See Ruth Schwartz Cowan, *More Work for Mother: The Ironies of Household Technology from the Open Hearth to the Microwave* (New York: Basic Books, 1983); Cowan, "Industrial Revolution in the Home"; Bonnie J. Fox, "Selling the Mechanized Household: 70 Years of Ads in *Ladies' Home Journal*," *Gender and Society* 4 (March 1990): 25–40; Philip Bereano, Christine Bose, and Erik Arnold, "Kitchen Technology and the Liberation of Women from Housework," in *Smothered by Invention: Technology in Women's Lives*, ed. Wendy Faulkner and Erik Arnold (London: Pluto Press, 1985), 162–81; and Phyllis Palmer, *Domesticity and Dirt: Housewives and Domestic Servants in the United States, 1920–1945* (Philadelphia: Temple University Press, 1989).
10. *Rural New Yorker* (January 20, 1900), quoted in Christine Kleinegger, "Out of the Barns and into the Kitchens: Transformations in Farm Women's Work in the First Half of the Twentieth Century," in *Women, Work, and Technology: Transformations*, ed. Barbara Drygulski Wright, et al. (Ann Arbor: University of Michigan Press, 1987), 178.
11. Cowan, "Industrial Revolution in the Home," 191; Fox, "Selling the Mechanized Household," 25; and Marilyn Irvin Holt, *Linoleum, Better Babies & the Modern Farm Woman, 1890–1930* (Albuquerque: University of New Mexico Press, 1995), 92.
12. Elna Harwood Wharton, "Uncle Sam's Model Kitchen," *McCall's*, November 1915, 19.
13. Isabel McDougall, "An Ideal Kitchen," *House Beautiful*, December 1902, 27.
14. Quoted in Eleanor Arnold, *Voices of American Homemakers* (Bloomington: Indiana University Press, 1993), 120.
15. Kleinegger, "Out of the Barns and into the Kitchens," 172.
16. Quoted in Arnold, *Voices of American Homemakers*, 126.
17. Kleinegger, "Out of the Barns and into the Kitchens," 172.
18. Quoted in Eleanor Arnold, *Memories of Hoosier Homemakers*, vol. 2 (Bloomington: Indiana University Press, 1984), 102.
19. Albert H. Leake, *The Means and Methods of Agricultural Education* (Boston: Houghton-Mifflin, 1915), quoted in Kleinegger, "Out of the Barns and into the Kitchens," 172–73.
20. See Arnold, *Voices of American Homemakers* and *Memories of Hoosier Homemakers*.
21. Marj D. Bennett, "Country Kitchen," *Chronicles of Oklahoma* 51, no. 3 (1973): 308.
22. Melanie Rich, "She Would Raise Her Hens to Aid the War: The Contributions of Oklahoma Women During World War I," *Chronicles of Oklahoma* 81 (2003), 334–35. For more on the history of food preservation, see Abigail Carroll, "'To Keep Green Peas till Christmas': A History of Domestic Food Preservation in the United States," unpublished report (2006), Historic New England Library and Archives.
23. Katherine Rosser Martin, "Food Preservation and the Folk Aesthetic," *Kentucky Folklore Record* 25 (1979), 1–5, cited in Caroll, "To Keep Green Peas," 110.
24. Leslie Prosterman, *Ordinary Life, Festival Days: Aesthetics in the Midwestern County Fair* (Washington, D.C.: Smithsonian Institution Press, 1995), 157.
25. See Katherine Leonard Turner, "Buying, Not Cooking: Ready-to-eat Food in American Urban Working-Class Neighborhoods, 1880–1930," *Food, Culture and Society: An International Journal of Multidisciplinary Research* 9, no. 1 (Spring 2006): 13–39. Government reports on labor conditions often described kitchens as work and living spaces, such as the Baltimore tenement kitchen described in *Report on Condition of Women and Child Wage-Earners in the United States, vol. 2, Men's Ready-Made Clothing* (Washington, D.C.: Government Printing Office, 1911), 292.
26. Ellen Richards, "The Relation of College Women to Progress in Domestic Science," paper presented to the Association of Collegiate Alumnae on October 24, 1890, quoted in Laura Shapiro, *Perfection Salad: Women and Cooking at the Turn of the Century* (New York: Modern Library, 2001), 42.
27. "Introduction," in *Rethinking Home Economics: Women and the History of a Profession*, ed. Sarah Stage and Virginia Vincenti (Ithaca, N.Y.: Cornell University Press, 1997), 9.
28. "Kansas State Agricultural College Extension Division, Annual Report for 1928," 96, quoted in Holt, *Linoleum . . . and the Modern Farm Woman*, 88.
29. Arnold, *Voices of American Homemakers*, 133.
30. Holt, *Linoleum . . . and the Modern Farm Woman*, 92.
31. "Dramatizing Kitchen Convenience," *American Gas Journal* 140, no. 1 (January 1934): 30. The U.S. government reinforced the importance of the single-family home with projects such as Better Homes in America and Herbert Hoover's Conference on Home Building and Home Ownership in December 1931. Dolores Hayden, *The Grand Domestic Revolution: A History of Feminist Design for American Homes, Neighborhoods, and Cities* (Cambridge, Mass.: MIT Press, 1981), 275–76, 286.
32. Cowan, "Industrial Revolution in the Home," 196–97.
33. Margaret H. Clarke, "Atmosphere in the Kitchen," in *Sweepings* (December 1926): 6.
34. Phyllis M. Ellin, "Now You're Cooking with Gas! or, From Black to White to Color in the Kitchen and Why," in *Preserving the Recent Past*, ed. Deborah Slaton and Rebecca A. Shiffer (Washington, D. C.: Historic Preservation Education Foundation, 1995), 137–44.
35. Laura Thornborough, *Interior Decorating for Everybody* (New York: Barse and Hopkins, 1925), 206–12.
36. Christine Frederick, *The New Housekeeping: Efficiency Studies in Home Management* (New York: Doubleday, Page & Co., 1913), 29; Janice Williams Rutherford, *Selling Mrs. Consumer: Christine Frederick and the Rise of Household Efficiency* (Athens: University of Georgia Press, 2003), 49. Catharine Beecher also taught how to wash dishes in exact detail in *Treatise on Domestic Economy*, rev. ed. (New York, 1851), 318–19.
37. Rutherford, *Selling Mrs. Consumer*
38. Other writers who made important contributions to the field of household efficiency include Mary Pattison, Georgie Boynton Child, and Martha and Robert Bruere. Laurel D. Graham, "Domesticating Efficiency: Lillian Gilbreth's Scientific Management of Homemakers, 1924–1930," *Signs* 24 (Spring 1999): 633–35.
39. Lillian Moller Gilbreth, *Management in the Home: Happier Living through Saving Time and Energy* (New York: Dodd, Mead, 1954), 80–81.

40. Susan R. Henderson, "A Revolution in the Woman's Sphere: Grete Lihotzky and the Frankfurt Kitchen," in *Architecture and Feminism*, ed. Debra Coleman, Elizabeth Danze, and Carol Henderson (New York: Princeton Architectural Press, 1996), 233–37.
41. The Gropius House, one of Historic New England's historic house museums, is open to the public.
42. *Buffer zone* is Ati's term. Ati Gropius Johansen, "Walter and Ise Gropius Living in Lincoln (1938–1983)," unpublished manuscript, rev. January 2005, Historic New England Library and Archives, 5.
43. Ise Gropius, *Gropius House: A History by Ise Gropius* (Boston: Society for the Preservation of New England Antiquities, 1996), 14.
44. Ibid.
45. "In good European fashion . . . [the Gropius] household—though modest—included a maid from the beginning." Johansen, "Walter and Ise Gropius," 3.
46. Ati Gropius Johansen, interview by Peter Gittleman, February 17, 1999, Historic New England Library and Archives.
47. Penny Ann Zaleta, memo to Marianne Zephir and Peter Gittleman, January 5, 2003. According to Ati, Gerdy was American and did not speak German. Ati Gropius Johansen, interview by Peter Gittleman, February 9, 2007, Historic New England Library and Archives.
48. Johansen, "Walter and Ise Gropius," 4.
49. Ibid.
50. Ibid., 5.
51. Ibid.
52. Gropius, *Gropius House*, 14.
53. Ati Gropius Johansen, interview, February 9, 2007.
54. Johansen, "Walter and Ise Gropius," 11.

### THE POSTWAR KITCHEN (1945-present)

1. Bill Sisson, interview with Sally Sondesky, March 15, 2002, Pennsylvania Historical and Museum Commission, Harrisburg; Melinda Talbot Nasardinov, telephone conversation with Sally Sondesky, October 4, 2006. In 2000 the Sondeskys donated their original Levittown kitchen to the State Museum of Pennsylvania, where it was part of the temporary exhibition "Levittown, Pa.: Building the Suburban Dream," between 2002 and 2003. An electronic version of the exhibition may be viewed at http://server1.fandm.edu/levittown/default.html.
2. When the Myerses moved to Levittown, they were already well acquainted with many in the community and shopped at the local Shop-a-Rama Shopping Center. Although they had a number of friends and neighbors who supported their right to move to Levittown, other neighbors protested their presence through various acts of intimidation. Among the most serious acts were the burning of crosses on the neighbors' lawns and the rental of an adjacent house by an opposition group, from which they could easily harass the family. Daisy Myers and Linda Shopes, "Breaking Down Barriers," *Pennsylvania Heritage* 28, no. 3 (Summer 2002): 6–13.
3. Mary Drake McFeely, *Can She Bake a Cherry Pie? American Women and the Kitchen in the Twentieth Century* (Amherst: University of Massachusetts Press, 2000), 71, 74–75.
4. Sherrie A. Inness, *Dinner Roles: American Women and Culinary Culture* (Iowa City: University of Iowa Press, 2001), 131.
5. Americans preserved 4.1 billion jars of food in 1943, the peak year for wartime canning. Amy Bentley, *Eating for Victory: Food Rationing and the Politics of Domesticity* (Urbana: University of Illinois Press, 1998), 131–32.
6. Quoted in Mark Jonathan Harris, Franklin D. Mitchell, and Steven J. Schechter, *The Homefront: America during World War II* (New York: G. P. Putnam's Sons, 1984), 70.
7. McFeely, *Can She Bake a Cherry Pie?* 69.
8. Quoted in Cynthia Lee Henthorn, *From Submarines to Suburbs: Selling a Better America, 1939–1959* (Athens: Ohio University Press, 2006), 66, 97, 99, 129.
9. During the war, Americans saved at a rate three times higher than in decades before or since. Stephanie Coontz, *The Way We Never Were: American Families and the Nostalgia Trap* (New York: Basic Books, 1992), 28.
10. Rosalyn Baxandall and Elizabeth Ewen, *Picture Windows: How the Suburbs Happened* (New York: Basic Books, 2000), 74–75.
11. Many veterans benefited from the GI Bill, but it was not universal in its financial support for housing. African American veterans had difficulty taking advantage of the VA program due to discriminatory lending practices. Baxandall and Ewen, *Picture Windows*, 170.
12. Barbara M. Kelly, *Expanding the American Dream: Building and Rebuilding Levittown* (Albany: State University of New York Press, 1993), 59.
13. Quoted in Craig Thompson, "Growing Pains of a Brand-New City," *Saturday Evening Post*, August 7, 1954, 72.
14. Baxandall and Ewen, *Picture Windows*, 57.
15. In 1953, 41 percent of Levittown residents were Protestant, 39 percent Catholic, 15 percent Jewish, and 5 percent nondenominational. Chad M. Kimmel, "Levittown, Pennsylvania: A Sociological Study" (PhD diss., Western Michigan University, 2004), 152.
16. Quoted in Brett Harvey, *The Fifties: A Women's Oral History* (New York: HarperCollins, 1993), 113.
17. Kimmel, "Levittown, Pennsylvania," 120.
18. Consumer spending on household furnishings and appliances increased by 240 percent nationwide. See Lizabeth Cohen, *A Consumer's Republic: The Politics of Mass Consumption in Postwar America* (New York: Alfred A. Knopf, 2003), 123, 195; and Coontz, *The Way We Never Were*, 25.
19. Mary Davis Gillies, *What Women Want in Their Kitchens of Tomorrow, A Report on the Kitchen of Tomorrow Contest Conducted by* McCall's *Magazine* (New York: McCall's, 1944), 11.
20. The Levitts were not the first to build homes with open plan kitchens. Frank Lloyd Wright pioneered this idea earlier in the century; Alfred Levitt, the architect/designer for Levitt and Sons, identified Wright as an influence. Kelly, *Expanding the American Dream*, 84–85, 94.
21. Data collected as part of the *McCall's* "My Kitchen" Contest of 1952, revealed that "Although over three quarters of respondents have dining facilities outside the kitchen, most meals are eaten in the kitchen. Eighty percent eat breakfast, 70 percent eat luncheon, and nearly 50 percent eat dinner in the kitchen all the time. . . . hence dining facilities become an important part of every kitchen plan." *My Kitchen: An Evaluation of Eighty-seven Products Commonly Found in the Kitchen as They Rank in the Minds of Homemakers* (New York: McCall's, 1952), 16.
22. "The Kitchen Opens Up," *House and Home*, June 1953, 130–31. Promotional material for Tracy stainless steel cabinets is in the collection of the Levittown Regional Library, Levittown, Pennsylvania.
23. Ibid., 131.
24. Karal Ann Marling, *As Seen on TV: The Visual Culture of Everyday Life in the 1950s* (Cambridge, Mass.: Harvard University Press, 1994), 263–64.
25. Shelley Nickels, "Object Lessons: Household Design and the American Middle Class, 1920–1960" (PhD diss., University of Virginia, 1999), 340.
26. Sally Sondesky also found the kitchen's design very efficient. Sally Sondesky, telephone conversation with Melinda Talbot Nasardinov, October 4, 2006.
27. Ellen Lupton and J. Abbott Miller, *The Bathroom, the Kitchen and the Aesthetics of Waste: A Process of Elimination* (Cambridge, Mass.: MIT List Visual Arts Center, 1992), 41.
28. Kelly, *Expanding the American Dream*, 97.
29. Alison J. Clarke, *Tupperware: The Promise of Plastic in 1950s America* (Washington, D.C.: Smithsonian Institution Press, 1999), 2, 126–27.
30. Quoted in ibid., 114.

31. Alice Kessler-Harris, *Out to Work: A History of Wage-Earning Women in the United States* (New York: Oxford University Press, 1982), 279.
32. Joan Vanek, "Time Spent in Housework," *Scientific American* 231 (November 1974): 116–20, reprinted in *History of Women in the United States*, vol. 4, pt. 1, *Domestic Ideology and Domestic Work*, ed. Nancy F. Cott (Munich: K. G. Saur, 1992), 434. See also Ruth Schwartz Cowan, *More Work for Mother: The Ironies of Household Technology from the Open Hearth to the Microwave* (New York: Basic Books, 1983).
33. Jessamyn Neuhaus, *Manly Meals and Mom's Home Cooking: Cookbooks and Gender in Modern America* (Baltimore, Md.,: Johns Hopkins University Press, 2003). See chapter 9, "'King of the Kitchen': Food and Cookery Instruction for Men."
34. Joanne Meyerowitz, ed., *Not June Cleaver: Women and Gender in Postwar America, 1945–1960* (Philadelphia: Temple University Press, 1994).
35. Betty Friedan, *The Feminine Mystique* (New York: Dell, 1963), 236.
36. Kessler-Harris, *Out to Work*, 301–2.
37. Sherrie A. Inness, *Secret Ingredients: Race, Gender, and Class at the Dinner Table* (New York: Palgrave Macmillan, 2006), 67.
38. Christopher Holmes Smith, "Freeze Frames: Frozen Foods and Memories of the Postwar American Family," in *Kitchen Culture in America: Popular Representations of Food, Gender, and Race*, ed. Sherrie Inness (Philadelphia: University of Pennsylvania Press, 2001), 184; Laura Shapiro, *Something from the Oven: Reinventing Dinner in 1950s America* (New York: Viking, 2004), 11–12, 16.
39. Shane Hamilton, "The Economies and Conveniences of Modern-Day Living: Frozen Foods and Mass Marketing, 1945–1965," *Business History Review* 77 (Spring 2003): 34, 42.
40. Ibid., 55.
41. See Marling, *As Seen on TV*, 232–33, 235; and Sylvia Lovegren, *Fashionable Food: Seven Decades of Food Fads* (Chicago: University of Chicago Press, 2005), 214–15.
42. Shapiro, *Something from the Oven*, 19.
43. Ibid., 39.
44. Marling, *As Seen on TV*, 209, 214.
45. Simone Beck, Louisette Bertholle, and Julia Child, *Mastering the Art of French Cooking* (New York: Alfred A. Knopf, 1964), vii.
46. Laura Shapiro, *Julia Child* (New York: Viking, 2007), xvii.
47. McFeely, *Can She Bake a Cherry Pie?* 115.
48. Inness, *Secret Ingredients*, 30, 52–53.
49. Quoted in Lee Rainwater, Richard P. Coleman, and Gerald Handel, *Workingman's Wife: Her Personality, World and Life Style* (New York: Oceana Publications, 1959), 173.
50. Shapiro, *Something from the Oven*, 83.
51. Stephen Gdula offers many examples of small appliances that made cooking easier for families in which both parents worked outside the home, including Rival's Crock-Pot, Presto's PrestoBurger, and Fry Daddy. *The Warmest Room in the House: How the Kitchen Became the Heart of the Twentieth-Century American Home* (New York: Bloomsbury, 2008), 141.
52. Results of a national survey of 450 households, statistically projectable to all U.S. households, conducted in June 2007 by Leo J. Shapiro & Associates, communicated to Nancy Carlisle by telephone.
53. McFeely, *Can She Bake a Cherry Pie?* 135–37.
54. Alice Waters, who opened Chez Panisse in Berkeley in 1971, has been influential in the promotion of eating locally. By varying the restaurant's menu to feature locally grown foods that were available seasonally, she encouraged farmers to increase and diversify their production. Ibid., 150.
55. In his May 4, 2003, *New York Times Magazine* article "The Futures of Food," Michael Pollan offers examples of what are now called "food systems": "TreeTop, Inc. has developed a 'low-moisture, naturally sweetened apple piece infused with a red-wine extract.' Just 18 grams of these 'apple pieces' have the same amount of cancer-fighting 'flavonoid phenols as five glasses of wine and the dietary fiber of one whole apple.'" Available at http://www.michaelpollan.com/article.php?id=27.
56. Cameron Stracher, "Much Depends on Dinner," *Wall Street Journal*, July 29, 2005, Weekend Section, 13.
57. Nancy Gibbs, "The Magic of the Family Meal," *Time*, June 4, 2006, http://www.time.com/time/magazine/article/0,9171,1200760,00.html.
58. E. B. White, "Coon Tree," *The Points of My Compass: Letters from the East, the West, the North, the South* (New York: Harper & Row, 1962), 69.

# SELECTED BIBLIOGRAPHY


## COOKBOOKS AND HOUSEHOLD MANUALS

Beck, Simone, Louisette Bertholle, and Julia Child. *Mastering the Art of French Cooking*. New York: Alfred A. Knopf, 1964.

Beecher, Catharine. *Miss Beecher's Domestic Receipt Book*. 3rd ed. New York, 1850.

———. *Treatise on Domestic Economy*. Rev. ed. New York, 1851.

Beecher, Catharine, and Harriet Beecher Stowe. *The American Woman's Home; or, Principles of Domestic Science, Being a Guide to the Formation and Maintenance of Economical, Healthful, Beautiful, and Christian Homes*. 1869. Reprint. Watkins Glen, N.Y.: Library of Victorian Culture, 1979.

Bracken, Peg. *The I Hate to Cook Book*. New York: Harcourt, Brace and World, 1960.

Cannon, Poppy. *The Can-Opener Cookbook*. New York: Thomas Y. Crowell, 1952.

Child, Lydia Maria Francis. *The Frugal Housewife: Dedicated To Those Who Are Not Ashamed of Economy*. 8th ed. London, 1832.

Darden, Norma Jean, and Carole Darden. *Spoonbread and Strawberry Wine: Recipes and Reminiscences of a Family*. Garden City, N.Y.: Doubleday, 1978.

Farmer, Fannie Merritt. *The Boston Cooking-School Cook Book*. Rev. ed. Boston: Little, Brown, 1911.

Fisher, Abby. *What Mrs. Fisher Knows about Old Southern Cooking*. San Francisco, 1881.

Gilbert, Fabiola Cabeza de Baca. *Historic Cookery*. 1939. Reprint. Santa Fe, N.M.: Ancient City Press, 1970.

Glasse, Hannah. *The Art of Cookery Made Plain and Easy*. Rev. ed. London, 1784.

Hale, Sarah Josepha. *The Good Housekeeper; or, The Way to Live Well and to be Well While We Live*. Boston, 1839.

Harland, Marion [Mary Virginia Terhune]. *Common Sense in the Household*. New York, 1873.

Kander, Mrs. Simon [Lizzie Black]. *The Settlement Cookbook: Containing Many Recipes Used in Settlement Cooking Classes, the Milwaukee Public School Cooking Centers, and Gathered from Various Other Reliable Sources*. Milwaukee, Wis.: J. H. Yewdale & Sons, 1901.

Leslie, Eliza. *Miss Leslie's Lady's House-Book; A Manual of Domestic Economy Containing Directions for Washing, Dress-Making . . . &c.* 11th ed. Philadelphia, 1850.

Lewis, Edna. *The Taste of Country Cooking*. New York: Alfred A. Knopf, 1987.

Lincoln, Mary Johnson Bailey. *Mrs. Lincoln's Boston Cook Book*. Boston, 1884.

Parloa, Maria. *Miss Parloa's Kitchen Companion*. 20th ed. Boston, 1887.

———. *Miss Parloa's New Cook Book*. New York, 1882.

*Presbyterian Cook Book*, by the Ladies of the First Presbyterian Church, Dayton, Ohio. Dayton, 1873.

Randolph, Mary. *The Virginia Housewife; or, Methodical Cook*. Baltimore, Md., 1838.

Russell, Malinda. *A Domestic Cook Book: Containing a Careful Selection of Useful Receipts for the Kitchen*. 1866. Reprint. Detroit: Inland Press, 2007.

Simmons, Amelia. *American Cookery; or, The Art of Dressing Viands, Fish, Poultry, and Vegetables, and the Best Modes of Making Pastes, Puffs, Pies, Tarts, Puddings, Custards and Preserves, and All Kinds of Cakes, from the Imperial Plumb to Plain Cake, and All Grades of Life*. Hartford, Conn., 1798.

Smart-Grosvenor, Vertamae. *Vibration Cooking; or, The Travel Notes of a Geechee Girl*. Garden City, N.Y.: Doubleday, 1970.

Tucker, Jane Armstrong, comp. *State of Maine Cook Book*. Wiscasset: Democratic Women of Maine, 1924.

Wilcox, Estelle Woods. *Buckeye Cookery and Practical Housekeeping*. Minneapolis, Minn., 1877.

## GENERAL RESOURCES

Ackerman, Phyllis. "Color in the Kitchen." *House Beautiful*, September 1922.

"An Unexpected Kitchen: The George Foreman Grill, Story Note from The Kitchen Sisters." NPR's *Morning Edition*. October 8, 2004. http//www.npr.org/templates/story/story.php?storyId=4075302.

Arnold, Eleanor, ed. *Memories of Hoosier Homemakers*. 6 vols. Bloomington: Indiana University Press, 1983–94.

———. *Voices of American Homemakers*. Bloomington: Indiana University Press, 1993.

Avakian, Arlene Voski, ed. *Through the Kitchen Window: Women Explore the Intimate Meanings of Food and Cooking*. Boston: Beacon Press, 1997.

Bailey, Pearl. *Pearl's Kitchen*. New York: Harcourt Brace Jovanovich, 1973.

Baxandall, Rosalyn, and Elizabeth Ewen. *Picture Windows: How the Suburbs Happened*. New York: Basic Books, 2000.

Beck, Margaret E. "Dinner Preparation in the Modern United States." *British Food Journal* 109, no. 7 (2007): 531–47.

Benes, Peter, ed. *Foodways in the Northeast*. Dublin Seminar for New England Folklife, Annual Proceedings 7 (1982). Boston: Boston University, 1984.

Bentley, Amy. *Eating for Victory: Food Rationing and the Politics of Domesticity*. Urbana: University of Illinois Press, 1998.

Berzok, Linda Murray. *American Indian Food*. Westport, Conn.: Greenwood Press, 2005.

Braunstein, Susan L., and Jenna Weissman Joselit, eds. *Getting Comfortable in New York: The American Jewish Home, 1880–1950*. New York: The Jewish Museum, 1990.

Brewer, Priscilla J. *From Fireplace to Cookstove: Technology and the Domestic Ideal in America*. Syracuse, N.Y.: Syracuse University Press, 2000.

Brown, Sanborn C., ed. *Collected Works of Count Rumford*. 5 vols. Cambridge, Mass.: Belknap Press of Harvard University Press, 1968–70.

Brumfel, Elizabeth M. "Weaving and Cooking: Women's Production in Aztec Mexico." In *Engendering Archaeology: Women and Prehistory*, edited by Joan M. Gero and Margaret W. Conkey, 224–51. Oxford, U.K.: Basil Blackwell, 1991.

Bunting, Bainbridge. *Early Architecture in New Mexico*. Albuquerque: University of New Mexico Press, 1976.

Campbell, Edward D.C., Drew Gilpin Faust, and Kym S. Rice, eds. *Before Freedom Came: African-American Life in the Antebellum South*. Charlottesville: University Press of Virginia, 1991.

Clark-Lewis, Elizabeth. *Living In, Living Out: African American Domestics in Washington, D.C., 1910–1940*. Washington, D.C.: Smithsonian Institution Press, 1994.

Clarke, Alison J. *Tupperware: The Promise of Plastic in 1950s America*. Washington, D.C.: Smithsonian Institution Press, 1999.

Clinton, Catherine. *The Plantation Mistress: Woman's World in the Old South*. New York: Pantheon, 1982.

Coffin, Joshua. *A Sketch of the History of Newbury, Newburyport, and West Newbury, from 1635 to 1845*. Boston, 1845.

Cohen, Lizabeth. *A Consumer's Republic: The Politics of Mass Consumption in Postwar America*. New York: Alfred A. Knopf, 2003.

Coontz, Stephanie. *The Way We Never Were: American Families and the Nostalgia Trap*. New York: Basic Books, 1992.

Cowan, Ruth Schwartz. *More Work for Mother: The Ironies of Household Technology from the Open Hearth to the Microwave*. New York: Basic Books, 1983.

Cushing, Frank Hamilton. *Zuni Breadstuff*. 1884–1885. Reprint. New York: Museum of the American Indian, Heye Foundation, 1920.

DeSalvo, Louise. *Crazy in the Kitchen: Food, Feuds, and Forgiveness in an Italian American Family*. New York: Bloomsbury, 2004.

Diner, Hasia R. *Hungering for America: Italian, Irish, and Jewish Foodways in the Age of Immigration*. Cambridge, Mass.: Harvard University Press, 2001.

*Domestic Needs of Farm Women: Extracts from Letters Received from Farm Women in Response to an Inquiry "How the U. S. Department of Agriculture Can Better Meet the Needs of Farm Housewives," with Special Reference to the Provision of Instruction and Practical Demonstrations in Home Economics under the Act of May 8, 1914, Providing for Cooperative Agricultural Extension Work, etc.* Washington, D.C.: Government Printing Office, 1915.

Douglas, Helen C. "Well-planned Work Centers Organized for Easier Living in Kitchen, Laundry and All Through the House." *Small Homes Guide*, Summer–Fall 1952.

Drumm, Stella M., ed. *Down the Santa Fé Trail and into Mexico: The Diary of Susan Shelby Magoffin 1846–1847*. New Haven, Conn.: Yale University Press, 1926.

Dudden, Faye. *Serving Women: Household Service in Nineteenth-Century America*. Middletown, Conn.: Wesleyan University Press, 1983.

Ehrlich, Elizabeth. *Miriam's Kitchen: A Memoir*. New York: Viking, 1997.

Emery, Sarah Anna. *Reminiscences of a Nonagenarian*. Newburyport, Mass., 1879.

Faulkner, Wendy, and Erik Arnold, eds. *Smothered by Invention: Technology in Women's Lives*. London: Pluto Press, 1985.

Faust, Drew Gilpin. *Mothers of Invention: Women in the Slaveholding South in the American Civil War*. Chapel Hill: University of North Carolina Press, 1996.

Ferris, Marcie Cohen. *Matzoh Ball Gumbo: Culinary Tales of the Jewish South*. Chapel Hill: University of North Carolina Press, 2005.

Foner, Philip S., ed. *Frederick Douglass: Selected Speeches and Writings*. Chicago: Lawrence Hill Books, 1999.

Foote, Cheryl J. "What's in [the spelling] of a Name? Chile, Chili?" *Food History News* 17, no. 2 (2005): 1, 7–8.

———. *Women of the New Mexico Frontier, 1846–1912*. Albuquerque: University of New Mexico Press, 2005.

Fowler, Damon Lee, ed. *Dining at Monticello: In Good Taste and Abundance*. Charlottesville, Va.: Thomas Jefferson Memorial Foundation, 2005.

Fox-Genovese, Elizabeth. *Within the Plantation Household: Black and White Women of the Old South*. Chapel Hill: University of North Carolina Press, 1988.

Frederick, Christine. *Household Engineering: Scientific Management in the Home*. Chicago: American School of Home Economics, 1920.

Friedan, Betty. *The Feminine Mystique*. New York: Dell, 1963.

Gabaccia, Donna. *We Are What We Eat: Ethnic Food and the Making of Americans*. Cambridge, Mass.: Harvard University Press, 1998.

Garrard, Lewis H. *Wah-to-yah and the Taos Trail*. 1850. Reprint. Norman: University of Oklahoma Press, 1955.

Gdula, Stephen. *The Warmest Room in the House: How the Kitchen Became the Heart of the Twentieth-Century American Home*. New York: Bloomsbury, 2008.

Genovese, Eugene D. *Roll, Jordan, Roll: The World the Slaves Made*. New York: Pantheon, 1974.

Gilbert, Fabiola Cabeza de Baca. *We Fed Them Cactus*. Albuquerque: University of New Mexico Press, 1954.

Gilbreth, Lillian Moller. *Management in the Home: Happier Living through Saving Time and Energy*. New York: Dodd, Mead, 1954.

Gillies, Mary Davis. *What Women Want in Their Kitchens of Tomorrow: A Report on the Kitchen of Tomorrow Contest Conducted by McCall's Magazine*. New York: McCall's, 1944.

Gilman, Charlotte Perkins Stetson. *Women and Economics*. Boston, 1898.

Gregg, Josiah. *The Commerce of the Prairies*. 1844. Reprint, edited by Max Moorhead. Norman: University of Oklahoma Press, 1954.

Gutiérrez, Ramón A. *When Jesus Came, the Corn Mothers Went Away: Marriage, Sexuality, and Power in New Mexico, 1500–1846*. Stanford, Calif.: Stanford University Press, 1991.

Guzman, Pilar. "Hey Man, What's for Dinner?" *New York Times*, August 28, 2002.

Haber, Barbara. *From Hardtack to Home Fries: An Uncommon History of American Cooks and Meals*. New York: Free Press, 2002.

Harland, Marion [Mary Virginia Terhune]. *Home Making*. Boston: Hall and Locke, 1911.

———. *Marion Harland's Autobiography: The Story of a Long Life*. New York: Harper and Brothers, 1910.

Harris, Jessica B. *Iron Pots and Wooden Spoons: Africa's Gifts to New World Cooking*. New York: Atheneum, 1989.

Harris, Mark Jonathan, Franklin D. Mitchell, and Steven J. Schechter. *The Homefront: America during World War II*. New York: G.P. Putnam's Sons, 1984.

Harvey, Brett. *The Fifties: A Women's Oral History*. New York: HarperCollins, 1993.

Hayden, Dolores. *The Grand Domestic Revolution: A History of Feminist Design for American Homes, Neighborhoods, and Cities*. Cambridge, Mass.: MIT Press, 1981.

Hemenway, Abby Maria. *The Vermont Historical Gazetteer*. Vol. 3. Burlington, Vt., 1877.

Henthorn, Cynthia Lee. *From Submarines to Suburbs: Selling a Better America, 1939–1959*. Athens: Ohio University Press, 2006.

Hilliard, Sam Bowers. *Hog Meat and Hoecake: Food Supply in the Old South, 1840–1860*. Carbondale: Southern Illinois University Press, 1972.

Hines, Mary Anne, Gordon Marshall, and William Woys Weaver. *The Larder Invaded: Reflections on Three Centuries of Philadelphia Food and Drink*. Philadelphia: Library Company of Philadelphia and The Historical Society of Pennsylvania, 1987.

Holt, Marilyn Irvin. *Linoleum, Better Babies & the Modern Farm Woman, 1890–1930*. Albuquerque: University of New Mexico Press, 1995.

Home Improvement Research Institute. "Weaknesses in Housing and the Overall Economy Seen to Result in Two Successive Years of Market Declines," February 2008, http://www.hiri.org/inside.asp?id=21#2.

Hudgeons, Thomas E., ed. *The Official From Hearth to Cookstove: An American Domestic History of Gadgets and Utensils Made or Used in America from 1700 to 1930*. 3rd ed. Orlando, Fla.: House of Collectibles, 1985.

[Huse, Caleb]. "The Coffin House in the Early Nineteenth Century." *Old-Time New England* 27, no. 2 (October 1936): 69–72.

Inness, Sherrie A. *Dinner Roles: American Women and Culinary Culture*. Iowa City: University of Iowa Press, 2001.

———. *Secret Ingredients: Race, Gender, and Class at the Dinner Table*. New York: Palgrave Macmillan, 2006.

———, ed. *Kitchen Culture in America: Popular Representations of Food, Gender, and Race*. Philadelphia: University of Pennsylvania Press, 2001.

———, ed. *Pilaf, Pozole, and Pad Thai: American Women and Ethnic Food*. Amherst: University of Massachusetts Press, 2001.

Jaramillo, Cleofas M. *Shadows of the Past (Sombras del Pasado)*. 1941. Reprint. Santa Fe, N.M.: Ancient City Press, 1972.

Katzman, David M. *Seven Days a Week: Women and Domestic Service in Industrializing America*. New York: Oxford University Press, 1978.

Kelly, Barbara M. *Expanding the American Dream: Building and Rebuilding Levittown*. Albany: State University of New York Press, 1993.

Kessler-Harris, Alice. *Out to Work: A History of Wage-Earning Women in the United States*. New York: Oxford University Press, 1982.

Kleinegger, Christine. "Out of the Barns and into the Kitchens: Transformations in Farm Women's Work in the First Half of the Twentieth Century." In *Women, Work, and Technology: Transformations*, edited by Barbara Drygulski Wright, et al., 162–81. Ann Arbor: University of Michigan Press, 1987.

Kreidberg, Marjorie. *Food on the Frontier: Minnesota Cooking from 1850 to 1900 with Selected Recipes*. St. Paul: Minnesota Historical Society Press, 1975.

Larcom, Lucy. *A New England Girlhood, Outlined from Memory*. Boston, 1889.

Laughlin, Helen. "The Farm Home Kitchen." *Colman's Rural World*, November 21, 1900.
Levenstein, Harvey. *Revolution at the Table: The Transformation of the American Diet.* New York: Oxford University Press, 1988.
Lifshey, Earl. *The Housewares Story: A History of the American Housewares Industry.* Chicago: National Housewares Manufacturers, 1973.
Lovegren, Sylvia. *Fashionable Food: Seven Decades of Food Fads.* Chicago: University of Chicago Press, 2005.
Lupton, Ellen, and J. Abbott Miller. *The Bathroom, the Kitchen and the Aesthetics of Waste: A Process of Elimination.* Cambridge, Mass.: MIT List Visual Arts Center, 1992.
Manring, M. M. *Slave in a Box: The Strange Career of Aunt Jemima.* Charlottesville: University Press of Virginia, 1998.
Marling, Karal Ann. *As Seen on TV: The Visual Culture of Everyday Life in the 1950s.* Cambridge, Mass.: Harvard University Press, 1994.
McFeely, Mary Drake. *Can She Bake a Cherry Pie? American Women and the Kitchen in the Twentieth Century.* Amherst: University of Massachusetts Press, 2000.
McInnis, D. Maurie. *The Politics of Taste in Antebellum Charleston.* Chapel Hill: University of North Carolina Press, 2005.
Melish, Joanne Pope. *Disowning Slavery: Gradual Emancipation and "Race" in New England, 1780–1860.* Ithaca, N.Y.: Cornell University Press, 1998.
Meyerowitz, Joanne, ed. *Not June Cleaver: Women and Gender in Postwar America, 1945–1960.* Philadelphia: Temple University Press, 1994.
Miner, Curtis. "Picture Window Paradise." *Pennsylvania Heritage* 28, no. 2 (Spring 2002): 12–21.
Moore, John Hammond, ed. *A Plantation Mistress on the Eve of the Civil War: The Diary of Keziah Goodwyn Hopkins Brevard, 1860–1861.* Columbia: University of South Carolina Press, 1993.
Morrison, Hetty A. *My Summer in the Kitchen.* Indianapolis, Ind.: Douglas and Carlon, 1878.
Myers, Daisy, and Linda Shopes. "Breaking Down Barriers." *Pennsylvania Heritage* 28, no. 3 (Summer 2002): 6–13.
Myers, Robert Mason, ed. *The Children of Pride: Selected Letters of the Family of the Rev. Dr. Charles Colcock Jones from the Years 1860–1868.* New Haven, Conn.: Yale University Press, 1984.
Neuhaus, Jessamyn. *Manly Meals and Mom's Home Cooking: Cookbooks and Gender in Modern America.* Baltimore, Md.: Johns Hopkins University Press, 2003.
New York State College of Home Economics. *Cornell Bulletin for Homemakers*, part 5, no. 578. Ithaca, N.Y., March 1943.
Nylander, Jane. *Our Own Snug Fireside: Images of the New England Home, 1760–1860.* New York: Alfred A. Knopf, 1993.
Oliver, Sandra L. *Food in Colonial and Federal America.* Westport, Conn.: Greenwood Press, 2005.
———. *Saltwater Foodways: New Englanders and Their Food, at Sea and Ashore, in the Nineteenth Century.* Mystic, Conn.: Mystic Seaport Museum, 1995.
Palmer, Phyllis. *Domesticity and Dirt: Housewives and Domestic Servants in the United States, 1920–1945.* Philadelphia: Temple University Press, 1989.
Pierson, William Dillon. *Black Yankees.* Amherst: University of Massachusetts Press, 1988.
"Planning Your New Kitchen." *Small Homes Guide*, Winter 1953–Spring 1954.
Plante, Ellen M. *The American Kitchen, 1700 to the Present: From Hearth to Highrise.* New York: Facts on File, 1995.
Rainwater, Lee, Richard P. Coleman, and Gerald Handel. *Workingman's Wife: Her Personality, World and Life Style.* New York: Oceana Publications, 1959.
Reichl, Ruth. *Tender at the Bone: Growing Up at the Table.* New York: Broadway Books, 1998.
Russell, Marian. *Land of Enchantment: Memoirs of Marian Russell along the Santa Fe Trail.* 1954. Reprint. Albuquerque: University of New Mexico Press, 1981.
Rutherford, Janice Williams. *Selling Mrs. Consumer: Christine Frederick and the Rise of Household Efficiency.* Athens: University of Georgia Press, 2003.
Ruxton, George Frederick Augustus. *Adventures in Mexico and the Rocky Mountains.* 1848. Reprint. Glorieta, N.M.: Rio Grande Press, 1973.
Saporito, Bill. "Inside the New American Home." *Time*, October 14, 2002.
Schenone, Laura. *A Thousand Years Over a Hot Stove: A History of American Women Told through Food, Recipes, and Remembrances.* New York: W. W. Norton, 2003.
Shapiro, Laura. *Julia Child.* New York: Viking, 2007.
———. *Perfection Salad: Women and Cooking at the Turn of the Century.* New York: Modern Library, 2001.
———. *Something from the Oven: Reinventing Dinner in 1950s America.* New York: Viking, 2004.
Sloan, A. Elizabeth. "What, When, and Where America Eats." *Food Technology* 62, no. 1 (January 2008): 20–29.
Smith, Andrew F., ed. *The Oxford Encyclopedia of Food and Drink in America.* 2 vols. New York: Oxford University Press, 2004.
Spofford, Harriet Prescott. *The Servant Girl Question.* Boston, 1881.
Stage, Sarah, and Virginia Vincenti, eds. *Rethinking Home Economics: Women and the History of a Profession.* Ithaca, N.Y.: Cornell University Press, 1997.
Stowe, Charles Edward, ed. *Life of Harriet Beecher Stowe.* Boston, 1889.
Strasser, Susan. *Never Done: A History of American Housework.* New York: Pantheon Books, 1982.
Sutherland, Kate. "Cooks." *Godey's Lady's Book and Magazine*, May 1852.
Swint, Henry L. *Dear Ones at Home: Letters from Contraband Camps.* Nashville, Tenn.: Vanderbilt University Press, 1966.
Taylor, Joe Gray. *Eating, Drinking, and Visiting in the South: An Informal History.* Baton Rouge: Louisiana State University Press, 1982.
Towner, Lawrence. *A Good Master Well Served: Masters and Servants in Colonial Massachusetts, 1620–1750.* New York: Garland, 1998.
Twain, Mark. "Putting Up Stoves." *Scientific American*, n.s., 22, January 1, 1870.
Ulrich, Laurel Thatcher. *Good Wives: Image and Reality in the Lives of Women in Northern New England, 1650–1750.* New York: Vintage, 1980.
University of California–Los Angeles. "'Convenience' Foods Save Little Time for Working Families at Dinner." *Science Daily*, August 13, 2007, http://www.sciencedaily.com/releases/2007/08/070807135415.htm.
Vickers, Daniel. *Farmers and Fishermen: Two Centuries of Work in Essex County, Massachusetts, 1630–1850.* Chapel Hill: University of North Carolina Press, 1994.
Vlach, John Michael. *Back of the Big House: The Architecture of Plantation Slavery.* Chapel Hill: University of North Carolina Press, 1993.
Ward, Barbara McLean, ed. *Produce & Conserve, Share & Play Square: The Grocer and Consumer on the Home-Front Battlefield During World War II.* Portsmouth, N.H.: Strawbery Banke Museum, 1994.
Washington, Booker T. *Up From Slavery: An Autobiography.* New York: Doubleday, Page, 1904.
Weiner, Marli F. *Mistresses and Slaves: Plantation Women in South Carolina, 1830–80.* Urbana: University of Illinois Press, 1998.
White, Deborah Gray. *Ar'n't I a Woman? Female Slaves in the Plantation South.* New York: W. W. Norton, 1999.
White, E. B. "Coon Tree." In *The Points of My Compass: Letters from the East, the West, the North, the South.* New York: Harper & Row, 1962.
Williams, Jacqueline B. *The Way We Ate: Pacific Northwest Cooking, 1843–1900.* Pullman: Washington State University Press, 1996.
Williams, Michael Ann. *Homeplace: The Social Use and Meaning of the Folk Dwelling in Southwestern North Carolina.* Athens: University of Georgia Press, 1991.
Wood, Kristen E. *Masterful Women: Slaveholding Widows from the American Revolution through the Civil War.* Chapel Hill: University of North Carolina Press, 2004.
Wright, Barbara Drygulski, et al., ed. *Women, Work, and Technology: Transformations.* Ann Arbor: University of Michigan Press, 1987.

## DIGITAL COLLECTIONS

Cornell University, Albert R. Mann Library. "Home Economics Archive: Research, Tradition, History (HEARTH)." http://hearth.library.cornell.edu/.

Harvard University Libraries, Open Collections Program. "Women Working, 1800–1930." http://ocp.hul.harvard.edu/ww.

Library of Congress, Federal Writers' Project, Works Progress Administration. *Slave Narratives: A Folk History of Slavery in the United States from Interviews with Former Slaves*. 17 vols. Washington, D.C., 1941. Published online as *American Memory, Born in Slavery: Slave Narratives from the Federal Writers' Project, 1936–1938*. http://memory.loc.gov/ammem/snhtml/snhome.html.

Michigan State University Library and Michigan State University Museum. "Feeding America: The Historic American Cookbook Project." http://digital.lib.msu.edu/projects/cookbooks/.

# ILLUSTRATION CREDITS

OPPOSITE INSIDE FRONT FLAP: Sondesky family kitchen, Levittown, Penn., ca. 1960. Courtesy the Pennsylvania Historical and Museum Commission and Sara V. and Jack Sondesky.
FRONTISPIECE: Cover of *You and Your Kitchen* by Christine Frederick (New Castle, Ind.: Hoosier Manufacturing Co., 1914). Promised gift to Historic New England from private collection.
OPPOSITE TABLE OF CONTENTS: Detail of Armour-brand products from the second edition of *The Business of Being a Housewife: A Manual to Promote Household Efficiency and Economy* by Mrs. Jean Prescott Adams (Chicago: Armour, 1921). Promised gift to Historic New England from private collection.
OPPOSITE FOREWORD: Tiled kitchen from the trade catalogue "Home Suggestions," 1922. Associated Tile Manufacturers, Beaver Falls, Penn., publisher. Promised gift to Historic New England from private collection.

### THE KITCHEN IN AMERICAN LIFE

1: Colonial Homestead Dinner Plate. Marshall-Burns, Chicago, Ill., ca. 1955. Transfer print on earthenware. Gift of Johanna McBrien. (1999.105.2) David Carmack, photographer. Collection of Historic New England.
2: *Making Buckwheat Pancakes*, September 13, 1949. Frederick L. Holmes, photographer. Courtesy Wisconsin Historical Society. (WHi-6844)
3: Chase Wissler at play, 2007. Adrienne Sage, photographer. Courtesy Gwendolyn Wissler.
4: *The Ghost Story*, by William Verplanck Birney (1858–1909), ca. 1895. Oil on canvas. Courtesy Cincinnati Art Museum, Gift of The Procter & Gamble Company. (2003.54)
5: *The Wind Mill*, by Francis W. Edmonds, ca. 1858. Oil on canvas. Courtesy Collection of The New-York Historical Society. (Accession S-217)
6: Kitchen, Altgeld Gardens, Chicago, Ill. Courtesy Library of Congress, Prints & Photographs Division. (LC-USZ62-51415)
7: Youngstown Kitchen by Mullins from the trade catalogue "Dream Kitchens for a Song," 1948. Mullins Manufacturing Corporation, Warren, Ohio, publisher. Promised gift to Historic New England from private collection.
8: "Eastern Woodland Indians Cooking Succotash," by Theodor de Bry (1528–1598), second edition of *Les Grands Voyages, Parts I–V* (Frankfort am Mayn: Matthies Merian, 1624). Courtesy Mashantucket Pequot Museum and Research Center, Archives and Special Collections. (MSS 115)
9: "The Detached Oven," *American Agriculturist*, June 1873. Collection of Historic New England.
10: Photograph from *Today's Woman Prize Kitchens* by Victor Civkin, A.I.A. (Greenwich, Conn.: Fawcett Publications, 1952). Promised gift to Historic New England from private collection.
11. Min-A-Kitchen models for Youngstown Kitchens by Mullins from the trade catalogue "Dream Kitchens for a Song," 1948. Mullins Manufacturing Corp., Warren, Ohio, publisher. Promised gift to Historic New England from private collection.
12–13: Mrs. Monroe Jones in her kitchen, Kentucky Straight Creek Coal Company, Belva Mine, Four Mile, Bell County, Ky., 1946. Courtesy the U.S. National Archives and Records Administration.
15: CATHY comic strip. CATHY ©1994 Cathy Guisewite. Reprinted with permission of Universal Press Syndicate. All rights reserved.
16–17: *Tamalada*, by Carmen Lomas Garza, 1988. Oil on linen mounted on wood. Courtesy the artist, www.carmenlomasgarza.com.
18: J.T. Aldridge, Boston, Mass. Courtesy Cheryl Aldridge.
19: Sintros family kitchen, North Andover, Mass., 2007. Collection of Historic New England.
20–21: Nesco Oil Cook Stove and Nesco Royal Granite Ware from the trade catalogue "Nesco Better Kitchens," 1925. National Enameling & Stamping Co., Milwaukee, Wis., publisher. Promised gift to Historic New England from private collection.

### THE NEW ENGLAND HEARTH (1720-1840)

22: Hearth cooking, Bixby House, Old Sturbridge Village, Sturbridge, Mass., 1999. Thomas Neill, photographer. Courtesy Old Sturbridge Village.
23: Stereo view of the Coffin House, Newbury, Mass., ca. 1872. Collection of Historic New England.
24: TOP: Axonometric drawing of Coffin House kitchen, Newbury, Mass., by Gerald L. Foster, 2008. Ink and colored pencil on paper. BOTTOM: Coffin House, Newbury, Mass., 2007. Peter Harholdt, photographer. Both from the collection of Historic New England.
25: Coffee mill, Coffin House kitchen, Newbury, Mass., 2007. Peter Harholdt, photographer. Collection of Historic New England.
26: Apprentice indenture, 1793. Courtesy Delaware Public Archives.
27: Iron kettle dated 1801. Henry Peach, photographer. Courtesy Old Sturbridge Village. (Artifact #2.47.143. B14070)
29: Title page of *American Cookery*, by Amelia Simmons (Hartford, Conn.: Hudson & Goodwin, 1796). Courtesy Library of Congress, Rare Books and Special Collections Division.
31: Broadside printed in London by Felix Kyngston and tipped into *A Declaration of the State of the Colony and State of Affairs in Virginia*, by Edward Waterhouse (London: G. Eld., for R. Mylbourne, 1622). Courtesy Virginia Historical Society, Richmond, Va.
32: Reenactment of hearth cooking, Plimoth Plantation, Plymouth, Mass. Courtesy Plimoth Plantation.
33: *Woman Baking Pancakes*, by Pieter Gierritz van Roestraten (1632–1700), 1678. Oil on canvas. Courtesy Bredius Collection, Museum Bredius, The Hague, Netherlands.
34: Rundlet-May House, Portsmouth, N.H. David Bohl, photographer. Collection of Historic New England.
35: Hermann-Grima House, New Orleans, La. Paul Taylor, photographer. Courtesy Hermann-Grima/Gallier Historic Houses.
36–37: "Scalded in the Kitchen" from *The Two Fawns*, by Mary Martha Butts Sherwood (New Haven, Conn.: S. Babcock, 1833). Courtesy Old Sturbridge Village.
38: Tin kitchen from *Miss Parloa's New Cook Book*, by Maria Parloa (Boston: Estes and Lauriat, 1881). Collection of Historic New England.
39: Frontispiece for *The New England Economical Housekeeper, and Family Receipt Book*, by Mrs. E.A. Howland (Worcester, Mass.: S. A. Howland, 1845). Courtesy Library of Congress, Prints & Photographs Division. (LC-USZ62-83637)
40: TOP: "Baking in a Bake-Kettle," *American Agriculturist*, June 1873. BOTTOM: "7 times 11 are 77 . . .," from *Marmaduke Multiply*, by John Harris (Boston: Munroe and Francis, 1845). Both from the collection of Historic New England.
41: *Making Sausage in the Old Manner*, by Henry Barrat, 1879. Woodcut. Courtesy York County Heritage Trust Library and Archives.
42: "Straining and Skimming," from *The Progress of the Dairy: Descriptive of the Method of Making Butter and Cheese for the Information of Youth* (New York:

Samuel Wood & Sons; Baltimore: Samuel S. Wood, 1819). Courtesy Sinclair Hamilton Collection No. 1424, Graphic Arts Division, Department of Rare Books and Special Collections, Princeton University Library.
43: Buttery, Coffin House, Newbury, Mass. David Bohl, photographer. Collection of Historic New England.
44–45: "Possum am Sweet," 1898. H.P. Cook, photographer. Courtesy Cook Collection, Valentine Richmond History Center.

## KITCHENS IN THE PLANTATION SOUTH (1830-1860)

46: Unidentified walkway from kitchen to main house. H.P. Cook, photographer. Courtesy Cook Collection, Valentine Richmond History Center.
47: Main House, Green Hill Plantation, Campbell County, Va., ca. 1933. Courtesy Library of Congress, Prints & Photographs Division. (HABS VA, 16-LONI.V, 1-3)
48: TOP: Kitchen building, Green Hill Plantation, Campbell County, Va., ca. 1960. Courtesy Commonwealth of Virginia, Department of Historic Resources. BOTTOM: Axonometric drawing of Green Hill Plantation kitchen, Campbell County, Va., by Gerald L. Foster, 2008. Ink and colored pencil on paper. Collection of Historic New England.
49: TOP: Axonometric drawing of Green Hill Plantation, Campbell County, Va., by Gerald L. Foster, 2008. Ink and colored pencil on paper. Collection of Historic New England. BOTTOM: Dining room door, Main House, Green Hill Plantation, Campbell County, Va., ca. 1933. Courtesy Library of Congress, Prints & Photographs Division. (HABS VA, 16-LONI.V, 1-8)
50: Green Hill Plantation, Campbell County, Va., ca. 1933. Courtesy Library of Congress, Prints & Photographs Division. (HABS VA, 16-LONI.V, 1-va1)
51: East end of kitchen walkway, Kenworthy Hall, Marion, Ala., January 9, 1937. Alex Bush, photographer. Courtesy Library of Congress, Prints & Photographs Division. (HABS ALA, 53-MARI.V, 5-23)
52: CLOCKWISE FROM TOP LEFT: Historic American Buildings Survey photographs, courtesy Library of Congress, Prints & Photographs Division: Icehouse, Green Hill Plantation, Campbell County, Va., ca. 1933. (HABS VA, 16-LONI.V, 1H-1); Stone smokehouse, Mount Lebanon, Paris, Ky., March 28, 1934. Theodore Webb, photographer. (HABS KY, 9-PAR.V, 1-11); Dairy, Hayes Manor, Edenton vicinity, N.C., May 5, 1940. C.O. Greene, photographer. (HABS NC, 21-EDET.V, 1-14); Dairy, Mount Airy (John Tayloe Plantation), Richmond County, Va., ca. 1933. (HABS VA, 80 WAR.V, 4B-1); and Woodlands Dairy Building, Northampton County, Va., ca. 1933. (HABS VA, 66-NASA.V, 1-9)
53: Ephraim Bumgarner cabins, Deep Creek, N.C., 1937. Courtesy Great Smoky Mountains National Park.
54: *A Visit from the Old Mistress*, by Winslow Homer (1836–1910), 1876. Oil on canvas. Courtesy Smithsonian American Art Museum, Gift of William T. Evans.
56: TOP: "The Virginia Housekeeper," by S.C. Richardson-Cox, *Harper's Monthly*, December 1854. Courtesy Old Sturbridge Village. BOTTOM: Notice, *Alexandria Gazette & Daily Advertiser*, March 16, 1818. Courtesy the American Antiquarian Society.
59: *The Kitchen at Mount Vernon*, by Eastman Johnson (1824–1906), ca. 1857. Oil on panel. Bequest of Ninah M. H. Cummer, C.0.117.1. Courtesy The Cummer Museum of Art & Gardens, Jacksonville, Fla.
60: Refuge Plantation, Camden County, Ga. Reproduced by L.D. Andrew from an old photograph in possession of B.C. Heyward. Courtesy Library of Congress, Prints & Photographs Division. (HABS GA, 20-WOBI.V, 1-3)
63: TOP: African Americans in front of log cabin, nineteenth century. Courtesy Virginia Historical Society, Richmond, Va. (2000.92.1). BOTTOM: Slave cabins, Hermitage Plantation, Chatham County, Ga., ca. 1934. C.E. Peterson, photographer. Courtesy Library of Congress, Prints & Photographs Division. (HABS GA, 26-SAV.V, 1-9)
64: Thornhill Plantation, Watsonia, Ala., December 30, 1934. Alex Bush, photographer. Courtesy Library of Congress, Prints & Photographs Division. (HABS ALA, 32-WATSO, 1-27)
65: Sketch of Spotsylvania Court House, Va., by Edwin Forbes (1839–1895), May 14, 1864. Courtesy Library of Congress, Civil War Drawings Collection. (LC-USZC4-2041)
66: *Noon on a Plantation*, by William Waud, 1860–1869. Ink wash, pencil, Chinese white, and watercolor on paper. Courtesy The Historic New Orleans Collection, Museum/Research Center, Accession 1977.137.4.10.
69: Frontispiece for *The Blue Grass Cookbook*, compiled by Minnie C. Fox (New York: Fox, Duffield, 1904). Courtesy Special Collections, Michigan State University Libraries.

## COOKSTOVES AND SERVANTS (1850-1890)

70: CLOCKWISE FROM TOP LEFT: Trade cards from the collection of Historic New England: New American Cookstove, Perry & Co., 1874; Kitchen Furnishing Goods, Thayer & Stiles, Newton, Mass.; New Hub Range, Smith & Anthony Stove Co., Boston; Sun Dial Gas Stove, the Goodwin Gas Stove & Meter Co., Philadelphia and New York; and New Model Grand Portable Range, Spicers & Peckham, Providence, R.I.
71, 72: David Davis Mansion, Bloomington, Ill. Ken Kashian, photographer. Courtesy Illinois Historic Preservation Agency: David Davis Mansion State Historic Site, Bloomington, Ill.
73: TOP: "Josiah Moving the Stove" from *Samantha Among the Brethren*, by Marietta Holley (1890. Reprint. New York: Garland, 1987). Courtesy Schlesinger Library on the History of Women in America, Radcliffe Institute, Harvard University. BOTTOM: Trade card for the Sun Dial Gas Stove by the Goodwin Gas Stove & Meter Co., Philadelphia. Collection of Historic New England.
74: *A Pastoral Visit*, by Richard Norris Brooke, 1881. Oil on canvas. Courtesy Corcoran Gallery of Art, Washington, D.C.
75: *Mother and Child*, by Eastman Johnson (1824–1906), 1869. Oil on board. Courtesy Godel & Co. Fine Art, New York, N.Y.
76–77: Homesteader's house, Dakota Territory, 1885. Courtesy South Dakota State Historical Society, State Archives.
78: Lithograph "Prang's Aids for Object Teaching—The Kitchen," 1874. L. Prang & Co., publisher. Courtesy Library of Congress, Prints & Photographs Division. (LC-USZC4-5155)
79: TOP: Eggbeater, Castle Tucker kitchen, Wiscasset, Me., 2007. Peter Harholdt, photographer. Collection of Historic New England. BOTTOM: "Backgrounds of Civilization . . .," *New York Illustrated News*, February 11, 1860. Courtesy New York State Library, Manuscripts and Special Collections.
80: Title page for *The American Woman's Home*, by Catharine E. Beecher and Harriet Beecher Stowe (New York: J.B. Ford, 1869). Collection of Historic New England.
81: CLOCKWISE FROM TOP LEFT: Trade materials from the Collection of Historic New England: Mixer and Kneader from a trade catalogue for Sparrow and Noble kitchen appliances, 1881; Little Giant Meat Cutter by the Peck, Stow & Wilcox Co., Southington, Conn. and New York; Improved potato paring machine by Chas. E. Gee, Lowell, Mass.; and Enterprise Raisin Seeder by the Enterprise Manufacturing Company, Philadelphia.
83: "Love in a Cottage," by Sol Eytinge, Jr., *Harper's Weekly*, April 3, 1875. Courtesy the Boston Public Library.
84: Sketch of cellar kitchen, 2 Chestnut St., Salem, Mass., by L.J. Bridgman, ca. 1915. Ink, graphite, and wash on board. Collection of Historic New England.
85: "A New England Kitchen," by C. Meeder, *Hearth and Home*, July 22, 1871. Courtesy the Boston Public Library.
86: TOP: *Interior of an Adirondack Shanty*, by George Bacon Wood, Jr., ca. 1880. Oil on canvas. Courtesy the Adirondack Museum, Blue Mountain Lake, N.Y. BOTTOM: Back cover of the trade catalogue "Ayer's Preserve

Book," 1891. Dr. J.C. Ayer, Lowell, Mass., publisher. Collection of Historic New England.
88: Trade card for Kirchberg & Keenan, Furniture Manufacturers and Dealers, Detroit, Mich. Collection of Historic New England.
90: Detail from the lithograph "Life in Philadelphia. Sketches of Character: At Home. Abroad," by H. Harrison, ca. 1833. Courtesy the Library Company of Philadelphia.
92–93: LEFT: Axonometric drawing of David Davis Mansion kitchen, Bloomington, Ill., by Gerald L. Foster, 2008. Ink and colored pencil on paper. Collection of Historic New England. RIGHT: Portrait of Sarah Davis. Courtesy the Abraham Lincoln Presidential Library.

## KITCHENS ALONG THE RIO GRANDE (1821-1912)

94: *Hornos*, El Rancho de las Golondrinas, Santa Fe, N.M., 2007. Kirk Gittings, photographer. Collection of Historic New England.
95: Carts, El Rancho de las Golondrinas, Santa Fe, N.M., 2007. Kirk Gittings, photographer. Collection of Historic New England.
96: Girls delivering food before Easter, El Cerrito, N.M., April 1941. Courtesy the U.S. National Archives and Records Administration.
97: "Fort Marcy and the Parroquia, Santa Fe," from *Notes of a Military Reconnaissance from Fort Leavenworth, in Missouri, to San Diego, in California, including part of the Arkansas, Del Norte, and Gila Rivers*, by Lieut. Col. W.H. Emory, with the Advanced Guard of the "Army of the West," United States Army, Corps of Topographical Engineers (Washington, D.C.: Wendell and Van Benthuysen, 1848). Yale Collection of Western Americana, Beinecke Rare Book and Manuscript Library.
98: Lithograph "Women Grinding Corn, Pueblo Zuni," by R. Ackerman (artist) and H. Kern (delineator), from *Report of an Expedition Down the Zuni and Colorado Rivers*, by the United States Army Corps of Topographical Engineers (Washington, D.C.: R. Armstrong, 1853). Courtesy Library of Congress, Prints & Photographs Division. (LC-USZ62-46905)
99: Zuni woman making bread, N.M., ca. 1903. Edward S. Curtis, photographer. Courtesy Library of Congress, Prints & Photographs Division, Edward S. Curtis Collection. (LC-USZ62-102040)
100: Frontispiece for *Commerce of the Prairies, or, The Journal of a Santa Fé Trader during Eight Expeditions Across the Great Western Prairie, and a Residence of Nearly Nine Years in Northern Mexico* by Josiah Gregg (New York: H.G. Langley, 1844). Yale Collection of Western Americana, Beinecke Rare Book and Manuscript Library.
101: Baking in an earthen oven, "Par-dah-weh," Southwestern U.S., ca. 1908. Milton E. Porter, photographer. Courtesy Library of Congress, Prints & Photographs Division. (LC-USZ62-45112)
102: *Indian Home Life, Pueblo of Zuni*, by Warren E. Rollins, ca. 1918. Oil on canvas. Courtesy the Collection of The Albuquerque Museum of Art.
103: *Mexican Courtyard at Cañada Alamosa, New Mexico*, by Vincent Colyer (1825–1888), 1871. Watercolor on paper. Courtesy the Collection of The Albuquerque Museum of Art.
104: Axonometric drawing of El Rancho de las Golondrinas, Santa Fe, N.M. by Gerald L. Foster, 2008. Ink and colored pencil on paper. Collection of Historic New England.
105: Fireplace, El Rancho de las Golondrinas, Santa Fe, N.M., 2007. Kirk Gittings, photographer. Collection of Historic New England.
106: CLOCKWISE, FROM TOP LEFT: Baking in an outdoors earthen oven, Taos County, N.M., 1939. Russell Lee, photographer. All courtesy Library of Congress, Prints & Photographs Division. Pulling out hot coals (LC-USF33-012422-M4, LC-USF33-012423-M1); Putting loaf into oven (LC-USF33-012420-M2); Removing bread from oven (LC-USF34-034214-D); Covering oven while baking (LC-USF34-034316-D); and Testing temperature (LC-USF33-012420-M5).
107: Removing bread from oven near Taos, N.M., September 1939. Russell Lee, photographer. Courtesy Library of Congress, Prints & Photographs Division. (LC-USF34-034215-D)
108: *Olla* on trivet, El Rancho de las Golondrinas, Santa Fe, N.M., 2007. Kirk Gittings, photographer. Collection of Historic New England.
109: Hanging meat, Chamisal, N.M., July 1940. Russell Lee, photographer. Courtesy Library of Congress, Prints & Photographs Division. (LC-USF33-012833-M2)
110: Picking over chili peppers, Concho, Ariz., October 1940. Courtesy Library of Congress, Prints & Photographs Division. (LC-USF34-037877-D)
111: Grinding corn, ca. 1908. Milton E. Porter, photographer. Courtesy Library of Congress, Prints & Photographs Division. (LC-USZ62-101335)
112: Wife of Spanish-American farmer, Chamisal, N.M., July 1940. Courtesy Library of Congress, Prints & Photographs Division. (LC-USF34-037140-D)
113: *Dispensa*, El Rancho de las Golondrinas, Santa Fe, N.M., 2007. Kirk Gittings, photographer. Collection of Historic New England.
115: Navajo preparing a meal, ca. 1950. Russell Lee, photographer. Courtesy Palace of the Governors (MNM/DCA), 183450.
116: Making tortillas near Taos, N.M., September 1939. Courtesy Library of Congress, Prints & Photographs Division. (LC-USF34-034220-D)
117: Zuni man, ca. 1903. Edward S. Curtis, photographer. Courtesy Library of Congress, Prints & Photographs Division, Edward S. Curtis Collection. (LC-USZ62-83960)

## TOWARD THE MODERN KITCHEN (1890-1945)

118: Hoosier cabinet, Castle Tucker kitchen, Wiscasset, Me., 2007. Peter Harholdt, photographer. Collection of Historic New England.
119: Castle Tucker, Wiscasset, Me. David Bohl, photographer. Collection of Historic New England.
120: Axonometric drawing of Castle Tucker kitchen, Wiscasset, Me., by Gerald L. Foster, 2008. Ink and colored pencil on paper. Collection of Historic New England.
121: Advertisement for Hoosier cabinet, 1924, by the Hoosier Manufacturing Co., Newcastle, Ind. Collection of Historic New England.
122: Advertisement for "Standard" Plumbing Fixtures, 1922, by the Standard Sanitary Manufacturing Company, Pittsburgh, Penn. Collection of Historic New England.
123: Domestic servant, Atlanta, Ga., May 1939. Marion Post Wolcott, photographer. Courtesy Schomburg Center for Research in Black Culture, Photographs and Prints Division, The New York Public Library, Astor, Lenox, and Tilden Foundations.
124: Detail from Whitehead Monel Kitchens trade catalogue "That's the Kitchen I Want," ca. 1940. Excel Metal Cabinet Company, Inc., New York, N.Y., publisher. Collection of Historic New England.
125: Farm stove in Norfolk, Conn., ca. 1890. Marie Hartig Kendall, photographer. Courtesy the Norfolk Historical Society.
126: Summer kitchen, Turville family farmhouse, Madison, Wis., August 1898. Blanchard Harper, photographer. Courtesy Wisconsin Historical Society. (WHi-25054)
127: Installation of power lines, November 10, 1937. Courtesy Schenectady Museum. (GE 559489)
128: Poster "Win the Next War Now . . . ," ca. 1918. J. Paul Verrees, graphic designer. Courtesy the U. S. National Archives and Records Administration.
129: Trade card for Pure Refined Paraffine by the Standard Oil Company. Collection of Historic New England.
130–131: Jorena Pettway sorting peas, Gee's Bend, Ala., May 1939. Marion Post Wolcott, photographer. Courtesy Library of Congress, Prints & Photographs Division. (LC-USF34-051542-D)
132: Market, Indianapolis, Ind., August 1908. Lewis Wickes Hine (1874–1940), photographer. Courtesy Library of Congress, Prints & Photographs Division. (LC-DIG-nclc-03213)
133: Antoinette Fazzino making Irish lace, 303 E. 149th St., New York, N.Y., January 1912. Lewis Wickes Hine (1874–1940), photographer.

Courtesy Library of Congress, Prints & Photographs Division. (LC-DIG-nclc-04131)
134: Cooking class, Hampton Normal and Agricultural Institute, Hampton, Va., ca. 1900. Frances Benjamin Johnston, photographer. Courtesy Library of Congress, Prints & Photographs Division, Frances Benjamin Johnston Collection. (LC-USZ62-95109)
135: Miss Chappelle helping Mrs. Smith can beans, Saint Mary's County, Md., September 1940. John Vachon, photographer. Courtesy Library of Congress, Prints & Photographs Division. (LC-USF34-061399-D)
136: "Work-saving kitchen" from the trade catalogue "Floors That Keep Homes in Fashion," 1936. Armstrong Cork Products Company, Lancaster, Penn., publisher. Promised gift to Historic New England from private collection. Courtesy Armstrong World Industries.
137: Cover of *Better Homes & Gardens*, November 1930. Cover design by Isabelle Vaughan. Promised gift to Historic New England from private collection.
138–139: Kitchen from the trade catalogue "Your Dream Kitchen," ca. 1928. Curtis Companies Service Bureau, Clinton, Iowa, publisher. Promised gift to Historic New England from private collection.
140: Time-motion study, Applecroft Home Experiment Station, Greenlawn, N.Y., ca. 1913. Underwood & Underwood, photographer. Courtesy Schlesinger Library on the History of Women in America, Radcliffe Institute, Harvard University.
141: Frankfurt Kitchen, Am Höhenblick housing estate, Ginheim, Frankfurt, Germany, ca. 1926. Margarete Schütte-Lihotzky (1897–2000), architect. Courtesy Dorothea Stransky and the University of Applied Art, Vienna.
142: Kitchen, Gropius House, Lincoln, Mass., 2007. Peter Harholdt, photographer. Collection of Historic New England.
143: Gropius House, Lincoln, Mass. David Bohl, photographer. Collection of Historic New England.
144: Axonometric drawing of Gropius House kitchen, Lincoln, Mass., by Gerald L. Foster, 2008. Ink and colored pencil on paper. Collection of Historic New England.
145: Mrs. Walter [Ise] Gropius in her kitchen, Lincoln, Mass., January 1960. Ann Rosener, photographer. Courtesy Ann Rosener/Stringer/Time & Life Pictures/Getty Images.

## THE POSTWAR KITCHEN (1945-present)

146: Mrs. Turner and her son, Flavet Village, Gainsville, Fla., 1946. Courtesy State Library and Archives of Florida.
147: Sally Sondesky with her children and friends, Levittown, Penn., ca. 1960. Courtesy the Pennsylvania Historical and Museum Commission and Sara V. and Jack Sondesky.
148: TOP: Axonometric drawing of Sondesky house kitchen, Levittown, Penn., by Gerald L. Foster, 2008. Ink and colored pencil on paper. Collection of Historic New England. BOTTOM: Daisy Myers and daughter Lynda in their kitchen, Levittown, Penn., 1957. Courtesy Charlotte Brooks, photographer, *Look Magazine* Collection, Library of Congress, Prints & Photographs Division. (L-9-57-7621-M, #6)
150: Office of War Information Poster No. 57, "We'll have lots to eat this winter, won't we mother?" Alfred Parker (1906–1985), graphic designer (Washington, D.C.: United States Office of War Information, Division of Public Inquiries, 1943). Promised gift to Historic New England from private collection.
152: Quonset hut home kitchen, 1948. Courtesy Archives and Special Collections at the Thomas J. Dodd Research Center, University of Connecticut Libraries.
153: Postcard of Levittown, Penn., ca. 1955. Eastern News, publisher. Courtesy Simeon David Marable, Proprietor for Levittown Exhibit Center North, Levittown, Penn.
154: *Portrait: Rochna Family in Kitchen*, Pittsburgh, Penn., 1950. Photograph by Sol Libsohn (1914–2001). Carnegie Museum of Art, Pittsburgh, Gift of the Carnegie Library of Pittsburgh (86.16.134).
155: Parker Kitchen, Coconut Grove, Fla., 1954. Alfred Browning Parker, Architect. Photograph by Ezra Stoller. Courtesy Ezra Stoller/Esto/IPNstock.
156: Advertisement for General Electric's Wall Refrigerator-Freezer, *House Beautiful*, July 1955. Collection of Historic New England.
157: Sondesky house kitchen, Levittown, Penn., as installed for the exhibit "Levittown, Pa.: Building the Suburban Dream" at the State Museum of Pennsylvania, Harrisburg, Penn., in 2002. Courtesy the Pennsylvania Historical and Museum Commission.
158: "U-Shaped" kitchen from *Sparkling Kitchens for Modern Homemakers* (Chicago: National Plan Service, 1954). Collection of Historic New England.
159: Nikita S. Khrushchev and Richard M. Nixon, American National Exhibition, Moscow, Russia, July 1, 1959. Courtesy Time & Life Pictures/Getty Images.
160: Advertisement for S.O.S.® Magic Scouring Pads, 1952, by The S.O.S. Company, Chicago, Ill. Collection of Historic New England. S.O.S.® is a registered trademark of The Clorox Company.
161: Advertisement for Tupperware®, *House Beautiful*, December 1958. Collection of Historic New England. Courtesy Earl S. Tupper Papers, Archives Center, National Museum of American History, Smithsonian Institution, and Tupperware Home Parties, Inc., Orlando, Fla.
162: Advertisement for Republic Steel Kitchens, *House and Garden*, September 1955. Collection of Historic New England.
164–165: "Kitchen No. 7," from the trade catalogue "Kitchen Hints," 1947. The Kitchen Maid Corporation, Andrews, Ind., publisher. Collection of Historic New England.
166: Advertisement for Swanson TV Brand® dinners, 1956. Collection of Historic New England. Swanson® is a registered trademark of CSC Brands, Inc., used with the permission of Pinnacle Foods Group LLC.
167: Sondesky house kitchen, Levittown, Penn., ca. 1960. Courtesy the Pennsylvania Historical and Museum Commission and Sara V. and Jack Sondesky.
168: Julia Child on the set of *The French Chef*, WGBH, Boston, ca. 1968. Courtesy WGBH Educational Foundation. Copyright © 2008. WGBH/Boston.
169: Radarange® microwave by Amana®, 1970s. Frederic Lewis, photographer. Courtesy Frederic Lewis/Getty Images.
170: TOP: Advertisement for Revco Bilt-In refrigerator, *House & Garden's Book of Building* (Fall-Winter, 1959–1960). Promised gift to Historic New England from private collection. Courtesy Thermo Fisher Scientific Inc. BOTTOM: Cover of *Crock-Pot® Cooking* by Marilyn Neill (New York: Golden Press, for the Rival Manufacturing Company, 1975). Cover photograph by Victor Scocozza. Courtesy Sunbeam Products Inc., doing business as Jarden Consumer Solutions; Teresa Mach; and Victor Scocozza.
171: Advertisement for Long-Bell kitchen cabinets, *House Beautiful's Houses and Plans*, 1972 edition. Promised gift to Historic New England from private collection. Courtesy International Paper Company.
172–173: LEFT TO RIGHT: Advertisement for Brown Soilfree Oven, *House Beautiful's Houses and Plans*, 1972 edition. Courtesy Brown Stove Works, Inc.; Baking bread, Messiah's World urban commune, San Francisco, Calif., 1969. Dennis Stock, photographer. Courtesy Dennis Stock/Magnum Photos; and Advertisement for Corning Counterange™, *House Beautiful's Houses and Plans*, 1972 edition. Courtesy Corning Incorporated.
174: Mayer kitchen, New Canaan, Conn. Courtesy Maureen Mayer.
175: *Selectman and His Wife*, Deerfield, Mass., ca. 1899. Frances S. and Mary E. Allen, photographers. Collection of Historic New England.
176: Carlisle house, Newport, R.I., ca. 1914. Collection of Historic New England.

# INDEX

**Page numbers in boldface type indicate illustrations.**

## DONOR ACKNOWLEDGMENTS

An Anonymous Foundation
The Acorn Foundation
Mars Foundation
National Endowment for the Humanities*

Mr. and Mrs. Theodore Alfond
Ms. Deborah Allinson and Mr. Thomas Lamb
Mr. and Mrs. Edward P. Bousa
Mr. and Mrs. Richard Cheek
Mr. and Mrs. Philip J. Edmundson
Mr. and Mrs. Joseph Junkin
Mr. and Mrs. Newton Levee
Mr. and Mrs. John B. McDowell
Mrs. Stephen D. Paine
Mr. Andrew Spindler-Roesle and Mr. Hiram Butler
Mr. and Mrs. William P. Veillette

**NANCY CARLISLE** has been a curator for more than twenty years at Historic New England where she works with some of the most important historic kitchens in the country. Ms. Carlisle, author of *Cherished Possessions: A New England Legacy*, has written and lectured widely on the material culture of domestic life from the seventeenth century to the twenty-first.

**MELINDA TALBOT NASARDINOV** is a former assistant curator at Historic New England. A graduate of the Winterthur Program in Early American Culture, Ms. Nasardinov writes about American decorative arts and the history of domestic life.

**JENNIFER PUSTZ** is the museum historian at Historic New England. She holds a PhD in American studies from the University of Iowa. Dr. Pustz is the author of a forthcoming book on interpreting domestic service at historic house museums.

* Any views, findings, conclusions, or recommendations expressed in this publication do not necessarily reflect those of the National Endowment for the Humanities.

Published by Historic New England
141 Cambridge Street
Boston, Massachusetts 02114
www.HistoricNewEngland.org

Distributed by Tilbury House, Publishers
103 Brunswick Avenue
Gardiner, Maine 04345
www.tilburyhouse.com
800-582-1899



First Edition 2008

*Library of Congress Cataloging-in-Publication Data*

Carlisle, Nancy Camilla.
America's kitchens / Nancy Carlisle and Melinda Talbot Nasardinov, with Jennifer Pustz. — 1st ed.
p. cm.
Includes bibliographical references and index.
ISBN 978-0-88448-308-3 (pbk. : alk. paper)
1. Kitchens—United States—History. 2. Kitchens—Social aspects—United States. 3. Cookery—United States—History. I. Nasardinov, Melinda Talbot, 1974- II. Pustz, Jennifer. III. Title.
TX653.C325 2008
643'.30973–dc22

2008028576

FRONT COVER: Lithograph "Prang's Aids for Object Teaching—The Kitchen," 1874. L. Prang & Co., publisher. Courtesy Library of Congress, Prints & Photographs Division, reproduction number LC-USZC4-5155 (top); Kitchen accessories from the trade catalogue "243 New Ideas for Your Kitchen," ca. 1955. Kalamazoo Stoves and Furnaces, Kalamazoo, Mich., publisher (bottom). Promised gift to Historic New England from private collection.
BACK COVER: Matisse, September 2005. David Carmack, photographer.
FRONT INSIDE COVER: Tenement family, New York, N.Y., ca. 1908. Lewis Wickes Hine (1874–1940), photographer. Courtesy Photography Collection, Miriam and Ida D. Wallach Division of Art, Prints and Photographs, The New York Public Library, Astor, Lenox, and Tilden Foundations.
BACK INSIDE COVER: Tupperware party from the trade catalogue "Tupperware: Beauty on Your Table . . . Utility in Your Kitchen," 1970. Tupperware Home Parties, Dart Industries, Inc., Orlando, Fla., publisher. Promised gift to Historic New England from private collection. Courtesy Tupperware Home Parties, Inc., Orlando, Fla.
FRONT AND BACK FLAPS: Details of the Hoosier cabinet in the kitchen at Castle Tucker, Wiscasset, Me., 2007. Peter Harholdt, photographer. Collection of Historic New England.



Book and cover design by Julia Sedykh Design

Illustrations edited by Nancy Carlisle, Melinda Talbot Nasardinov, Jennifer Pustz, and Richard Cheek

Editorial production managed by Lorna Condon

Printed and bound in China by C&C Offset Printing Co., Ltd.